THE SERIALS

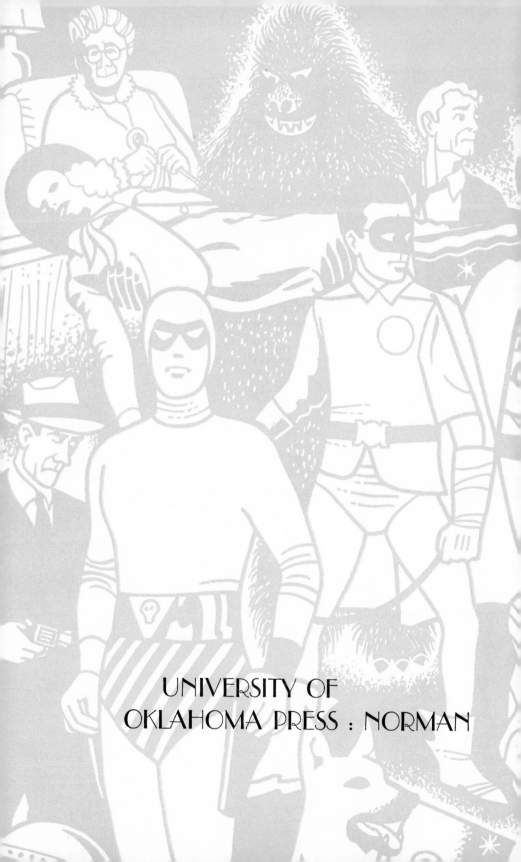

UNIVERSITY OF
OKLAHOMA PRESS : NORMAN

THE
SERIALS

SUSPENSE AND DRAMA
BY INSTALLMENT

BY
RAYMOND WILLIAM STEDMAN

The paper on which this book is printed bears the watermark of the University of Oklahoma Press and has an effective life of at least three hundred years.

International Standard Book Number: 0–8061–0927–0

Library of Congress Catalog Card Number: 74–123343

Copyright 1971 by the University of Oklahoma Press, Publishing Division of the University. Composed and printed at Norman, Oklahoma, U.S.A., by the University of Oklahoma Press. First edition.

PREFACE

In 1912, a year in which many things seemed to be coming to an end, the serial drama was born. Films had been telling stories for about ten years. Magazines had been telling continued stories for decades. And in more and more newspapers appeared a new medium for gradually unfolding a story in visual form: the daily comic strip.

Here—at times in broad brushstrokes—is the story of the dramatic serial in America, its beginnings, its glorious cul de sacs, its continued good health in an electronic medium not even in existence when the genre began. Assuredly I will have neglected some favorite of each reader, and I expect to suffer accordingly. Serial followers are fiercely loyal. I only can ask indulgence with my effort to emphasize the wide view, hoping that the reader will recognize, as I once had to, that the greatest serial ever to play the Orpheum in one town may not have passed through a projector in a hamlet twenty miles down the road. Not even the soap operas and thrillers of network broadcasting have had the uniformity of distribution or presentation time that might be assumed.

If *Kitty Keene, Daredevils of the Red Circle, Those We Love,* and others appear slighted, many of their sisters, cousins, and aunts are not. It is the flow of the genre that I have tried to represent historically, not simply the ripples and rapids. *Amanda of Honeymoon Hill* can be evoked by *Our Gal Sunday; Mysterious Dr. Satan,* by *The Phantom Creeps.* After so long a historical slighting of a whole form—and America's unique contribution to drama at that—I trust that the reader will accept this attempt to capture the essence of its story, as it could be seen almost six decades after the birth date.

RAYMOND WILLIAM STEDMAN

Newtown, Pennsylvania
September 15, 1970

ACKNOWLEDGMENTS

For their recollections and comments: Frank Hummert, Irna Phillips, Hector Chevigny, Gordon Hughes, Mrs. Marian Jordan (Molly McGee), Patrick McGuirk, Cecil Smith, Mrs. Jack Warfield, Milton Dickens, Mark Frutchey, and a grandmother, a mother, and a wife who explained that part of the daytime-serial genre which to a male is unfathomable.

For their assistance in gathering and preparing materials: Willis Duniway; Mrs. Marion Hopkins; Louis Murphy; Kenneth Harwood; A. W. Moise and J. W. Wiley, of Ralston-Purina; Robert Wogan and Alfred Haber, of NBC Radio; Charles F. Darden, of Procter and Gamble Company; Bruce Handshu, of Crosley Broadcasting; A. Louis Champlin, Jr., of General Mills; Keir's Photos; Robert D. Wood, of CBS Television; the staffs of the Program Analysis Department, NBC, and the Program Information Department, CBS; Movie Star News; Kalton C. Lahue and Blackhawk Films. Bruce Katsiff graciously assisted in the preparation of photographs.

The Serials

For permission to include excerpts of programs: Columbia Broadcasting System, for *The Romance of Helen Trent*; General Mills, Inc., for *Jack Armstrong, the All-American Boy*; National Broadcasting Company, for *Vic and Sade* (by Paul Rhymer); Procter and Gamble Company, for *Ma Perkins*.

CONTENTS

The Serials

ILLUSTRATIONS

The Serials

Illustrations

THE SERIALS

1234567891011121314151617181920212223224

DRAMA BY INSTALLMENT

Then the king shut himself up with his brother and related to him that which had betided him with the Wazir's daughter, Schehera-zade . . . and told him what he had heard from her of proverbs and parables, chronicles and pleasantries, quips and jests, stories and anecdotes, dialogues and histories and elegies and other verses. . .

THE THOUSAND AND ONE NIGHTS
(from the translation by Sir Richard Francis Burton)

On the cover was a stunning portrait of a beautiful young woman, obviously the creation of that eminent artist of 1912, Charles Dana Gibson. Her name was Mary, and it was plain that some grand adventure lay in store for her within the pages of that August issue of *The Ladies' World* magazine. If the Gibson Girl portrait was not enough to lead the reader to page three of the journal, newly acquired by the McClure syndicate, the legend across the bottom of the attractive cover surely would have done so. In large letters it read:

3

The Serials

What did happen to Mary was part of cinema history, but no one could know that when the otherwise undistinguished issue of *The Ladies' World* went to press. Certainly the anonymous author was unaware that he was creating the first chapter-play heroine when he began his "remarkable story of a remarkable girl": "Mary's eyes were smoldering that day with the fire of strange yearnings. She moved about her work as one walking in a dream—burning with life that was not the life around her. Under her old print gown, her bosom rose and fell with soft regularity like that of slumber; her lips were parted."

The unnamed writer then unfolded the tale of a baby left on the doorstep of a small-town storekeeper, Billy Peart. In the basket beside the child lay five hundred dollars in cash and a note promising a thousand more if the shopkeeper would rear the girl and find her a husband from among the local bachelors. As might be expected, eighteen years later Peart was busily trying to marry off pretty Mary to get that thousand—not an altogether vile action in that he surely had spent more than his five hundred dollars in her upbringing.

Mary, however, would have nothing to do with Tuck Wintergreen, Peart's confederate and principal nominee. When, by accident, she discovered the circumstances of her "adoption," the young woman took a hundred dollars that she felt was rightfully hers and slipped away from home. Here is how the narrative ended:

> It came upon her heavily, the seriousness of her act. A girl of nineteen . . . going to a life of which she knew nothing. How long would the hundred dollars last? What would she do when it was gone? She drew a deep sigh. Then, resolutely, she turned her face toward town and walked down the dock and up the street to the railroad station.

What would happen to Mary? A note on page 4 of *The Ladies' World* gave a clue. Whatever it was, it would occur within twenty minutes of the time the reader last saw her. To the reader who could guess the events of those twenty minutes—in three hundred words or less—the magazine promised a prize of one hundred dollars, a more than generous sum in 1912.

We do not know how many three-hundred-word entries poured into the magazine in this prelude to the many contests and premium offers eventually to be associated with the serial drama. We do know, however, the name of that pioneer prize-winner. Lucy Proctor of Armstrong, California, guessed correctly that, as Billy Peart and Tuck Wintergreen closed in on Mary at the railroad station, a young man would sweep in and carry her off in his rig.

This rescue was included in another story about Mary that appeared in the September, 1912, *The Ladies' World*. But much more noteworthy than the story itself were the illustrations for "Her First Night in the Big City." They were stills from a motion picture. Something extraordinary *had* happened to the fictional heroine, and it was a complete surprise to her creators.

On page one editor Charles Dwyer shared with his readers what was clearly for him an exciting exposure to a new and dazzling medium. Caught up in the fascination that even then surrounded the movie business, Dwyer revealed the thrilling details in several paragraphs that combined the overstatement of the press release with the inside information of the movie column. After claiming that Mary would "take her place among the great fictional characters like Sherlock Holmes, Raffles, and Wallingford," Dwyer described for his readers how Mary got into the movies. He was, at the same time, describing the birth of serial drama.

The new concept of dramatic entertainment came into being in the summer of 1912, when Dwyer met a man named Horace G. Plimpton. Plimpton was manager of Thomas Edison's Kineto-scope Company, one of the more significant film-producing concerns of the time. As Dwyer and Plimpton chatted, the motion-picture executive was "plainly attracted" to the editor's plan to put a Mary story in each issue of *The Ladies' World*, with prizes for readers who guessed correctly what would happen next. A few days later Plimpton called Dwyer to suggest that the scheme be taken a step farther. Why not, suggested Plimpton, let the Edison company make a film version of each month's narrative and release it to theaters all over the country in the same week the magazine was published? The two ventures would be mutually supporting.

Dwyer was delighted by the idea. Swiftly the first adventures of Mary were put before the camera, with Mary Fuller, a popular member of the Edison acting company, in the title role. Miss Fuller, whose screen career had begun at Vitagraph in 1907, was sufficiently attractive and athletic to fulfill the requirements of the role that would assure her at least a footnote in cinema history. The first serial villain, Billy Peart, was played by William Wadsworth.

As the one-reelers and magazine stories made their parallel appearances, Mary's wanderings took her to places that in her isolated childhood she would not have dreamed of seeing: Broadway, Wall Street, London at Yuletide, the back alleys of the underworld. Seemingly just beyond her grasp was an inheritance—hers if she could claim it before her twenty-first birthday, Peart's (through a confederate) if she failed.

Although Mary's convoluted quest for her birthright continued chapter after chapter, each segment could be understood and appreciated in itself without much initial summary. Audiences were left to wonder how and when she would obtain her fortune—but not, as would be true of later serials, how she would escape a peril menacing her at each episode's end. In Chapter 9, for example, there is a good action sequence—Miss Fuller lowering herself from a seventh-story window by a rope of knotted bedclothes—but it comes at the three-quarter mark of the episode, not at the end. The chapter concludes on a quiet note with Mary finding refuge in the Salvation Army.

Does this mean that *What Happened to Mary* was not a serial? Of course not. The individual installments followed the heroine and her associates through a particular phase of her life, the characters and basic situation continued from episode to episode, the episodes appeared at regular intervals, and the audiences knew when to expect the next installment—especially if they were readers of *The Ladies' World. What Happened to Mary* was a serial, a narrative with continuing characters broken into a series of regularly appearing installments.

Because it lacked high-suspense endings, *Mary* is sometimes called a series film, a misguided segregation which overlooks the fact that all chapter plays are, technically, sequential series. Hairsplitting aside, I propose that series films are best represented by the Blondie and the Hardy-family pictures or by those with Francis, the talking mule. Characters and sometimes locales continued; yet the individual motion pictures appeared in random and never-specified fashion. Audiences did not go to the theater with the idea that they were seeing part of a whole, nor did they know with certainty that there would ever be another such film. (Indeed, MGM itself did not project a set of sequels when it made the first Hardy picture.)

Earlier and more germane examples of the series picture were the short, self-contained films—the 119 *Hazards of Helen* railroading movies being good examples—which thrust the featured performer into hair-raising situations in movie after movie. But while such films were tied together by the continuance of the leading character, and perhaps by a general theme, they lacked true connection with each other. Further, they were represented not as parts of a whole but as parts of a series and did not appear with the sequential regularity that one associates with a motion-picture serial. Theaters could, and did, show only parts of these series, and *in any order*, a situation scarcely conceivable with what is generally understood to be a chapter play.

And yet many who saw these series films recall them as serials. They are sometimes listed as such in reprint catalogues. If I exclude them from consideration in this book, assigning them to the convenient category of series films, I do so to keep this book under two thousand pages, not to banish them forever beyond the pale. These ancient series films, remember, were the antecedents of the B-picture adventure series of the sound era—the Boston Blackie, Lone Wolf, Saint, Falcon, and Philo Vance detective dramas, and, of course, the Westerns of Charles Starrett, Tim Holt, and others. It would be a broad meadow in which to roam, and I must resist that temptation. Not even the easy rationalization that *on television* the old Blondie and Blackie films and many other B series were given the regularity in presentation and advertising that I have ascribed to serials will sway me from my appointed rounds. The lure, however, is great.

In 1913, while the first film serial was still running in theaters, Edison used Mary Fuller in *Who Will Marry Mary?* This six-chapter drama, only half as long as its predecessor, is now forgotten. The other serial of 1913 was the important one. It too was a stepchild of the publishing industry. At the time the newspapers of Chicago were involved in a spectacular circulation war. Leading the scramble for readers were the *Daily News*, the *Inter Ocean*, the *Times-Herald*, the *American*, and the *Tribune*, the last in the final year of the regency of Medill McCormick.[1] The managing editor of the *Tribune* was English-born James Keeley, an energetic journalist who mounted the crusade to recall United States Senator William Lorimer for allegedly using bribery to gain his office. Under the pressure of competition, particularly from Hearst's new *American* and morning *Examiner*, Keeley led the *Tribune* to increasing dependency upon sensationalism, spurred, no doubt, by new circulation manager Max Annenberg and demon city editor Walter Howey. Howey (whose brash news-gathering exploits were the inspiration for the play *The Front Page*) may, in fact, have conceived a promotional project which film producer William Selig was eager to work out with the *Tribune*.

Selig was head of the Chicago-based Selig Polyscope Company, a firm now remembered more for the giant zoo which supported its productions than for the productions themselves. The *Tribune*-Selig plan was to combine a newspaper serial with a biweekly film version, just as *What Happened to Mary* had joined magazine and screen. Using a Harold MacGrath story, Gilson Willets put together a screenplay for *The Adventures of Kathlyn* that made ample use of the Selig lions—in India—amid

[1] Medill gave way to his brother, Colonel Robert R. McCormick, whose *Tribune* radio station, WGN, played an important role in the development of the serial drama, as will be seen.

8

much more man-made and natural violence than Mary's adventures displayed. Like many other early serials, this one had a correspondence of names in title, heroine, and actress. Kathlyn Williams played Kathlyn Hare, daughter of Colonel Hare, a Frank Buck–type character who loved to surround himself and his household with the creatures he brought back alive.

The Adventures of Kathlyn is lost to general view today, but pioneer serial writer Frank Leon Smith recalled it in a letter to *Films in Review* in February, 1958:

> The girl was given a packet "to be opened at midnight December 31st," and the villain, Umballah by name, gets to it before she learns its contents. So, when she gets to India, Umballah is on the job, and Episode 1 ends with Kathlyn, against her will, being crowned "queen" by the natives, and Umballah being brought forward as the man chosen for her husband. That was a "situation" ending, but other episodes wound up with sensational action or stunts, broken for holdover suspense.

Even without the Selig lions, Kathlyn had more to worry about than Mary did. Where Billy Peart was inclined to be wishy-washy at times, generally employing others to do his evil deeds for him while he faded into the scenery, Umballah (played by Charles Clary) lent his forceful presence to every reel, in the manner of the heavies in the *Fantomas* series pictures which appeared in France about the same time. Colonel Hare's daughter had the added discomfort of having to wait a fortnight to escape the chapter-ending perils which beset her, whereas Peart's foster child had things tidied up, more or less, at episode end.

Frank Leon Smith, who considered both *Mary* and *Kathlyn* bona fide serials, believed that in emphasizing holdover suspense, as opposed to situational endings, writer Willets "gave the serial both the key to its success and the assurance of its doom." Why he linked the chapter play's destiny to cliffhanging will soon be seen. For the present suffice it to say that business for the first true cliffhanger was good. The *Tribune* reportedly enjoyed a 10 per cent increase in circulation, duly observed by other newspapers, which soon developed their own serial projects.

9

The Serials

By coincidence the sudden interest in chapter plays came at the time the motion picture was in transition from one- and two-reelers to feature films. Although the motion-picture Establishment resisted the "manufacture" of longer photoplays, Adolph Zukor and others were importing European films running four or more reels and showing them in legitimate theaters or in the new movie houses which were replacing the tiny nickelodeons. Further, in 1913, D. W. Griffith was quietly completing *Judith of Bethulia*, a drama of almost feature length, which served as his steppingstone to *The Birth of a Nation.*

But making longer films in this country was a precarious undertaking at the time because of expense (which smaller companies feared to undertake) or because of the direct resistance of the old guard (which had money but not foresight). Biograph, for instance, was furious when it discovered that Griffith had made a film *four* reels long.

Serials, therefore, were a nice compromise. They did not cost much per unit, but they could run to a dozen or more installments, thus surpassing a feature in total length. Audiences, moreover, obviously liked the new genre. They returned to the theaters time after time to see successive chapters—which made the new drama form popular with exhibitors. Finally, financial support for chapter plays could be found without great difficulty because of the promotional interests of newspaper executives.

The year 1914 thus brought extraordinary activity in the production and distribution of chapter plays, beginning with *The Active Life of Dolly of the Dailies*, another episodic serial of the Edison Company starring Mary Fuller. This production, not so much thriller as career-girl drama, concerned a girl reporter trying to make a go of it in the big time while also putting marital harness upon a handsome fellow worker. *Dolly* was, in fact, a precursor of several of the early soap operas of radio, and innumerable nighttime television programs could call it sister.

The title *Lucille Love, Girl of Mystery* might suggest that Universal Pictures' first chapter play likewise foreshadowed broadcasting's daytime serials. Actually it was a spy drama, set in the Pacific and featuring Grace Cunard and Francis Ford, the

10

movies' first serial team. Soon afterward they starred for Universal in *The Broken Coin* (1915), *The Adventures of Peg o' the Ring* (1916), and *The Purple Mask* (1916).[2]

Well aware of the added readership which *The Adventures of Kathlyn* had brought the *Tribune*, the rival Hearst empire prepared its own serial for prompt release. William Randolph Hearst himself apparently took an interest in the development of the plot. Certainly he was sufficiently interested to be present at Loew's Broadway Theatre on March 23, 1914, for the premiere of *The Perils of Pauline*.[3]

Pathé Film Company made this famous motion picture for Hearst. It was the film company's first serial. Louis Gasnier, the supervising director, and Donald MacKenzie divided the directing duties. The narrative (by Charles W. Goddard) required alteration by George W. Seitz, a newcomer to Pathé, who tried unsuccessfully to make the episode endings follow the cliff-hanging pattern of *The Adventures of Kathlyn*. Despite his efforts each installment was largely self-contained. Crane Wilbur played Harry Marvin, the hero. Paul Panzer was the villainous Koerner (called Owen in the first print). On the promise of copious publicity a twenty-five-year-old Pathé actress was induced to portray Pauline—Pearl Fay White.

I shall make no attempt to provide a detailed biography of Pearl White; the errors and variations in available source material are too many. Miss White's autobiography contains strange distortions of seemingly unimportant matters. I can state with some certainty, though, that she was born in Missouri in 1889.

---

[2] Grace Cunard, one of the last surviving chapter-play heroines, died in the Motion Picture Country Home in January, 1967, half a century after giving up regular serial work. Francis Ford worked for many years in serials and features as both actor and director. In fact, he directed all the Cunard-Ford films and in *The Broken Coin* featured his now-famous brother, John Ford, in a small part. The scenario for that twenty-two-episode film was written by Miss Cunard, whose imaginary Gretzhoffen seemed more like Graustark.

[3] This date is given by Wallace E. Davies in "The Truth About Pearl White" (*Films in Review*, November, 1959, 541). *The Perils of Pauline* went into general release about the first of April, 1914. At Keith's Alhambra Theatre in New York City the first episode was part of a vaudeville bill headed by Mr. and Mrs. Carter DeHaven. In the theatrical notes it was called "a motion picture play." Hearst advertising for the printed counterpart called *The Perils of Pauline* "the 25,000 prize novel, which you can see in stirring MOTION PICTURES."

11

At age eighteen she left home to tour with a stock company (not a circus, as is often stated) and at about that time acquired a husband, actor Victor Sutherland, of the same company.

Pearl White's screen career began in 1910 at the studios of the Powers Film Company in New York. Subsequently she worked for the Lubin Company in Philadelphia, Pathé in New Jersey, and Crystal Films in the Bronx. At the last studio she performed in one-reel farces and in a series of light films in which her own name was used in the titles: *Pearl's Romance, Pearl's Adventure, Pearl's Dilemma,* and so on. In 1914 she returned to Pathé (with a new wardrobe purchased with winnings at gambling tables in Monte Carlo), having divorced Sutherland.

The chapter play into which the outgoing, energetic actress was thrust was roughhewn, even by 1914 standards, but not without entertainment value. Certainly it was more polished than *What Happened to Mary.* The writers provided good action sequences, which Miss White carried out with unusual zest. Her personality was so effervescent that audiences readily overlooked the theatrical and literary deficiencies of the scenes in which she was framed. Pearl was having fun, even in peril, and viewers in darkened movie houses had fun along with her.

During her escapades as Pauline, Miss White proved herself (and womankind?) more than equal to the assaults of pirates, gypsies, sailors, cowhands, and renegade Indians. She could race down a hill only a few steps ahead of a crashing boulder without so much as mussing the blonde wig that became her trademark. Though not graceful, Pearl had resilience, a definite asset for an actress seldom aided by doubles in her early serials. During the filming of one episode, she fell and permanently injured her back (and possibly brought on her premature death at forty-nine). Even more terrifying to her fellow workers on *Pauline* was an errant balloon ascent which carried the plucky actress across the Palisades and New York City and into a sudden storm before the craft was brought to the ground miles from its starting point.

The twenty loosely connected chapters of *The Perils of Pauline,* which appeared in theaters and Hearst papers throughout most of 1914, follow waters navigated earlier in *What Happened to Mary*. Heroine Pauline has a lost inheritance that Koerner hopes to snatch from her. Although more active than Billy Peart, Pauline's adversary uses second-string heavies to perform his unpleasant tasks, all the while remaining friendly with the maiden. The action roams all over the continental United States and surrounding waters, Koerner's schemings linking the otherwise independent installments. The filming, however, was done entirely in the East.

Louis Gasnier and his associates at the French-run Pathé Company have been blamed for the horrendous illiteracies of the *Pauline* subtitles. In the prints still available simple words like *one* and *help* are misspelled; cowboys use unnatural expressions, such as "Comrades, wheel round!" and Pauline asks for aid by calling, "Hey, man! Get me out of this hole!" The prize orthographic lapse occurs in the second chapter, in which Pearl's Indian captors, suspecting that she is a goddess, decide to test "her immoral strength."

While Gasnier did have difficulty communicating in English, the *Pauline* cameraman, Arthur C. Miller, in *One Reel a Week* (published in 1967) states that the errors were not in the original film. The intelligent George Seitz, who prepared the subtitles with Bertram Milhauser, could never have produced such illiteracies, contends Miller. They were, instead, the result of retranslation from twenty-eight-millimeter safety-film copies made in Europe—the only prints of the famous serial that had survived by the time its historical value became evident. Film historian William K. Everson also espouses this theory, which has internal support in the European-style construction and lettering, Koerner, for instance, appears in the subtitles as Kœrner.

In case the reader wonders what happened to Pauline's chief tormentor, by the way, it should be recorded that he exits permanently in "The Floating Coffin." In his last attempt at homicide Koerner scuttles Pauline's dinghy, but the heroine and her dog find haven on what turns out to be a navy target vessel. As shells from shipboard cannons tear apart her improvised life

13

raft, Pauline scribbles a note which the dog carries through the waves to the astonished cannoneers.[4] Meanwhile, an elderly yacht captain who has befriended Pauline recognizes Koerner's treachery and in a scuffle elbows him into the waves. As Koerner's straining hands disappear into the ocean, heroine and hero are reunited. The girl pledges to renounce her life of peril and become Mrs. Harry Marvin. We can believe that she kept her word, too, for when Pearl White next appeared in a serial she was not Pauline.

Before Pearl White's second brush with danger, another spectacular serial event confronted the nation's film audiences. Delighted with its circulation profit from *The Adventures of Kathlyn*, the *Chicago Tribune* outlined a new serial project. From only a title the Thanhouser Company prepared on order the twenty-three chapters of *The Million Dollar Mystery*. Once again a scramble for money occupied the principals in the story. This time the funds were not an inheritance (in fact, they may have been a trifle tainted), but moviegoers enjoyed watching innumerable attempts to steal them go awry. So great was the enjoyment that the $125,000 or so expended in the filming brought a gross profit half again as large as the amount mentioned in the film's title. According to some reports the return to the stockholders was 700 per cent.

The Million Dollar Mystery demonstrated that significant financial as well as circulation profits could be derived from serials. That success in turn led to chapter-play productions not directly related to journalistic promotions. The latter half of 1914 brought *The Beloved Adventurer* from the Lubin Company and *The Trey o' Hearts* and *The Master Key* from Universal.[5] Ventures tied in with publications continued to over-

---

[4] The occupied-target-boat situation was durable enough for 20th Century Fox to use it as the climax to a 1942 Technicolor feature, *To the Shores of Tripoli*.

[5] I have not made any attempt to summarize the plots of all film serials, thinking it better to describe only the more significant or representative ones of the hundreds produced. For the most part, of course, the plots were little more than props upon which to hang action sequences. Readers wishing to obtain story information are referred to the back issues of the several publications for film exhibitors—*Moving Picture World*, for example—or to Kalton Lahue's

shadow the independent productions, however. *The Million Dollar Mystery* was followed by *Zudora,* which was renamed *The Twenty Million Dollar Mystery* before it ended its run. It disappointed its enthusiastic backers, partly because of script problems and partly because audiences were disconcerted to see James Cruze (the hero of the first mystery) in the ominous characterization of a mystic named Hassam Ali. In a midcourse correction Cruze was abruptly assigned an additional role of more heroic proportions, the title change was made, and Harold Mac-Grath, author of *The Adventures of Kathlyn* and *The Million Dollar Mystery,* was brought in to complete the story.

These changes improved things immeasurably. The finished production ran to twenty chapters (later condensed to half that number for rerelease in 1919 as *The Demon Shadow*). The final retitling may have reflected the damage to the film's dignity inflicted by a 1915 Vitagraph spoof, *The Fates and Flora Fourflush,* or *The Ten Billion Dollar Vitagraph Mystery Serial.* A serial parody as early as 1915 is not surprising when one considers the burst of success of the form. It can also be taken as evidence that in the midst of this success there were moviegoers who viewed chapter-play goings on with something other than the naïveté frequently attributed to the film audience of that era.

A follow-up to earlier success that proved more profitable than *Zudora* was Hearst-Pathé's *The Exploits of Elaine.* Avoiding the mistake Thanhouser made in transforming hero to villain, Pathé's managers, Theodore and Leopold Wharton, presented the new serial as a spectacular encore for their new action star, Pearl White. Was it she or serial heroine Elaine Dodge who was described in the opening pages of the printed serial which accompanied the film:

> Elaine Dodge was both the ingenue and the athlete—the thoroughly modern type of girl—equally at home with tennis and tango, table talk and tea. Vivacious eyes that hinted at a stunning amber brown sparkled beneath masses of the most wonderful auburn hair. Her pearly teeth, when she smiled, were marvelous.

Continued Next Week, which presents much of the exhibitor material on *silent* serials, along with synopses derived from other writers. Screen Facts Press offers several soft-cover books of synopses of serials of the sound era.

And she smiled often, for life to her seemed a continuous film of enjoyment.

As a published work in hard covers and Hearst syndication, *The Exploits of Elaine* was part of the *Craig Kennedy, Scientific Detective* series, written by Arthur B. Reeve, possibly the most popular mystery writer in the United States in the years immediately following Kennedy's first appearance in *Cosmopolitan* in 1910. To play the American Sherlock, Pathé hired Broadway's Arnold Daley, who brought stature to serial acting at no little salary expense to the studio. Other able members of the cast were Creighton Hale as the reporter, Jameson (narrator of the printed story), and Sheldon Lewis as the handsome young attorney, Perry Bennett.

In a major surprise Bennett was exposed as the first in the serial genre's long parade of unknown menaces. As seen by the audiences and author Reeve, this shadowy figure was

> masked by a handkerchief drawn tightly about his lower face, leaving only his eyes visible beneath the cap with visor pulled down over his forehead. He had a peculiar stoop of the shoulders and wore his coat collar turned up. One hand, the right, seemed almost deformed. It was that which gave him his name in the underworld—the Clutching Hand.

The presence of an unknown malefactor in a serial enhanced interest by adding carry-over mystery to the customary visual action. It was an excellent device for maintaining audience interest during the months in which a continued drama might run. When properly handled, it could surpass cliffhanging.

In 1916, incidentally, a Pearl White serial contained the less common reversal of the masked-villain situation: the unknown agent for good. Throughout *The Iron Claw* (Pathé) Miss White was helped by a hooded crime fighter known as the Laughing Mask. Though lacking the dash and sharp tailoring of a Batman, he was a good match for the one-armed, Fagin-like Iron Claw, who tutored Pearl in the ways of crime to revenge himself upon the father he had stolen her from years before. At the end of each episode the audience was presented with a question which grew more intriguing with each chapter: "Who is the Laughing Mask?" Not until Republic's *The Lone Ranger* of 1938 did a film serial gain more from the mounting curiosity surrounding the identity of a hero.

Although audiences of today find *The Exploits of Elaine* mildly amusing, by comparison with *The Perils of Pauline* it was a finished production, with better scriptwriting and acting. The directing was also improved by the employment of scriptwriter George B. Seitz as codirector with Louis Gasnier. Seitz, who ended his career as the director of the Hardy-family films for MGM, became the first master planner of the chapter-play world. He directed Pearl White's last five serials, *The Fatal Ring* (1917), *The House of Hate* (1918), *The Lightning Raider* and *The Black Secret* (1919), and *Plunder* (1923). His serial work continued until the mid-1920s. By that time he had set the pattern for producing continued films, had starred in a few light-hearted ones himself, and had trained some able protégés, such as Spencer Bennet (whose own association with the serial would span four decades).

Despite its comparative polish, however, *The Exploits of Elaine* does not have the interest for later audiences of *The Perils of Pauline*. Elaine's adventures are cluttered with once-fascinating but no longer startling gadgetry and the scientific detection of Craig Kennedy. Fingerprinting, for example, is something Kennedy has to explain in dramatic fashion to his unbelieving listeners. And one episode hinges on the vocaphone, an invention no more out of the ordinary today than an intercom or a telephone amplifier. *The Perils of Pauline*, by contrast, was free of fanciness and, like *The Great Train Robbery*, was anchored in outdoor action and settings which glossed over theatrical crudities. Yet, dated as it is, *The Exploits of Elaine* remains the prototype of the scientific mystery serial that gave much service to chapter-play makers over the years. It was the proving ground for suspenseful action *within four walls* and the point of departure for the death ray, the hypnotic drug, the life-restoring machine. Arthur B. Reeve was guiding the hands of dozens of serial writers of the sound era when he wrote for the

17

printed installment of "The Poisoned Room" these words addressed by Kennedy to a pale Elaine:

> That wall paper has been loaded down with arsenic, probably Paris green or Schweinfurth green, which is acetoarsenite of copper. Every minute you are here, you are breathing arseniuretted hydrogen. The Clutching Hand has cleverly contrived to introduce the nascent gas into the room. That acts on the arsenic compounds in the wall paper and hangings and sets free the gas. I thought I knew the smell the moment I got a whiff of it. You are slowly being poisoned by minute quantities of the deadly gas. This Clutching Hand is a diabolical genius. Think of it—poisoned wall paper!

Think of it indeed! Fourteen chapters of such agony might seem enough for one heroine, but when Pathé began counting the profits these episodes brought in, the studio was not long in creating *The New Exploits of Elaine* (ten chapters) and *The Romance of Elaine* (twelve chapters). George Seitz was largely responsible for the production of both these serials, which reached theaters in 1915. In the cast of the last of the trilogy was another prominent actor from Broadway, who reached the land of cliffhanging via a submarine. The vessel's nose broke through the surface of a lonely inlet, its conning tower opened, and out stepped a sneering Lionel Barrymore.

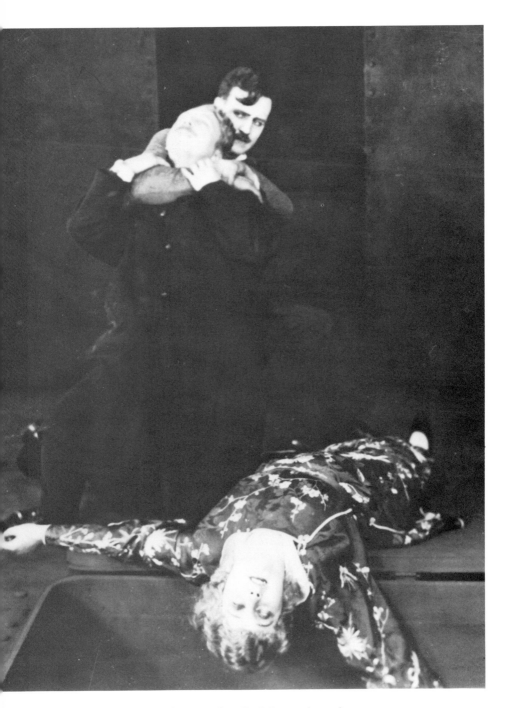

Pearl White in *The Black Secret* (1919).

Mary Fuller, who in
What Happened to Mary (1912)
became the first serial heroine.

Advertisement for
The Adventures of Kathlyn (1913),
the first serial with
cliffhanging chapter endings.

Kathlyn Williams, star of *The Adventures of Kathlyn*.

The poster above hails *The Million Dollar Mystery*, a highly profitable chapter play of 1914, underwritten by the *Chicago Tribune*. A prize of ten thousand dollars for the best suggestion for a sequel chapter brought letters from thousands of readers, including winner Ida Damon, a secretary in St. Louis. In the first significant press-agent hoax, an imaginary heiress (whose name was that of the serial heroine) was reported missing. Details paralleling those of the scenario were fed to the police and newspapers for seven days before the stunt was exposed.

OPPOSITE: Serial quee
Pearl Whit

Ruth Roland in still frames
from one of her cliffhanging triumphs,
The Timber Queen (1922).

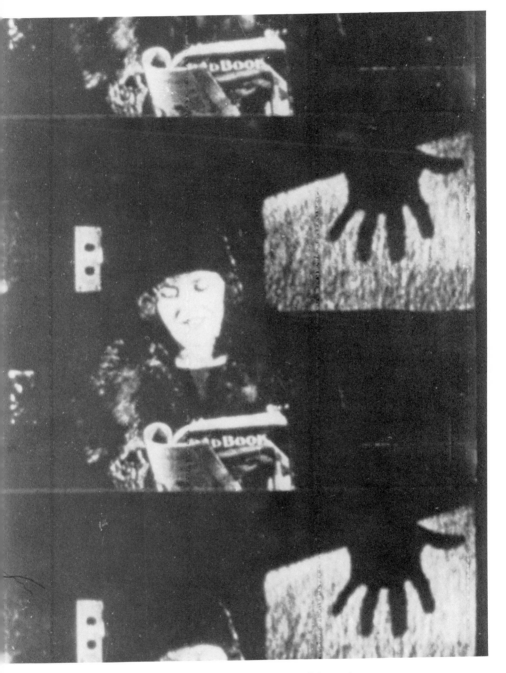

Ruth Roland in *The Tiger's Trail* (1919).

The chapter play and the yellow menace. ABOVE AND RIGHT: Pearl White confronts the treacherous Wu Fang (Warner Oland) in *The Lightning Warrior* (1919). BELOW: Henry Brandon instructs a dacoit (John Merton) in *Drums of Fu Manchu* (1940).

Strong men of the chapter play.
LEFT: Joe Bonomo. ABOVE: Jack Dempsey.
OPPOSITE: Buster Crabbe (left), one of
the serial Tarzans, enjoys the company
of, from the top, Herman Brix,
Elmo Lincoln, and Frank Merrill.

Antedating Republic's masked avengers
of the 1930s were those played by William
Desmond in *The Riddle Rider* (1924),
The Return of the Riddle Rider (1927),
The Vanishing Rider (1928), above, and
The Mystery Rider (1928). Desmond's
nine silent serials were filmed by
Universal. (Photograph courtesy of
Howard Nelson and Kalton C. Lahue.)

OPPOSITE: Reed Hadley (above) carrie
on the Desmond tradition in *Zorro'*
Fighting Legion (1939). Linda Stirlin
(below, with George Lewis) traded o
the Zorro name in *Zorro'*
Black Whip (1944)

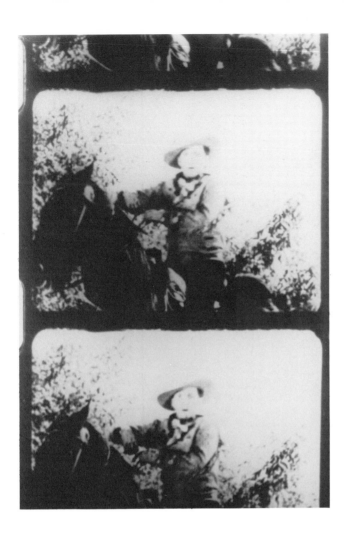

OPPOSITE: Serial hero of the 1920s Walter Miller, above, in a scene from *Queen of the Northwoods* (1929). The poster, below, advertises the last serial in which Miller and Allene Ray costarred. It was also Pathé's last chapter play (1929).
ABOVE: Tim McCoy and scenes from *The Indians Are Coming* (1930), the first successful sound serial.

33

Leading serial cowboy star Buck Jones.

THE PERILS OF SUCCESS

I have set my life upon a cast,
And I will stand the hazard of the die.

WILLIAM SHAKESPEARE, *Richard III*

Even without Elaine's adventures, 1915 would have been a rich year for serial production. Universal and Pathé released four each and six other studios also contributed continued dramas. Vitagraph balanced the comic *Flora Fourflush* with *The Goddess*, an admixture of *Trilby*, *Strife*, and *The Miracle Man* that was as much women's drama as thriller. Another flirtation with what was to be the substance of soap opera was Reliance's *Runaway June*, presenting Norma Phillips as a foolish bride unable to face a minor domestic crisis.

From Mutual came *The Girl and the Game*, with Helen Holmes of the *Hazards of Helen* series. American Films' ambitious *The Diamond from the Sky* (featuring Lottie Pickford in a role originally intended for her sister, Mary) traced in thirty

35

chapters the passage of a meteoritic diamond from rightful to wrongful possessors and back again. A director-to-be, Irving Cummings, was guided through the hero role by William Desmond Taylor (whose real-life murder six years later still remains unsolved).

In addition to parody there was experimentation in 1915. Universal's *Graft* (starring Harry Carey) was written round robin, for press and screen, by a dozen or so writers. Lubin's *Road o' Strife* presented its dialogue on dark backgrounds within the scenes. Cinema producer–historian Kenneth MacGowan recalled the noninterruptive visual technique of this Crane Wilbur film with pleasure but found it used again in only one other serial, the French-made *Judex* of Louis Feuillade (about 1916). In another variation of 1915, Kalem's episodic *The Ventures of Marguerite* drew upon a labors of Hercules motif, as heroine Marguerite Courtot thrust aside fifteen formidable obstacles before getting her man.

In 1915, in addition to the second and third Elaine serials, Pathé released *Neal of the Navy*, noteworthy for its use of a man's name in the title, and *The Red Circle*, the first of eleven serials made by the only true rival to Pearl White's crown in the chapter-play kingdom, Ruth Roland.[1] Miss Roland's first chapter play might now be called a psychological thriller. The title described a circular stigma on the heroine's right hand which drove her, Dr. Jekyll–style, to criminal actions she could not govern. (Frank Mayo played a detective whose love helped wipe away the curse.) Possibly confused by the psychology, the general serial audience was cool to the drama. Ruth Roland's rise to the cliffhanging pinnacle was to be deferred for a time.

The accelerated chapter-play activity of 1915 extended over the next two years. Ten companies released about twenty continued films in 1916 alone, Pathé and Universal again issuing eight between them. A dash to the serial gold fields had clearly begun—though the lure of the quick profit sometimes led only to

[1] Miss Roland had earlier appeared in series films—*The Girl Detectives* and *Who Pays?*—but *The Red Circle*, produced by the Balboa Company for Pathé, introduced this former vaudevillian and already popular film performer to the genre to which her talents proved best suited.

pyrite. Kleine, for instance, paid Billie Burke $150,000 to appear in *Gloria's Romance* (1916), which, despite elaborate mounting and a cast from the legitimate theater, failed to gain the rewards of the less fancy cliffhangers with which it competed.

Gloria's Romance did, however, become the first (and possibly the only) chapter play to garner a formal review in the *New York Times*—no doubt because it was the first one to be shown in a legitimate theater on Broadway. In that engagement the Globe played it two episodes at a time to audiences who paid twenty-five and fifty cents. The *Times* reviewer liked Miss Burke as a hoydenish girl "Lost in the Everglades" and "Caught by the Seminoles" but opined that "she would be more of a vision if her frocks were longer." Nonetheless, the critic conceded, "one should not demand everything." The last line of his review is of interest to latter-day readers: "Jerome Kern, master of insinuating melody, has composed a score for the serial, and last night he conducted the orchestra."

Another ill-starred attempt to substitute prestige for chapter-play basics was *The Great Secret* (1916), Louis B. Mayer's first venture into film production. The drama had little but its somewhat reluctant stars to commend it. They were well-remunerated Francis X. Bushman and Beverly Bayne, the screen's leading romantic team of that day. For all his persistence in corralling the film idols, Mayer (and Metro) made little or nothing from the production. The failure was doubly painful to Metro, which shortly before had undergone similar misfortune with a serial showcase for Maurice Costello, *The Crimson Stain Mystery*.

The unfortunate sorties into chapter-play production by theatrical and film celebrities demonstrated that making successful serials required an unidentified constituent of artisanship—perhaps it was earnestness or sincerity—that not every performer or production staff could muster. George Seitz developed techniques that could smooth the way to success; yet even they mattered little if those using them believed that in making chapter plays they were demeaning themselves. The creation of continued films was no longer for the uninitiated and assuredly not for unbelievers.

37

The early serial era was established upon the heroines, of course. As they would a few decades later in soap opera, male stars often had to operate in feminine shadows, providing rescues when needed and reacting to situations created by the struggle between villain and leading lady. Although chapter-play titles were emerging from the name-the-heroine pattern which they had originally followed, 1916 still had its share of girl-oriented serials, including *Lass of the Lumberlands*, *Perils of Our Girl Reporters*, *Beatrice Fairfax*, Essanay's *The Strange Case of Mary Page*, and *The Mysteries of Myra.*

The Mysteries of Myra epitomized the chapter play's increasingly frequent exploration of the occult and the bizarre. Portraying a secret order resembling a group of Rosicrucians gone mad, the serial dealt in thought transference, witchcraft, death wishes, levitation, and mysticism in general. The filming techniques accentuated the grotesque elements of the narrative, which were abundant. At one point Myra's fiance, Dr. Payson Alden (played by Howard Estabrook), had to raise up some water elementals to douse a fire in Myra's home that had been ignited by the black order's fire elementals.

Myra was the group's target because she had inherited some incriminating papers from her father, a defrocked member of the hooded set. Her good fortune in having an occult scientist as a promised mate repeatedly saved her from the vampires, spirits, and ambulatory oak trees sent her way. As Charles Beaumont once suggested, it is difficult to see how those who as youngsters sat through fifteen chapters of such terror could later worry about the comparatively innocent pleasures provided by the entertainment media to their own offspring in the 1930s.

Admittedly, *The Mysteries of Myra* was the continued film's *ne plus ultra* in horror fantasy. Nevertheless, serial doings before World War I often wandered noticeably beyond the ordinary course of adventure. In 1916, *The Shielding Shadow* (Pathé) featured an unusual cloak which brought invisibility to its wearer—long before such devices were employed in the *Invisible Man* films or Bela Lugosi's *The Phantom Creeps*. Prominent also was an apparently amphibious squid which dragged Ralph

Kellard to the deep when he tried some light reading at the water's edge.

By that time even Pearl White was facing perils far more sinister than the rough-and-tumble encounters with which she began her career. Late in *The Exploits of Elaine* there was a hint of what was to come in the appearance of one Long Sin. At first he was conspicuous only because of the drooping mustache which accented his conventional American dress. A short time later Arthur B. Reeve's debt to Sax Rohmer became obvious:

> Long Sin, now in rich Oriental costume, was reclining on a divan smoking a strange looking pipe and playing with two pet white rats. Each white rat had a gold band around his leg, to which was connected a gold chain about a foot in length, and the chains ended in rings which were slipped over Long's little fingers. Ordinarily, he carried the pets up the capacious arm of each sleeve.

Despite this promising beginning, Long Sin was more or less absorbed by another Oriental, Wu Fang, in the second Elaine serial. As Reeve explained it: "Beside Wu, the inscrutable, Long Sin, astute though he was, was a mere pigmy—his slave, his advance agent, as it were, a tentacle sent out to discover the most promising outlet for the nefarious talents of his master."

In other words, Pathé had recognized the growing commercial viability of the yellow peril and was going to make much more of it. The name Wu Fang had the right ring.[2] Through a remarkable ability to spring back from death, Wu Fang became Miss White's personal Fu Manchu in several continued dramas. Indeed, in *The Lightning Raider* (1919) he was played by Warner Oland, the screen's great Oriental impersonator, whose film repertoire also included portrayals of Rohmer's mysterious character. (One criticism of Oland's Fu Manchu films was that there was too much Wu Fang in them; it is an inscrutable point.)

A contemporary of Pearl White's Long and Wu was Ali Singh,

[2] It may not be remembered, but there was a real Wu Fang. He in no way resembled his fictional namesake spiritually. Formerly the Chinese minister to Washington, Wu Ting Fang wrote a book called *America Through Oriental Spectacles,* which reached bookstores less than a year before the fictional Mr. Wu turned up in Reeve's story. On March 22, 1914, the *New York Times* devoted a full page to prepublication excerpts.

Mongolian by birth and known to 1916 serial audiences as *The Yellow Menace*. While Long Sin was content to obtain the Clutching Hand's treasure map by placing that defeated villain in suspended animation, Singh was bent upon world supremacy for his race. The open hostility toward those of other races displayed by Americans in the film no doubt strengthened his incentive. In this sorry affair the Secret Service—and thus the white race—was too much for Ali Singh, who perished in his cause. If he had seen how Neal of the Navy had dismantled "The Yellow Peril" a short time earlier, Singh might have used greater caution.

The vicious racial assassination of *The Yellow Menace* and other films, both serial and feature, was offered under the guise of "preparedness." Europe had been at war since 1914, and many Americans were urging that their country ready itself to join the fray. The motion-picture medium was employed to depict all sides of the question, though prowar, antialien films soon outnumbered the few pro-German efforts and the pacifistic dramas such as *Be Neutral*, a 1915 nonserial starring Francis Ford and Grace Cunard. In their film exports Great Britain and Germany were far from neutral. Balfour, Kitchener, and Lloyd George authorized a documentary, *How Britain Prepared* (1916), designed to show Americans how the British forces were geared for action. During this country's period of neutrality it was bombarded by similar propaganda vehicles from both sides, although Germany's propaganda was generally ineffective.

There was confusion for serialgoers, nonetheless, about which side to be on. The exact origin of Marcius Del Mar (alias Martin), the character portrayed by Lionel Barrymore in *The Romance of Elaine*, was obscure. But that leader of saboteurs and former head of the Anti-American League had a Prussian air about him—and he made a memorable entrance by emerging from the symbol of Germanic disregard for civilian life, a U-boat. More pleasing to the kaiser would have been Mutual's *The Secret of the Submarine* (1916), attributed after some legal action to the pen of war correspondent Richard Barry. This film, which served as actress Juanita Hansen's serial debut, told of the efforts of the heroine and Lieutenant Jarvis Hope (Tom

Chatterton) to keep an oxygen-breathing sub from falling into the hands of the Japanese or the Russians, ironically enough, eventual allies of the United States in World War I.

Equally anti-Japanese in sentiment was Pathé's *Patria* (1917). The fifteen-chapter production was financed to the amount of about $90,000 by William Randolph Hearst. It gave every indication that the United States would soon be at war with the Japanese, as well as with Mexico (which supposedly would launch a Japanese-inspired invasion of the southern states). The title role in this polemic mistake was given to ballroom dancer Irene Castle, whose partner and husband, Vernon Castle, shortly lost his life in the allied cause.

Patria incurred the deep displeasure of President Woodrow Wilson, who asked Hearst to withdraw it from circulation so that its more severe anti-Japanese sections could be eliminated. They were, at some cost to the film's momentum and with the result that the film appeared primarily anti-Mexican—even to an Oriental-appearing advance guard with Japanese uniforms and Mexican names. To be anti-Mexican was not distressing to administration officials at the time because of the unsettled conditions south of the border. In fact, the expeditionary force under Pershing was in Mexico when the picture was released.

Immediately after World War I the whole *Patria* matter was placed before a Senate committee investigating German propaganda—which *Patria* was in character if not in intent. It was revealed that a German propagandist named Fox, whose articles had appeared in Hearst newspapers, had written a letter to Franz von Papen explaining a scheme to use a motion picture to deprecate Japan. Whether some of Hearst's executives knew that Fox was in the pay of the German government is uncertain, but, as Captain G. C. Lester, of United States Military Intelligence, testified, "*Patria* exploited the very idea which was set forth generally in Fox's statement."

The Mexican situation was touched on more directly, and possibly more realistically, in *Liberty, a Daughter of the U.S.A.* (1916). Jack Holt and Marie Walcamp starred in this Universal serial, about an American heiress named Liberty who was kid-

41

napped by a scheming Mexican needing the ransom money for his rebel cause. Codirector Henry McRae went on to become Universal's leading serial overseer in the 1920s and later.

Naturally, the chapter-play kingdom could not achieve full preparedness without some contribution by the reigning monarch. Pearl White was therefore presented by Pathé in *Pearl of the Army*, released in December, 1916. Her assignment was nothing less than to save the Panama Canal from a band of Oriental spies headed by the Silent Menace. (She did.) When the United States actually entered the war, however, Pearl was out of uniform. Her wartime chapter play, *The House of Hate*, bore upon a munitions firm whose operators thought only of profit. Pearl, the heiress apparent, battled a strong tide in her efforts to make the amoral House of Walden a constructive outlet of society. Harassment came from the Hooded Terror and from a vampish cousin named Zelda. Antonio Moreno, playing the hero, did so well at keeping from being obscured by Miss White that he almost became a serial actor permanently, making four consecutive chapter plays for Vitagraph before returning to feature work.

Counterespionage, as opposed to battlefield action, was the main occupation of the principals in war-oriented serials. In *A Daughter of Uncle Sam* (1918) wireless was used to trap enemy agents. Starting as a Western, *Wolves of Kultur* (1918) shifted after a few reels to a metropolitan setting, where spies and saboteurs were more likely to be found. The male star of this adventure was Charles Hutchison, a husky actor who appeared in a string of serials noted mainly for their vigorous outdoor action.[3]

Although *Wolves of Kultur* had some strong anti-German chapter titles (such as "The Huns' Hell Trap"), they were as nothing compared with the chapter headings of *The Eagle's Eye*. King Baggot chased a hundred or more aliens through "The

[3] After *Wolves of Kultur* Hutchison appeared in *The Great Gamble* (1919), *The Whirlwind* (1920), and *The Double Adventure* (1921). Then came three films directed by Seitz: *Hurricane Hutch* (1921), *Go Get 'Em Hutch* (1922), and *Speed* (1922). All but *Whirlwind* were Pathé releases. In 1926, Hutchison directed his comeback film, *Lightning Hutch*. Financial as well as production difficulties buried the film, but it is still shown occasionally, giving younger audiences a disappointing example of the chapter play in the late silent period.

Naval Ball Conspiracy," "The Plot Against Organized Labor," "The Invasion of Canada," "The Infantile Paralysis Epidemic," "The Campaign Against Cotton," "The Great Hindu Conspiracy," "The Menace of the I.W.W.," and other amazing installments. Evidently Baggot's adversaries left absolutely no stone, germ, or phobia unturned in attempting to destroy America.

By comparison with *The Eagle's Eye* other serials were only on the periphery of the war action. Vitagraph's *The Fighting Trail*, which brought William Duncan to serial prominence in 1917, revolved about a secret mine containing munitions materials of great interest to German agents. Another hidden-mine story was *The Red Ace* (1917), a Universal film with Marie Walcamp. The foreign agents in such stories were no more than stand-ins for badmen who in peacetime sought mineral wealth or treasure for financial gain alone.

Definitely topical was *A Woman in a Web*, a Vitagraph drama about a Russian princess caught in the overthrow of the czar. Here was the introduction of a new cinematic menace, this one red. In another 1918 chapter play with political overtones, Universal's *The Lion's Claw*, Marie Walcamp resisted a holy war being fused by the Central Powers in Africa. A quarter-century later this idea underlay several talking serials.

Some wartime chapter plays, of course, had little or no relationship to the conflict. After all, civilian crime did not cease for the duration. Serialgoers in 1917–18 were able to slip away from worries about spies, the western front, and the influenza epidemic while enjoying mufti heroics of several new cliffhanging favorites, the colorful Eddie Polo for one. *The Voice on the Wire*, a 1917 journey into the occult and the macabre, brought together Ben Wilson and Neva Gerber, successors to Ford and Cunard at Universal. These well-liked adventure performers joined talents for nine continued dramas, including *The Mystery Ship* (1917).[4]

[4] The better Wilson-Gerber efforts were produced between 1919 and 1921: *Trail of the Octopus, The Screaming Shadow, The Branded Four,* and *The Mysterious Pearl.* In 1925–26 the two performers teamed again, less effectively, for *The Power God, The Mystery Box,* and *Officer 444.* Wilson's work actually spanned the silent era, for he had supported Mary Fuller in *What Happened to Mary.*

Two 1917–18 serials I have thus far withheld: *The Neglected Wife* and *Hands Up*. *The Neglected Wife*, a plodding story of a romantic triangle, had little to commend it. But it had as its star Ruth Roland, who in *Hands Up* was at last allowed to show her value in a chapter play with extensive action. *Hands Up*, written by Gilson Willets, was in the dramatic mold of his earlier *Adventures of Kathlyn*. The temples were Inca, not those of India, but the heroine faced the same kind of problems one faces when mistaken for native royalty.

Within five years of her triumph in *Hands Up*, Ruth Roland appeared in eight serials for Pathé, most of them good representatives of the high-action chapter play, all of them money earners. In *The Tiger's Trail* (1919) she was entangled with both a Hindu tiger cult (real tigers courtesy the Selig zoo) and a gang of western badmen. The strange juxtaposition came when Louis Gasnier required Frank Leon Smith to relocate some of the metropolitan scenes of the source work, C. A. Logue's *The Long Arm*. Train travelers watching *The Tiger's Trail* may have developed a sense of uneasiness after seeing a famous sequence in which some daring wranglers jumped onto the roof of Ruth's train and by forming a human chain were able to reach into her compartment and snatch the valuable parcel she was carrying.

As Miss Roland's reputation increased, Pathé capitalized upon it by including her name in the titles; hence *The Adventures of Ruth* and *Ruth of the Rockies* (1920). According to the count of her *Films in Review* biographer, George Geltzer, Miss Roland used thirty-five disguises in *The Adventures of Ruth*, which was advertised as written, produced, and directed by the actress. She did produce the movie, but the script was by Gilson Willets, and George Marshall was the director. Marshall also directed *Ruth of the Rockies*, based upon a published work by Johnston McCulley, whose Zorro would one day become a serial fixture.

After *The Avenging Arrow* (1921) came two pictures noted for some extraordinary, and highly unlikely, action sequences. In *White Eagle*, almost a reworking of *Hands Up*, Miss Roland made a spectacular departure from a moving train by climbing a rope ladder suspended from a plane overhead. In *The Timber*

Queen, remembered for its runaway-boxcar sequence, the heroine (or her double) rode down a high wire holding onto a pulley and made another breathtaking exit from a train, this time by catching a swinging rope. The Roland-Pathé chapter-play cycle was concluded with (in order of release) *Haunted Valley* and *Ruth of the Range.*

Because Ruth Roland's serials contained an unusual amount of daredevil action, it is interesting to note that she had strong opinions on the importance of developing empathy between the audience and the character she was portraying. Perhaps her position as serial heroine second only to Pearl White is explained by her statement that "unless audiences look on you as a dear old friend, they won't get half the fun out of seeing you in danger."

In retrospect, the correctness of Miss Roland's words becomes apparent. Never successful as a dramatic actress, she did succeed in allowing her warm personality to emerge in her chapter-play characterizations. Whatever the name of the character she was playing, she was Ruth in danger—just as Pearl White was always an imperiled Pearl. The ability to transfer personality to celluloid brought both Pearl White and Ruth Roland to pre-eminent serial positions; it gave them their places in memory.

Miss White especially gave the impression of enjoying her work. In her later serials even the subtitles conveyed a happy approach to danger. In *The Lightning Raider,* needing a quick hiding place in a museum, Pearl hit upon a mummy's sarcophagus. "Here, Rameses, you old bigamist," she chuckled. "You haven't done anything for a lady in a thousand years." Later on, confronting Wu Fang in his snare-filled parlor, Pearl asked, "Eh, where do you keep your poisonous snakes these days, Wu Fang?"

Perhaps there was other value (or meaning) in the comic-book-style dialogue Miss White's writers were using in 1919. On the eve of the Roaring Twenties, the chapter-play genre, not yet ten years old, had settled all its frontiers. Everything it would do in its remaining one-third century of life it had already done. Sound would add another pathway to the sensory organs of the viewer, but serials themselves did not change significantly by virtue of being heard. They might have clangorous sound tracks, they might enjoy clearer photography, they might present more spectacular stunt work, but chapter plays remained what they had been almost from the beginning: thrillers by installment with high suspense at the end.

In the 1950s Frank Leon Smith decried the quick adoption of cliffhanging endings, because it was the easy way out and because it predestined the serial to an audience change to be considered in Chapter 3. But right or not, the situational endings Smith preferred did not become the vogue, and the motion-picture-serial mode was fixed before the form could grow. As Smith noted, the basic perils were established in Pearl White's productions: water, fire, height, depth, weight, speed, and edged tools. The techniques for dispelling the perils in subsequent episodes were quickly refined. Falls were broken by overhanging limbs or canopies. Diabolical devices were deactivated a hairbreadth from the completion of their deadly missions. Onrushing water was cut off by a desperate turning of a valve no one had seen before—for the key to fooling amateur peril solvers lay in keeping the saving agent unseen until the resolving episode.

In some instances the characters escaped by normal reflex action, although they frequently had to regain consciousness to do so. They rolled away from falling objects. They swam to safety after plunging into raging currents from amazing heights. They found miraculous paths through blazing infernos. And, more often than anything else, they jumped—out of cars, out of planes, out of buildings about to explode, out of crashing wagons or coaches. The explosion or crash was all the eye could see in Episode A, but in Episode B a short piece of footage depicted the last-second awakening and desperate self-ejection of the person in danger.

Studios developed fondnesses for certain of these scenes. Scarcely a Western serial was made at Republic in the sound era that did not use the shots of a mine car racing through twisting corridors before hurtling over a precipice to the seeming doom of a chap who it later turned out had already exited his chariot.

The sequence could be varied by having the out-of-control car appear to overtake and crush the hero.

Ingenuity of a certainty was often used in devising these escapes. Yet even youngsters who fretted about the outcome while waiting for the next installment recognized their artificiality. And by the end of the chapter-play cycle there was not even ingenuity in ending. Characters mechanically jumped or rolled from danger in episode after episode without the slightest evidence of imagination on the part of the serial makers. No wonder Frank Smith wished that in the glory days there had been more of "The Lady or the Tiger?" in chapter breaks and less of the lady tied to the tracks.

Before leaving this formative period of the motion-picture serial it should be mentioned that along with the fixing of suspense patterns came the conventions of serial titles. Obviously the dominant form was *The Adventures of . . .* or its variations: *Exploits of, Perils of, Great Adventures of, New Adventures of,* and so on. But other forms were used heavily. From the serial studios came *The Mysterious: Airman, Pearl, Mr. M, Dr. Satan, Pilot,* and *Island; Mystery: Pilot, Rider, Ship, Mountain, Box, Mind,* and *Squadron;* and *The Mystery of: the Double Cross, 13,* and *the Riverboat.*

Close to the mysterious was the secret. The silent and sound eras produced *Secret: Four, Kingdom, Service Saunders, Agent X-9* (produced twice), plus *Secret Service in Darkest Africa, Secret of the Submarine, Secret of Treasure Island, Secret Code,* and *The Great Secret.* During silent days magnitude in title, apparently not too important in the sound era, brought not only *The Great Secret* but *The Great Gamble, The Great Reward,* and, in double-barreled approach, *The Great Radium Mystery* and *The Great Circus Mystery.* Also on display were gigantic financial dealings: *A Fight for Millions, The Million Dollar Mystery, The $1,000,000 Reward,* and *The Twenty Million Dollar Mystery.*

Color also was a characteristic fetish of the silent serials: *The Black Book, The Black Box, The Black Secret, The Blue Fox, The*

Crimson Flash, The Crimson Stain Mystery, The Golden Stallion, The Gray Ghost, The Green Archer, The Purple Mask, The Red Circle, The Red Glove, The Scarlet Arrow, The Scarlet Brand, The Scarlet Runner, The Scarlet Streak, White Eagle, A Woman in Gray, The Yellow Cameo, and, not so lustrous, *The Yellow Menace* and *The Yellow Arm*.

Title makers in the sound-serial period made little use of color. In fact—and the point may not be without significance—the production at Republic Pictures of such efforts as *The Purple Monster Strikes, The Crimson Ghost*, and *The Black Widow* coincided with the final decline of the motion-picture chapter play. But if the titles of talking serials reflected little nomenclatorial interest in color, they did reveal a receptivity somewhere to things of the jungle, things lost, and things majestic. Audiences of the 1930s to 1950s watched *Jungle Drums of Africa, Jungle Girl, Jungle Jim, Jungle Raiders, The Jungle Menace*, and *The Jungle Mystery*, as well as *Panther Girl of the Kongo, Congo Bill*, and several Tarzan serials. Among the "lost" were a city, a planet, and a special train. And filling the ranks of royalty were *King of the: Carnival, Forest Rangers, Mounties, Rocket Men, Royal Mounted*, and *Texas Rangers*. Impressive combinations appeared in *The Lost Jungle, King of the Congo* (and *Kongo*), *Jungle Queen*, and *Queen of the Jungle*.

Though it never appeared, the ultimate serial title of the sound days would certainly have been *King of the Lost Jungle*. Perhaps even a Phantom King would have been in order, for there were almost as many specters around as there were kings, not the least being *The Phantom* himself. Others were *The Phantom Empire, The Phantom of the Air, The Phantom of the West, The Phantom Rider* (two of them), and *The Phantom Creeps*.

A unique titling syndrome of the sound period was the *versus* label. *Canadian Mounties v. Atomic Invaders* is an example of a title fad that was perhaps symptomatic of waning creativity. That, however, is material for a later chapter.

There is danger in reading too much into serial titles. It may be equally unwise to disregard them entirely. In looking at the designations given to chapter plays of any vintage, any period, we somehow find the words of that old Roman, Pliny the Younger, coming to mind: "I have said everything when I have named the man."

AT THIS THEATER NEXT WEEK

The one cruel fact about heroes is that they are made of flesh and blood.

HENRY ARTHUR JONES, *The Liars*

In 1922 two wonder women of the silver screen quietly let out the news. No longer would they earn their livelihood by being thrown in front of onrushing locomotives or bounding boulders or rampaging horses. Their bones and their artistic dignities had suffered enough. They would go on to other things.

Ordinarily the retirement of two actresses from the business of cliffhanging would have done no harm to the profession. At least a dozen experienced serial heroines stood in reserve, and hundreds of young hopefuls were willing to risk a few bumps to get a toehold in the film industry. But in this instance the ladies deserting the genre that had brought them worldwide attention were Pearl White and Ruth Roland, first and second goddesses of the chapter-play pantheon. They were performers who could not be replaced.

50

Pathé's simultaneous loss of its primary box-office attractions was one more indication of the declining fortunes of the film serial. It was, however, by no means the starting point. Even before the 1920s the serial's time in the sun had passed. Its usefulness as a compromise between two-reeler and feature film ended when the full-length picture became the dominant form. Its value as a promotional gimmick for newspapers and magazines eroded from overuse. And its appeal to the adult segment of the motion-picture audience diminished as that audience changed.

Discerning moviegoers—whose number increased each year as the 1920s approached—were unmoved by the fantastic exploits of serialdom that had thrilled both old and young in earlier years. At the same time the serial makers, who might have reduced the gap between happenings on the screen and the sensibilities of those over twenty-one, allowed it to widen by devising situations that appeared ever more implausible. As the motion-picture audience, drawn by the films of Griffith and others, grew in sophistication, the chapter play developed along physical lines. Its creative artists in the 1920s were, in fact, the stunt men.

Yet the greater their daredevil achievements—the more they stretched reality—the farther the stunt men took the serial from a position of significance in the motion-picture industry. While those of tender years might catch their breath as a heroine leaped from a moving train to a low-flying Spad, others were sadly aware that such things did not happen, save in the world of Douglas Fairbanks, who could make it all seem reasonable with a smile and a wink.

So, by accident or design, the movie serial was given to the young, undoubtedly its rightful possessors. It was they who measured the derring-do of Charles Hutchison or Ben Wilson or William Duncan against that of Art Acord or William Desmond. It was they (never admitting it, of course) who breathed silent prayers for the safety of Neva Gerber and Eileen Sedgwick, Edith Johnson and Louise Lorraine. And it was they who gave point to the efforts of the serial directors—the Spencer Bennets, Ray Taylors, and Robert Hills who continued with the form till the end, the George Marshalls, W. S. Van Dykes, and Richard

Thorpes who went on to bigger things. Whatever the indifference of the older generation, the kids could be counted among
the faithful each Saturday afternoon.

But when those kids grew up, something puzzling happened.
Unlike serialgoers of earlier and later eras, those of the post–Pearl
White period discarded their celluloid heroes and heroines with
scarcely a backward glance. In recollections of childhood in the
Roaring Twenties, where are the paeans to the serial gods?

Walter Miller is a case in point. Between 1925 and 1929 he
starred in twelve major serials, a record in number and frequency approached by no other actor. Ten of Miller's roles were
in Pathé films with Allene Ray—not the queen, but certainly the
crown princess of the chapter play after the White and Roland
abdications. The Miller and Ray heroics included the popular
Hawk of the Hills and *The Green Archer*, as well as Pathé's final
serial, *The Black Book*. Not just a he-man, Miller was talented
enough to handle character parts in later years. He was Sylvia
Sidney's boss in *Street Scene*.

Why, then, don't we hear more about Walter Miller and his
contemporaries today? Their names and faces must have been
well known to the several million youngsters who went to serials
during the 1920s. Can it be that the inhabitants of the shadow
world of chapter plays made no lasting impression in an era noted
for its unrestrained adulation of the celebrated?

Perhaps that was exactly the problem. The day's flesh-and-
blood heroes overwhelmed the pretend ones. While Miller was
making his twelve serials, Charles A. Lindbergh was flying the
Atlantic, Babe Ruth was hitting home runs, Red Grange was running wild on middle western gridirons, Jack Dempsey was fighting Gene Tunney, and Admiral Richard M. Byrd was exploring
the South Pole. What two-reel-a-week hero could compete with
a horde of living legends?

In the years following World War I even the serial makers
turned several times to real-life champions. Summoned to cliffhanging in those days of ticker-tape parades were Dempsey,
Tunney, and Grange, not to mention assorted Olympic medalists
and the 1925 New York Giants.

The first to heed the call to higher duty were James J. Corbett and Harry Houdini. At fifty-three, Gentleman Jim was too old to be a convincing hero in his 1919 adventure, *The Midnight Man*, though to some extent his athletic ability and experience in theatrical melodrama helped him overcome the handicap of age. Houdini, only eight years younger, also failed to strike fire that year, but not because of his age. If the silent serial needed a conclusive demonstration of its incompatibility with the mature cinema audience, Houdini's *The Master Mystery* was it.

Attracted by the Houdini name, blinking adults were confronted by something that can be viewed only as a curiosity today and must have seemed just as absurd in 1919. Its only saving grace—some acrobatic escape work by Houdini—was far from sufficient to distract spectators from the amusement afforded by a Machiavelli who happened to be a clanking robot, by a forerunner of a James Bond supersecret eavesdropping device called the Dictagraph, and, above all, by a husky vamp named DeLuxe Dora.

Audiences who sit through a revival of *The Master Mystery* encounter a nasty gang of crooks known as International Patents, Inc., whose aim is to stop progress—that's right, progress. Under a castle on a roaring river they maintain a hidden vault—the Graveyard of Genius—to stow away mock-ups of supposedly dazzling inventions—the water motor for example—that might reduce their profits. Masterminding this buy-and-hide combine is the Automaton, who will do most anything to achieve his fiendish purposes. If need be, he'll use that rare Oriental poison Dhatura Stramonium on a member of his own gang. A pinch of this derivative of the nightshade family, he has discovered, is just the thing for defectors.

When Federal Agent Quentin Locke (Houdini) gets on his trail, the Automaton offers an incredible case study in avoiding the obvious in disposing of an adversary. Starting by shoving the government man into a strait jacket—child's play for a great escape artist—he moves on to hanging the Master Magician by his thumbs. This fruitless measure convinces the Automaton that he must bring into play more serious means of liquidation. Locke is shackled and tossed into a river, only to pop up before his tormentors have left the scene. As an encore, he performs the same trick encased in a wooden box.

The frustrated Automaton now begins to improvise. Quentin is bound with barbed wire prior to an acid sauna, strapped in an electric chair, suspended over a vat of highly corrosive liquid, stationed as a bumper for a plunging elevator, engulfed in poison gas, handed a package which makes an odd ticking noise, and thrust into an elaborate garroting apparatus by the Madagascar Strangler. He survives all, even DeLuxe Dora, and at last gets to the heart of the case, and the Automaton, who turns out to be a man in a metal suit, caught working controls and pulling levers like the Wizard of Oz.

Poor Houdini! He deserved better, though it must be said that he had a hand in forming the plot, along with Arthur B. Reeve, the creator of Craig Kennedy, the scientific detective of *The Exploits of Elaine*. In the end the great escape artist was forced to sue Octagon Films to obtain his modest share of the picture's earnings.

Jack Dempsey found his encounter with cliffhanging more profitable—or at least less trying. Shortly after winning the heavyweight title from Jess Willard, he took on a fifteen-chapter opponent called *Daredevil Jack*. If he did better than might have been expected in an arena as menacing as the motion-picture studio, credit should be given to W. S. Van Dyke, a director adept at making nonactors look good—as his work with jungle animals in *Trader Horn* and Asta in *The Thin Man* would prove. The presence in the cast of the experienced Lon Chaney also may have stabilized the champion.

Although his film brought a fine profit, Dempsey's impersonation of Jack Derry, college Achilles, did not lead him to give up the ring. Later in 1920 he squared off with one Billy Miske in Benton Harbor, Michigan, disposing of his opponent before the end of the third episode.

The only challenger the Manassa Mauler couldn't handle, Gene Tunney, had his turn in serials in 1925, just before his first

fight with Dempsey. Frank Leon Smith rushed a plot to completion, while Tunney was shown the basics of motion-picture
acting by Spencer Bennet. Despite an unpublicized injury to
the young fighter's hand, *The Fighting Marine* was ready for
theaters at the time of the championship bout. Tunney's victory
prevented what might have been a financial disaster for Pathé
if Jack Dempsey had won. In the tradition of the chapter play
the hero saved the mortgage, if only by a ten-round decision.

Another strong man called upon for serial service in the early
1920s was Joe Bonomo, sometimes known as the Modern Apollo
or the Cinema Colossus. Bonomo entered film production as a
stunt man, working out many of the remarkable tricks which
characterized serials of the time. Racing a motorcycle along a
dock and onto a ferryboat was one of his early specialties, but
he soon progressed to leaping from fire escapes to flagpoles and
diving into water from a plane sans parachute. His most widely
viewed feat was less spectacular than most of the stunts he performed. It survives because it was done for a historic film. Bonomo, doubling for Lon Chaney, made the breathtaking slide on
a rope down the cathedral wall in *The Hunchback of Notre
Dame.*

Setting a pattern for later stunt men, notably Yakima Canutt,
Kermit Maynard, David Sharpe, Rod Cameron, Clayton Moore,
Jock Mahoney, and Ben Johnson, Bonomo advanced to hero
roles. In 1925 he starred in two serials, *Perils of the Wild*, based
loosely upon *Swiss Family Robinson*, and *The Great Circus Mystery.* For the latter film he devised a plan of shooting consecu-
tively all the scenes in a given location, regardless of their subsequent placement in the finished film. That economy stratagem
endeared him to Universal president Carl Laemmle, whether or
not Bonomo was, as has been claimed, the first to use it.

After *The Great Circus Mystery*, Bonomo appeared in several
other serials, though the cliffhanging part that might have kept
him on the star level slipped from his grasp. In the early shooting
of *Tarzan the Mighty* he broke his leg and was replaced in the
title role by actor and stunt man Frank Merrill. When his film

career ended a few years later, Bonomo, ever a good business-man, moved to the pages of men's magazines, eyes staring, muscles flexed, in his well-known body-building ads.

Frank Merrill was the screen's fourth Tarzan. The first was Elmo Lincoln, who pounded his awesome chest in the well-received *Tarzan of the Apes* and *Romance of Tarzan* only six years after the October, 1912, issue of *All Story* magazine intro-duced Edgar Rice Burroughs' durable creation. But Elmo Lin-coln was not the first serial Tarzan. That distinction belonged to an actor-singer named P. Dempsey Tabler. Tabler actually was a background character in National Film's 1920 chapter play *Son of Tarzan*. As Lord Greystoke, now a middle-aged ex-Ape Man, he strode about his English estate in tweeds and toupee, leaving most of the jungle heroics to son Korak (played by Kamuela Searle, who was fatally injured in the filming).

Tarzan, however, was too colorful a character to be left in retirement. In 1921 he was rejuvenated for a fifteen-chapter serial, *The Adventures of Tarzan*. This time the impersonator was Lincoln, who had been busy with the serials *Elmo the Mighty* and *Elmo the Fearless* while Tabler and an alleged fire-man, Gene Pollar, enacted the role he had created. (Pollar played Tarzan in a dismal Goldwyn feature of 1920, *The Return of Tarzan*.)

Lincoln's posturings, bobbed hair, and off-the-shoulder animal skin amuse audiences today; yet old-timers insist that he was a convincing Tarzan. Physically striking—though a little over-weight—he had impressed filmgoers as the giant warrior in Grif-fith's *Intolerance*. To his advantage (or disadvantage, if other roles were considered), Elmo Lincoln, born Linkenhelt, could project the mien of one raised in the jungle and molded by simian society. He and perhaps Frank Merrill (who doubled for him in *The Adventures of Tarzan*) were the only screen Tarzans to possess this uncommon qualification, the others seeming closer to Western civilization, anthropologically speaking.

The Adventures of Tarzan was Elmo Lincoln's last bow as the Ape Man. No new Tarzan film would appear for six years. During the hiatus fashions in jungle kings changed. When *Tarzan and the Golden Lion,* a feature film, was made in 1927, a streamlined he-man, James Pierce, got the job. The no-longer-wanted Lincoln spent the last half of his life waiting for a role equal to the one that brought him worldwide recognition. Instead, the parts became smaller and smaller until, in a final irony, he appeared once more in a Tarzan film. Someone mindful of the publicity possibilities gave him a walk-on in *Tarzan's Magic Fountain,* a Lex Barker epic of 1948. Four years later Elmo Lincoln was dead. Until the end he hoped for one more good role.

If Elmo Lincoln found that being the originator of the Tarzan role gave him no hold on the part, James Pierce found it no surer to marry the boss's daughter. He wooed Joan Burroughs while making *Tarzan and the Golden Lion* and married her the next year. Yet when the chapters of *Tarzan the Mighty* (1928) were shot, Bonomo's stand-in, Frank Merrill, did the swinging on vines. Pierce had to content himself with the radio role in the early 1930s.

Merrill was Tarzan in two serials. The first was stretched to fifteen episodes when Universal saw the popularity of the early installments. The sequel, *Tarzan the Tiger,* is remembered as the film in which the Lord of the Jungle had amnesia. From Chapter 3 to Chapter 13 the poor fellow never knew quite whom to pounce upon.

The advertising for *Tarzan the Tiger* stressed other things, however. Those not content with the usual line of "thundering elephant herds, sabre-toothed tigers, man-eating lions, giant gorillas, hyenas, and other jungle denizens" were enticed by bait less mundane as jungle attractions go. If they beheld the fifteen episodes they would assuredly see:

1. The amazing palace of Opar, where pure gold is hidden in tons;
2. The beautiful high priestess who wants Tarzan for her mate;
3. The slave market, where beautiful women are put on the auction block—where souls are sold for a few grains of sand—or less;
4. Tarzan's beautiful wife, captured by the giant gorilla, dragged off to a jungle retreat—as the gorilla's revenge on his enemy. AND . . .

5. A beautiful white woman snatched from her gorgeous boudoir and dragged to the innermost reaches of the inaccessible jungle.

It is said that fathers sometimes accompanied their sons to showings of *Tarzan the Tiger*.

Former stunt man Frank Merrill was the last Tarzan whose every grunt and "ah-ee-ya-ee-ya-ee-ya-wa-hoo!" was not recorded for posterity—though *Tarzan the Tiger*, coming as it did during the transition to talking pictures, was augmented by music and sound effects, an occasional Merrill yowl included. (The first all-talking Tarzan was Johnny Weissmuller, who in MGM's 1932 feature *Tarzan the Ape Man* provided W. S. Van Dyke with another opportunity to demonstrate his ability with nonactors.)

While sound rescued the motion-picture business in a period of financial depression and heavy radio competition, many thought that it meant the end of the serial. Early talkies, entrusted to stage directors and encumbered by immovable sound apparatus over which technicians presided with exasperating inflexibility, too often resembled tableaus rather than moving pictures. The fast action of the chapter play seemed incompatible with the new form of picture making. Serial production almost came to a halt. When Joseph P. Kennedy, special adviser turned chairman of the board, pulled Pathé out of serial production in 1929, only Universal and Nat Levine's young company, Mascot, were left to carry on the form. Mascot had the backing of Herbert Yates's Consolidated Film Corporation, but other independents found the making of sound serials too expensive during this period of change.

Eventually the obstinacy of the sound technicians was overcome, effective dubbing techniques were devised, recording equipment was improved, and films started moving again. Universal expressed confidence in sound serials by giving full promotional support to Henry McRae's *The Indians Are Coming*, starring Tim McCoy and Allene Ray. Just to be sure, the company prepared a silent version for theaters not yet equipped for sound and theater managers not interested in talking serials.

But when the talking edition played major film palaces throughout the country, it pushed aside the myth that the serial was doomed by sound.

Had the judges been grownups and not youngsters, the decision might have been different. The makers of *The Indians Are Coming* had much to learn about spoken drama. As in many other early talkies, the dialogue sections stand apart from the action sequences much as the librettos of operettas do from the songs. Moreover, these conversational interludes are unbelievably melodramatic when viewed today—and we can wonder whether they looked much better in 1930. The scene in which McCoy is reunited with the brother he thought lost "out there somewhere"—while his sweetheart and faithful dog portray despair turned exultation—is camp exemplified. McCoy, a flamboyant performer, who would, however, become one of the better actors in Westerns when he discovered the subtleties, was given lines that had not been uttered in drama since the days of Buffalo Bill. He declaimed them with a fervor more appropriate to 1880 than to 1930, unintentionally communicating the ingenuous resolution that Adam West would strive to produce as television's Batman years later.

Even so, Tim McCoy's performance as Jack Manning was more restrained than that of others in the film. Only the dog managed not to fall victim to the natural tendency of actors groomed in the silent film to overplay when thrust into a talkie. And even that poor animal was forced to carry out several bits of stage business that are embarrassingly cloying. Had it not been for the rip-roaring action sequences—the truly important scenes, after all—the motion-picture serial, and Tim McCoy, might have found it difficult to recover from *The Indians Are Coming*.

But we must not be too aesthetic in evaluating a pioneer sound serial. Its most concerned audience found every episode highly satisfactory, from "Pals in Buckskin" to "Trail's End." Film sovereign Will Hays was delighted that the picture brought the kids back to the movies. Carl Laemmle's delight lay in the near-million-dollar profit the inexpensive production brought to Universal. He hoped that it would happen again. The motion-picture serial, having passed its own sound barrier, would have another quarter-century of life.

The serial heroes of the sound era were not those of the 1920s, although many of the new he-men had their roots in silent films. The first talking chapter plays drew upon actors—Rin Tin Tin included—who in the earlier period had played leads in features. The old serial stars—William Desmond, Joe Bonomo, and others —were shunted into secondary roles. Walter Miller wound up playing villains.

Many of the heroes in the first wave of talking cliffhangers seemed to be stopping in the land of the serials on the way to other things. Tim McCoy, who had starred in several high-budget frontier dramas before *The Indians Are Coming*, made a second serial, *Heroes of the Flames* (1931), before beginning the long parade of Westerns for which he is best remembered. Harry Carey, whose simple Westerner was no longer in vogue after Tom Mix changed cowboy styles, returned to serials in Mascot's *Vanishing Legion* (1931) en route to the fine character roles which rounded out his career. Mix himself made his only serial, *The Miracle Rider*, in 1935. It was Mascot's longest, fifteen episodes, but unimpressive. The fifty-five-year-old range rider decided that it was time to withdraw from films and spent the last five years of his life with the Tom Mix Circus.

Another longtime Western star, Ken Maynard, made his one serial, *Mystery Mountain*, in 1934. Supporting him was, ironically, a young Mascot performer whose warbling would spell the decline of Maynard's vigorous breed of Westerns. Yet Gene Autry was not, technically, the first singing cowboy. In earlier films Maynard himself had sung in situations natural to cowboy life.

Bob Steele, Ken Maynard's screen pardner in an inexpensive series near the end of the feature trail, was one more short-term serial hero. He put on aviator's goggles for *Mystery Squadron* (1933) but soon returned to feature work. In 1965 he turned up as Duffy, a regular in television's *F Troop*, a vastly different kind of frontier drama from that he had worked in for many years.

For most actors who had been leading men in features a stopover in serials meant another step on the way down, but for one, Marion Morrison, it was a prelude to greater success—though it may not have seemed so at the time. In a brief period Morrison had moved from the Southern California football team to prop work in Tom Mix pictures and to a small part in John Ford's *Men Without Women*. Then, renamed John Wayne, he was given what seemed to be his great chance, the principal role in a pioneer wide-screen epic, *The Big Trail*. But 1930 was no year to ask exhibitors, who despite a financial depression had installed expensive sound equipment, to add seventy-millimeter projectors and larger screens to their budgets. The wide-screen processes were deferred until the early 1950s, when they were revived by television competition. Wayne turned to B Westerns (interesting ones) and serials. He made three twelve-episoders for Mascot in 1932–33. None were Westerns. *Hurricane Express* was a railroad thriller; *Shadow of the Eagle*, a drama of carnival life; and *The Three Musketeers*, a tale of the Foreign Legion. In *The Three Musketeers* Wayne had the eminent support of Raymond Hatton, Jack Mulhall, William Desmond, and the juniors Noah Beery, Francis X. Bushman, and Creighton/Lon Chaney. Wayne finished out the 1930s with several series of well-made B Westerns and the film that did bring him major status, John Ford's much-admired *Stagecoach* (1939).

Another football-player-turned-actor was assigned to a wide-screen Western epic in 1930. His *Billy the Kid* was no more successful than *The Big Trail* in setting off a change to the wider screen, and soon he too was acting in low-budget Westerns and serials. This actor's descent to the Saturday-afternoon valley was not as rapid as John Wayne's, but, unlike Wayne, Johnny Mack Brown remained there.

Brown was three years older than Wayne and had achieved prominence slightly earlier. He was an established leading man in romantic films of the late 1920s, appearing with Marion Davies, Mary Pickford, and Greta Garbo. He was one of Joan

61

Crawford's beaus in *Our Dancing Daughters*. Somehow Brown's warm drawl and husky build made him seem more natural in buckskins than in dinner jacket. After *Billy the Kid* he made a few more conventional features (if a film with Mae West can be considered conventional) and then fell into the profitable serial-Western pattern he would continue until the mid-1950s. Brown was a B-Western star over a longer period than anyone else in the sound era. His serial work, however, was confined to the 1930s.

Mascot's *Fighting with Kit Carson* (1933) was Brown's first serial. The others were Universal's *Rustlers of Red Dog* (1935), *Wild West Days* (1937), *Flaming Frontiers* (1938), and *The Oregon Trail* (1939). Brown's serials contained more Indians, rustlers, land grabbers, Pony Express riders, and heroines named Lucy than those of any other sagebrush star, a fact well known to the short-pants set.

Only one actor played the lead in more Western serials than Johnny Mack Brown. He was Buck Jones, whose chapter plays brought youngsters back to the theaters week after week in the years before World War II. In the sound era audiences seldom were drawn to serials by the actors who appeared in them. If there was an attraction beyond the normal mystery and action, it was some celebrated fictional avenger. The famed Lone Ranger was the magnet, not Lee Powell, who first played him. The Shadow beckoned, not Victor Jory. Yet in Buck Jones's serials the attraction was Buck himself. He was the only actor whose name consistently appeared above the title in the newspaper ads. Others are regarded as more noteworthy serial performers in retrospect, but in the 1930s Buck Jones was the ranking star.

From 1933 to 1936 Jones starred in a Universal serial each year—first the well-produced *Gordon of Ghost City*, then *The Red Rider, Roaring West,* and *The Phantom Rider*. Exhibitors welcomed them all. Whatever the title, it was the "new Buck Jones serial" they advertised. There was apprehension about only one thing: the episode in each serial which ended with Buck and his white horse leaping from a cliff into water far below. One theater owner called the device old hat and suggested that Universal scrap it. The company didn't, of course. Good chapter-ending predicaments were too hard to come by in Western serials, which couldn't draw upon poison gas, falling elevators, crashing planes, or electrical contraptions. In *Raiders of Ghost City*, a Universal release of 1944, Dennis Moore and mount jumped into a lake that Jones undoubtedly had used a decade earlier.

A dispute with management broke Jones's Universal serial cycle after *The Phantom Rider*, in which he played a masked crusader on a white horse, a role similar to one he had performed in feature films and enjoyed doing. Jones's last two serials were issued in 1941, when he was no longer one of the leading cowboy performers; he had not, in fact, made a Western for several years. Nevertheless, in that year Columbia placed his name above the title of the one he made for the studio, *White Eagle*. And Universal brought him back for what it claimed was the most expensive serial ever made, *Riders of Death Valley*. Jones shared the marquee in that vehicle, not surprisingly, because much of the high budget for the film was used to round up a cast that included Dick Foran, Leo Carrillo, Charles Bickford, and Lon Chaney, Jr.

Meanwhile, Jones was also making a modest comeback in feature Westerns as one of the Rough Riders. His pardners in this inexpensive but entertaining Monogram series were fellow old-timers Tim McCoy and Raymond Hatton. Though McCoy did most of the heavy acting, Buck was the principal figure. His horse was usually a nose ahead of those of his buddies, and in the last reel he faced down the prime villain, after slowly inserting a stick of chewing gum in his mouth—the sign that the malefactor's end was at hand. Buck was being discovered by youngsters who had not seen his older films when tragedy ended his career. On November 28, 1942, some eastern exhibitors were honoring him with a party at the Cocoanut Grove in Boston when the club burst into flames. Jones apparently made it safely outside the building and then returned to the inferno to help others escape. The luck that had saved him so many times on the screen was not with him that night. He was overcome by smoke and severely burned. Two days later Buck Jones was dead. The serial prairie would not see his like again.

From the films mentioned thus far in this chapter the reader may wonder whether all the serials made in the early sound era were Westerns. They were not, of course. But the Western serial was always the prevalent form and was especially prominent in the first half of the 1930s, when the influence of science fiction and the comic strip upon chapter-play production was slight. Though sound may have affected the form of other motion pictures, the low-budget Western retained essentially the same character it had had in the silent days and, on the whole, suffered little from the addition of the sound track—at least, until the singing cowboy came along. Individual stars, such as Art Acord, could not survive the requirements of spoken dialogue, but the Western itself, serial or feature, quickly adapted to its new environment, while comedy, romantic, and even mystery films, so often placed in the hands of stage-trained writers and directors, floundered under a surfeit of talk. Moreover, the sounds of horses' hooves, Indian yells, and rifle fire undoubtedly increased the effectiveness of Western serials, certainly the large-scale ones, such as RKO's only cliffhanger, *The Last Frontier* (1932), which starred Lon Chaney, Jr., and Universal's *Battling with Buffalo Bill*, a Tom Tyler film of 1931.

Tom Tyler was the busiest hero of chapter plays in the early 1930s. Between 1930 and 1933 he made five serials, starting with Mascot's *The Phantom of the West*. Although two of them were Westerns (three if one includes *Clancy of the Mounted*), Tyler was comfortable in the other two popular serial milieus of depression days, the sky and the jungle. In 1932 he made *The Jungle Mystery* for Universal; the next year, *The Phantom of the Air*.

For a time it was thought that the airplane film might supplant the Western in the affection of the young, but, air age and all, it didn't happen. Situations involving airplanes were woven into many serials and adventure features; yet the number of serials centering upon aviation never matched that of films set in the West. Nonetheless, in the New Deal era at least one air adventure could be expected to appear each year among the ranks of serial dramas. In the same year that Tom Tyler was seen in *The Phantom of the Air*, his future rangeland associate, Bob Steele, made *Mystery Squadron*. Then in 1934 came *Tailspin Tommy*, a highly popular production starring Maurice Murphy. It was the first film serial based upon a comic strip, and as such its fortunes were closely observed. The warm response it received from young moviegoers encouraged Universal's serial makers to produce a sequel, *Tailspin Tommy and the Great Air Mystery* (1935), as well as *Ace Drummond* (1936), another serial derived from an adventure strip.[1]

Tailspin Tommy's greatest importance, however, was not in providing a stimulus to aviation subjects but in opening the chapter-play door to comic-strip features. As a matter of fact, the aviation cycle would soon be lost in space—and in war clouds. Not many old-fashioned, seat-of-the-pants flying films would be made after Flash Gordon took off for Mongo and World War II revolutionized aeronautics.

A product of the old school was *The Mysterious Pilot* (1937), in which Commander Frank Hawks, after battling gangsters for two reels in a drama of Canada's air police, returned to the screen to give a few tips on flying. Hawks was directed by the able Spencer Bennet and surrounded by a good cast that included Rex Lease, Dorothy Sebastian, Kenneth Harlan, Esther Ralston, Clara Kimball Young, and that magnificent portrayer of native villains, Frank Lackteen.

In 1938 the memorable *Fighting Devil Dogs* brought the aviation serial to its zenith—and at the same time outdated the kind of airways adventure that had been made up to that time. Heroes Herman Brix and Lee Powell had more to do than win air races or chase minor gangsters. Their challenge was the Lightning. The two Orient-based marines discovered how dangerous that fellow could be when he eliminated all occupants of a war lord's

---

[1] *Ace Drummond* was a Sunday-comic feature with a story line attributed to Captain Eddie Rickenbacker and drawings by Clayton Knight.

castle with an electrically charged aerial torpedo. (That's right: the episode was called "The Lightning Strikes.") While the boys were investigating the disaster, another mysterious missile wiped out their waiting detachment. Marine Powell, facing charges of negligence, returned to the States to clear himself by flushing out the source of his difficulty. But the incendiary genius who concealed his identity under a black metal hood and flowing cloak was not easy to corner, especially when aboard his airship —then only an engineer's dream—the flying wing.

Perhaps it was the scientific wizardry. Perhaps it was the striking ebony costume, so close to the cape and cowl garb soon to be affected by the heroes in comic books. Whatever it was, the Lightning was the remembered figure in *The Fighting Devil Dogs*. When he received his comeuppance in Chapter 12, it was almost a shame. Simply learning his identity, after a long guessing game, was satisfaction enough.

Yet, even when he had been blown to smithereens, the Lightning's influence was felt. After the flying wing, no twin-cockpit biplane could arouse much excitement in an aerial extravaganza. Universal made a few old-style skyhangers in the early 1940s, using the Dead End Kids. And figures from other media, notably Hop Harrigan, Smilin' Jack, and Bruce Gentry, zoomed by occasionally. But the old barnstormers, the Tailspin Tommys, disappeared in the roar of jets and the blast of rockets.

Less affected than the sky by temporal events was the jungle. The lush tropical undergrowth of Africa or India or the South Pacific served the chapter play well, from *The Adventures of Kathlyn* in 1913 to *Panther Girl of the Kongo* in 1955. Did it matter that the undergrowth looked like a mass of potted palms on the studio's back lot or that the cannibals spoke with distinctly southern accents? Not on Saturday afternoon.

One jungle figure, of course, surpassed all others, and Hollywood had a talking Tarzan in action by 1933 and another one in 1935. Oddly, these were the only motion-picture serial adventures of Burroughs' character produced in the sound era. And even then the producers hedged their bets by releasing the stories

A fiendish partnership existing only in imagination. Bela Lugosi, top left (in *SOS Coast Guard*), contacts Charles Middleton, top right (of the Flash Gordon series), while Frank Coghlan, Jr., below (Billy Batson in *The Adventures of Captain Marvel*) eavesdrops.

Another imposing serial villain, the Scorpion, wisely takes cover from Tom Tyler in *The Adventures of Captain Marvel* (1941).

When a superhero went into action against lesser villains, he often ignored the amenities. Captain Marvel had a way of devastating a sitting room.

In outer space there sometimes were no amenities at all. Arriving on the planet Mongo, Dr. Zarkov (Frank Shannon), Dale Arden (Jean Rogers), and Flash Gordon (Buster Crabbe) find a cold welcome from the local constabulary in Universal's *Flash Gordon* (1936).

Kindlier treatment of interplanetary visitors could be expected from the leonine King Thun (James Pierce) and Prince Barin (Richard Alexander), though Flash's complexion is somewhat the worse for one of his many scuffles with the denizens of Mongo.

The mayhem in *Flash Gordon* at times reached prodigious proportions. Restrained by Princess Aura (Priscilla Lawson), Buster Crabbe
as Flash stands victorious over a sampling of the gladiators he has
felled.

Sex, serial style. Awesome Aura lays claim to a stupefied Flash Gordon. Such overt indications of romantic interest were rare in chapter plays, rarer yet when emanating from the supposedly submissive sex.

Youngsters delighted in the rococo rockets of *Flash Gordon*. Earnest performers Crabbe and Rogers managed to convey the impression that the gadget-filled mock-ups actually could get off the ground.

The second Flash Gordon serial, though less dependent upon pugilistic exhibitions than its predecessor, was not without its livelier moments. Here Flash and pals enjoy a light workout in *Flash Gordon's Trip to Mars* (Universal, 1938).

Ralph Byrd as Dick Tracy, right, fixes
his eyes on former serial hero Walter
Miller in a sequence from
Dick Tracy's G-Men (1939).

The invisible ghost stalks his prey in *Dick Tracy vs. Crime, Inc.* (1941).

ABOVE: The first Lone Ranger of the screen, Lee Powell, right, shares a 1938 photograph with, from left, Hal Taliaferro, Herman Brix, George (Letz) Montgomery, Chief Thundercloud, Lynn Roberts, and Lane Chandler. BELOW LEFT: A *Lone Ranger* poster. BELOW RIGHT: The second movie Ranger, Robert Livingston, minus mask but with Tonto (Thundercloud).

Frances Gifford brings out the terpsichorean tendencies of a normally uncooperative gorilla in *Jungle Girl* (Republic, 1941).

What's a girl going to do? Facing the Mysterious Dr. Satan, Ella Neal
has the not inconsiderable encumbrance of Eduardo Cianelli's wide-
ranging robot.

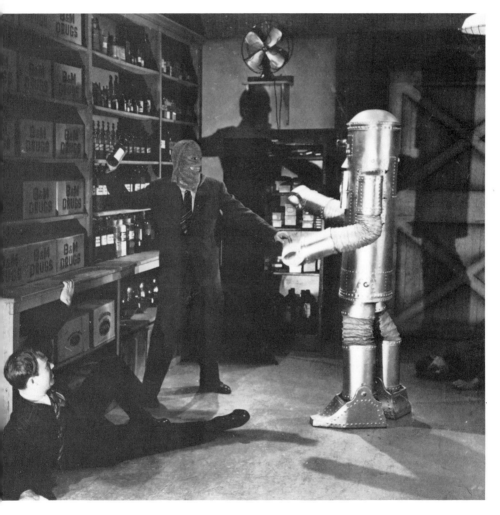

Robert Wilcox, as the Copperhead in another scene from *The Mysterious Dr. Satan* (Republic, 1940), tries to stop the automaton with a bottle of volatile chemicals.

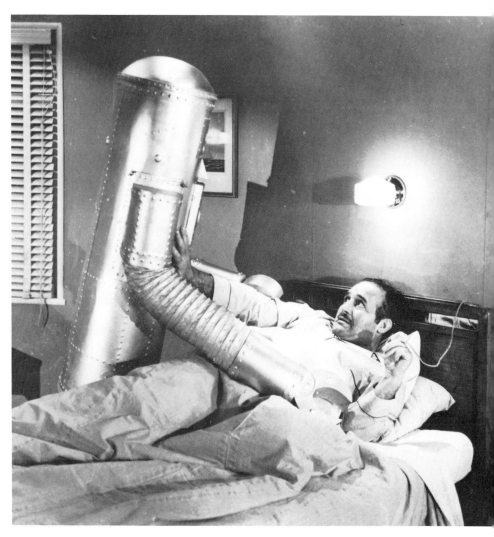

Was there no sanctuary from Dr. Satan's robot?

Kay Aldridge, as Nyoka, momentarily pinned by Vultura (Lorna Gray) in *The Perils of Nyoka* (1942).

Much less aggressive than Nyoka was Laura Graham (Frances Robinson), of *Tim Tyler's Luck* (Universal, 1937). Her reaction to tense situations was often a dead faint.

In twelve chapters Miss Robinson advanced
from the supportive arms of Tim Tyler (Frank
Thomas, Jr.) to the hirsute ones of a
short-tempered gorilla.

Not all serial perils were reserved for heroines.
In Republic's first chapter play, *Darkest Africa*
(1936), Clyde Beatty and the youthful Baru (Manuel
King) face the Bat-Men of Joba.

OPPOSITE: Betty Wallace (Louise Currie)
and Billy Batson (Frank Coghlan, Jr.)
seemingly at the mercy of the Scorpion
and associates in *The Adventures of
Captain Marvel*. But Batson is only
a "SHAZAM!" away from becoming
a superhero.

The hardest-working serial villain, Roy Barcroft,
has Linda Stirling in his net in *Manhunt of
Mystery Island* (1945).

One of the chapter play's last hooded menaces, the title character of *The Crimson Ghost* (Republic, 1946), intimidates a normally villainous Kenne Duncan, while a normally heroic Clayton Moore (TV's Lone Ranger) looks on, pistol in hand.

A study in contrasts. Bolo, the giant elephant of *Tim Tyler's Luck*, stands nose-to-nose with Professor Tyler's jungle cruiser. The fancy vehicle had stalled before this shot, and it was necessary for Bolo (played by a lady pachyderm named Anna May) to push it up the incline.

in both feature and chapter versions, a common practice of independent film companies, who needed to strain every ounce of gold from the few sound serials they made before leaving chapter-play production to the major studios around 1937.

The jungle king in Principal's *Tarzan the Fearless* (1933) was Buster Crabbe, whose ultimate cliffhanging glory was yet to come. Herman Brix played the Ape Man role in *The New Adventures of Tarzan*, made by a company in which Burroughs had a financial interest. This chapter play was turned into not one but two feature versions: *Tarzan and the Green Goddess* and *Tarzan in Guatemala*. The action scenes were good, though sometimes they seemed forever in coming. The Brix adventure was the chattiest Tarzan serial made. Guatemala, an odd place for the Ape Man to be operating, provided an interesting and obviously nonartificial background for the tale of a scientific expedition employing Tarzan as technical adviser. The problems of recording the sound on location, however, were sufficient to cause the producers to "crave the audience's indulgence" in a foreword to the picture.

Physically Brix, a 1928 Olympic medalist from the University of Washington, was an excellent Tarzan. Moreover, he was an articulate one. In this production Tarzan was the fluent Lord Greystoke of Burroughs' novel, not the "Me Tarzan, you Jane" noble savage of the Weissmuller films for MGM. By the time Brix had captured the part, however, the Weissmuller portrayal had become the norm, thanks to two well-made and extremely popular features. Loquacious or not, Johnny Weissmuller was a Tarzan the public liked, and that was that. The role would be played in his image for years after he left the series. A conversational Lord Greystoke would not reappear till the fall of 1966 in the person of Ron Ely of the television series. Ex-Tarzan Brix, by the way, continued in serial work for several years after *The New Adventures of Tarzan* and then enjoyed success as a leading man and character actor under the name Bruce Bennett.[2]

[2] Brix, according to one account, was MGM's initial choice for *Tarzan the Ape Man*, but an injury he sustained during the filming of *Touchdown* (Paramount, 1931) caused the search for an actor-athlete to be continued till Johnny Weissmuller was found. Weissmuller recalls going to the studio for a test without

Not every athlete found the transition in thespian service as easy as Herman Brix did. That's why a good old jungle setting often came in handy. It provided a means of concealing a lack of talent behind thick vines—or at least muffling it under drumbeats. Red Grange had no such protection in *The Galloping Ghost* (1931), a Stateside adventure. When not in action he had the look of someone who suddenly had found himself on the wrong subway train. But when wild-animal trainer Clyde Beatty said his lines in the 1934 Mascot thriller *The Lost Jungle*, the big cats of the Hagenbeck-Wallace Circus and those infernal *drums* were there to mask the primitive histrionics.

Beatty, who handled animals as no other trainer could, was given a second serial role in *Darkest Africa* (1936). This time, instead of hacking his way through the shrubbery looking for heroine Cecilia Parker, he hacked his way toward Elaine Shephard. In both cases his quarry was more appealing than the kind Frank Buck forever tried to bring back alive. In fact, when Buck himself landed in the serial jungle in 1937, it was neither Miss Parker nor Miss Shephard he pursued, but *The Jungle Menace*.

To tell the truth, old Frank missed out on a lot of the fun that went on in the chapter-play jungle. Noah Beery, Jr., didn't. In 1935 he played a junior Tarzan in Universal's *Call of the Savage*, based upon Otis Adelbert Kline's character Jan of the Jungle. It was Beery's pleasure in this drama to be shipwrecked somewhere along the African coast with baby-faced heroine Dorothy Short. When not occupied with the serial's twelve thousand thrills— "Lions and Tigers! Elephants and Monkeys! Chimpanzees and Crocodiles! Battling each other for jungle supremacy! Attacking man for survival!"—Beery could observe the film's twelve-thou-

---

thinking too seriously of becoming a film actor. The salary first offered him did not compare favorably to what he could earn in promotional appearances and testimonials. While Edgar Rice Burroughs never understood the pidgin-English characterization of the MGM Tarzan, it was the only one that would have worked for Weissmuller, who would have sounded absurd imitating an English lord. Brix, no doubt, would have had more dialogue, and he did make an impressive Tarzan when he finally got the role; but without the peculiar Weissmuller-Tarzan chemistry it's doubtful that MGM would have had so lucrative a series of jungle films.

sand-and-first thrill, Miss Short, bathing in a jungle stream or filling a leopard skin as no shipwrecked teenager should.

The plot of *Call of the Savage* involved a search for a lost polio vaccine (the badmen planned to sell it for a big profit), but it may have been difficult for all but the youngest spectator to bear this in mind while Miss Short was on the screen. Though serials generally were devoid of all the elements of feminine sex appeal found in feature films, the jungle adventures were the exception. The intellectual attraction of a scantily clad maiden in peril of being burned at the stake or thrown into an active volcano seldom was overlooked by the producers of Hollywood, even those who made cliffhangers.

Filmgoers who recall Noah Beery, Jr., as a grizzled wrangler in countless Western dramas may find it difficult to think of him as the hero of a tropical thriller. Yet what about the most unlikely rescuer of fair damsels ever to trod a south-sea island, the matchless Bela Lugosi? Aside from viewers of the late late show, only those of middle years remember Bela as Chandu the Magician. He played Dr. Chandler, counterconjurer, for the first time in Universal's 1932 feature adaptation of the old radio mystery. Two years later he again was Chandler, alias Chandu, in a serial sequel for Principal. The title (what else but *The Return of Chandu?*) also was used for one of two features compiled from the collected chapters. The other was called *Chandu on the Magic Island*.

For those who wonder in what kind of situation Bela Lugosi found himself as a serial good guy, let us say that his assignment was to protect an Egyptian princess from the forces of black magic. This involved, as a beginning, snatching a poisoned cup from her fingers just as she raised it to her lips, then eluding the disappointed poisoners by vanishing magically. From there on the audience followed a running battle between Chandu and a band of nasty necromancers headed by Lucien Prival. During a stopover on a tropical island these scoundrels went so far as to begin sacrificial rites with the princess the honored victim. Bela, who probably was inclined to cheer them on from force of habit, stepped in at the climactic moment to break up the fun. It was just about the last time Bela Lugosi did anything nice in a motion picture.

In his first serial work he was more in character. Mascot's *Whispering Shadow* (1933) found him playing Professor Strang, proprietor of a waxworks inspired by the Grand Guignol. After his deviation as Chandu he returned to stride as Victor Poten, mad inventor, in Victory's *Shadow of Chinatown* (1936). Herman Brix brought Lugosi's wild schemes to an end in fifteen chapters. In 1937 Lugosi was another mad inventor, Boroff by name, in *SOS Coast Guard*. This time hero Ralph Byrd was too much for him.

Bela gave it one last try in *The Phantom Creeps* (1939). And as Doctor Alex Zorka, a scientist with designs on ruling the world, he had a lot going for him. First was a giant robot, somewhat more menacing than Houdini's Automaton. Zorka developed it as a prototype of what he expected would be an army of mechanical warriors if he could swing the right deal. Most of the time the robot stood idle behind a panel in the scientist's home. But when Bela pressed the button on the control box strapped to his wrist and the panel slid open, juveniles in darkened theaters across the land bit down hard on their Milk Duds and twisted their Tootsie Rolls into misshapen masses.

Alex Zorka, nevertheless, was too versatile a mad inventor to rely solely upon a robot. He had a G man in a state of suspended animation by the end of Chapter 1. Shortly before that, one of his highly explosive mechanical spiders went off in midair, causing a plane crash in which Zorka's wife was an unintended victim. Zorka, at the crash scene but concealing his identity, was forced as a physician to choke back his emotion and pronounce his wife dead during a wild hubbub—in the midst of which the heroine, a nosy reporter, shook off a restraining policeman with the cry, "Leave go of me!"

Dr. Zorka also had defensive armor: if the police or a band of Nazilike agents became annoying, he pressed another button on his wrist and faded to invisibility. This power also helped him several times to recover his most prized secret, a chunk of a meteorite he had found in Africa. With it he could fashion an arsenal of powerful hand bombs and a potent ray gun—just as potent as the one Boris Karloff had devised in Universal's 1936 feature *The Invisible Ray*, which co-starred Lugosi. The similarity in weaponry is not surprising. Part of the African sequence from *The Invisible Ray* (showing the discovery of a meteorite) was used in *The Phantom Creeps* to reveal how Lugosi discovered the hidden source of his power.

Borrowing was common in chapter-play making. To keep costs low, the serial units appropriated everything at hand, from sets and costumes to stock shots and background music. Thus *The Phantom Creeps* profited from the *mysterioso* theme of the Frankenstein films, as well as from some striking shots of a streamliner roaring past the snow-covered terrain used in every Universal serial of the day calling for a train chase—whether or not the snow was appropriate. Also drawn upon were the tricks in simulating invisibility acquired by the studio's special-effects department in the concurrent cycle of *Invisible Man* pictures; the dockside, airport, and rural locales utilized in countless thrillers; and chase music that was not new when heard in *Flash Gordon*. The contribution of *The Phantom Creeps* to later serials was an auto chase in which a 1939 black Nash pursued an ancient touring car. The appearance of a vintage vehicle in a chase was a sure sign that sooner or later it would go over a cliff and burn. New cars didn't match those in crashes in the stock-film library, and stock shots were meant to last many years.

But all this is not helping Bela Lugosi conquer the world. To tell the truth, he doesn't quite make it. For each of his weapons a defense is devised by the film's good scientist, Dr. Mallory, described by Zorka as a "genius second only to me." The frustrations mount. Mallory brews an antidote for suspended animation in Chapter 3 and later catches the terrible tinkerer with his invisibility down by means of an antidematerialization ray.

When his precious robot is blasted into a pile of nuts and bolts, Zorka takes to the skies, determined to bring the world to its knees with the hand bombs he begins dropping in key areas. Like a child with the ultimate toy, he sits in the rear cockpit of an open plane, letting go his explosives while his man Monk

95

pilots the craft in full chauffeur's regalia and dark glasses. Then the inevitable pursuit planes surround him, as they did King Kong. Announcing, "I'll take them all with me!" Zorka prepares to destroy most of North America by detonating all his lethal hardware. Only Monk's lack of receptivity to the idea saves the situation. The two airborne threats to humanity scuffle and plummet into the ocean, ending Dr. Alex Zorka's career as a world-beater and Bela Lugosi's as a serial villain.

Bela, as is well known, went on working in the laboratories of low-budget features for many years after 1939, sharing with cronies Boris Karloff, Lionel Atwill, and George Zucco the wild desire to revolutionize the processes of life and smarting under the ridicule of medical colleagues. In serials, though, the day of the do-it-yourself mad scientist and robot maker was almost over. Eduardo Cianelli tried it in *The Mysterious Dr. Satan* (1940). He sent his mechanical monster off to a spectacular bank robbery but was no more successful than the Automaton in disposing of the hero—possibly because he employed several of the bizarre methods of assassination used in the old Houdini movie.

Once again it was a matter of the real world pushing its way into that of the motion-picture serial. World War II provided more than enough real madmen bent upon taking over the world. Some of the free-enterprise, home-workshop schemers went to work for the Axis powers, but most closed shop. And when the war was over, they were among the technologically unemployed. They hadn't noticed it, but as early as 1936 the sphere of dangerous inventors had begun shifting—to outer space.

PERILOUS SATURDAYS

Ah! happy years! once more who would not be a boy!
LORD BYRON, *Childe Harold's Pilgrimage*

The gray-haired scientist took his eyes from the telescope that magnified an angry heaven and turned toward his distinguished colleague.

"We are doomed, Professor Gordon," he said. "The planet is rushing madly toward Earth and no human power can stop it."

With these words—at once a death song and a call to final glory—the motion-picture serial began a last bid to recapture its lost audience. The effort failed, of course. Filmgoers past teen-age found only momentary amusement in the chapter play that was intended to win them back. But critics in corduroy knickers and striped polo shirts, unaware that adults had ever supported cliffhangers, saw nothing trivial in the new adventure from Universal. To them, *Flash Gordon* was a step beyond what they had come to expect at the Majestic or Oriental on Saturday afternoon. They slid forward in theater seats scarred by numberless matinee skirmishes to witness the beginning of if not the Golden at least the Silver Age of the motion-picture serial.

Flash Gordon was not the serial's first brush with science fiction in the sound era. A year earlier, in February, 1935, Mascot had put forth an incredible piece of nonsense called *Phantom Empire*. History shows it to be the only singing Western set 25,000 feet underground. To be honest, not all the action took place below tumbleweed level. Some was unfolded in and around the ranch of the hero, who was none other than Gene Autry, in the first of his many attempts to meet the challenging assignment of playing himself. Autry's Radio Ranch was just an ordinary spread, except for three things: it was the site of his weekly broadcasts to the nation, it was the stomping ground for a pack of kids who put sheets on their shoulders and pots on their heads to become the Junior Thunder Riders, and it accommodated, on one corner of the grazing land, a hard-to-miss "unknown" entrance to the "glamorous" kingdom of Murania.

Murania was a scientifically advanced but sartorially retarded empire presided over by Queen Tika. At times her cavalry, the senior Thunder Riders, took the long elevator ride to the surface for special missions, rumbling across the countryside with a roar most annoying to a performing artist with a broadcast to do. Gene went below to see what was going on. In no time he was enmeshed in a palace revolt planned by the traitorous Lord Argo. In fact, the rascals did him in. This awkward situation—a dead hero with half the chapters still to go—was rectified almost immediately by order of the queen. Her dutiful scientists speedily brought Gene back to life in a glass-enclosed resuscitation chamber. The operation was nothing special in Murania. It didn't even damage a yodeler's tonsils.

Despite all his difficulties, Autry managed to get back to Radio Ranch at the end of each episode to do his show. During trips to the surface he also was able to thwart the dishonest efforts of a group of scientists searching for a deposit of radium around the Muranian entrance. And, as might be expected, he sneaked in a few Western ballads before Murania vanished forever in an enormous explosion.

Phantom Empire undoubtedly was the most unusual serial of the 1930s—and perhaps of the entire sound era. It was an amalgam of everything and everybody on the Mascot lot: cowboys in customary costume playing ranch hands, cowboys in Flash Gordon costumes playing Muranians, character actors chewing upon the papier-mâché scenery of the underground palace, worn-out Shakespeareans struggling through dialogue with imperial guards who sounded fresh from the prairie. Towering above this cross section of mask and wig was Dorothy Christie, in regal décolletage, shouting every line as if the microphone were not to be trusted. Then too, we must not forget Gene Autry and pals Smiley Burnette, Frankie Darro, and a young girl named Betsy K. Ross, billed as the World's Champion Trick Rider. Autry, incidentally, gave every evidence of thoroughly enjoying his first big part. He carried out all the foolishness in superbly guileless manner, with no apparent apprehension about his dramatic limitations.

For all its weaknesses—and they have to be seen to be believed —*Phantom Empire* was a good investment for Mascot. Youngsters reacted well to the science-fiction folderol, whatever the confusions of plot. They were fascinated by the idea of an underground kingdom. More important to Mascot, they liked Gene Autry, who was soon to begin his long career in cowboy features.

Did *Phantom Empire* play a part in the thinking of those at Universal who, after the success of *Tailspin Tommy*, were wondering whether other features from the comic pages might make good serial subjects? It's possible. The Autry film was released fourteen months before *Flash Gordon*, and there was a fair amount of crossover from studio to studio among serial personnel in those days. More likely, however, both *Phantom Empire* and *Flash Gordon* were reflections of the increasing interest in science fiction at the time. The scientific-fantasy magazines had gained an impressive foothold at the newstands in the early 1930s. And in the comic sections and on the radio Buck Rogers was entertaining youngsters and more than a few adults with his escapades in the twenty-fifth century. The newspapers had introduced him in 1929. Flash Gordon appeared in the Sunday comics on January 7, 1934. By 1936 he was a logical candidate for serial stardom. The only real surprise is that Buck Rogers did not precede him in films. Possibly it was because Buck's popularity peak had passed by the time the movie serial turned to the comic pages, while Flash's was just being reached.

Then too, when the two newspaper features were placed side by side, the pictorial superiority of *Flash Gordon* was evident. Alex Raymond, who had polished his comic-strip style while drawing Dashiell Hammett's *Secret Agent X-9* and later would create *Jungle Jim* and *Rip Kirby*, was one of the pre-eminent artists of the comic field. He drew *Flash Gordon* with the care and draftsmanship that also marked the work of Harold Foster in *Tarzan* and *Prince Valiant* and Milton Caniff in *Terry and the Pirates* and *Steve Canyon*. These artists used cinematic effects and light and shadow in a manner seldom approached by other craftsmen of the funny pages. Raymond kept dialogue balloons from intruding upon his panels. He ran his narration and dialogue at the top or bottom of each picture.

Within a matter of months Raymond's striking illustrations and lively narratives made *Flash Gordon* a leading Sunday feature. With its exotic settings and creatures, its half-Graustark, half-Ziegfeld costumes, and its imposing arch villain it was a natural chapter-play subject for a studio willing to spend the money necessary to translate it to the screen. Universal was willing to do so. The budget for *Flash Gordon* reportedly was $350,000, a figure unheard of for a cliffhanger. *Phantom Empire*, for example, cost no more than $100,000, and few serials of the 1930s exceeded $150,000 in outlay.

Flash Gordon was further enhanced by the wealth of loan material available on the Universal lot at the time, the laboratory set of *The Bride of Frankenstein* and a giant idol of *The Mummy* being the most conspicuous appropriations. Film buffs still delight in tracing the musical borrowings of the *Flash Gordon* sound track to their feature-film origins, notably Franz Waxman's score for *The Bride of Frankenstein* and Heinz Roemheld's compositions or variations for *The Invisible Man, The Black Cat, Bombay Mail,* and *The Werewolf of London.*

The *Flash Gordon* plot line devised by writer-director Fred Stephani and three cowriters closely followed the comic strip's initial narrative: to save Earth from deadly emanations from the planet Mongo, Dr. Zarkov and two unexpected companions, Flash Gordon and Dale Arden, fly to Mongo in Zarkov's untested rocket and there do battle with the creator of the lethal disturbances, the emperor Ming.

This faithful reproduction of the original was in itself something of a novelty in serial making. In fact, *Flash Gordon* probably was closer in every way to its source than any other chapter play. A person not knowing otherwise might have thought the Sunday strip was based upon the film version, so similar were the narratives, costumes, settings, and even physical characteristics of the principals.

Certainly Larry ("Buster") Crabbe was a perfect Flash Gordon. It was necessary only to lighten the hair color of the former Olympic swimmer to give him an uncanny resemblance to Raymond's pen-and-ink hero. *Flash Gordon* was a second experience in serial starring for the 1932 graduate of the University of Southern California, his first having come in *Tarzan the Fearless.* In the three years and dozen or so appearances in features that lay between his first and second serial roles the six-foot-one-inch athlete added a few acting skills to his natural élan. When one watches an episode of the old serial today, he can see that Crabbe, in a thoroughly fantastic setting, gave a convincing performance. An actor of the serious tradition might have betrayed his lack of belief in the part, but nothing in Crabbe's manner or voice could be interpreted as a message to the audience that the whole thing was nonsense.

Crabbe could enter a strange flying craft, scan the dials and mechanisms for a few seconds in nonchalant manner, and then put the ship in the air moments later to engage in a dogfight with a fleet of suddenly appearing rocket ships. Preposterous? Of course. But remember, Flash Gordon was capable of doing such things, and without flying lessons. Buster Crabbe's accomplishment lay in not destroying the illusion. With dialogue that could have choked any actor (and seldom exceeded in depth his oft-parodied "Steady, Dale!"), young Crabbe succeeded to a remarkable degree in making the incredible credible.

But Buster was not the only well-cast actor in *Flash Gordon*. Frank Shannon was an exemplary Dr. Zarkov. And Charles Middleton devoured the role of Ming the Merciless. (Some said that he also devoured the carpets and walls.) He was an awesome Emperor of Mongo, from his glistening head to his ornate footwear. It would be difficult to imagine a better antagonist for Gordon than the one given being by Middleton. He could switch from keen interest in the diabolical doings of the scientists in his laboratory to an equally keen interest in the slender charms of Dale Arden, Gordon's girl friend, without losing a beat or a particle of majesty.

Playing the pretty Arden girl, by the way, was Jean Rogers, the only one of the principals who was not a perfect physical match of her comic-strip counterpart. Her hair was given an entirely wrong hue—blonde—and her figure, though attractive, was not as full as that of Raymond's original. Still, Miss Rogers, who had made her serial debut in *Tailspin Tommy*, was excellent as a woman in distress. Her fragile beauty caused the lechery directed her way to seem all the more sinister—whether it came from the always thwarted Ming, whose mistake was the insistence on the formality of a wedding ceremony, or from the gargantuan King Vultan, who stalked Miss Arden for the very fun of it and came a lot closer to getting somewhere.

Vultan's cornering of his frail quarry at the end of Chapter 5 stands as one of the more erotic bits of film footage turned out by Hollywood after the reins of censorship were tightened in 1934. Moments after the earth girl is brought to him as a prisoner, Vultan (John Lipson) begins his game by using a pet bear to terrify his prey and force her, trembling, against a wall. Then, ridding the chamber of pets and underlings, he closes in on the nearly hysterical damsel for what clearly is not the kill. The focus at the end of this chapter is not upon the more serious concurrent action—Flash's rocket, about to be blasted from the sky by one of Vultan's ray guns—but upon the predicament of Dale Arden, her slender form pressed against the wall, her midriff sucked in till it will go no farther, her bosom thrust forward to the limit of its dimensions. Shots of the approaching rocket intercut this sequence, each shift to the menaced maiden showing her breathing deeper, ever deeper, until, with Vultan only a few steps away, the closing titles suspend her agony for another week.

Flash Gordon is interlaced with such business as this. The minor strain of the erotic is never far from the major one of thrills and spills. At times it comes to the fore, as in Chapter 5, only to recede so that the action stuff can take over. In Chapter 6 the Vultan sequence is recast in such a way as to bear scarcely any resemblance in tone to the scene of the preceding episode. Dale, frightened into a state of shock by the king's huge pet, promptly collapses in Vultan's arms as Flash, miraculously untouched by the ray gun, rushes to her side. The patently lustful aims of Vultan are never again suggested. Dale now has only Ming to worry about, as far as lasciviousness goes.

A still-present physical peril for her, however, is Ming's crafty daughter. The unfortunate Dale is to Princess Aura what Flash is to Ming: an obstacle in the path of romance. Just as the Emperor of Mongo would dispose of Flash so that he might marry the Arden girl, his daughter would eliminate Dale to take possession of her boy friend. Aura asks Daddy for the blond earthman in the first chapter, then dogs her dream *innamorato* with the utmost vigor reel after reel. (Priscilla Lawson brought to the role of Aura a pursuit technique worthy of Mae West.)

Flash, apparently, sees more in a woman than sweater size. He remains true to Dale and manages to hold the overpowering princess at bay until he can redirect her ardor to someone, *anyone*, who loves her. The sacrificial victim, by his own choice, is Prince Barin, rightful ruler of Mongo. Flash, nevertheless, does not risk the chance that Aura might renew her interest in earthlings. In Chapter 13, with Ming seemingly dead by his own hand, the handsome spaceman heads back to Earth with his two companions, and *Flash Gordon* comes to an end.

It was all good fun, even in 1936, when *Flash Gordon* had not

103

yet achieved its status in the world of camp. The kids accepted the serial without skepticism. The adults, drawn by an extensive publicity campaign, enjoyed it as escapist material—and for the pieces of humor not too subtly planted in each chapter. Some of the asides cannot be accidental, especially the line in the first episode asserting the nobility and sacrificial nature of the hero. Let it be recorded that Flash Gordon "left his polo game" to be with his father at the dissolution of Earth.

In Chapter 6 the actors obviously are having fun with lines that may or may not have been in the original script—lines that bring to mind things topical on this planet, not Mongo, in 1936. The marital exploits of Tommy Manville seem to have been the inspiration for Ming's matter-of-fact prediction that Vultan, the playboy of Mongo, will marry the captive Dale. "He makes a habit of it," clucks the all-powerful potentate with uncharacteristic levity. Vultan (or actor Lipson) has his turn a scene or two later when Zarkov complains that Flash and Barin are being exposed to too much radium as slaves in Vultan's furnace room. The corpulent king, smiling in the manner of Oliver Hardy, muses, "It's . . . a pleasant death." Watching this scene, one almost expects the flip of the little necktie—that is, if one overlooks the fact that Vultan is wearing a vest of molded armor from which sprout a pair of huge wings. (Whether these wings are Vultan's or just part of his armor is the abiding mystery of *Flash Gordon*.) Vultan is allowed one more digression. When Flash and his fellow stokers break out in revolt, the wordplay involves a movie title of the day. With undisguised pleasure Vultan offers—not as an alarm, but as a caption—"Mutiny in the Furnace Room."

The light banter did not spoil things for the kids or prevent a sequel from appearing. In 1938, Universal released *Flash Gordon's Trip to Mars* (where an unexplainedly alive Ming, a somewhat pushy visitor from Mongo, was at it again). Though made without the generous budget of the original, the second film had some impressive special effects. There were clay people who oozed magically from the walls of caves, capes which allowed the wearers to soar through the Martian heavens, strato-sleds for sport travel, and tiny subway cars that roared through secret tunnels, not to mention a villainess who, while a trifle drab after Princess Aura, could vanish in a puff of smoke.

In addition to the special effects there were the principal performers from the first serial: Crabbe, Shannon, Middleton, Richard Alexander as Prince Barin, and heroine Jean Rogers (now a proper brunette). The several flashbacks to the first serial also let the audience see again John Lipson as Vultan and one-time Tarzan James Pierce as Thun, King of the Lion Men. Everyone was there except good old Princess Aura, who, presumably, was on Mongo, perhaps getting things ready in the nursery.

Flash Gordon's Trip to Mars received good treatment from the press. (*Look* did a three-part photo summary.) Some writers hold that *Trip to Mars* was a better serial than its twice-as-expensive predecessor, primarily because the action sections were less repetitive and better staged and because the dialogue was more polished. The wearisome stopping for man-to-man combat of *Flash Gordon* was not present in the second chapter play. On the other hand, the dialogue may not have been significantly improved the second time around—just more expansive. It's true that Flash was allowed more than the "Steady, Dale!" and "Hold on, Zarkov!" lines he had to work with on Mongo. But in the second chapter of his visit to Mars he most definitely can be heard warning Zarkov, "Head for the hills, Doc! We may be able to give them the slip in the canyon!" And the chapter play ends after a less-than-distinguished utterance by Hap, a wholly unnecessary comic character, who crowns the party's return to Earth with, "Look out, Broadway, here we come!"

Not long after the release of *Flash Gordon's Trip to Mars*, Orson Welles electrified the nation with his Halloween broadcast of H. G. Wells's *War of the Worlds*, a story of an invasion from the red planet. The furor surrounding the broadcast, which by its simulated news technique fooled thousands of people, caused Universal to hurry into release a feature version of its new serial. As *Mars Attacks the World* the film played to good audiences in many cities, sometimes alongside a feature version of the first serial, titled *Rocketship*. These feature editions of the old serials turned up in theaters once again in the early 1950s to capitalize on the rising interest in outer space. At about the same time the chapter versions began winning new admirers on television. Also reaching the home screen was the third, and weakest, of the Flash Gordon serials, *Flash Gordon Conquers the Universe*, as well as another Buster Crabbe film much in the Flash Gordon mold, *Buck Rogers* (1939). The already well-traveled Universal cliffhangers did so well in their new environment that a new television series of Flash Gordon adventures was shot in West Germany. This 1954 package, with Steve Holland playing Flash, suffered badly in comparison with the Crabbe films and disappeared quickly. A dozen years later, the original Flash Gordon serials were still running on major television stations, in the daytime for the kids and at night for adults with a bent toward nostalgia or camp savoring. Could anyone have foreseen the durability of these space sagas back in 1936?

Not that there was no optimism surrounding the serial form in that year. After all, it was then that Republic Pictures entered the serial market for the first time. From that studio would come a memorable line of chapter plays.

Republic Pictures Corporation was set up by Herbert J. Yates in 1935. It was not so much a new production organization as a combination of several existing ones, principally Monogram Pictures and Mascot Films (Nat Levine's serial-making outfit which had been financed by Yates's Consolidated Film Industries). Monogram brought to the merger of independents a large number of desirable film exchanges in leading cities, while Mascot brought a good reputation as a producer of adventure thrillers. Bulwarking the new operation was Consolidated Industries, probably the best concentration of technical facilities in Hollywood.

It was expected that Republic would bring production quality and good distribution to the kind of films which up to that time had been made on a quickie basis and given less than satisfactory distribution. And that's exactly what happened. Though Monogram shortly withdrew from the new organization, Republic in a few years gained a reputation as the unexcelled producer of Western and serial films, enjoying an extraordinary financial success while doing so. Republic was the studio of Gene Autry, Roy Rogers, the Three Mesquiteers, and half a dozen other Western figures, John Wayne included. Its serial productions embraced the tales of Zorro, the Lone Ranger, Dick Tracy, Captain Marvel, Nyoka, and Captain America, as well as such sagas as *The Fighting Devil Dogs, The Drums of Fu Manchu, The Mysterious Dr. Satan,* and *The Painted Stallion.*

Thanks to Republic's care in fashioning the adventure films in which it specialized, theaters in large cities which had shunned serials and modest-budget Westerns began to show them. Republic's ranch locations, laboratory facilities, mobile gear, skilled crews, and talented composers gave its thrillers a slick look that was matched by sound not heard before in the productions of smaller companies. At Republic adventure films were not unwanted bones tossed to lesser lights or beginners; they were the firm's principal product. It made a difference. Republic's thrill makers took pride in their work, however humble it may have seemed to those in the prestige companies. Academy Awards may have been few, but support from the kids of the 1930s and 1940s could not have been greater.

All this does not mean that as soon as the Republic trademark appeared before a serial title all traces of the old Mascot flavor were gone. Republic's first serial, Clyde Beatty's *Darkest Africa,* was *Phantom Empire* in a jungle setting. Its second serial, *Undersea Kingdom,* was the same thing at the ocean's floor. Indeed, action expert B. Reeves Eason was codirector of all three films. Each of the plots he had to work with presented a hero who found himself captive in a strange world—one advanced in science and weaponry, but seemingly unable to discard the armaments and costuming of another era. Thus powerful ray guns were brandished by tyrants whose Hittite-clad palace guards carried sword and spear. Horse-drawn chariots were followed into battle by armored tanks. Opulence of production set *Darkest Africa* and *Undersea Kingdom* apart from Nat Levine's inexpensive cliffhangers. But never far from center stage was the familiar Mascot blood and thunder, dressed up in *nouveau riche* fashion in a lot of fancy clothes.

Although Republic would make money over the years with far-out scientific fantasy, this kind of thing was not really the studio's forte. It was too good at genuine adventure to get mixed up with out-and-out hokum. Now the wild West was another matter. It seemed made for Republic. The company went there for its third serial and found itself on firm ground. Yet how could it miss? *The Vigilantes Are Coming* (1936) let the studio test-drive its most durable hero figure, the mystery rider. This one was Don Loring, the Eagle, and he looked for all the world like those disguised heroes to come: Zorro and the Lone Ranger.

The Vigilantes Are Coming was a reworking of *The Eagle*, Rudolph Valentino's silent film. It served as a showcase for Robert Livingston, one of Republic's popular leading men. Livingston, a handsome, virile performer and a competent actor, had the misfortune to come to Republic in the bloom of the singing-cowboy craze. Otherwise he might have been the company's top Western star. He is best remembered for his role as Stony Brooke, the lead cowboy in the well-liked Three Mesquiteer films. Livingston played in twenty-nine of them between 1936 and 1941, except for a stretch in 1938–39, when he was promoted to romantic melodramas and replaced by John Wayne. Wayne moved from the Stony Brooke role to his career-making portrayal of the Ringo Kid in *Stagecoach*. Livingston, on the other hand, met with little success in non-Western parts and returned to the Mesquiteers' range, replacing his replacement.

The night-rider device that Robert Livingston made work so well was not original with Republic. It was at least as old as the Klansmen of D. W. Griffith's *Birth of a Nation*. It served William Desmond nicely in serials of the 1920s and in *The Mark of Zorro* (1920) was the trick that set Douglas Fairbanks on the swashbuckling path. In the sound era Lon Chaney, Jr., was the Black Ghost in RKO's serial *The Last Frontier* (1932), while Buck Jones more than once donned a cloak or hood to set things right on the western countryside. His *The Phantom Rider*, for Universal, appeared two months before *The Vigilantes Are Coming*.

No studio, however, achieved greater mileage from the mounted avenger than Republic did. Robert Livingston had scarcely finished playing the Eagle when he was transformed into the sound film's first Zorro for a pioneer color feature, *The Bold Caballero*. In 1937, Republic drew upon the mystery rider for the central figure in two of its four serials.

The Painted Stallion, a well-made covered-wagon epic starring Ray Corrigan and Hoot Gibson, had as its pinto-borne *deus ex machina* an unknown Indian whose arrows went whistling through the air to warn the wagon train or forestall a villain. As elusive and omnipresent as a ghost rider, the protector of the caravan to Santa Fe was ultimately revealed to be not a youthful brave but a young woman. Julia Thayer played her, quietly yet impressively. Among the beneficiaries of her Athena-like intervention were Davy Crockett (Jack Perrin), Jim Bowie (Hal Taliaferro), and a juvenile Kit Carson (Sammy McKim). *The Painted Stallion*'s sweeping camera work was by William Nobles, photographer for twenty of Republic's first twenty-one serials. Raoul Krausharr contributed a musical score that was a bridge between the synthetic fusions of early sound serials and the creative scorings of his successors at the studio, notably Alberto Colombo, William Lava, and Cy Feuer.

In November, 1937, Republic released *Zorro Rides Again*, with John Carroll playing James Vega, great-grandson of Don Diego Vega, the original avenger. A reminder of the first Zorro adventure was a full-length portrait of a beaming Don Diego, bearing no slight resemblance to the senior Fairbanks. The painting swung away to reveal a secret passage leading to Zorro's ready room. There a paint horse and black riding outfit awaited Carroll, who changed simultaneously into both Zorro and Yakima Canutt. Without denigrating Carroll's performance, one could say that Canutt's stunt work contributed as much to the success of *Zorro Rides Again* as did the actor's dialogue scenes. In fact, Canutt probably was on the screen longer as Zorro than was Carroll, who spent much of his time in the idling dandy pose James Vega assumed to cover his tracks. The actor's best moments *in the Zorro costume* came post escapade, when, as he returned to his lair, he could burst into song. "Zorro rides again into the night . . .," he began, in the ringing baritone that would be heard in MGM's *Rio Rita* a few years later.

While obviously influenced by the emerging vogue of the singing cowboy, Zorro's first serial dramatization remained, nonetheless, solid adventure. John Carroll's singing, as Zorro or Vega, was kept in proportion, and neither Carroll the actor nor Canutt the stunt man succumbed to the cuteness that the Fairbanks inheritance might have inspired in them.

A no-nonsense directorial approach may have been the principal cause of the restraint. *Zorro Rides Again* had behind-the-scenes significance as the first joint effort of that peerless serial partnership John English and William Witney. It was customary economy for chapter plays to be guided by two directors, one shooting while the other prepared the next day's work, or one doing the locations while his associate filmed the interior sequences. No other team shared assignments as well as English and Witney. Together they piloted seventeen consecutive serials for Republic, including the well-received *Fighting Devil Dogs*, *Mysterious Dr. Satan*, *Adventures of Captain Marvel*, *Jungle Girl*, and the last three *Dick Tracy* episoders.

The intermixture of galloping horses, roaring locomotives, and racing aircraft was for Witney and English a highly polished skill. This basic *Rides Again* recipe they took pleasure in augmenting through the years, with motorcycles, flying wings, dirigibles. Never, when Witney and English prepared it, did the broth seem too rich. And yet, one of their less mechanized admixtures secured their reputations. In 1938, with Zorro's great-grandson behind them, the two embraced the hardiest of all masked riders, the airwaves' Lone Ranger.

The arrival of the celluloid embodiment of radio's champion of justice was clarioned by neighborhood theaters throughout the country. *The Lone Ranger* was the biggest serial event since *Flash Gordon*. For it Republic called upon a mystery technique as old as *The Iron Claw*, yet never used more effectively. The puzzle for viewers to solve in fifteen chapters was the identity not of the badman but of the hero himself. Five identically clad free-lance rangers stood against the well-equipped guerrilla army of the cruel "General" Jeffries. As the drama advanced, the westerners died valiantly, one by one, until, after an evolutionary process more complex than the original radio legend (described in Chapter 7), there was indeed a Lone Ranger.

But who was he? Each member of the audience had a favorite, and a surprising number of adults found themselves taking part in the guessing game. The available nominees were five solid adventure actors, any one of whom would have been a worthy rider of the great horse Silver. The youngest, Jim Clark, played by George Letz (now George Montgomery) died early in the action. Did this mean that the Lone Ranger was Dick Forrest, enacted by Lane Chandler, once a rival of Gary Cooper at Paramount, or Bob Stuart, portrayed by Hal Taliaferro?

As personal favorites were killed off, the mental wagering shifted to other candidates, while backyard or rumpus-room seminars analyzed the merits of each potential titleholder. Many things seemed to be pointing toward ex-Tarzan Herman Brix, in the role of Bert Rogers. Unquestionably, he had that daring and resourceful look. Almost no one was prepared for the surprise in the last chapter when actor Lee Powell, as the real Lone Ranger, removed his mask for a few friends. The audience, in voice as well as spirit, joined heroine Lynn Roberts in her astonished, "Allen King!"

It was a moment pressed into the minds and inner ears of those who had waited almost four months for that revelation. And it cannot be described to those who knew not Joseph. The sudden release from the splendid agony of watchful waiting was one of the things that perished with the film serial. Not even the television reruns of the old thrillers bring the impact that accrued from active participation—from hurrying past a blur of sandwich-board posters, swirling popcorn, and sepia-toned stills to a seat nine rows down on the left side; from watching the screen come to life at the instant the cry of "Hi-Yo Silver!" resounded through the tinseled auditorium; from adding a not-yet-baritone voice to the wave of cheers that greeted the first

111

appearance of the masked rider—in sum, from *being there*. The bemused observation of tiny heroes and villains flitting across a small glass tube could never match the excitement of sitting in the presence of the gods, even flickering ones formed of silver nitrate.

For those who were there to see *The Lone Ranger*, the images and sounds were the kind that could be transferred to innumerable backyard rounds of cowboys and Indians. Waiting to be invoked when needed were silver bullets molded by the Lone Ranger himself, glistening revolvers with handles of pure-white pearl, a custom-made mask that covered the whole face (keeping the audience as well as the villains from recognizing the countenance of actor Powell), and, of course, the familiar challenge to adventure, the "Hi-Yo Silver!" Incidentals? Yes. But in the twenty minutes between the opening and closing titles of a serial, an apparently minor ornament, property, or effect could make a deep impression on the juvenile mind. Actors' names could be forgotten; silver bullets, never.

The right disguise or gun draw or Stetson crease could elevate a cliffhanger from run-of-the-mill to extra-special production. When Zorro's pistols were placed in his holsters butts forward, the fashion was more than duly noted; when a year or so later Bill Elliott as Wild Bill Hickok perfected a rapid draw with pistols so oriented, his technique was emulated in just about every town in America. Yet, if clever introduction of the little things could add luster to a serial, minor carelessness could mar the veneer of an otherwise adequate effort. No ten-year-old worth his popcorn was unaware that the Green Hornet's Black Beauty was a Lincoln Zephyr with fancy mudguards or that Batman's cowl had absurd projections resembling horns more than ears or that the Phantom's long underwear was baggy at the knees. The economic logic of customizing an existing car a youngster could recognize and overlook, but the costuming aberrations of the other films were inexcusable. None of these films, we should mention, came from Republic, which had the cleanest, neatest, best-dressed, best-armed heroes around.

Mere haberdashery and sporting goods did not, of course,

make successful serials out of bad ones. But in a competitive market they could put one picture a step ahead of the cliffhanger playing at the theater down the street. In Republic serials the trimmings were additional signs of the care that was present in the whole undertaking, be it an important chapter play such as *The Lone Ranger* or a lower-budget work such as *Daredevils of the Red Circle*.

The exceptional response to *The Lone Ranger* made a follow-up almost certain. *The Lone Ranger Rides Again* appeared in 1939, with Robert Livingston, not Lee Powell, in the title role. Powell had been assigned the lead in *The Fighting Devil Dogs* immediately after *The Lone Ranger*, but from there his trip was downhill. His contract with Republic expired, and after doing a minor Western feature, he toured with a small circus as the Lone Ranger of the Movies. The undertaking was doubtful at best. Because of the guessing game about the masked man's identity, Powell never had been billed as the Lone Ranger. Not many followers of the film could have recalled the name of the actor who played the role. Moreover, seeing the claimant in the flesh, reduced to a meager center ring that the day before had been a farmer's field, was somehow discomforting. The crackdown on his appearances by the copyright owners may have been an act of kindness.

Still, Lee Powell deserved more of a finish to his career than the half-dozen cheap Westerns he made for Producers Releasing Corporation after the circus fiasco. Things might have worked out had it not been for World War II. In 1942, in a manner fitting for a veteran of *The Fighting Devil Dogs*, Powell enlisted in the United States Marine Corps. And though he served in a manner worthy of a serial star, for him there would be no postwar comeback. Lee Powell lost his life on Tinian Island on July 29, 1944. Thirty-nine months after an auto crash that killed radio's Lone Ranger (Earle Graser), a second portrayer of the masked rider had met violent death. The coincidence was little noted. With a war going on, the press had scant space for the passing of a serial star. Most of Powell's admirers of six years earlier never learned of it.

As the screen's new Lone Ranger, ex-Eagle, ex-Zorro Robert Livingston was completely at home. He was much too prominent, however, to keep behind a mask for fifteen chapters. Livingston played many of the scenes of *The Lone Ranger Rides Again* without facial concealment of any kind. Except for the brief unveiling scene of the first serial, that was the only production in which the natural likeness of the actor playing the Lone Ranger was revealed to a film or television audience.

The uncovering by Livingston was not without logic. It was performed in the presence of his companion, Tonto, capably portrayed for the second time by Victor Daniels, better known as Chief Thundercloud. This motion-picture Indian was one of the best. He could supply the solidness coupled with warmth that was required of the Tonto character and then, in a film such as *Geronimo* (1940), give a thoroughly terrifying impersonation of the classical bad Indian.

A second confederate of the masked rider in *The Lone Ranger Rides Again* was Juan Vásquez, played by Duncan Renaldo, one of Republic's foremost hero-helpers. Renaldo, who first achieved prominence in the early sound film *Trader Horn*, had been John Carroll's ally in *Zorro Rides Again*. Helping Robert Livingston came almost as second nature. In fact, the good-looking Latin actor became Livingston's saddle pal in a string of features made in the early 1940s. He also aided Sammy Baugh, the football player, in the serial *King of the Texas Rangers* (1941) and Rod Cameron in *Secret Service in Darkest Africa* (1943). Many years later, the devoted service paid off. Renaldo became television's Cisco Kid, acquiring in the process his own man Friday, as well as a considerable accumulation of residuals.

Although few filmgoers were aware of it, Robert Livingston was not the only replacement in the second Lone Ranger serial. Lee Powell had ridden a horse billed as Silver King, while Livingston's steed was Silver Chief. It didn't actually matter. Both stallions bore up well under all the hearty hi-yo-ing. What's more, they innocently delineated equine fashion for the next few years. Galloping along trails outlined in the late 1920s by Ken Maynard's Tarzan, Fred Thomson's Silver King, and Buck

Jones's Silver, they at last confirmed the white horse as the mount nonpareil of the cowboy hero.

Now it may seem surprising that in the matter of horseflesh the youngsters of the middle Roosevelt years were color-conscious, but the conventions were well set. The trihero teams so popular in that period gave testimony to that fact. If the Three Mesquiteers or Rough Riders sauntered toward a hitching post, there was no doubt about which Westerner would climb onto the white courser. It would be the lead cowboy—the John Wayne or Robert Livingston or Buck Jones. Since the top hand always rode slightly ahead of his confreres, that meant, by indirection, that white horses were faster than darker ones. The two-tone or calico cow ponies that had predominated in the Tom Mix and William S. Hart days had hit a decline. Fritz and Tony were gone, leaving the brunette Champion of Gene Autry to uphold the cause of the nonalabaster cayuse. It was a hopeless assignment, for among male juveniles Hopalong Cassidy's snow-covered Topper more than offset the thoroughbred of a *singing* cowboy.

The traditional color of purity had in the Western film completed the flow from Stetson and revolver handle to Old Faithful. Not until milkiness had been overdone could an off-white charger again achieve status. Roy Rogers' golden Palomino, Trigger, attracted attention not because his hair color matched Roy's but because it was something different after all the frostiness. Perhaps that shows how unwise it is to read much symbolism into the color schemes of serials and Westerns. Kids were interested in the little touches all right, but hidden meanings meant nothing. Symbolism was for film critics.

After *The Lone Ranger Rides Again*, Republic's serial makers called upon a masked rider one more time before letting the device rest awhile. Their fourth chapter play of 1939 was *Zorro's Fighting Legion*, in which the founder of the sword-and-whip dynasty made his first appearance in serial form. Don Diego, visiting in Mexico, assumed command of a volunteer legion assembled by his uncle to oppose Don Del Oro, an empire seeker posing as a Yaqui god to steal the gold of a terrified band of

Indians. The ritual revelation of the charlatan in Chapter 12 ("Unmasked") was executed by Reed Hadley, an elongated but effective Zorro. Hadley's days as Captain Braddock of television's *Racket Squad* lay far ahead.

A more famous racket buster kept directors Witney and English occupied during much of the time they were not busy with Zorro and the Lone Ranger. Six years after his introduction in newspapers, a hook-nosed policeman was available in new form, packaged in the fifteen chapters of *Dick Tracy* (1937). Ray Taylor and Alan James were in charge of this picture, but the Witney-English team took over the three sequels.

Chester Gould's detective strip was approaching its zenith at the time Republic adapted it for the screen; therefore, the title role had to be cast with care. The producers selected a new adventure actor, Ralph Byrd, fresh from basic training in Victory's serial *Blake of Scotland Yard* (1937). He was an excellent choice for the role, so much so that he would fill it, on and off, until his death in 1952.

Although Byrd lacked the jagged nose that the cartoon character somehow acquired with time, he clearly possessed the firm jaw and stern visage necessary for a convincing characterization. His rightness in the part was not appreciated fully until 1945, when RKO made two Tracy features with another actor. Byrd was quickly recalled to service to complete the series. He also was used in the television version filmed in 1951.

Dick Tracy's motion-picture adventures were begun without benefit of the cast of friendly characters he leaned upon in the papers. Junior was the only carryover. Instead of Tess Trueheart, Dick had only a girl named Gwen (Kay Hughes) for feminine companionship. Gwen was around for this film and two more despite the fact that she wasn't the easy source of free meals that Tess was. Papa Trueheart, for those who have forgotten, was in the right business for a hungry flatfoot. Dick Tracy's historic first words (in the daily strip) were, "Good evening, Mr. Trueheart—how's the delicatessen business this evening?"

The actual reason for scuttling Tess Trueheart was, of course, the recognition that kids wouldn't buy a film heroine with that name any more than they would sit still for the free-meal business parodied by Al Capp in *Fearless Fosdick*. Dick Tracy's fifteen chapters were too full of action to tolerate a heroine who could call a virile detective "my very bestest boy friend." (Tess did—on October 12, 1931.) The screen Tracy battled mystery rays, wingless airships, and a deranged brother to get to a crook known sometimes as the Spider, sometimes as the Lame One. Drollery was delegated to the almost obligatory comedy-relief character of thrillers, this one being Smiley Burnette as Mike McGurk.

Mike and Gwen were back in *Dick Tracy Returns* (1938), but the actors were Lee Ford and Lynn Roberts. Cast as the heavy was the redoubtable Charles Middleton, on vacation from Flash Gordon and from that point of view in the wrong Tracy film. In an odd reversal of sequence *Dick Tracy Returns* came closer to the cops-and-robbers stuff of the early Tracy comic strip than did the first Dick Tracy serial, which, with its futuristic inventions and grotesque menace, presaged (and possibly influenced) the newspaper feature's later years. Middleton's empire in *Dick Tracy Returns* was nothing more than a gang of crooks comprising himself and his no-good sons. Yet, as Pa Stark (a male Ma Barker), Mongo's absent ruler showed that he could inject formidable villainy into a serial even if reduced to wearing a pinstripe business suit.

The third Tracy serial, *Dick Tracy's G-Men* (1939), was a return to near fantasy. The detective's crafty adversary, Zarnoff (Irving Pichel), sent to the gas chamber as a result of Dick's earlier sleuthing, had the foresight to plan a resurrection. After a little postmidnight technical maneuvering by his associates, Zarnoff was back in the business of worldwide espionage and ruckus raising. Had Zarnoff not paused to sip from a poisoned water hole, Tracy might still be chasing him. (The suspiciously punlike title of the chapter depicting Zarnoff's poorly selected refreshment facility: "The Last Stand.")

Aside from the appearance of Irving Pichel, who subsequently won favor as a director, *Dick Tracy's G-Men* is noteworthy because of the presence in the cast of a future Academy Award

117

winner. This time Gwen was played by Phyllis Isley, not far away from her role in *The Song of Bernadette* under the name Jennifer Jones. A sadder footnote involves old-time serial hero Walter Miller, who played Zarnoff's henchman, Robal. This was Miller's last cliffhanger. A strenuous fight scene for a Gene Autry picture a short time afterward brought on a fatal heart attack.

The final Tracy episoder, released in 1941, continued the supernatural touches, combining them with gangster fighting. In *Dick Tracy vs. Crime, Inc.* (later called *Dick Tracy vs. the Phantom Empire*), Dick pursued an invisible criminal known as the Ghost. Although the Ghost's identity was intended to be a mystery, the presence in the cast of Ralph Morgan was something of a giveaway. Morgan so far outshone his fellow actors in stature that there was little doubt that the choicest of supporting roles was his—unless the producers were hoping to fool the audience by setting up just such an assumption, a possibility no serialgoer could overlook.

The Dick Tracy serial quartet, when concluded, ran to sixty chapters, making it the most extended serial series since the days of Pearl White's Elaine. Not even the Zorro films, with their several heroes, exceeded it in total episodes. Tracy's exploits are remembered for some spectacular action sequences and cinematic effects, in sky, on land, in water, underground, and underwater. The driverless automobile that carried an *hors de combat* Tracy careening down the ramps of an indoor parking garage was a frightening spectacle, instilling a permanent uneasiness about such parking facilities in the minds of many witnesses of the scene. The use of negative film to show the accidental electrocution of the Ghost revealed how effective a simple motion-picture trick could be when used at the right time.

In the main, the motion picture had been kind to Chester Gould's demon investigator—at least in his serial years, 1937 to 1941. Those years, incidentally, happened to be the peak ones for comics-based cliffhangers, what with the Tracy and Flash Gordon cycles and *Buck Rogers*, *Mandrake the Magician*, *Red Ryder*, *Terry and the Pirates*, *Don Winslow*, *Red Barry*, and *King of the Royal Mounted* as well.

118

1937 alone brought, in addition to *Dick Tracy, Jungle Jim, Radio Patrol, Secret Agent X-9*, and *Tim Tyler's Luck*. All but the Tracy film came from Universal, the studio most closely wed to the feature syndicates. Of the four Universal films *Tim Tyler's Luck* was the most interesting. Some think it the best of the many jungle thrillers from that studio.

Frank Thomas, Jr., played Tim, a teenager in search of his lost professor father. Tyler senior, using an armor-clad jungle cruiser, had wandered into the brush to study gorillas and their habits. In the process, he also stumbled across the fabled elephant's burial ground (for the moment not occupied by Jack Armstrong and pals). This discovery made him a source of much-desired information for the likes of Spider Webb and his gang.

Tim finds his father—as a result of a ruse by Webb—but the reunion is short-lived. Professor Tyler is killed in a skirmish, causing Tim to dedicate the rest of his chapters to bringing Webb to justice. His allies are Sergeant Gates (Jack Mulhall) and the mounted Ivory Patrol. Auxiliaries are Laura Graham (Frances Robinson), Lazarre, a softhearted member of Webb's gang, and Fang, a pet black panther. In addition Tim can muster a herd of friendly elephants when it is necessary to tear up a village or to offer opposition to the jungle cruiser, in the hands of Webb and cronies most of the time. Disappointingly, the apes whom the elder Tyler chummed and even chatted with take an impartial stance, charging anyone in sight once the professor is gone.

In outline *Tim Tyler's Luck* seems absurd. Yet good direction by Ford Beebe and Wyndham Gittens and convincing performances, especially that of metallic-voiced Norman Willis as Webb, brushed aside the obstacles to believability. The confluence of elephants, jungle cats, horse cavalry, and armored vehicles—not to mention an army of apes—kept the screen overflowing with crisp action. And present to balance the frenzy were quiet touches not often found in cliffhangers, for instance, the attempt of the sympathetic Lazarre to cheer the captive Tim with a bit of song. This badman's gradual transfer from evil to good was developed in greater detail than chapter plays normally took

119

time for. Then too, the passing of Tim's gentle father added a contrasting note (despite Papa's inexplicable Smith and Dale accent).

Though by no means profound, the nuances in characterization and interaction in this adaptation of Lyman Young's comic strip went beyond what might have been expected in an action serial. These aspects of legitimate drama were inserted in Universal serials much more often than they were in the chapter plays of other studios. How much they added to, or subtracted from, a cliffhanger was never determined. Republic and Columbia had no time for them.

SHAZAM AND GOOD-BY

A hero cannot be a hero unless in an heroic world.
NATHANIEL HAWTHORNE, *Journals*, May 7, 1850

Columbia, the last of the sound era's serial big three to begin chapter-play production, often seemed unable to come up with thrillers containing strong plot lines, let alone narrative nuances. Yet, in the few years before the Sam Katzman touch turned Columbia's serials into almost complete absurdities, the studio did turn out some popular continued dramas. Its first three were Frank Buck's *Jungle Menace* (1937), Frank Hawks's *The Mysterious Pilot* (1937), already mentioned, and *The Secret of Treasure Island* (1938), starring Don Terry.

Although none of Columbia's pioneer trio is remembered much today, its fourth serial is. *The Great Adventures of Wild Bill Hickok* (1938) was, as the *Motion Picture Herald* put it, "a complement to its title." It completely transformed the career of an actor named Gordon Elliott, who was cast in the title role.

121

Elliott's quiet firmness as the marshal of Abilene won him an immediate following. Soon he was no longer making films as Gordon Elliott. He was Wild Bill Elliott, to some critics the cowboy actor who came closest to the William S. Hart conception of the Westerner. Elliott's buckskin shirt and reversed holsters became trademarks, as did a line of dialogue he used several times in each film: "I'm a peaceable man." In the last reel of an Elliott feature this statement was assurance that his rough-handled, long-barreled Colts were about to be put in action.

Columbia used Elliott in another serial, *Overland with Kit Carson*, a year after his first portrayal of Wild Bill. In the meantime, the studio had released a chapter play of an entirely different sort, foreshadowing a new direction of the motion-picture serial. Having tapped the comic strip and the radio drama, the makers of cliffhangers now turned to the pulps. Passing over Doc Savage, who would have been a magnificent serial character, Columbia selected an upcoming crime fighter, much akin to The Shadow, and billed in his own magazine as the Master of Men. To the citizens of his community Richard Wentworth was a member of the four hundred who dabbled in criminology, but for confrontations with the criminal element Wentworth put on black mask and cloak to become the Spider.

Columbia's fifteen-chapter serial was called *The Spider's Web*. Starring in it was Warren Hull, a good leading man who today is associated with audience-participation radio and television shows (*Vox Pop*, for example) rather than with movie thrillers. Nevertheless, Hull was entirely competent in the action category and possessed dramatic talent that came in handy when Wentworth assumed yet another guise, that of Blinky McQuade.

McQuade, a sniveling underworld hanger-on, was Wentworth's means of obtaining inside information on gangland activities. As a matter of fact, it was in this disguise, which included steel-rimmed glasses *and* eye patch, that Wentworth stumbled across the clue that at last led him to the stronghold of the villain of the piece, the Octopus.

One of the memorable chapter-play villains, the white-robed Octopus headed a black-robed underworld combine bent on controlling the country by taking over the major industries. McQuade's discovery of an unusual deflection tube put Wentworth on the right trail to the phony radio school that served as a front for Octopus headquarters. For some reason radio schools, language schools, and the like were popular covers in cliffhangers.

Those who saw the Spider-Octopus showdown remember the robed one's last ploy. Throughout the film he had presided over his power-mad clan in a magnificent oak-and-marble chamber, seated behind an impressive desk on which rested the microphone he used to disguise his voice. At the final confrontation, the Octopus sat calmly facing his costumed adversary, one hand on the desk, one on the microphone. But things were not as they appeared. The Octopus' right hand was artificial. From under his robe came the real one, holding a revolver that would have meant the end of the Spider had not Wentworth fired just in time.

The Octopus was dispatched to the land of fallen villains, there to review his mistakes with that other superb schemer of 1938, the Lightning. Presumably, as the years went along, they were joined in their discussion by the Wasp (*Mandrake the Magician*, 1939), the Scorpion (*The Adventures of Captain Marvel*, 1941), the Ghost (*Dick Tracy vs. Crime, Inc.*, 1941), the Gargoyle (*The Spider Returns*, 1941), and those other misguided geniuses who hid under hood or mask in chapter land, never seeming to profit from their predecessors' examples.

The Spider's Web—aside from its significance in allying the pulp thriller with the cinema—is noteworthy for two reasons. First, it transferred the long-used masked-avenger concept from the old West to the contemporary East, bringing into visual dramatic form a device that to that time had been confined to pulp literature and radio (*The Shadow* and *The Green Hornet*). The premise of *The Spider's Web* was that a hero could, as a regular practice, solve crimes and catch criminals by putting on a weird costume and dashing about a twentieth-century metropolis. That was quite a different thing from a Western hero who assumed a disguise to correct a situation of the moment.

While a hooded avenger in the wide-open spaces was unlikely —but not impossible, as the Ku Klux Klan demonstrated for different purpose—a costumed crime fighter in a modern congested city was the material of fantasy. The premise was that of the comic book. And that is the second noteworthy aspect of *The Spider's Web*. In a remarkable coincidence the Spider reached the screen at just the time the first tights-and-cape hero, Superman, appeared on comic-book racks. What is more, as the Spider's adventures played in theaters, radio's first *visible* masked avenger of modern day, the Green Hornet, reached national attention after starting in the Middle West in 1936. The cycle of the superhero was beginning, and it was beginning simultaneously in comic book, radio, and film.

As if to underline his place with the new guard, the Spider of the cinema wore a costume far gaudier than that used in the illustrations for his magazine, and certainly surpassing that of the pulp version of The Shadow, whose costume in his radio adventures, of course, was incidental in that because of his hypnotic powers no one could see him. In his pulp stories The Shadow wore black to be inconspicuous. Dressed for action, the cinematized Spider, and the Superman brotherhood, were about as hard to miss as anyone would care to be.

The way having been pointed by the pulps, the full amplification of the twentieth-century avenger was performed by more prosperous media—the youngest and most chromatic of which would hasten the demise of its pulp-paper cousin while doing no little altering of chapter-play history. The origin of the comic-book crusaders I leave to a later chapter, but their impact upon the motion-picture serial should be noted here. As the ultramen cropped up in one prismatic booklet after another, the film serial moved toward its rendezvous with them, though not in headlong fashion. *The Spider's Web* was released in late October, 1938. Its effectiveness, therefore, could not be measured and related to that of radio's *Green Hornet,* or the comic book marvels until

124

the next year. 1939, accordingly, brought only *Mandrake the Magician* (starring Spider portrayer Hull) in the way of offbeat contemporary heroes with unusual powers. By 1940, however, the thinking of the serial producers was obvious. In January, Columbia issued *The Shadow*, with Victor Jory perfectly cast as Lamont Cranston. Four days later Universal was out with *The Green Hornet*, whose sequel issued forth the same year.

Republic, still preferring bizarre villains to bizarre heroes, offered as its non-Western serials of 1940 *The Drums of Fu Manchu* and *The Mysterious Dr. Satan* (with Eduardo Cianelli). Fu Manchu, splendidly played by Henry Brandon, was, though not a superhero, most certainly a supervillain. That put Republic in the spirit of things. Furthermore, the crime fighter in *The Mysterious Dr. Satan* wore a snakeskin cowl with his business suit to disguise himself as the Copperhead. The pretext for this was more sentimental than logical: the skintight mask had been worn many years earlier by his father as he avenged injustice in the West. In unconscious fashion Republic was observing the transfer of the costumed crusader from prairie to pavement.

The next year Republic took the ultimate step. The first super-hero taken directly from the comic book appeared in a serial. And, giving no indication of what the flying avengers one day would do to the chapter play, *The Adventures of Captain Marvel* was roaring-good juvenile entertainment.

The twelve-chapter serial was a good example of what happens when the right people undertake a project at the right time. 1941 was the right time because the comic-book era was at its creative peak—it had one—and Republic's serial unit had come to full stride. World War II had not yet begun to drain the studio's production personnel or work its sometimes distorting influence on story lines.

The right people for *The Adventures of Captain Marvel* were directors William Witney and John English of the Republic serial unit and leading man Tom Tyler. Witney and English were in the last year of their fruitful megaphone partnership (the war would break it), and never were they more essential to a successful finished product. Not only did they have to make a superman look believable on the screen, they also had to cope with one who gained his powers by uttering a magic word.[1] The project might have defeated other men; but in the hands of Witney and English, Captain Marvel was not a bad choice to introduce the superhero to serial fans. He may have been even more suitable than Superman (who was used in some excellent short cartoons around that time).

It was a tossup which superhero-origin story was harder to swallow: a baby from a race of supermen shot to earth in a rocket or a boy suddenly entrusted with an open sesame to immense strength and wisdom. From that point on, however, Captain Marvel had advantages for a continued thriller that Superman did not possess. Superman was impervious to the usual cliffhanging dangers; Captain Marvel, only when in super-form. The Man of Steel, moreover, had a ridiculous transformation problem that passed (barely) in comic books and radio but never was viable on film. To become Clark Kent, he put on a business suit and spectacles—a disguise that, as anyone could see, would fool no one, not even the obnoxious Lois Lane. To become Superman he had to find that empty room in which to disrobe, no matter how pressing the danger. It was a blasted nuisance, slowing the action and containing the dramatic value of a deodorant commercial.

With Captain Marvel, on the other hand, it was the magic word and "BANG!" Young Billy Batson had a new self. In a cliffhanger a lightning bolt was infinitely more exciting than a string of double-breasted suits and accessories, neatly laid out in phone booths, storerooms, and rock shelters about the nation. (How much time, we wonder, did Superman spend recovering them? And how many piles of clothes were found by

---

[1] The word, of course, was "SHAZAM!" and it brought youthful Billy Batson the wisdom of Solomon and the strength of Hercules, as well as the stamina of Atlas, the power of Zeus, the courage of Achilles, and the speed of Mercury. The writers of television's *Andy Griffith Show* and *Gomer Pyle* revived the acronym in the 1960s, passing over, oddly enough, Billy's characteristic "Holy Moley!" That exclamation found its way into the Batman television series as the basis for Robin's tiresome "Holy . . .!" ejaculations. As his former readers know, in comic books Robin never said anything of the sort.

puzzled cleaning men before the strong one got back? And, more perplexing yet, what did Kent do with his wallet?)

No, Superman, king of the comic books, probably would not have launched the superhero in serials with the flourish of Fawcett Publications' seeming second-best avenger. It would have been interesting, though, to see what Witney and English would have done with the Man of Steel. To judge from their handling of Captain Marvel, Republic's serial makers would have been kinder to him than were those who finally brought him to serials under Sam Katzman's auspices at Columbia.

The plot of *The Adventures of Captain Marvel* centered upon a multilensed metal transmutation device that also emitted a powerful ray when the arms of a golden scorpion that held the lenses were arranged correctly. The potent figurine was discovered by the Malcolm Scientific Expedition in Siam. There also young Billy Batson, radio operator for the group, was given his special powers by the ancient guardian of those forces. Witney and English built to this scene with a sequence resembling the opening of King Tutankhamen's tomb. The suspense, and the accomplished playing of the ancient seer by Nigel de Brulier, saved the serial from what could have been a ludicrous beginning and set the tone for Captain Marvel's twelve-chapter struggle with a human Scorpion—a member of the expedition who was trying to take possession of the high-powered lenses, which for safety's sake had been distributed among various members of the scientific party.

There was mayhem aplenty—what with a two-hundred-horse-power hero—yet it was mayhem well executed. Much of the credit for the exciting action should go to stunt man David Sharpe, who with the utmost verve overwhelmed the baddies by diving upon them from midair, somersaulting under their chins, and hurling in their direction anything from a machine gun to a fair-sized tree. What's more, a good combination of clever camera angles, concealed wires, and artful faking by Sharpe and Tyler made it appear that Captain Marvel really could fly through the air. It was the most successful illusion of such aerobatics ever put upon the screen, in serial or feature. Kids knew that they were being fooled but were dazzled by the skill with which it was done.

To those kids, of course, the elements of direction and stunt work that made *Captain Marvel* an outstanding serial were to be appreciated only indirectly. Their attention was caught by the new kind of hero brought to life by Tom Tyler. The use of Tyler in this role was every bit as inspired as that of Buster Crabbe for Flash Gordon—perhaps more so. Never did a serial actor fit his role any better. Not only did Tyler have the powerful build necessary for a playing a superman, he had the acting experience and the piercing countenance to make his part believable.

Tom Tyler possessed the ability to bring conviction to a wide range of roles. He could be the Hollywood cowboy—as he was much of the time during his early career—or turn with equal ease to a portrayal of a vicious heavy, such as Luke Plummer, the man waiting to gun down John Wayne in *Stagecoach*. He even had a turn as a monster in Universal's *The Mummy's Hand* (1940). Not a romantic type, though possessing masculine good looks, Tyler was one of the motion picture's accomplished, but seldom heralded, stars. His work is overlooked today, except by a million or so former serialgoers who recognized a magnificent performance even if the Motion Picture Academy didn't. The crippling arthritis that cut down Tom Tyler deprived the screen of one of its more virile performers. His sixth and last chapter play, *The Phantom*, was made in 1943. A necessary withdrawal from films came a few years later and death from a heart attack in 1954.

The Adventures of Captain Marvel gave Republic a head start in the business of making celluloid supermen. The studio exploited the opportunity without selling out to the pulp-paper medium. After making three serials of conventional type, Republic called upon another creation of Fawcett Publications, *Spy Smasher*. That was a nice way of trading upon the reputation of the Captain Marvel serial in promotional material appearing in Fawcett's comic books but also meant that Republic would not be drawing upon the characters of the top comic-book chain,

National Comics, which wound up selling the serial rights to Superman, Batman, and others to Columbia.

Spy Smasher (1942) broke the Witney-English directing cycle, Witney doing it with W. J. O'Sullivan. The serial was a swift-moving adventure in which Kane Richmond played a costumed, but not superhuman, Axis fighter. Richmond also played Spy Smasher's twin brother, who died impersonating him late in the serial.

Spy Smasher's costume was little more than a tight-fitting old-style aviator's outfit, complete with boots, cap, and goggles. But Republic's tailors made sure that he was well turned out, just as Captain Marvel had been. The distance between the costumes of Republic's caped crusaders and those of other studios had to be measured in light-years. If a distinctive outfit, even an improbable one, was important to a characterization, it had to look right, reasoned Republic's producers. A superhero at another lot might have to appear dashing after pulling swim trunks over two-piece woolen underwear; Republic's crusaders would look fresh from Bond Street.

The key to Spy Smasher's intrepid appearance was a long silk cape which, when he crouched atop a speeding train or raced along on a motorcycle, gave the illusion of swifter motion. Clearly it was a clumsy thing to have to contend with when fighting Nazis, but that only mattered to actor Richmond and his double. To the junior Spy Smashers of America, it looked just fine.

After *Spy Smasher*, Republic lost its monopoly on comic-book heroes. *Batman* was brought to the screen by Columbia Pictures in 1943. Starring Lewis Wilson as the Caped Crusader and Douglas Croft as the Boy Wonder, this wartime serial garnered some good press notices, although, from the vantage point of the 1970s, it scarcely deserved them. Wilson was a paunchy Batman, little helped by a baggy costume that was topped by a pair of devil's horns. His adversary, Dr. Daka, borrowing an idea that hadn't been very good when used in *Buck Rogers*, whipped up a line of electric skullcaps to jam onto the heads of those he wished to make zombies. Long before the chapter in which Daka—brazenly overplayed by J. Carroll Naish—slipped one that looked like a hair dryer over Batman's horns, there was little that could be taken seriously in *Batman*.

As much as Houdini's old *The Master Mystery*, this midwar cliffhanger was unintentional farce. Recognizing this fact twenty-two years later, some clever individuals spliced together all fifteen episodes, called them *An Evening with Batman and Robin*, and watched the profits roll in. When Batman came to television a few months later, Columbia transferred the chapters to eight-millimeter film and sold them to home-movie fans. They remain a staple of film sellers, showing that if a film is bad enough its possibilities for long-term dividends are enormous.

Republic's 1943 derivation from the comic book, *The Masked Marvel*, failed to enjoy the later-day success of *Batman*, perhaps because it wasn't as brilliantly bad. Then too, the principal character of Republic's new serial was not the kind to be prominent in a surge of nostalgia or among things called low camp. In the hierarchy of comic-book avengers the Masked Marvel was one of the lesser nobles. There was nothing distinctive about him when he came to Hollywood, and the same could be said after his departure. To add some interest, the writers tried to rework the "Who's the hero?" format that had been so effective in *The Lone Ranger*. (Ronald Davidson served on the writing team of both serials.) The Marvel—as the actors had to refer to him —was one of four "investigators" digging into the sabotage activities directed by Sakima, a former Japanese envoy. By Chapter 9 three of the original four men remained; by Chapter 10, only two. Because the blurbs for the final episode advised that when the true Marvel revealed himself to the camera he refused any newspaper publicity, "preferring to keep his identity secret so that he might again resume his role when needed," I won't tell whether it was Bob Barton or Terry Morton. I will say, however, that the guessing game wasn't nearly as interesting as that in *The Lone Ranger*. And today it has comic overtones owing to changing fashions. One "investigator" in overpadded, light-colored, double-breasted suit, white handkerchief, and Clark Kent hat is not easy to overlook. But four . . . !

Republic Pictures brought the wartime comic-book cycle to a close with *Captain America* (1944), a much better serial than either *Batman* or *The Masked Marvel*. John English, doing his last serial for Republic, was in charge, along with Elmer Clifton. (Spencer Bennet had done *The Masked Marvel*.) The Captain America character was significantly transformed for films, from a GI with scientifically created superstrength to a fighting district attorney possessing somewhat less muscle power. The change probably was for the better. The Simon and Kirby creation named Steve Rogers had to sneak away from his army base in story after story to fight the Axis baddies. It was an inconvenience equal to Clark Kent's dressing problem. Grant Gardner, the Captain America of filmland, at least did not have to go AWOL constantly. And when an avenger was up against a villain played by the magnificent Lionel Atwill, the fewer the inconveniences the better.

Captain America was played by Dick Purcell, known primarily for his work in low-budget thrillers made by Monogram —the productions that turned up on television with such titles as *King of the Zombies* and *Phantom Killer*. Purcell's serial role was strenuous, despite the extraordinary assistance he and his fellow actors received in the elaborate fight scenes from a team of stunt men. Only a few weeks after completing *Captain America*, Purcell collapsed in the locker room of a Los Angeles country club and died. The strain of his vigorous assignment had taxed his heart too heavily.

After *Captain America* there was a lull in the making of chapter plays based upon comic-book powerhouses. Producers no doubt thought that the cycle had run its course. World War II was over, as was the golden period of the comic magazines. In addition, Republic Pictures was in the midst of another cycle, not too far removed in concept from that of the superhero but going back to the very beginning of serials.

In 1941, after releasing *The Adventures of Captain Marvel*, Republic gave juvenile audiences something of a counterpart

131

to the superman in the adventures of an exceptional young woman. Named Nyoka, she was a female Tarzan, which was appropriate in that she was created by Edgar Rice Burroughs. There was no better source for such a heroine.

By filming *Jungle Girl*, Republic was making a direct return to the days of Pearl White and Ruth Roland. In the years following the actresses' retirements there had, naturally, been leading women in almost every serial. At times they could rightfully be called heroines. But normally the leading ladies were secondary to the male principals, the exception perhaps being the unimpressive Universal remake of *The Perils of Pauline* (1934).

The advertising for *Jungle Girl* revealed that Republic was attempting to revive the kind of heroine upon which cliffhanging had been built. "The screen hails a new serial queen . . . ," ran the lead of one announcement. And to some extent the promotional material was correct. Nyoka, the Jungle Girl, was very much in the tradition of the White-Roland heroines. She swung through the trees on vines, battled fearlessly with diamond hunters and gorillas, and, when captured and powerless, graciously let her boy friend save her. Moreover, she did all this in an attractive costume considerably skimpier than anything worn by Pearl White.

Playing Nyoka was a strikingly attractive young actress named Frances Gifford. She had the beauty and the manner to charm even the ten-to-twelve-year-old woman haters who formed the bulk of the serial audience in 1941. Who knows how far Miss Gifford might have gone in recapturing the Pearl White summit had she not been on loan to Republic from another studio. When a second Nyoka film was decided upon, she was unavailable.

The next Nyoka was former Powers model Kay Aldridge, whose old-fashioned beauty and honey-colored hair may have reminded senior filmgoers of Pearl White. Her 1942 serial bow was *The Perils of Nyoka*. It was a sequel to *Jungle Girl* only in that both heroines bore the name Nyoka. Though both were reared in Africa, one grew up in the jungle, the other in the desert. The father of Nyoka Meredith, Jungle Girl, had fled civilization to escape blame for a crime committed by his twin

132

brother. The professor father of Nyoka Gordon suffered amnesia as a result of a blow on the head and became the chieftain of the fierce Tuaregs, leaving his daughter fatherless. Nyoka II was reunited with her father, while Nyoka I lost hers when the criminally inclined twin killed him and took his place.

Pearl White would have been at home in either Nyoka serial. Each had what she called "weenies"—objects that the villains strove to take away from the heroine. Bad brother Trevor Bardette, aided by Gerald Mohr and Frank Lacteen (as a tribal witch doctor), were after Jungle Girl's amulet, which bore the key to a treasure in diamonds. Bad guy Tristram Coffin, aided by George Lewis and Charles Middleton (as a tribal cavalry leader), were trying to beat Nyoka Gordon to the lost Tablets of Hippocrates, which contained an ancient cure for cancer as well as a guide to hidden treasure.

Although the second Nyoka had an additional adversary in the evil Princess Vultura, a specialist in torture devices, she didn't have to wrestle Mr. Mohr, which may have evened things out. In any event, the girls had the strong right arms of good-looking men to lean upon. Frances Gifford's Jack Stanton was played by Tom Neal; Kay Aldridge's Larry (a surgeon), by Clayton Moore. At those moments when male help was not at hand, the Nyokas knew how to handle things, provided the odds were no more than two to one. In the last chapter of her serial Nyoka Gordon had it out toe to toe with Vultura, ridding the earth of that wretched female without resorting to hair pulling. (Actress Lorna Gray, who played Vultura, was able to make amends for her wrongdoing in 1946, when, under the name Adrian Booth, she had her turn as a chapter-play heroine in *The Daughter of Don Q.*)

After *The Perils of Nyoka*, Kay Aldridge moved on to *Daredevils of the West* (1943), directed by John English. She shared billing with Allan Lane (*King of the Royal Mounted*), but it scarcely was an imposition in that they were hailed as "their Majesties, the King and Queen of Serials." Miss Aldridge looked pretty in her Western outfit, while Lane seemed tolerant of the necessity of teaming with a girl. Nevertheless, one of their majesties must have been fickle. 1944 found actress Aldridge opposite Kane Richmond in *Haunted Harbor* and Lane working with a new serial queen, Linda Stirling, in *The Tiger Woman.*

Actually, Miss Aldridge had abdicated her throne in favor of a more comfortable off-screen life.[2] Miss Stirling, the new monarch, enthusiastically began a six-serial reign that would exceed the combined terms of Gifford and Aldridge in duration if not in distinction. After *The Tiger Woman* she made *Zorro's Black Whip* (which had no Zorro) in 1944, *Manhunt of Mystery Island* and *The Purple Monster Strikes* in 1945, *The Crimson Ghost* in 1946, and, her last serial, *Jesse James Rides Again*, in 1947.

Though set in the jungle, *The Tiger Woman* could have been one of the many "Will the oil well come through in time?" Westerns that Republic made so often. It also used the steal-the-heroine's-inheritance motif of *What Happened to Mary* and *The Perils of Pauline.* After some initial doubts about Inter-Ocean Oil, the Tiger Woman (her only name) helps chief engineer Lane bring in the well. Lane, in turn, helps the heroine—if the reader will pardon me—bring in the will, too.

The *Tiger Woman* was directed by Spencer Bennet with the help of Wallace Grissell, John English having done his last serial work for Republic in *Captain America* and William Witney also having done almost all of his work in the form. When things are wrong in a film, it is not always possible to isolate responsibility —if indeed it can be isolated. But clearly *The Tiger Woman* contained elements not characteristic of the Republic serial in the Witney-English era. Obvious carelessness was in evidence each time the Tiger Woman was on screen; her brief costume was trimmed with *leopard* fur. Yet this little thing could be overlooked were there not other little things to suggest that something was happening to the motion picture serial as World War II moved toward its end. The natives of the Tiger Woman's domain, somewhere across the sea, had definite peculiarities of attire. Outdoors they dressed like Navahos; indoors, like Aztecs. And when they threw a ceremonial dance before an execution,

---

[2] Coregent Lane, after his salad days as a Republic Western star, attracted the public's ear as the voice of television's talking horse, Mr. Ed.

the warriors were assisted by an embarrassingly out-of-place line of chorus cuties in the harem-girl attire associated with Yvonne de Carlo. Even men from the civilized world had their fashion idiosyncrasies in *The Tiger Woman*. Inside or out, they never removed their hats.

As I suggested, it is difficult to fix responsibility for cinematic aberrations. Those of *The Tiger Woman* and subsequent Republic serials no doubt reflected in part a front-office decision that the chapter play had had its day and that budgets would not be increased to offset rising production costs. This conclusion would seem to be borne out by Universal's decision to discontinue serial production not long after the war.

On the other hand, a full budget does not in itself ensure a good production. *The Tiger Woman*, for example, would have cost less and been better without the line of chorus girls. Someone, remember, had to ask for—or not object to using—them. That is where the value of Witney and English is revealed. They eschewed hokum and held the line against it when other directors were letting it creep in.

But Witney and English were largely out of serial making when the lean years came. It was Spencer Bennet who directed or codirected thirteen of the eighteen Republic serials in the 1943–47 transitional period. And it was Bennet who, after moving to Columbia in 1947, guided twenty of that studio's last twenty-one serials. In other words, more than any other director, this former stunt man, who learned the serial business in the Pearl White days, presided over the death and burial of the chapter play. He was at the helm of almost half of those made after 1946.

Does that imply that Spencer Bennet was responsible for the demise of the motion-picture serial? Not at all. It does mean that he had more than a little part in forming the image offered by cliffhangers in their last years. To the extent that he improved upon the material delivered him for the Sam Katzman quickies at Columbia, he should be praised. It must have been a horrifying ordeal to grind out episodes at breakneck speed while working with actors who scarcely knew the plot.

At the same time, Bennet's ability to improve upon the seemingly hopeless, to make do with what he had, may, ironically, have made him the wrong director to be at Republic when management began losing interest in serials and suggestions were coming from all sides about ways of improving them. Where Witney and English, established team members, may have protested a piece of nonsense designed to "add production values," Bennet may have tried to make that nonsense look as good as possible. Moreover, he liked broad comedy, something the chapter play could have done without when it was starting to come apart at the seams.

Let me illustrate with two Republic serials of 1943, both with the same producer (W. J. O'Sullivan) and the same fictional hero. *G-Men vs. the Black Dragon*, directed by William Witney and introducing government agent Rex Bennett, is an interesting, if unspectacular, adventure film. While there are many scuffles, they are the conventional sort of serial engagement—nothing fancy. The only uncommon touch in the picture is the Japanese villain, Haruchi, who arrives in America disguised as a mummy. He was well played by Nino Pipitone in Oriental make-up that gave him an odd resemblance to silent comedian Snub Pollard.

Secret Service in Darkest Africa, Spencer Bennet's serial, is obviously a more elaborate production. The locale is exotic: northern Africa, somewhere in Nyoka's old territory, from the look of the exterior sets. Rex Bennett's business suit and flowered tie have been exchanged for a snappy new uniform, combining the best elements of the dress of Generals MacArthur and Patton. The villain's hideout in Casablanca boasts as fancy a sliding panel as one could find: a press of a button causes rug and furniture to slide into a fireplace, revealing a secret stairway. Here and there are some diabolical murder and torture devices, including a racklike wheel that spins under a descending Sword of Damocles. And in this action-filled cliffhanger—as lively as any ever made—there is a bang-up chapter ending in which agent Bennett is trapped in a field of explosive-laden open graves that suddenly erupt in a lethal chain reaction.

Not blending very well with these colorful, but still legitimate, chapter-play elements is an oversupply of hokum, commencing with one of several contrived sword fights. Discovered in Gestapo headquarters, the hero gives the full Errol Flynn treatment to a duel with a German instructed to take him prisoner. With time at a premium and a plane waiting for him nearby, Bennett disarms the Nazi and then flips his weapon back to his enemy so that the duel can continue. After finally disposing of his opponent, hero Rex takes some more time to pick up a sword and hurl it into a portrait of Adolf Hitler.

That is not the end of the cute things done by Rex Bennett—played a bit self-consciously by towering Rod Cameron, who was not the kind of performer to imitate Errol Flynn. In one fight Cameron and his adversary battle their way inside an overturned wardrobe and then burst out the side of it a moment later, still swinging away. Later on, Cameron conceals himself in a large wicker basket, popping up like a grinning jack-in-the-box to confront some startled Nazis.

If this sequence reminds the reader of the *Batman* television program, he has recognized the difference between straight serial adventure and what turned up too often in *Secret Service in Darkest Africa*. In fact, one can almost hear the Caped Crusader and his pal as Bennett and his helper analyze an important clue left for them by Pierre LaSalle of the Free French:

"Two face cards, lying face up."
"With holes in them."
"Wait a minute! Holes? No, they're 'O's. Aces with 'O's!"
" 'O'—Aces!"
"Oasis Cafe! Let's go!"

And so it went in *Secret Service in Darkest Africa,* a chapter play with more than its share of thrills—and more than its share of silliness. Fortunately, no subsequent Republic serial would equal it in smarty-pants heroics, not even one of those done by Bennet, who toned down the comic bravado considerably after his first serial for the studio. On the other hand, few later Republic serials equaled *Secret Service in Darkest Africa* in interest and excitement. The motion-picture serial was an ailing form, and no film doctor knew how to cure it without expensive treatment.

Universal tried to improve its last cliffhangers by eliminating that necessary appendage, the written synopsis of happenings in earlier episodes. For a long time this familiar chapter-play feature had annoyed those at Carl Laemmle's old studio. In the latter half of the 1930s some elegant variations appeared in Universal's episode-opening summaries. Simulated comic strips were used to tell what had gone before in *Tim Tyler's Luck* and *Flash Gordon's Trip to Mars*. In *The Phantom Creeps* a crawl device was used to make the superimposed words rise slowly to the top of the screen and disappear in the sky above a menacing promontory.

But these variations remained written summaries, not dramatic action. During World War II, Universal decided to scrap the written summary entirely and substitute exposition within the action. Sometimes it worked; sometimes it didn't. The episodes in *Jungle Queen* opened in Nazi Germany, where a partly seen official declaimed upon Africa's importance to the Third Reich, sometimes asking a subordinate how the fifth column work was progressing in the jungle locale where most of the action took place. The rest of the updating was left to the characters in Africa. Much the same technique was used in *Raiders of Ghost City*, the opening action in each episode occurring in Washington, D.C., where there was concern about the doings of the Confederacy in the West. Universal did eliminate the ordinary synopsis by this method, but often at the price of slowed action and artificial dialogue. Nevertheless, the studio was trying to improve the serial form.

What Columbia was trying to do in the mid-1940s was trade upon—some would say tarnish—the reputations of heroes of other media. Beginning in 1945, when "Produced by Sam Katzman" was stamped upon every Columbia serial, the borrowings were regular and frequent. The funny papers' *Brenda Starr, Reporter* began the procession, to be followed in 1946 by *Hop Harrigan*, of comic book and radio, and by *Chick Carter, Detective*, a Street and Smith character associated with the better-known

Nick Carter, but not so closely as to bring down the displeasure of MGM, maker of the Nick Carter series with Walter Pidgeon.

Columbia's 1947 serial output contained not one original hero. *Jack Armstrong* and *The Sea Hound* (with Buster Crabbe) were based upon radio programs. *The Vigilante* (Ralph Byrd) came from *Action Comics*; and *Brick Bradford* (Kane Richmond), from the funnies. In 1948, when Columbia's serial productions dropped from four to three a year (as Republic's had a year earlier), the comic book provided the source for Katzman's *Tex Granger, Superman* (starring Kirk Allyn), and *Congo Bill*. Appropriations of 1949–52 were, from comic pages, *Bruce Gentry* (1949); from comic magazines, *Batman and Robin* (1949), *Atom Man vs. Superman* (1950), *King of the Congo* (1952), and *Blackhawk*, (1952); from the pen of Jules Verne, *Mysterious Island* (1951); and most significantly, from television, *Captain Video* (1951).

The use of a television hero—even a pastiche one such as Captain Video—dramatized the problem of the motion-picture chapter play. Its function of entertaining youngsters was being transferred to the half-hour adventure thrillers of a new medium. What is more, that new medium was forcing the film serial to compete with itself by showing such well-made cliffhangers of earlier days as *Flash Gordon*. The low-budget, often uninspired serials of the postwar years were involved in a losing battle. Universal left it early. Republic and Columbia stayed with it until the mid-1950s, using rereleases to fill out the schedule.

For a brief time it seemed that salvation might lie in outer space. On the heels of the interest generated by *Destination Moon* and other films (including the Flash Gordon feature versions) came a flurry of cliffhangers depicting interplanetary difficulties: *King of the Rocket Men* (1949), *Flying Disc Man from Mars* (1951), *Radar Men from the Moon* (1952), and *Zombies from the Stratosphere* (1952), fashioned by Republic; and *Captain Video* and *The Lost Planet* (1953), from Columbia. These pictures could in no way be compared with *Destination Moon* or with the old Flash Gordon serials. Essentially, they were variations upon the old conquer-the-world-through-science

139

themes, the Earth-based mad inventors of earlier days being replaced by aliens from other worlds.

Cast as Retik, the outer-space heavy in *Radar Men from the Moon*, was Roy Barcroft, making his thirteenth and last appearance as a badman in Republic serials. Beginning with *Haunted Harbor*, the Kay Aldridge film of 1944, Barcroft made a career of bullying Republic's chapter-play heroes and heroines—when he wasn't busy annoying its cowboy stars. In *Manhunt of Mystery Island* he was Captain Mephisto, a legendary pirate into whose form the villain of the piece could transform himself by means of an incredible machine. Barcroft was back the same year as the Purple Monster. Then came a run of miscellaneous chicanery in *Daughter of Don Q* (1946), *Son of Zorro* and *Jesse James Rides Again* (1947), *G-Men Never Forget* (1948), *Federal Agents vs. Underworld, Inc.* and *Ghost of Zorro* (1949), *The James Brothers of Missouri* and *Desperadoes of the West* (1950), and *Don Daredevil Rides Again* (1951). Somehow he managed to get the role of the marshal in *The Phantom Rider* (1946). And he was both good guy and bad in his dual role in *G-Men Never Forget*.

These titles give the reader a fair idea of what Republic's serial factory was up to during those years, when the studio was not producing space sagas. By the close of the 1940s the plots of the studio's cliffhangers had lost the touches of imagination that had distinguished its earlier efforts. While the action scenes were reasonably well staged, the plots degenerated into tedious skirmishing between the goodies and the baddies. The titles themselves sometimes betrayed what went on in these jousting dramas: *Federal Agents vs. Underworld, Inc.*, *Radar Patrol vs. Spy King* (1950), *Government Agents vs. Phantom Legion* (1951), *Canadian Mounties vs. Atomic Invaders* (1953).

Following plots that would have worked in Tom and Jerry cartoons, the villains set innumerable traps for the hero or heroine, only to have the quarry escape and deliver a few blows of his or her own. Often the same predicament was presented to a hero several times in a single serial. Clayton Moore, the Lone Ranger of television, survived the twelve chapters of

Ghost of Zorro primarily because of his ability to regain consciousness and roll away from a falling object in a fraction of a second. Walter Reed got through *Flying Disc Man from Mars* by bailing out of every conceivable aircraft, as well as jumping out of crashing cars.

Certainly one reason for the lack of imagination in Republic's last serials was the necessity for the writers to construct the episodes around footage from older efforts. It was no coincidence that the outfit of *Panther Girl of the Kongo* (1955) matched to the last detail that of *Jungle Girl*; it was designed to take advantage of scenes filmed for the earlier cliffhanger. The same could be said about the uniform of Mota, the alien villain of *Flying Disc Man from Mars*, who dressed like the Purple Monster. Sadder yet, the heroes of *Don Daredevil Rides Again* and *Man With the Steel Whip* (1954) suffered the disgrace of wearing caballero suits of a design used by Linda Stirling in *Zorro's Black Whip*. (Ken Curtis and Dick Simmons overcame this humiliation to become television's Festus and Sergeant Preston.) In a hard-to-conceal costume revival, the memorable bank-robbery-by-robot of *Mysterious Dr. Satan* was reconstructed for *Zombies of the Stratosphere*.

Sometimes the scene juggling was obvious even to those unacquainted with earlier serials. Harry Lauter and Fran Bennett had to don decidedly old-fashioned costumes to make usable some scenes shot for a 1937 feature starring Robert Livingston. The only latter-day Republic heroine to rate a bit of chic was Phyllis Coates, who in *Jungle Drums of Africa* (1953) wore a matching cap, blouse, shorts, and knee-length-hose ensemble of a striking dark hue. But two years later, as Panther Girl of the Kongo, she was in Frances Gifford's old miniskirt.

King of the Carnival was Republic's last serial. Franklin Adreon was both director and producer, as he was for the studio's four preceding episoders. Carrying the entire writing burden in this and Adreon's other double-duty efforts was Ronald Davidson, who never had fewer than four script collaborators in the good old days. With "Vengeance Under the Big Top," Chapter 12 of this last adventure, ended twenty years of serial making

141

that had begun with "Baru—Son of the Jungle," the first installment of *Darkest Africa*.

If the outpourings of the second decade of those twenty years
at Republic are undistinguished by earlier standards, those of
the first decade brought scenes to savor in memory. In wistful
moments yesterday's youngsters can call up images that once
brought hushed awe or tingling excitement: a hovering protector
on a painted stallion outlined against the horizon, a heavy mine
car hurtling toward a seemingly trapped Lone Ranger, a secret
hanger entrance drawing aside to reveal the Flying Wing, as
the Lightning prepares to strike! Only reluctantly, we conjecture, would witnesses to those flickering events of another time
accept a gaudy evening with James Bond in trade for the remembrance of more solid stuff. Could, in fact, an exchange value
be placed upon Captain Marvel confidently surveying the situation while gliding through the air—or Frank Lackteen fixing his
evil eye upon Jungle Girl—or Captain America lashing into
Maldor's men as giant sparks illuminate the power plant in which
he is fighting? Probably not by those who drank this heady wine
in days before the world crashed in upon juvenile fancies. Let
the record read that Republic Pictures fulfilled its duties as
caterer of thrills extraordinaire.

In 1956, Columbia Pictures, the only remaining maker of chapter plays, released Spencer Bennet's *Blazing the Overland Trail*.
An unremembered drama with unremembered heroes, it stands
as the last serial fashioned for viewing in those darkened trans-
ports to adventure that were the Rialto or the Cameo or the
Grand. With much less notice than had attended its arrival, a
distinctive form of entertainment disappeared—but not without
trace, and not without the gratitude of those who had known it
when.

1234**56**789101112131415161718192021222324

SLEUTH AND SHADOW

Oh! scenes in strong remembrance set!
Scenes never, never to return!

ROBERT BURNS, *The Lament*

The invasion began quietly enough. The small advance guard gave little suggestion of the horde that lay so close behind. Yet when we look back at the year 1929, we can see that there were definite signs of what was about to break loose—not economic depression in this instance, but an explosion of chills and thrills without parallel in American history.

Readers of the comic pages had the most conspicuous clue to what was soon to happen. Into a region that had been, just as its name indicated, comic, came two heroic characters unlike all earlier denizens of the territory. In a blast of rocketry arrived a smiling Buck Rogers; and, swinging on a vine, a stern-browed Tarzan. The funnies would never recover their pristine state.

Other areas of publishing showed stirrings of a similar nature.

At the newsstands the latest manifestations of the story papers and dime novels, the pulps, were multiplying as rapidly as their fast-working writers could grind them out. And a new genre was competing for the attention of the magazine browser: science fiction.

In movieland the evidences of the impending thriller explosion were less easy to detect, for derring-do had been a part of the motion picture since the days of the flickers. Furthermore, in 1929 the chapter play, making its precarious transition from silence to sound, stood in danger of dying prematurely. Nonetheless, there were measurable rumblings of new dimensions in screen excitement. Possibly it was the addition of the sound track that stimulated an unusual emphasis on action—or at least an unusual appreciation of it by those not addicted to thrills and chills. Nods of approval could have been anticipated for Warner Oland's portrayal of *The Mysterious Dr. Fu Manchu*, but could it have been expected that Warner Baxter would win an Academy Award for playing the Cisco Kid?

Baxter's picture, *In Old Arizona*, ranked seventh in *Film Daily*'s list of the ten best films of 1929. If that level of critical approval seems dizzying for a Cisco Kid picture, consider the film that nosed it out for sixth place: *Bulldog Drummond*. Was not response such as this fair warning of the imminent arrival of the two cycles of violence indelibly associated with the 1930s and paralleling the rise of explosive action in comics and radio? I mean, of course, the gangster pictures, starting with *Little Caesar* (1930) and *Public Enemy* (1931), and the round of horror films set off by the two 1931 classics, *Dracula* and *Frankenstein*.

Although radio took a little longer than the other media to gather its high-adventure momentum, the appearance of its first network thrillers coincided with the newspaper debuts of Messrs. Rogers and Greystoke—and, accidentally or not, with the advent of the depression. *Empire Builders, Forty Fathom Trawlers*, and *True Detective Mysteries* may not have been as exotic as the accounts of Buck and the Ape Man, but they were just as distinct departures from the established pattern of their medium as the comic-strip adventures were from theirs. Two major forms of entertainment thus began the trip into the realm of danger almost simultaneously.

Radio in 1929 was less than ten years old as an entertainment medium, and radio drama was even younger. Although the date of the first radio play is uncertain, we do know that on August 3, 1922, a stage melodrama, *The Wolf*, was aired by WGY, Schenectady. The determined listener heard a broadcast two and a half hours long—that is, if he didn't have to surrender his earphones to curious friends and relatives. In those days the novelty of a play coming over the air would have been more impressive than the drama itself, and possibly few listeners spent an uninterrupted evening with *The Wolf*.

Be that as it may, a month later WGY began presenting dramas each week, some of them full-length plays from Broadway. By 1923 the station was offering prizes for original scripts. That same year, according to one survey of radio drama, a mystery serial, *The Waddington Cipher*, was heard on WJZ, New York. While it might appear that the motion-picture serial, already come upon leaner days, now faced competition of its own kind, *The Waddington Cipher* would have been merely one of several short-run, local efforts which affected the chapter play not at all. Thriller drama played no real part in radio programing until 1929 and did not ripen until the 1930s.

Network radio's first thrillers owed both their being and their subject matter to their anything-but-modest sponsors. Great Northern Railroad, for example, hoped to profit by association with *Empire Builders*, a tribute to enterprises such as itself, heard on the Blue Network of NBC (now ABC). *Forty Fathom Trawlers* (CBS) was created with great care by the Bay State Fishing Company, the identification being carried to the point of having the program supposedly presented from the deck of one of its vessels. The weekly adventure story—a play within a play—was a seaman's yarn, told by old Forty Fathom to his shipmates following a bit of shipboard singing and chatter. In an early use of the integrated commercial, the client's message was delivered by an announcer "visiting" on board. *Forty*

Fathom Trawlers also anticipated radio and television dramas of later years by presenting a minute or two of dialogue before the opening titles, a good device for holding the listener.

The artificial genesis of the air thriller was not confined to tales of general adventure. The detective and mystery dramatization was also the result of some commercially tainted program creation. Although technically unsponsored, *True Detective Mysteries*, which appeared in the 1929–30 season, and the *Detective Story Program* of the following season amounted to promotionals for the magazines from which their stories purportedly derived. At about the same time, the National Surety Company, using its name in the title, as was the custom then, sponsored a series of NBC dramas about one of its operators, a Detective Harkness. Harkness no doubt was a fictional character, but the dramas had some root in actual company cases.

To show how well established the radio-detective pattern was by late 1930—or perhaps how much later shows copied from National Surety—here is a bit of the program presented on November 12, 1930:

ANNOUNCER: The police whistle and the siren bring again for your entertainment one of the secret cases of the National Surety Company. Tonight's story is based on a residence burglary that baffled Detective Harkness until he became perplexed over an incidental phase of the case. But the detective will explain all this himself. Detective Harkness . . .

HARKNESS: I'm not going to waste any time or words getting into tonight's story. One day, not so long ago, I entered my office in the National Surety Company's building just as the phone was ringing.

Having moved quickly into the first-person-narrative technique that would reach its apex with *Sam Spade*, the show's writer gets things going with the soon-to-be-cliché expository phone call. Through Harkness' careful repeating, the audience learns that the call is from Mrs. Whiteside, who has been robbed of fifteen thousand dollars in jewelry. Harkness tells about checking the home, suspecting an inside job, and making the rounds of pawnshops. Dialogue commences at the shop of the detective's friend

146

Jake, where Harkness spots a diamond ring and the writer inserts some ethnic speech patterns:

JAKE: Well, Mr. Harkness, if that's the ring, then half your job is done.

HARKNESS: Yes—all I have to do is to find the thief. . . . What name did he give you?

JAKE: Name? I should remember names?

HARKNESS: He signed a receipt for the money, didn't he?

JAKE: You should be a business man already! Sure, he signed a receipt.

HARKNESS: Then break out the receipt and let's see what he signed himself.

JAKE: Here you are, Mr. Harkness—"received two hundred and fifty dollars for diamond ring."

HARKNESS: Mmmmmm—John Smith—that's an unusual name.

JAKE: Oh, he's an unusual fellow.

HARKNESS: 740 Third Avenue—well, I'll write that down, but I don't expect it to mean much. I may need this receipt as a sample of his handwriting, Jake—when I come across him. I'll take it if you don't mind.

JAKE: Sure, go ahead—but give me a receipt for that ring.

HARKNESS: Of course. Now, Jake, do you remember what this fellow looked like?

JAKE: Say, for two hundred and fifty dollars I should remember a lot! He was a regular tough customer, all right, with a big scar over his eye like someone hit him in a fight. He had black eyes and black hair, and one of them little sheik moustaches.

HARKNESS: Mmmmmm—that could be anyone by the name of John Smith.

JAKE: You said it! He was one of those little guys what don't look you straight in the eye, and mamma! What a sob story he give me! I should laugh!

After listening to Jake's account of the singular-looking Mr. Smith's tale of financial woe and of his odd interest in some cameos under Jake's counter, Harkness takes the ring to Mrs. Whiteside's home for identification. There he is met by Maria, the comely maid. Maria tells him of her devotion to domestic duty and to her invalid mother, at the same time assuring him of her lack of interest in diamonds and such. The old family cameo she is wearing is her only jewelry, she says, aside from a ring her daddy gave her the day before he died.

Harkness goes on to check out the diamond with Mrs. White-side, but soon he is on his way to pick up Jake for a midnight visit to the house where the detective thinks he will find his man. The show's final scene could have appeared in innumerable police and detective dramas of the next quarter century:

HARKNESS: Here we are. Quiet, now.
JAKE: Do we ring the bell?
HARKNESS: No, I've had a key made for the door. (Open door) (Whisper) Now, not a sound, Jake. (Close door softly) Follow me up the stairs.
JAKE: (Whisper) You shouldn't go so fast, Mr. Harkness—I ain't got such long legs.
HARKNESS: Sh—it's the last door at the end of the hall.
JAKE: This must be the one.
HARKNESS: All right now—in we go. (Aloud) Hello, Marie!
MARIE: Harry, it's the detective.
HARKNESS: Well, Marie, won't you introduce me to your boy friend?
HARRY: Say, what do you want here, anyhow!
HARKNESS: Why, I just came over to see how Marie's mother was get-ting on.
HARRY: Funny, aintcha. Marie ain't got no mother.
MARIE: Harry! Shut up!
HARKNESS: That was a beautiful act you put on for me this afternoon, Marie. Well, Jake, is that the man who pawned the dia-mond ring?
JAKE: Is it him? I should hope to smile!
HARRY: Oh yeah? Well, you gotta catch me first!
(Marie screams, chair knocked down, door slam)
JAKE: You find him and let him get away, Mr. Harkness?
HARKNESS: He won't get far, Jake. The cop on the corner followed us up here—he's just outside the door. Well, there's the clue you gave me, Jake—see the brand new cameo pin Marie is wearing? A gift from Harry. Your cameo gave him the idea, but he didn't dare buy one in your store.
JAKE: Well, if that don't beat two and two makes four.

(*Pause*)

HARKNESS: Marie's old family cameo looked too new for me, and, remembering what Jake had said about Harry's enquiries about cameos, I had trailed Marie to the house at Number

39. And that is how we discovered Mrs. Whiteside's jewelry without loss of a single piece . . . .

And that is how Detective Harkness and *National Surety's Secret Cases* pointed the way to the capture-them-at-their-hideout finishes of *Gang Busters, Mr. District Attorney, Counterspy, The FBI in Peace and War, Dragnet,* and dozens of others that would follow along on the trail of crime.

An investigator much more famous than Detective Harkness also came to radio in 1930. He was the immortal resident of 221B Baker Street, Mr. Sherlock Holmes. Here radio had a mystery drama in which the characters and stories were not forced feedings of a commercial enterprise. The sponsor was G. Washington Coffee, and the extent of the patronage could have been no more than some harmless enjoyment of the distillate of the bean by Holmes and Watson.

Sir Arthur Conan Doyle died in the year the program began, three years after the last magazine appearance of an original Holmes story. The Doyle estate entrusted the NBC dramatizations to Edith Meiser, who did a good job of maintaining the integrity of the characters. Before coming to radio Miss Meiser had worked on several of the Garrick Gaieties revues on Broadway, which made for an odd coincidence, for it was at the Garrick Theatre that actor William Gillette had introduced New Yorkers to a flesh-and-blood Sherlock Holmes back in 1899. Gillette pieced together his drama from several Doyle stories and was so successful in it he did not take off the deerstalker for the last time on Broadway until the very year the radio episodes commenced. The space of a few months, in fact, brought the death of the great detective's creator, the last representation of Holmes on the New York stage by the actor who many believed best fit the part, and the beginning of his long, if occasionally interrupted, sojourn on the airwaves.

When the Holmes program went on the air on October 20, 1930, with "The Speckled Band," Gillette was in his mid-seventies and may have seemed a poor risk for a continuing part. But he took it on, ensuring the program an auspicious beginning. When Gillette resumed his theatrical touring, the Holmes role was entrusted to the very British Clive Brook and to Richard Gordon, like Gillette, an American actor born in Connecticut. Amazingly, Gillette survived, as an active performer, the first six-year radio run of *The Adventures of Sherlock Holmes*. Indeed, on November 18, 1935, he managed to share again with a nationwide audience his memorable interpretation when he impersonated the supreme investigator one last time on the *Lux Radio Theatre*.[1]

A British actor whose association with the master criminologist now stands as strong as Gillette's came to the role in both radio and motion pictures in 1939. Early that year 20th Century Fox released *The Hound of the Baskervilles*, with Basil Rathbone in the principal role and Nigel Bruce as his physician-associate. Several months later the two were starring in a revived *Adventures of Sherlock Holmes*, again on NBC, and sponsored now by Bromo Quinine Cold Tablets—a product as fortifying against the British weather as was G. Washington Coffee.

Edith Meiser once more adapted Doyle's stories, though at one point during the Rathbone era she gave way to two established mystery writers, Leslie Charteris, creator of the Saint, and Anthony (White) Boucher, who, using other pen names, devised "new adventures of Sherlock Holmes" based upon minor references in the original mysteries. Regardless of adapter, *Sherlock Holmes* normally held to an episodic-serial framework —that is, the major characters continued in the Baker Street setting from program to program, solving a different case each week. When *The Hound of the Baskervilles* roamed the moors, however, the dramatization was extended to about two months. How else could a writer properly treat a work with the most famous of all chapter-ending hooks: "Mr. Holmes, they were the footprints of a gigantic hound"?

Throughout Sherlock Holmes's stay on American radio, the Victorian, or at latest the Edwardian, backdrop of his earlier

---

[1] Gillette's final stage appearance as Holmes had been in Wilmington, Delaware, in March, 1932. Death came to the actor in 1937. An interesting account of Gillette's debut as the radio Holmes is found in the radio section of the *New York Times* of October 26, 1930. The *Lux Radio Theatre* appearance is described in the issue of November 24, 1935.

adventures was employed. Indeed, it was emphasized, with horse-drawn hansom cabs rolling over cobblestone streets as efficient sound men produced clip-clops, rumbles, and squeaks which seemed muted by heavy fog. While Watson might tell the night's story to the program's announcer in the comfortable setting of his study, he was recalling events of many years before. Holmes was gone—to his final rest or to beekeeping in Sussex. Never did he join his old friend in the preludes, only in the stories themselves.

For Rathbone and Bruce the *fin-de-siècle* backdrop necessitated some mental adjustment, because three years after filming *The Adventures of Sherlock Holmes* in 1939 for Fox, they undertook the familiar multipicture series for Universal in which Holmes was confronted by criminals of the 1940s, Nazis and spider women included. (By that time his hair style had changed from Victorian elegant to barber-shop American.) Since some of the movie plots derived from Doyle stories, in the mid-1940s Rathbone was presented with enigmas he had solved in Victorian settings on radio. The ultimate in adjustment, though, occurred on a radio comedy show in which Rathbone and Bruce appeared as themselves. For the program they exchanged fictional roles, Rathbone playing a fumbling Watson and Bruce dropping his faltering delivery to play Holmes. The two carried it off masterfully, Rathbone's imitation of Bruce convulsing the studio audience.

It is sad that Basil Rathbone came to resent the part of Sherlock Holmes; he served it so well. And only after his death can it be seen how well it served him. Rathbone believed that his acting art, and his identity, were being submerged in the Holmes role and that he must leave it or stagnate. Therefore, the radio part he surrendered to Tom Conway, and the film role he abandoned when his contractual obligation ended. But to Americans who did not know Gillette, Basil Rathbone *was* Sherlock Holmes. So it would have been had he made only half the pictures he did, or had he not returned to the radio role in the late 1940s.

It was not just accumulation of performances that made people think of Rathbone as Holmes; it was the performances themselves. During the balance of this century when the Holmes name is mentioned, millions of Americans will hear no other voice, see no other visage than that of the sharp-nosed, stern-jawed actor from South Africa who, in one of those magic feats of casting, had found his part. In his last years the actor must have realized that the portrayal of Holmes would keep his memory alive long after his other, more demanding characterizations had been covered by time. We can hope that he finally found some satisfaction in this kind of immortality. Other acting assignments may have challenged Rathbone more; none was fulfilled so completely.

The Adventures of Sherlock Holmes, while exciting radio drama, was not really a counterpart of the motion-picture cliff-hanger. Aside from being more intellectual in its appeal, it lacked the slam-bang action and rapid pace of a chapter play. Less intellectual, but no more breakneck in pace, was a hardy non-serial adventure drama introduced along with Holmes in the 1930–31 broadcast season, *Death Valley Days*. A commercial fabrication, but an entertaining one, it recalled the color of the West for 20 Mule Team Borax through the Old Ranger's true tales, which were closer in bearing to those of *Empire Builders* and *Forty Fathom Trawlers* than to the full-blown thrillers of screen and radio.

Unrestrained action came to radio with shows such as *Rin-Tin-Tin* (1931 to 1934, for Ken-L-Ration) and the short-lived dramas of 1931–32, *Count Von Luckner's Adventures* (for Scott's Emulsion), *Danger Fighters* (for Feenamint), and *With Canada's Mounted* (sustaining). But most dramatically of all, action came in the persons of an unusual man about town and a thoroughly preposterous little girl. 1931, you see, was the year of *The Shadow* and *Little Orphan Annie*.

While the *Little Orphan Annie* radio program stemmed from the successful comic strip, the derivation of *The Shadow* is blurred in serendipity. Odd as it may seem, the colorful crime fighter was created almost by accident. At the beginning of his career he was nothing more than the disembodied voice he presented later to his opponents.

Earlier I mentioned the *Detective Story* program. This CBS feature was basically a narration of miscellaneous Street and Smith pulp mysteries dressed up by the use of a storyteller affecting a weird voice. The technique was not uncommon at the time. WOR, the station that one day would originate *The Shadow* for Mutual, used it starting in May, 1931, for *The Witch's Tale*, a bizarre mystery series written by Alonzo Dean Cole and starring Adelaide Fitzallen as Old Nancy, a Salem sorceress. The device also turned up on *The Hermit's Cave, Inner Sanctum Mysteries, The Mysterious Traveler, The Whistler,* and a number of other dramas of the radio era.

None of his successors, though, caught the fancy of listeners as did the narrator of the *Detective Story* program. The piercing voice, the macabre laugh, the ironic tones brought fan mail that reflected considerably less interest in the stories than in the mysterious "Shadow" who told them. Almost overnight two things happened. The radio program evolved into the eerie dramas in which The Shadow was not narrator but principal participant, and Street and Smith introduced this fascinating new character in *The Shadow* magazine. Both program and pulp magazine were destined to prosper for a good many years, generating excitement-filled offshoots that spanned the mass media from *Big Little Books* and comic magazines to serial and full-length films. In the mid-1960s, after a near decade in the graveyard of heroes, the character returned to attention through resurrected transcriptions of the old broadcasts plus a couple of paperback originals, and (to the chagrin of former fans) a comic-book reincarnation which saw him give in to the kind of attire more appropriate to Batman.

There has long been an argument whether The Shadow was better as a radio personality (1931–54) or as a character in pulp fiction (until 1948). The argument stemmed from the fact that he was not quite the same crime fighter in both media. He had the same civilian guise—most of the time—Lamont Cranston being his only alter ego in radio and his principal one in the pulps. But this name, according to his Street and Smith author, Walter Gibson, was simply one of several he used to confuse his adversaries. A little nose putty and a mustache made him Kent Allard, his second-most-common identity camouflage.

The essential distinctions between radio and pulp Shadow were in technique of tactical operation and constancy to mistress. While The Shadow of the periodical was a cloaked figure using darkness for concealment, the radio Shadow was nothing less than the Invisible Man gone straight. His ultimate weapon was his hypnotic ability to cloud men's minds so that they could not see him. By contrast the weaponry of the Street and Smith hero was almost prosaic, though no less effective:

> Roaring their accompaniment to The Shadow's weird, sardonic laugh, big automatics tongued their messages toward the walls. Chinese sharpshooters toppled before they could fire. Li Sheng's treacherous servants were as helpless as the racked targets in a shooting gallery, as The Shadow pumped his alternating fire, turning his head with every trigger tug.[2]

Judged dispassionately, both Shadows were suited perfectly to their media. The many assistants of the magazine crime stopper were in the best tradition of pulp fiction of the 1930s (witness the compleat pulp hero, Doc Savage, and his five talented helpers), while solo work was more effective in the medium of sound. Although the radio writers drew occasional criticism for ignoring Cranston's associate sleuths, multiple investigators would have been difficult to sort aurally. Only Carlton E. Morse in *I Love A Mystery* managed to amalgamate several continuing agents without confusion—partly by giving them distinct accents: Eastern, Texan, British, and sometimes Irish.

Because of an unwavering script pattern, consideration of the listening audience (its cross-sectional nature, not its aural dependency) also mandated the other point of difference between

---

[2] "Teeth of the Dragon," *The Shadow,* November 15, 1937, 87. The definite article in The Shadow's name was always capitalized in the pulp adventures. That practice has been followed in this book, even at the risk of offense to the Spider, the Green Hornet, the Lone Ranger, and others, who apparently were more modest about their definite articles.

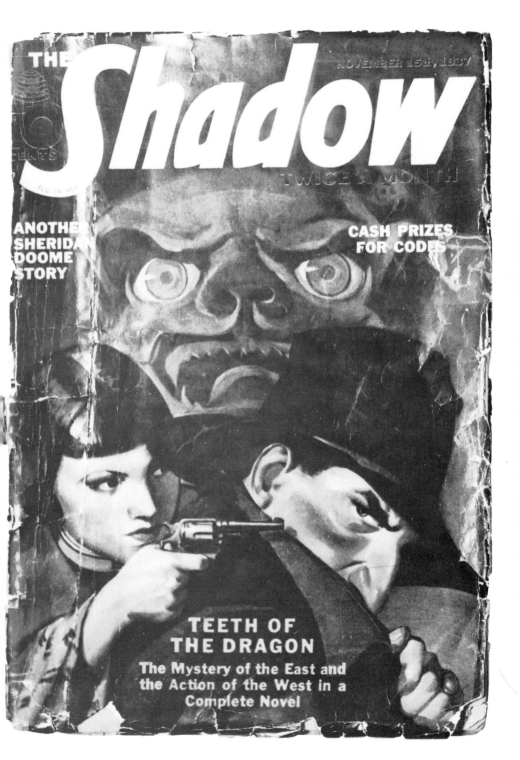

The Shadow was in the vanguard of radio's journey into thrills in the
1930s.

As Lieut. Wilma Deering in the Buck Rogers program, (Curtis Arnall playing the part of Buck), Adele Ronson flies about in a space ship between planets and fires rocket pistols with abandon

ABOVE: Tom Mix and a delighted Ralston executive (W. H. Danforth) survey the response to an early premium offer. BELOW LEFT: Billy Halop in sombrero for the Bobby Benson role. BELOW RIGHT: Buck Rogers (played by Curtis Arnall) and copilot Wilma Deering (played by Adele Ronson).

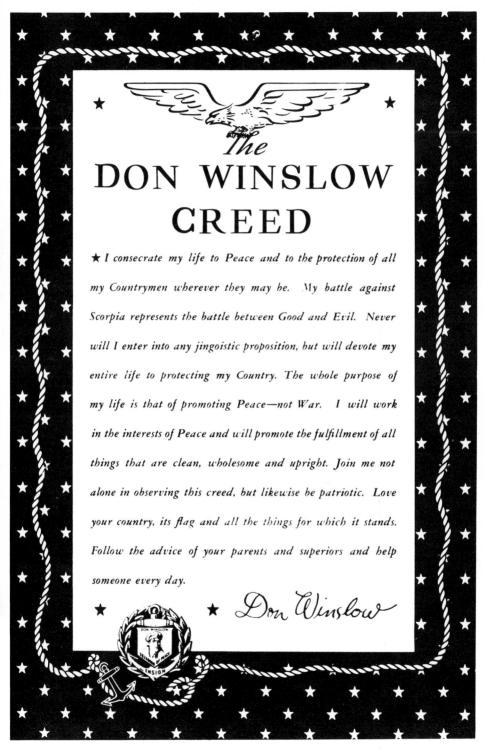

The DON WINSLOW CREED

★ I consecrate my life to Peace and to the protection of all my Countrymen wherever they may be. My battle against Scorpia represents the battle between Good and Evil. Never will I enter into any jingoistic proposition, but will devote my entire life to protecting my Country. The whole purpose of my life is that of promoting Peace—not War. I will work in the interests of Peace and will promote the fulfillment of all things that are clean, wholesome and upright. Join me not alone in observing this creed, but likewise be patriotic. Love your country, its flag and all the things for which it stands. Follow the advice of your parents and superiors and help someone every day.

Don Winslow

The Creed of the Squadron of Peace.

ABOVE LEFT: The Lightning, villain of *The Fighting Devil Dogs* as he would have appeared in a comic book. RIGHT, ABOVE AND BELOW: The Spider. These two gaudy dressers set apparel standards for the superheroes of pen and ink who reached the screen in the 1940s.

CLOCKWISE, FROM THE LEFT: The Phantom and dog Devil, Robin, Batman, Captain America, Spy Smasher, and the Masked Marvel.

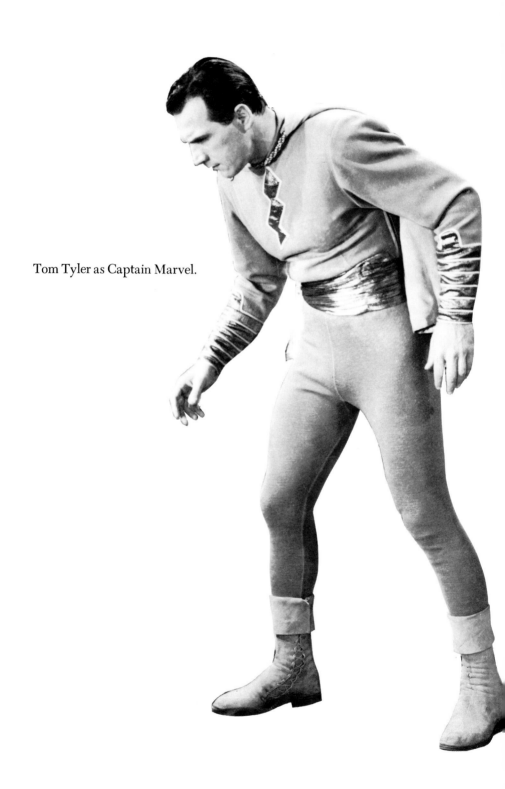

Tom Tyler as Captain Marvel.

SUPERMAN IN RADIO

"Jimmy, Jimmy! Where are you?" Superman made a quick dive . . . "Got him! Poor kid, he's as limp as a rag." . . . Superman's muscles tensed as he wrenched the shells apart to free Edwards' foot

The great heroes of National (Detective) Comics, copyright National Periodical Publications.

A Johnson Smith advertisement of 1941.

the two Shadows: the radio detective's notably higher fidelity to the lovely Margo Lane. Anyone who stopped to think for a moment could have had little doubt about the Cranston-Lane relationship, in the radio adventures at least. The two were always together, in train, plane, car, or apartment—and Margo's last name was Lane, not Cranston.

Why, then, was Margo only an in-and-out heroine in the pulps but a constantly present one on radio? The answer is that, while pulp readers (99 per cent male in this case) were not overly fussy about the romantic lives of their heroes and were conditioned to a wide variety of female companionship for them, a change of distressed damsel in the stereotyped radio adventures would have made Cranston seem a philanderer. After all, how many different women can an upright criminal stalker drive across state lines, spend nights with in haunted houses, and talk things over with afterward in penthouse apartments? Although in both pulp and air stories Cranston was seldom if ever observed so much as kissing a heroine, the nature of the media generated in one case a freewheeling detective and in the other a man true to his mistress, unacknowledged though she may have been.

The Shadow's immutable radio format alluded to above became one of the several most familiar of broadcasting. When refined to the ultimate degree, it began with a wheezy organ rendition of Saint-Saëns' symphonic poem *Le Rouet d'Omphale*, interrupted by that familiar question-answer posed by The Shadow himself: "Who knows—what evil—lurrrrrks—in the hearts of men? The *Shadow* knows! Hm-hm-hm-hm-hm-hm-hm."

Then the announcer explained:

> The Shadow, who aids the forces of law and order, is, in reality, Lamont Cranston, wealthy young man about town. Years ago in the Orient, Cranston learned a strange and mysterious secret, the hypnotic power to cloud men's minds so they cannot see him. Cranston's friend and companion, the lovely Margo Lane, is the only person who knows to whom the voice of the invisible Shadow belongs. Today's story . . . .

Now came a title to conjure with on cold or stormy Sundays:

"The Ghost Walks Again," "Isle of the Dead," "The House of Horror," "Murder from the Grave," or "The Terrible Legend of Crownshield Castle." Was there any doubt what a story with a title like that was going to be?

Almost invariably the drama itself opened to some cataclysm, major or minor, in mid-process. The lights of the city had failed, leaving darkness and terror; a logger was being torn apart by an apparent werewolf; a young woman was falling a shrieking victim to "something in this house." When the noise subsided, one could expect to hear Margo and Lamont in quiet conversation, sometimes discussing the catastrophe but more often happily driving along a lonely road somewhere, on the way to visit Cranston's old college chum—one Lansing Turnbull, perhaps—whom he hadn't seen in years. The reunion could be expected to end in hair-raising fashion. Many times, though, it never took place. A missed road sign, a flat tire, and Lamont and Margo were spending the night in that house with "something" in it.

Cranston would, by and by, discover what was amiss and begin puddling about with a view to its correction. Here a visit as The Shadow to a weak link in the chain of horror normally elicited a strong clue from the terrified underling. The invisible third degree never came in time, however, to save Miss Lane from the trying ordeal that dogged every one of those weekend trips with Lamont.

After falling through a trapdoor, locking herself in a windowless basement room "for safety," or following a thread trail to the lair of a man who thought himself a spider, this charming human guinea pig rounded off each episode with a bit of dire peril. Clamped into an ancient torture device, enmeshed in a spider's web, or strapped to an operating table, she awaited, at best, quick dispatch, at worst, transformation into a canine, primate, zombie, vampire, or whatever else preoccupied the villain of that Sunday. Once she was forced to ponder a switch of vocal cords with a family cat, another time a blending of portions of her brain with that of a gorilla.

Because most of these operations were doomed to failure, the second appearance of The Shadow was an absolute necessity for

164

the prolongation of the Cranston-Lane relationship. It was signaled by another "Hm-hm-hm-hm-hm" and a "Release that girl!" coming out of nowhere—or so it seemed to the bedeviled amateur surgeon caught with scalpel poised. A few wild thrusts of the knife, and the miscreant lost heart and rushed into the crushing arms of the gorilla. Soon Margo and Lamont were in auto, stateroom or apartment, talking it over with shuddered contemplation of what might have happened if things had not worked out. "I never want to look at another gorilla/spider/zombie/vampire/cat/mummy again!" was an invaluable closing line for Miss Lane, who, as sure as Sunday, would be looking at one of them the next week.

A closing commercial (for Blue Coal in the East) preceded the well-remembered tag The Shadow brought with him from the *Detective Story* program: "The weed of crime bears bitter fruit. Crime does not pay. The Shadow knows! Hm-hm-hm-hm-hm-hm."

Who listened to all of this? Just about everybody not tuned to a sports event late on Sunday afternoon, the time into which the program finally settled. Hackneyed though it was, *The Shadow* possessed a strange fascination for listeners of all ages. Was it the fun of being frightened to death in the perfect safety of the home? Was it the attraction of the hero nonpareil for radio —one whom *nobody* could see? Was it the end-of-weekend timing, which might have made listeners more susceptible to fictional escape that bordered on lunacy? Or was it *The Shadow's* undisguised, unpretentious invitation to get away from it all, logic included, for half an hour? It is too late now to say. But year after year the program rang up highly respectable ratings in a time slot that was not otherwise high in listenership. It became one of the few radio programs recognized or asked about by those growing up in the rock-and-roll age. It has a preferred chair in the house of trivia.

Whom should the world acknowledge for the long life of the man who wasn't there? At least a small roomful of broadcasters, some of whom are lost to history because time has obscured the switch from *Detective Story* to *The Shadow*. When The Shadow began his independent career, however, he had two writers: Walter Gibson (pen name Maxwell Grant) for the pulps and Harry Charlot for radio. Like a character in one of his stories, Charlot was found dead one day under mysterious circumstances. From that time on, the radio adventures were placed in the hands of free-lance writers, who sometimes found inspiration in the narratives of Gibson and his relief men, just as the writers of the twice-a-month pulp did in the air stories. More writers joined the brotherhood when The Shadow became a character in children's books and in films. For the revival in paperbacks the man at the typewriter was Gibson, who after three decades and 178 novels was allowed to use his own name.

The Shadow's impersonators were almost as numerous as his writers, a fact which may have contributed to the air of mystery surrounding him—mystery sparked by the magazine's repeated assertion that the real Shadow was somehow involved in the broadcasts as well as in the printed stories. The magazine certified that the adventures were from The Shadow's secret annals, as "set down by Mr. Maxwell Grant, my raconteur." Two unremembered early stand-ins for the invisible nemesis were Frank Readick and James LaCurto. They passed the black cloak to Robert Hardy Andrews, whom we shall encounter again several times in this book, though not as an actor.

In 1937, when the program needed a boost if it was not to disappear from the air as an outworn specimen of the less demanding days of thriller drama, it acquired just the actor to carry it through. Not yet twenty-three, and with "Invasion from Mars" still in the offing, Orson Welles assumed the role for which his rumbling tones were ideally suited. Braced by Welles, the anything-but-logical thriller-chiller was able to withstand the necessary comparisons with the highly polished prestige dramas that had come to the airwaves. When the actor left the show a year or so later, it had passed from novelty to institution. It could be laughed at, but not laughed away. For the last fifteen years of its life the series was accepted for what it was, absolute escapist entertainment.

Orson Welles's partner in his days as The Shadow was Agnes

Moorehead, perfecting her hysteria technique for her radio triumph, *Sorry, Wrong Number*. Welles's successor, Bill Johnstone, for a time also had the benefit of Miss Moorehead's piercing screams, and later those of Marjorie Anderson. The last radio Shadow, Bret Morrison, was joined by a Margo Lane portrayed by Gertrude Warner. Filling out the casts over the years were such radio stalwarts as Santos Ortega (playing Commissioner Weston), Everett Sloane, Ted de Corsia, Alice Frost, Kenny Delmar, Lawson Zerbe, Alan Reed, and Dwight Weist.

The *Shadow* cast lists left the realm of incidental history when transcriptions of the program were pulled out of vaults for re-release in the 1960s. Untangling the mystery of who played what role became a problem greater than any presented in the fictional dramas. A panel of former *Shadow* actors had to come to the rescue so that performers might be identified and compensated for their earlier efforts; otherwise the show could not have been cleared for broadcast.

The revival of *The Shadow* drew some play in newspapers throughout the country. More than one hundred radio stations picked up the series, according to *Time*, which was exuberant enough about the return of the program to term it a "Gothic Revival." The nostalgia was fine, but by the mid-1960s radio was too far down the line toward top-forty songs and talk formats to do more than flirt with drama—even though fan mail was encouraging. The return of The Shadow was essentially a glorious reprise for radio buffs, and a nice bit of profit for packager Charles Michelson.

12345678910111213141516171819202122324

LISTEN!

> *Trouble rides behind and gallops with him.*
>
> NICOLAS BOILEAU, *Épîtres*

Included in the block of old transcriptions offered to stations along with those of *The Shadow* were the shows of Cranston's two longtime partners in disguise, the Lone Ranger and the Green Hornet, who came to radio within five years of The Shadow's debut and rode with him most of the way to the last fade-off. The first to join The Shadow in radio's war against foul play was the Lone Ranger, whose fictitious labors, of course, ante-dated Cranston's by half a century. Of these three avengers under cloak or mask the Ranger was the most enduring and—probably not incidentally—the least complex. He was all that was right and good and courageous mounted on a white horse.

In light of The Shadow's Topsy-like origin it is interesting to note that the Lone Ranger was fabricated from drawing board to showroom as carefully as the newest Detroit product—which,

168

indeed, he was. During the fall of 1932, George W. Trendle, head of Detroit's WXYZ, decided that his station, newly disaffiliated from CBS but not yet an originating partner of Mutual, should have some identifying programing of its own, possibly an adventure drama for children. A little deliberation refined the idea to the point that the locale would be the old West and the hero a masked rider.

Zorro seems to have been foremost in Trendle's thinking, but Zorro as modified by the phantom riders of the chapter plays and B Westerns of the 1920s and 1930s. This hero was to be strictly American, without the Spanish elegance of Johnston McCulley's sword-and-whip daredevil. Moreover, he was to be not a one-crisis avenger but a hero dedicated enough to law and order to join the Texas Rangers *before* circumstances made him a masked paladin. When Trendle insisted that his new hero work independently of his former associates, the name for the projected series and its central character became almost inevitable. This title, incidentally, though superb for the series, was not entirely original. Fox had made a film called *Lone Ranger* in 1919, and not far removed in title was that company's *Lone Star Ranger* of 1923 (based upon Zane Grey's book and remade in 1930). Columbia's *The Lone Rider* was released only two and a half years before the debut of the radio series. These earlier (and several later) approximations of title had little significance once Trendle's character became *the* lone ranger.

Having decided in general the kind of hero they were creating, the Detroit program planners had more designing to do. During the closing weeks of 1932 the ideas came forth with uncanny rightness. Though the drama was designed to be heard and not seen, an extraordinary emphasis was given to visual elements. The color of the hero's horse—something that could have been ignored completely—was given central importance. He would be pure white, with silver horseshoes.

When writer Fran Striker arrived at the strategy chambers to flesh out the drama, the silver motif was extended. The Lone Ranger would use silver bullets (just as Robin Hood had used silver-tipped arrows in an earlier Striker dramatization). And what more appropriate name could be given the white stallion than Silver? (Again, the name was letter-perfect but not original. Until the Ranger came along, the best-known rider of a white horse named Silver was Buck Jones, the star of *The Lone Rider* in 1930.)

When *The Lone Ranger* at last reached the air on January 30, 1933, after innumerable script revisions and a much-analyzed pilot broadcast, it was the polished product Detroit was accustomed to turning out. An extended tag line more appropriate to Zorro or the Cisco Kid had been scrapped in favor of the famous "Hi-Yo-Silver!" The *William Tell* Overture had become the Lone Ranger's theme song. And neatly in place were those stirring opening lines that were set off by a burst of gunfire: "A cloud of dust—a galloping horse with the speed of light—a hearty Hi-Yo-Silver. The L-o-o-o-ne Ranger!"

The bugs were minor. The masked rider initially was too much alone. He needed someone to talk with other than his horse. So the faithful Tonto joined the cast—and the legend of the Lone Ranger was recited. Listeners learned how a band of six Texas Rangers, led by Captain Dan Reid, was ambushed by the Cavendish gang, the only survivor being Reid's younger brother, John. They learned of the cleverness of the Indian Tonto, who, finding Reid alive, dug six graves to deceive the outlaws into thinking there were no survivors, then nursed Reid back to health. And they learned how the Indian and the ex-Ranger, riding together, found the great wild stallion that became Silver. Once Tonto acquired his mount, the swift paint Scout, the Indian and the man he called Kemo Sabay (Trusty Scout) were off to adventures that still go on in one entertainment medium or another.

Although the fictional framework was set early, there was a little difficulty in settling upon an actor to play the title role. Three men filled it during the first six months. Jack Deeds, the originator, was followed by George Stenius (now film producer George Seaton) and then by WXYZ station manager Brace Beemer, who had helped plan the series. Had Beemer kept the part, what eventually would become an extraordinary tenure in a role would have been an even longer one. But Beemer left WXYZ for a fling at the advertising-agency business, and the Lone Ranger impersonation at last settled upon Earle Graser, who would retain it for eight years.

Graser (pronounced "Grah-zer") might have been the Lone Ranger for the remainder of the hero's radio days, but he fell victim to twentieth-century civilization in 1941, when an automobile accident took his life. Thousands attended his funeral, though his name probably was unknown to most of them before the accident.

Faced with a replacement in the role much more difficult than those of the program's shakedown days, the *Lone Ranger* production team came up with a brilliant ploy. The Ranger was seriously wounded at the outset of an episode and lay in a coma as Tonto carried on alone (it was virtually a re-creation of the Ranger's origin). When the masked rider revived, he spoke only a few halting words until several episodes had passed. Then the booming baritone of Brace Beemer once more burst forth in the role. Having returned to WXYZ, Beemer was doing the announcing for the Western adventure at the time of Graser's death, and he reassumed the role he had surrendered years before.

Brace Beemer, a real-life hero in the Rainbow Division during World War I, possessed the voice that most people now associate with the Lone Ranger. He was at the microphone when the radio series ended in September, 1954. He also dubbed the "Hi-Yo-Silver" for the long-running television series when the film actor's challenge to his mount seemed anemic compared with Beemer's booming cry. The veteran radio performer was about to revive a sound version of *The Lone Ranger* on long-playing records when death came to him in 1965. Newspaper obituaries were almost uniform in heading: "The Lone Ranger Dies," they said. And while association with the character had prevented him from getting other dramatic roles, Beemer probably would not have minded being remembered that way.

At least he did not toil in the near anonymity of his fellow actors on the radio show. Longtime announcer Fred Foy did get a credit at the end of each program, but not loyal Tonto. How many would recognize the late John Todd as the portrayer of the faithful Indian? Certainly his natural voice—one strengthened and disciplined by training for Shakespearean roles—did not suggest the broken-English phrases of Tonto. Nor did his appearance. Todd took the role when he was in his sixties, and he was an octogenarian when he enacted it for the last time on the program's final broadcast. Off-microphone, this performer was as much like a last-century Potawatomi as was Herbert Hoover sitting for his presidential portrait. One can only imagine Todd's reaction to an oft-recounted *faux pas*—the time habit caused him to respond, "Gettum-up, Scout," when the Ranger said, "Let's go, Tonto"—in a second-floor room!

John Todd can be excused that bit of carelessness; he often was required to play a second role in an episode. The principal parts, however, were handled by members of what amounted to a Trendle stock company. Rarely did their assignments vary. Paul Hughes was the heavy (in voice as well as character); John Hodiak, the young man in trouble; Jay Michael, the villainous Butch Cavendish and sundry other badmen. At the end of each episode it could be expected that a senior citizen of the plains would either ask, "Who was that feller in the mask?" or respond to that question with the penultimate line in nearly every drama: "Why, don't you know? That was the Lo-o-one Ranger!" Frank Russell was given this question/answer assignment more often than anyone else. For a time comedian Danny Thomas worked in the series under his real name, Amos Jacobs—not that stage names mattered when the most that could be hoped for in the way of credits was a quick announcement of participants, without reference to the roles they portrayed.

Before AFTRA minimum scales (and General Mills) came to the rescue, this small band of thespians, and writer Striker too, toiled long and hard for scarcely more than a ration of Silvercup Bread. Meanwhile, Trendle was gathering million-dollar profits from the radio enterprise, its offshoots in other media, and its authorized imitations. One of the facsimiles, *Challenge of the Yukon* (better known as *Sergeant Preston*), was set in Canadian gold-rush days. Instead of a great white horse, the hero of the series had a magnificent husky lead dog, King. "On, King! On, you huskies!" was the cry of Preston, played by actor Paul Sutton, whose voice seemed even more immense than Lone Ranger Beemer's. The blending of classical-music bridges, long sequences of narration, and slightly stilted dialogue that characterized the first Trendle drama was also evident in this adventure. So was the Trendle stock company.

Challenge of the Yukon turned up first in the late 1930s but did not come into prominence until NBC aired it during the 1947–48 season. It was in point of time and significance the third of a WXYZ-Trendle trilogy. Trendle's second big adventure series, though farther than *Challenge* from the Ranger's period and locale, was actually closer to the original in format and, perhaps for that reason, more profitable.

The Lone Ranger's surname, it will be recalled, was Reid. Young Dan Reid, who appeared frequently in the series over the years, was of course the Ranger's nephew, the son of the slain Ranger captain. Long after the Lone Ranger's frontier was a memory, Dan Reid was a background figure in another series. He was the white-haired father of a fighting newspaper editor who, like his range-riding great-uncle, donned a mask to fight wrongdoers. Dan Reid's son was Britt Reid, known to millions of Americans (but not to his pursuers) as the Green Hornet.

The Hornet program began modestly on WXYZ and the Michigan Radio Network in 1936. Although attracting much less juvenile attention in that region than *The Lone Ranger* had, it drew enough notice to cause NBC-Blue to try it on a sustaining basis in 1938. "The Green Hornet is coming!" the on-the-air promotional ads proclaimed, and soon many listeners were looking forward to the program. The first buzz of the sound-effects hornet, joined quickly by "The Flight of the Bumblebee," left no doubt that high-geared adventure was the essence of the series. Here was a modern-day equivalent of the man on horseback, buzzing around a large city in an uncatchable sedan called the

Black Beauty. At his side was a Japanese chauffeur-valet, and in his hand a pistol that could knock out crooks with the harmless pellets of gas it unleashed.

The mercy gun was not unimportant to the program concept, for just as the Lone Ranger never killed badmen, merely wounding them or shooting the guns out of their hands instead, his latter-day counterpart was also respectful of human life, even that belonging to society's undesirables. This unity of approach was not the only parallel between the two heroes, as is well known. Aside from their masks, the two were related in their unbeatable methods of transportation (one white, one black), their sidekicks of Asian descent, their stirring theme songs, their action lines ("The Lone Ranger rides again" and "The Green Hornet strikes again"), their unique calling cards (a silver bullet and a facsimile hornet), their solid financial undergirding (a silver mine and a newspaper enterprise), and so on. Sooner or later it came to juvenile listeners that the Green Hornet was the Lone Ranger in modern dress, facing the complications of trying to operate independently of the law in twentieth-century society. If the comic-book heroes had not come along in the late 1930s to saturate the avenger market—and openly copy the Green Hornet's *modus operandi*—the Ranger-Hornet link would have been much more obvious.

Unlike the Lone Ranger, the Green Hornet was the pursued as well as the pursuer, which makes it easier to trace his lineage, not simply to the Lone Ranger but also to an earlier hero in disguise to whom the Hornet, as well as Zorro, The Shadow, and the Superman-Batman gang were much indebted.

It is somewhat jarring to realize that the originator of the gaudy-avenger vogue of the twentieth century was a woman born in Hungary in 1865 and raised in baronial elegance in an environment that often included three of her father's friends: Wagner, Gounod, and Liszt. When she was fifteen, Emmuska, Baroness Orczy, learned English, the language in which she was destined to write for publication perhaps a million words. With her English husband, Montagu W. Barstow, she wrote a play called *The Scarlet Pimpernel* in 1905. In it she introduced the protector of the French aristocracy during the Reign of Terror, Sir Percy Blakeney, who also was the central character of her book version of the story, which was published the same year.

From this beginning—unimpressive to the critics, applauded by the public—came many other works based upon the Pimpernel figure: *The Triumph of the Scarlet Pimpernel, Sir Percy Hits Back, The League of the Scarlet Pimpernel, Percy and Rosemary,* and so on. The first film dramatization of the story was made in 1917. Baroness Orczy was still writing stories about her character five years after the most successful of the Scarlet Pimpernel films, the one starring Leslie Howard, was released in 1935.

So that Baroness Orczy's contribution to the Don Diego Vegas, Lamont Cranstons, Britt Reids, Clark Kents, and Bruce Waynes can be fully appreciated, let it be noted that Sir Percy Blakeney was born in comfortable circumstances, led a double life in order to fight injustice, was constantly in danger of discovery, concealed his identity with a carefree exterior, wore a disguise while going about his heroics, adopted an artificial name (containing a color), developed a symbol from it, worked in the shadow of legal authorities, and was noted for his elusiveness.

Johnston McCulley, twenty-two years old when the Pimpernel made his debut, used this framework for his 1919 continued magazine story, *The Curse of Capistrano.* Don Diego Vega (Zorro) acted the dandy while aiding the peons under the noses of Spanish colonial officials. Where Blakeney took the name of a flower, Vega took that of an animal, the fox. Blakeney's Pimpernel symbol became Zorro's slashing Z. The Pimpernel's color was scarlet; Zorro's, black.

On radio *The Shadow* brought the alter-ego motif to a contemporary metropolitan setting. The Shadow's disguise was one appropriate to radio: invisibility. So was his identifying symbol: a sinister laugh coming from nowhere. His very name, of course, carried out his theme and reflected his own kind of identifying color. If Lamont Cranston was less the fop than were Sir Percy and Don Diego, one can only reflect upon the perils of such an affectation in twentieth-century New York City. Interference

by the police while in the role of the avenger was sufficient
handicap without bringing upon the alter ego the harassment
of the Times Square vice squad's plainclothesmen.[1]

The enlargements upon Baroness Orczy's basic design presented in *The Green Hornet* were simply mechanical aids,
gadgetry that would be passed on to the comic-book superheroes.
Borrowing the double identity, the color-keyed name, the identifying symbol, the disguise, the need to stay clear of the law,
Trendle's writers added (with some debt to the Lone Ranger)
the flashy supercar and the trick weapon. Kato (and Tonto too,
of course) were nice additions, but could be traced at least as
far back as Don Quixote's Sancho Panza.

After the appearance of *The Green Hornet* radio appropriated
a few more costumed avengers, the Pimpernel included, but it
created no more twentieth-century ones, leaving that work to
the comic-book galaxies of "POW!" and "ZAM!" In transferring
Superman and Batman to electromagnetic form, broadcasting
actually had little interest to pay the comic-book medium. The
debt of the Clark Kent posture to Baroness Orczy is obvious,
and Batman is simply the Green Hornet with Superman's tailor.

The years following the advent of *Sherlock Holmes* and *The
Shadow* brought many other nighttime thrillers with continuing
characters: in 1937–38, the prestigious *Big Town*, with Edward
G. Robinson as a battling editor; in 1939–40, *Ellery Queen* and
Mr. District Attorney; in 1941–42, *Bulldog Drummond* and *The
Thin Man*; in 1942–43, *Counterspy* and *Mr. and Mrs. North*; and

---

[1] Little remembered today, and never the prominent motion-picture figure
that Zorro was, novelist Frank L. Packard's Jimmie Dale may, nonetheless, have
influenced the metropolitan branch of the Pimpernel family, Shadow and Spider
especially. Dale, who antedated Zorro by about two years, was a member of an
exclusive New York club who used three aliases to fight crime: the Gray Seal
(an expert safecracker whose "signature" gave him his name); Larry the Bat
(an underworld habitué); and Smarlinghue (a rejected artist). Guided by a
woman of mystery (sometimes called Margo), Dale, in the manner of Jimmy
Valentine, committed seeming crimes to correct wrongs.

About two million copies of books in the Dale series were sold, from *The Adventures of Jimmie Dale* (1917) to *Jimmie Dale and the Missing Hour* (1935).
A serial film, *Jimmie Dale Alias the Gray Seal*, appeared shortly after the first
book, but is almost completely forgotten.

then a legion of detective programs in the 1940s and 1950s, including *Nick Carter, The Saint, The Falcon, Crime Photographer, Michael Shane, Sam Spade, Mr. Chameleon,* and dozens of others.

All these dramas, like most other nonanthology thrillers of evening radio, were episodic serials. That is, while the broad narrative framework continued, the plots of each episode normally came to some resolution at the end of each program. The Shadow's war against evil did not end, but every week he faced and won a different battle of the war, a battle that could be followed from beginning to end with comprehension, whether or not the listener had heard an earlier program in the series. To use technical terminology, destroying the weed of crime was the prevailing *dramatic action* in *The Shadow* dramas, while catching a spider man was the *plot structure* for an individual episode.

Throughout the radio era and into that of television the episodic serial was the dominant form of continued drama in the nighttime hours. Principal exceptions were *I Love a Mystery* and *Mr. Keen,* among the adventure series, and *Easy Aces* and *Beulah,* among the comedies.

Mr. Keen, Tracer of Lost Persons, a Frank Hummert production, was first broadcast on October 12, 1937. Each week night the strains of Noel Coward's "Somewhere I'll Find You" introduced the fifteen-minute adventures of the kindly old investigator and his brawny assistant, Mike Clancy. Although Keen's ostensible purpose was to find missing persons within a reasonable number of episodes, he frequently found himself in the business of solving murders, without dropping his pince-nez or wrinkling his collar; Mike Clancy handled the rough work.

Anything but genteel, on the other hand, was the crack detective team of *I Love a Mystery.* Jack, Doc, and Reggie of Carlton E. Morse's suspense series delighted in a good fight. Their brawling started on the Pacific Coast network of NBC on January 16, 1939, and moved coast to coast the following fall. At first dispensed in fifteen-minute morsels each week night, the cliffhanging took on half-hour weekly proportions from 1940 to 1942 and then returned to quarter-hour form in 1943, when CBS picked up the series and Procter and Gamble replaced Fleischmann's Yeast as sponsor.

Readers of the Doc Savage and Shadow pulp tales were prepared for the hazards endured by the partners of the A-1 Detective Agency in the Temple of the Vampire or on the Island of Skulls as they probed "The Decapitation of Jefferson Monk," "The Thing That Cries in the Night," "The Fear That Crept like a Cat." The sound of a train whistle, the haunting "Valse Triste," and audiences steeled themselves for tests of courage. As a clock sounded the hour at which action had been frozen the night before, the listener dashed headlong into a land of escape, drawn by a bell surely forged alongside that which excited Pavlov's dog.

So adept were the makers of this mystery program that they could effect an extreme of terror through a sound that in itself was not frightening. The soft tinkling of a collar bell warned of the approach of the savage wolf dog Prometheus, who, save for the click of his paws on a bare floor, was totally silent. Gentle organ music, seemingly coming from nowhere, brought to another sequence possibly the most singularly chilling impression in the entire series, for it meant that a crazed murderer was once again announcing a new victim. Anomalous as it may seem, the melody that told of death was the lovely "Cradle Song" of Brahms. Those who remember the sequence know well how effective the juxtaposition of tenderness and horror can be.

Although related to the Doc Savage stories in its emphasis upon bizarre adventures, *I Love a Mystery* was somewhat different in its treatment of women and sex. Jack Packard (played by Michael Raffeto), the leader of the "three comrades," had little more to do with women than did Savage, but it wasn't because he was the perpetual celibate the Man of Bronze was. It was because some years before a girl had let him get her in trouble. Somehow Jack assumed that this disaster of his medical-school days was the inevitable result of becoming entangled with women—who as a group didn't have much sense. The girls kept after him, nevertheless, though they would have had much greater success with Jack's associate, a Texan named Doc Long (played by Barton Yarborough), who pursued women with great energy and a fair degree of success. Reggie York (played by Walter Paterson), the third of the three detectives (whose friendships dated back to days when they had fought the Japanese in war-torn China), offered some balance to the trio through his over-all restraint and good manners.

One of Carleton E. Morse's ventures into a kind of titillation rarely heard in radio, particularly in a thriller, was a two-day, on-the-air striptease. It happened when a pretty assistant of the A-1 team was suspected of having in her possession some small object desired by the other side. A femme fatale forced her to disrobe completely, "dress, shoes, everything," in the presence of an occasional member of the detective agency, Terence Burke, who, rogue that he was, seemed anything but willing to keep his back turned while the poor girl shucked down to the alto-gether. Not until every listener from coast to coast was well aware that the attractive and thoroughly infuriated damsel was excruciatingly naked did she find shelter in an oversize raincoat. This interesting diversion occurred during the five-night-a-week run on CBS, when there was time for pauses and digressions that added color—though at the cost of diluting the mood of sustained excitement so evident when the program had only half an hour each week to develop its story.

I Love a Mystery slipped from the air after a few years. It was revived (not too impressively) by Mutual in 1949, with scripts from the earlier series and a new cast that included Tony Randall as Reggie. Then it was lost forever to its dedicated admirers. An attempt to transfer the property to the motion-picture screen resulted in a weak kickoff film lacking the spark of the regular dramas.

The obvious glow that *I Love a Mystery*'s old listeners exhibit at the mention of the program is a source of puzzlement to those who for one reason or another never heard what followed the tolling of that clock. *I Love a Mystery* is one of a few radio dramas which lasted long enough to gather worshipers without becoming nostalgia for the multitudes. Grateful old fans of the drama (mostly males) may still be trying to figure out how to use Fleischmann's Yeast.

As the number of thrillers rocking the nighttime air increased, the alarm about them did also. Long before the peak of about three dozen sponsored thrillers a week was reached during the 1946–47 season, articles appeared with such titles as "Terrorism on Radio" (*NEA Journal*, May, 1935), "Radio Gore" (*Newsweek*, November 8, 1939), and "Slaughter, Sponsored by . . ." (*New Republic*, October 6, 1941). The articles resembled those on television violence which appeared in the wake of the assassinations of Dr. Martin Luther King and Robert Kennedy in 1968, along with the implication that mystery and suspense dramas imperiled society. A particular worry arose because the children were listening to evening fare which supposedly was for adults, a concern which has a familiar ring to it.

But the children had their own shows for the adults to worry about (enumerated in "Mothers Fighting Radio Bogies," in *Literary Digest*, March 18, 1933, and "Radio Horror for Children Only," in *The American Mercury*, July, 1938). The children's thrillers, with a few exceptions, were clustered in the late-afternoon hours, five to six P.M. being the prime period, with some overflow into the hours just before and after that hour (because of the different time zones, there were some variations in individual localities, particularly those on the edges of the zones).

The juvenile dramas were continued stories, divided into fifteen-minute time segments stretching from Monday through Friday. (For a few years they ran into Saturdays, too.) As suggested earlier, these daytime thrillers were not episodic serials in the mode of nighttime adventures but were open-ended, having suspenseful closings for each daily installment. Only when an adventure that had occupied the regular characters for weeks or months was at last wrapped up might an individual program end on a note of resolution. More often a new mystery was introduced—in what was called the revolving-plot technique—during the same episode in which the old one concluded, a device that drew the juvenile listeners to the next installment. Women's serials also employed this device, but soap-opera writers used many more episodes to sneak in the new plot and rarely ended one on the high note of suspense that marked the serials for children.

Daytime cliffhanging began on April 6, 1931, on the Blue Network of NBC. By coincidence, as it was with the pioneer movie serials, the afternoon radio genre had as its first principal character a female, and an underage one at that. Well, not much underage, for she had made her debut in Harold Grey's comic strip in 1924, and she then looked to be nine or ten years old. When she reached the airwaves seven years later, Little Orphan Annie seemed not a day older. It must have been disconcerting to Jack Armstrong, Tom Mix, Don Winslow, and the gang that a little child had led them, but that's the way it was. As a matter of fact, she didn't have a single ally for more than a year—and when he arrived, he too was a child—Bobby Benson.

There is a possibility of confusion on the part of those who recall the *Little Orphan Annie* series, because it was really two, or perhaps three, different programs. First of all, because of the imperfections in network connections in 1931, it was necessary to maintain two complete casts for the dramas, one in Chicago and one in San Francisco. Thus, until 1933, when the network lines were complete and available, listeners in the East and the Middle West heard the Shirley Bell company enacting the dramas, while those on the Pacific Coast heard a company with Floy Hughes in the title role. The scripts, fortunately, were identical, so the distinction amounted to having the same things happen to different-sounding people on the same days. This variation in aural images in the days before the Chicago cast took over coast to coast may or may not have affected the way the early Orphan Annie program is remembered by those of different areas.

The real dichotomy in Annie's radio existence, however, was chronological, not geographical. She had, if I may give them names, her Ovaltine period and her Puffed Wheat Sparkies period. The former was the longer (1931–40) and the more distinguished. Moreover, it was only in the earlier Ovaltine years that her listeners heard both words and melody of the Orphan Annie song, which began:

> Who's that little chatterbox,
> The one with pretty auburn locks . . . ?

Many of the later Orphan Annie fans had no idea that there were lyrics to go with the tune that was played on the organ at the beginning and end of each episode. No doubt they would have choked had they been confronted by the interjectional:

> "Arf!" says Sandy.

The adventures themselves initially corresponded to the kinds of things that went on in the Annie comic strip—and thus beggar description. Not that they were excessively exotic; they took place mostly in Tomkins Corners or Sunfield and were sprinkled with some American Gothic characters, including Mr. and Mrs. Silo and Annie's little pal Joe Corntassel. But there were those other people, notably Oliver Warbucks, the war profiteer's war profiteer, the capitalist's capitalist, who never had to take the law into his own hands because he had a law of his own. Violators faced dispatch at the hands of the giant Punjab or, worse yet, the silent Asp, Warbuck's favorite executioner. Although Daddy Warbucks was not always around to help Annie, when he was, villains could expect quick liquidation without the fuss of arrest and trial.

When Annie and Joe were on their own, the radio adventures were not so much bizarre as improbable, primarily because the two youngsters did things that real kids could only dream of doing. (For example, explore the logical aspects of, "Follow that cab!" when placed in the mouth of a ten-year-old.) Because the adventures represented wonderful wish fulfillment for a child —as Warbucks represented the child's concept of the all-powerful adult—*Little Orphan Annie* caught on quickly with younger children and remained *their* thriller when others came along. Announcer Pierre André has to be considered an important factor in the show's appeal to that age group; he had the youngsters hanging upon every word, whether it was about the day's adventure or the Wander Company's nourishing Ovaltine. Wander should erect a monument to André (and to Blackett-Sample-Hummert, the advertising agency which packaged the show) atop one of the Swiss mountains whence the idea for Ovaltine supposedly came.

Sometime around the beginning of World War II the makers of Orphan Annie's very own drink decided that they had milked her series for all it was worth and dropped it for *Captain Midnight*. Annie staggered along on the energy she had stored while drinking Ovaltine, but her producers, faced with the choice of canceling the program or selling Annie's soul, chose the sellout. Deserting Joe Corntassel (Mel Torme), Annie became the camp follower of Captain Sparks, an aviator who took the first part of his name from the figure he was imitating, Captain Midnight, and the second part from the sponsor's product, Puffed Wheat Sparkies. Such a hero had no chance of success, and poor Annie had no place at a combat pilot's elbow. Some razzle-dazzle with secret codes and an unusual giveaway of an Orphan Annie Cockpit stirred interest for a while, but the revised series was left behind by shows which could do the sky-spy job better. Even the cereal couldn't make it and went back to being plain old Puffed Wheat.

I am moving ahead of my story, however. Let us return to the days of dinnertime radio when an ensemble could be heard singing:

> Always wears a sunny smile,
> Now wouldn't it be worth your while
> If you could be
> Like little Orphan Annie?

It is hard to imagine grownups worrying about dramas containing sentiments like these. Nevertheless they did, despite the fact that things weren't too frightening of an afternoon in the early 1930s, not even when the impish title character of *Skippy*, who had his own secret code, was embroiled in a kidnap sequence dreamed up by Robert Hardy Andrews, then chief writer for Blackett-Sample-Hummert.

Skippy excepted, Little Orphan Annie's first true companion in afternoon adventure was Bobby Benson, whose escapades appeared initially on the eastern stations of CBS, beginning in the 1932–33 season. No doubt that is the reason one radio historian, reared in the Middle West, called it an imitation of *The Adventures of Tom Mix*, which began about a year later.

Peter Dixon (creator of *Raising Junior*), the principal writer of the *Bobby Benson* series during its formative days, claimed that the characters were inspired by people he knew or had known. Briefly, they were young Bobby, owner of a ranch in the Big Bend country of Texas near the Mexican border; Tex Mason, the ranch foreman; Windy Wales, a cowboy Baron Munchausen; Harka, an Indian ranch hand; and, when Wales was on vacation, Diogenes Dodwaddle (played by Tex Ritter), whose tales topped Windy's. Bobby's ranch was the H-Bar-O, until Hecker's H-O cereals stopped sponsoring the show. At that moment the ranch became the B-Bar-B.

The writing approach of *Bobby Benson* was lighthearted and certainly not very frightening to its principal intended audience, the younger children who liked *Little Orphan Annie*. An attempt was made to insert some educational elements into the dramas without going to the extreme of boring the listeners. Writer Dixon, in contrast to many authors of Westerns, checked his facts: Big Bend details with a former Texas Ranger and zoological ones with a distinguished reptile expert.

As the years went by and things got a little wilder in the afternoon, Bobby (played by Dead End Kid Billy Halop) came to be less a boy Orphan Annie and more a younger Jack Armstrong. As an example, let's compare two closing narrations in the series. The first followed an "overheard" election broadcast in behalf of Tex Mason, at the time candidate for sheriff. After some comedy at the expense of the rival candidate (a smuggler with the unterrifying name Jughead Wilson), Diogenes and friends unpack a wooden crate to reveal the exasperated Wilson, who unknowingly releases his venom to a large listening audience. At the episode's end some of Wilson's confederates appear outside the studio to rescue him:

Listen!

ANNOUNCER: What's this . . . they must have cut the microphone lines in station XOX, . . . and that ended the broadcast for Tex. What do you suppose is happening down there now the Scorpion and his men have shown up to rescue Jughead? We'll have to listen Friday to find out what happens next, . . . and anything is likely to happen.

Now here is the closing of Episode 690, which finds Bobby doing some slick "amateur" piloting in an around-the-world airplane race:

ANNOUNCER: What's this? Stranded fliers starving on an island in the Pacific and an old Spanish galleon under water in a reef enclosed lagoon. But the Lone Star can't stop for sunken treasure ships or anything else, . . . and now the crew of the Lone Star must get along without food until the non-stop race around the world ends. And it must end soon for the goal is less than twenty-four hours ahead. Be sure and listen Friday.

The distance between the disputed election in the Big Bend country and the Spanish galleon spotted in the Pacific was representative of the separation between the subject matter of earlier children's shows and those that came later. Within a few years it was nothing for a hero to range all over the world in search of something or someone. Orphan Annie herself landed on a desert isle and had to take refuge in a stockade that might have been left behind by Jim Hawkins and Dr. Livesey.

The symbolic beginning of such radio globe trotting took place on July 31, 1933, the date of the first broadcast of *Jack Armstrong, the All-American Boy.* Jack did not start to roam immediately, but he wasn't long in shaking the dust of Hudson High's athletic fields (where he was a latter-day Frank Merriwell), and starting his treks through Africa and his sails in the Sulu Sea. Although Jack paid lip service to his alma mater while overseas—the uranium he searched for in 1940 he planned to take back to his high-school science teachers so that they might split the atom—the institution that was the focal point of his earlier escapades became a shadow place remembered only in the song that opened the program:

The Serials

Wave the flag for Hudson High, boys,
Show them how we stand!
Ever shall our team be champ-yuns,
Known throughout the land.

After Jack sprang free from the trials caused him by envious fellow student, Monte Duval, the drama's regular supporting characters were the Fairfield kids, Billy and Betty, and their Uncle Jim. Radio's great uncle-figure, the owner of an aircraft factory, was seldom without some glamorous means of transportation: his hydroplane, the *Silver Albatross*; his yacht, the *Spindrift*; his efficient jungle cruiser; his handy autogyro; or his huge dirigible, the *Golden Secret*. *Jack Armstrong* was the adventure for boys who spent hours with Lionel trains or Gilbert chemistry sets, an aperitif for future engineers and scientists who built crystal sets and loved gadgetry. Once its Merriwell days were over, the show was of less interest to budding sports stars (despite the pitches for Wheaties) and of uncertain appeal to those without mechanical inclinations. Detail such as the following were not of interest to every listener:

JACK: . . . Look! Here comes Uncle Jim!
BILLY: We got those supplies unloaded just in time. Say! Look! I never can quite get used to that autogyro.
BETTY: (Laughing) Neither can I. With that windmill whirring above it, and no wings, it looks like a bad dream.
JACK: But it's a mighty useful machine just the same, Betty. The propeller drives it forward while the rotors keep it up, and it can stand still in one spot and still stay up.

Many listeners, we can conjecture, felt more comfortable with Billy or Betty than with the personable but perfect and always well-informed Jack. Sometimes, as was proper, Jack sat back and let Uncle Jim do the teaching. The following excerpt is from an episode of the mid-1930s. The gang is flying up the Congo River in the *Silver Albatross*:

BETTY: What are those specks . . . look . . . four, five of them, between that island and the river bank?
BILLY: Are they logs . . . or crocodiles . . . or what are they?
UNCLE: Those are native canoes.

186

Listen!

JACK: Gosh, those native boatmen must be pretty skillful!

UNCLE: You bet they are! Those are enormous canoes, and they're built of mahogany. There isn't any wood much stronger than mahogany. But one careless stroke with a paddle, and good-bye!

BETTY: I suppose the canoe would be all smashed to pieces.

UNCLE: Yes. Into pieces too small for matchwood.

BILLY: That current looks worse than Niagara.

JACK: It seems a pity that engineers can't do something about those sixty miles of rapids and make them navigable.

UNCLE: Engineers can do *anything*, Jack. There isn't a thing that the mind of man can imagine that the engineers can't do, if you only give them time and money.

BILLY: Then why don't they do it?

JACK: If engineers would make these rapids navigable, there'd be an open waterway, wouldn't there, right into the very middle of Africa?

UNCLE: Three thousand miles of it, Jack . . . and lots of it more than twenty miles wide. But it wouldn't pay. It would cost too much money. It was cheaper to build that railway line around the falls. You can see it winding through the forest there. And it wasn't any cinch to build that, I don't mind telling you!

I suppose that quite a few former listeners have forgotten how much there was to learn from an episode of Jack Armstrong —not included in the excerpt above was a discourse on railway building in face of harassment by lions.

The introductions to *Jack Armstrong* were unsurpassed in combining exposition with excitement. Here is the one which preceded the autogyro episode quoted earlier:

ANNOUNCER: Jack and Billy are rowing their hearts out—getting the last of the supplies aboard the two-masted schooner *Spindrift*. The *Spindrift* rides her mooring like a grey ghost while the San Francisco fog hides her from the view of hostile eyes on shore. The schooner is all ready to start on her perilous journey to the Sulu Sea to recover a precious cargo of Uranium, sunk off an uncharted reef. Jack and Billy, as they bend to the oars, know that other persons are trying desperately to get possession of a mysterious ring which Uncle Jim has just received—a ring which may contain the secret of

187

the Uranium. Betty, alone on the schooner in the fog, is having the fright of her life—but Jack doesn't know it —yet! Listen!

"Listen!" That daily command needed scarcely be given. The audience had been waiting too long (twenty-four hours or a weekend) to need encouragement. *Jack Armstrong* listeners in the 1930s would stay with a plot as much as half a year without complaining. In September, 1946, however, the plot lines shortened. Did that mean that children of postwar United States were less attentive than their older brothers and sisters? Whatever the answer, they were given nothing to match the prolonged search for the elephants' graveyard in the middle-Roosevelt years. It was Jack's chef-d'oeuvre. The Elephant Man, Booloola, "six feet four inches of bronze savage," remains a monumental figure of fiction to those who remember the months of excitement that followed this invitation from the previously silent protector of the burial ground:

BOOLOOLA: My home . . . down that road . . . long way . . . in jungle. You come.
JACK: When shall we come? Billy and I will be tickled to bits to visit you.
BILLY: He didn't ask me, did he?
JACK: You're in on it, Billy, or I'm out!
BOOLOOLA: You come tonight . . . in dark . . . no lantern my servant him meeting you . . . you not afraid . . . you follow servant. . . . Goo'bye!
JACK: Here, half a minute, come back! I want to talk to you!
K'MOTO: Uh-uh-uh-uh-uh, bwana! Let-um to'way! That Booloola . . . him Elephant Man. Him greatest magician in Africa. Make too much magic! Uh! Uh! Trouble tonight. Big trouble in jungle! (fade)
ANNOUNCER: What will Jack do? Do you think he'll accept that mysterious invitation to go into the jungle, after dark, without a lantern, to visit the Elephant Man, Booloola? What's going to happen? Listen in tomorrow, to an exciting and weird episode in the greatest adventure of all time—with Jack Armstrong, the All-American Boy.

After his creator, Robert Hardy Andrews, departed, *Jack Armstrong* was written by several writers, including Talbot

Mundy, Colonel Paschal Strong, and Jim Jewell (*The Lone Ranger's* first director). This multitude suggests that an annoying characteristic of many of its later scripts stemmed from a script supervisor at the advertising agency (Knox-Reeves, which took over from Blackett-Sample-Hummert). Apparently convinced that young listeners could not keep the day's cast in mind for more than thirty seconds, the guiding genius (or geniuses) insisted that each speaker identify the character who had just spoken or was being addressed. When the lines were short, the air was cluttered with first names, as in this reconstruction:

BILLY: Gosh, Jack, it's dark in this corridor!
JACK: Stay close behind me, Billy. We don't want to get separated.
BETTY: It's hard to keep from slipping on the wet floor, Jack.
JACK: Take hold of Uncle Jim's arm, Betty. He'll keep you from falling.
UNCLE: Right, Jack . . . if I don't slip myself. Here you go, Betty.
BETTY: Thanks, Uncle Jim.
UNCLE: Can you see an opening, Billy?
BILLY: No, Uncle Jim. Can you, Jack?
JACK: Not yet, Billy . . . .

In twelve minutes of dialogue the name count of *Jack Armstrong* could reach fantastic proportions.

Late in the 1940s a transformation almost as severe as that which had devastated *Little Orphan Annie* a few years earlier overcame the All-American Boy. Uncle Jim stepped aside in favor of a younger character named Vic Hardy. A reincarnated Craig Kennedy, Hardy was head of the Scientific Bureau of Investigation. (Do its initials sound like those of another agency?) Jack, Billy, and Betty were enrolled in the service of the bureau, and Jack spent his last years on the air thwarting the theft of superatomic knickknacks. Something had happened to the nice little science lessons that had once graced the program. In their place the youngsters heard:

BILLY: You mean, we've got to work with those two murderers, and pretend they're our friends, and . . .
JACK: That's just what I mean, Billy. It'll be a game of wits between us. We're after the energizer which Rowers has, and he's after that magnetic concentrator which we have.

189

VIC: Jack is right, Billy. It's going to be a dangerous game. But whoever wins it will have the complete cosmo-tomic energizer.

JACK: And if they win, they can't dispose of it in this country. They'd have to do it abroad.

VIC: And some foreign country having all the electrical energy they want for nothing, we'll be reduced to a pauper country.

BILLY: Golly! We *are* playing for big stakes!

Energizer by energizer, the All-American Boy was disappearing along with the era that could produce a hero of that designation.

When the last broadcast was presented in 1951, Charles Flynn was playing Jack. While no actor carried the role throughout the run of the show, Flynn played it longer than anyone else. He had matured from teenage to the threshold of his thirties in the part. It was fitting that he was present at the end. In 1933, Jack was played by Jim Ameche, the younger brother of Don Ameche (who had become radio's romantic idol in shows like *The First Nighter* and the soap opera *Betty and Bob*).

The identity of Jack's virile-sounding portrayer was top secret for a while; CBS feared that the younger Ameche's physique, though perfectly normal, would not appear to match that of a boy who could do the things Jack Armstrong could. In time *Radio Stars* magazine blabbed the news anyway.

St. John Terrell, later proprietor of the Lambertville, New Jersey, Music Circus, was another early Jack Armstrong. Later on, Stanley Harris and Rye Billsbury played the part for brief stretches. No matter who was in the title role, however, James Goss continued as Uncle Jim. If his part had not been removed from the show, doubtless he would have been the only actor to perform in it for the full eighteen years. As it was, he came close, maintaining his avuncular attitude whether Betty was played by Shaindel Kalish or Sarajane Wells, whether Billy was played by John Gannon or Dick York. Not much ruffled good old Uncle Jim.

12345678910111213141516171819202122232⁴

BOX TOPS AND DIMES

Straight shooters always win!

TOM MIX

Without question *Jack Armstrong, the All-American Boy* broadened the horizons of dinner-hour adventures, opening the world to vicarious exploration. Some of the stimulus for this departure from mainland America, however, came from a serial that lay somewhere between the afternoon and the evening in both hour of presentation and audience. On November 7, 1932, another comic-strip transplant, Buck Rogers, blasted off to his adventures in the twenty-fifth century. His series on CBS carried him not only to the ends of the earth but to the solar system of the future.

With a broadcast hour of 7:15 P.M., Monday through Friday, in the East, it was natural that the audience for *Buck Rogers in the Twenty-fifth Century* was a mingling of youngsters and grownups. Eventually the former prevailed, and the series moved closer to the children's hour, but not before parents got an earful of what their offspring were listening to. The agitated fantasy of *Buck Rogers* must have been at the heart of many of those articles expressing worry about radio's effect on young minds. Certainly it was not the kind of thing that could substitute for a lullaby. What Dick Calkins did not imagine for his newspaper strip, writer Jack Johnstone did for the air shows. While planets waged war against each other with death rays, gamma bombs, incendiary missiles, and massed flights of space ships, Buck, his lovely copilot Wilma Deering, and the brilliant Dr. Huer spent week after week trying to save the universe from total distruction. It was an anything but reassuring future to contemplate as bedtime approached.

When the scheming of the evil Killer Kane did not provide mothers with apprehension, the Rogers-Deering relationship did. Adele Ronson, the actress who played Wilma to Curtis Arnall's Buck, might complain in a fan magazine that Buck did not display enough romantic interest in his pretty pal, and the program's writer might strain to avoid suggesting anything improper in the relationship of the astronautical twosome he inherited from the comic strip, *but mothers knew better*. What did the pair do on those long flights or when they were marooned that time in the Arctic? Any couple who could use molecular contractors to shrink to figurine size would have no trouble putting one over on the pseudo chaperon, Dr. Huer—who generally was preoccupied anyway. (On the other hand, what secret knowledge was behind that incessant "heh-heh" of his?) There were such pleasantly unimportant things to worry about in those days, when nuclear weapons, jumping belts, television helmets, and such were too fantastic to consider. Think what anxiety might have resulted if *Flash Gordon* had caught on as a radio series! Buck's futuristic doings always were a bit tame romantically beside those of Flash in this century, whatever the medium.

As the fantasy of Buck Rogers was edging toward the late-afternoon time block, the first adult hero appeared in that territory. Another vocalized theme, to the melody of "When the Bloom Is on the Sage," hailed the favorite breakfast of Tom Mix and his Ralston Straight Shooters. "When it's Ralston time for breakfast," the theme began. By the end of the lyric an opening commercial had been extracted from the available program time with minimal pain.[1]

Tom Mix was the kind of hero who, if an agency had created him, would have been laughed at as impossible. He had done, or claimed he had done, the things that other cowboy heroes merely pretended to do. At one time his sponsor distributed a compact Tom Mix handbook which detailed the highlights of an incredible career: combat service in the Spanish-American War, the Philippine insurrection, and the Boxer Rebellion; horse wrangling (and soldiering) in the Boer War; some genuine cowpunching; rodeo stardom; law enforcing as a Texas Ranger, Kansas sheriff, and deputy United States marshal; a few secret-service duties not well defined; ranch owning; guerrilla duty with Madero's "army" in Mexico; and (after an earlier nonacting brush with motion pictures) stardom in films. A diagram in the handbook illustrated the extraordinary number of wounds Mix received along the way.[2]

[1] The lyric varied through the years, but in the pre-Instant-and-Shredded Ralston days it ran as follows:

First verse: When it's Ralston time for breakfast
Then it surely is a treat
To have some rich, full flavored Ralston
Made of golden western wheat.

Chorus: Wrangler says it is DE-E-E-E-LICIOUS
And you'll find before you're through
With a lot of cream—boy it sure tastes keen
It's the tops for breakfast too.

Second verse: Ask your mother in the morning
To serve you up a steaming plate
It's a grand, hot, whole wheat cereal
And the cowboys think it's great.

Chorus: Once you try it, you'll stay by it
Tom Mix says it's swell to eat
Jane and Jimmy, too, say it's best for you
Ralston cereal can't be beat.

[2] The extraordinary events of Mix's life mentioned in the handbook also ap-

Tom's moviemaking—sometimes as director and author as well as performer—began in 1911, when Broncho Billy Anderson was *the* movie cowboy, spanned the peak years of William S. Hart, and reached its ascendancy in the 1920s. In 1925 Mix's salary was reportedly seventeen thousand dollars a week, and the flamboyant movies he had made with his horse, Tony, had changed the pattern of Westerns from semirealism to spectacle.

When the radio program commenced on September 25, 1933, Mix was more interested in work in circuses or wild West shows than he was in the few talking pictures he made before he called a halt with the Mascot serial *The Miracle Rider* in 1935. Apparently he had no inclination to tie himself down to a weekday radio show and agreed to let a radio actor represent him. It was just as well, because Mix's voice and diction, though suitable for talking Westerns, were not refined to the degree necessary for effective radio work. The youthful listeners for the most part weren't aware of the substitution. Only if they listened to the last seconds of the closing credits did they hear: "Tom Mix was impersonated." It could take years for them to discover that the statement was not "Tom Mix was in person," and even longer to decipher the meaning of "impersonated." Although considerations of mortality played no part in the arrangement, the use of the substitute facilitated the continuation of the series after Mix's death in a car accident in 1940.

Despite the degree of excitement the Tom Mix adventures generated, mothers never seemed to worry too much about letting their children listen to them. There were several possible reasons for parental toleration of the program, one being the care Ralston took to insert some promotional advertising in *Parents' Magazine* showing the real Tom with the Jimmy and Jane characters of the radio show. That Tom Mix was an actual person surely made his path a little easier with mothers, as did the warm manner in which the Old Wrangler introduced the tales. A mother might listen to the relaxed storyteller's "Howdy, Straight

peared in his *Who's Who* entries and in his *New York Times* obituary. There are those who challenge the military and lawkeeping achievements—but this loyal Straight Shooter of yesterday has no heart to do so.

Shooters," follow his tale spinning long enough to be reassured that all was cozy, then slip back to her dinner preparations moments before all sorts of mayhem broke loose. Even then, the action seemed in character with the Texas countryside around Dobie. "After all, things like that happen in the West," was a deceptively easy rationalization with *Tom Mix and His Ralston Straight Shooters.*

Occasional songs, and bits of humor (provided mostly by Wash, a cook in the Stepin Fetchit mold), served further to disarm an eavesdropping mother. The epigram helped too: "Lawbreakers always lose. Straight shooters always win. It pays to shoot straight!" Buck Rogers never said anything like that. Jack Armstrong and Orphan Annie were too young to make such an utterance believable. But Tom Mix could speak from experience. His impersonators (Artells Dickson, Jack Holden, Russell Thorson, and Curley Bradley) were faced with a line as intimidating as, "It is a far, far better thing I do . . . ." As a matter of fact, the pronouncement seems to have dropped by the wayside before Bradley came to the part in 1943, after portraying Tom's singing lieutenant, Pecos, for several years.

All other attributes of *Tom Mix* aside, I suspect that it received charitable treatment from mothers because it got kids to eat cooked cereal. Ralston, while agreeable to the palate, was not a dish youngsters would tear into without a little prodding. Orphan Annie's Ovaltine and Buck Rogers' Cocomalt made milk attractive and even more nourishing. Ralston had to do it on its own. It lacked even the camouflage of the piles of fruit under which Jack Armstrong buried his Wheaties; the hot Ralston would have stewed them.

Loyalty to Tom Mix no doubt caused an increase in Ralston sales, but the real inducements to eating were the premiums. No thriller received greater mileage from this merchandising scheme than did the Mix dramas—though giveaways were part of almost every series. Most universally remembered, perhaps, were the Orphan Annie mugs, plain or shake-up. The shake-ups were handy vessels in which to mix Ovaltine and milk (one or two teaspoons of sugar optional). As the shaking proceeded, images of the urchin and her dog Sandy danced before the eyes of the youthful milk bartender, who could drink the mixture from the mug itself once the domed top was removed. First- and second-graders perfected their reading skills by scanning again and again the words in balloons coming from Annie's mouth. One year's mug read:

> Leapin' Lizards! For a swell summer drink there's nothing like a cold Ovaltine shake-up mug, eh, Sandy?

The sponsor's message never ended. It stared at the drinker between every gulp.

Cereal manufacturers could not come up with any such self-renewing encouragement to consume more of the product—a Tom Mix double boiler would have been absurd—so they tended to integrate the premium and the program. Jack Armstrong would make a fetish of a device for measuring and recording how far he had trekked, and, sure enough, his fans would be offered a pedometer just like Jack's. (The gadgets worked so noisily that many a schoolboy was asked to go back to guessing how far he had walked.)

Premiums that served the hero in his adventures were much more interesting to potential customers than were simple souvenirs, such as a photograph of Tom Mix. What could a junior cowboy do with a picture? Once an actual gold nugget was offered. It sounded wonderful, but after the first day's novelty it was just a piece of rock, worth very little at the local assay office. At least it was a real rock, however; Blue Coal, *The Shadow's* sponsor, once distributed rings, each one set with a small lump of imitation anthracite.

Success in a giveaway campaign for juveniles (and for grown-ups too, as will be seen later) lay in first cultivating a patch of pure envy in the hearts of young Straight Shooters. While for housewives' dramas it sufficed to have the characters become gaga over the symmetry of a purple-and-white cameo, youngsters had to "see" the gadget in action. Beauty alone was not enough for males who one day would look under the hoods of autos in dealers' showrooms while their wives examined upholstery swatches. Thus Tom Mix would find himself tied up and seemingly helpless as the villain imperiled the community. But wait! What about the handy foldaway magnifying glass Tom always carried with him? If the rays of the sun could be directed through the lens to Tom's bonds . . . .

Shortly after the ingenious escape Mix listeners were asked whether *they* would like a foldaway magnifying glass exactly like the one which had saved Tom. (Would they? Absolutely! A boy never knew when he might be bound and gagged in sunlight.) To get one of the dandy articles was easy. "Just tear off the boxtops of two packages of Regular Ralston or Instant Ralston," the announcer advised. "Put these boxtops (or facsimiles) in an envelope with a slip of paper containing your name and address, and send to Tom Mix, Checkerboard Square, St. Louis, Missouri. Please allow two weeks for delivery." (The admonition regarding patience was essential; mailboxes were examined by eager boxtop senders the next day.)

While the dreadful waiting went on, the as-yet-unrequited giftseekers satisfied the piper. The contents of two boxes of Ralston (or facsimile) had to be consumed. Wise premium seekers stayed ahead, in anticipation of the next premium, their neat little stacks of cereal boxtops rising on kitchen shelves. Sometimes, however, the transaction was on a one-time-only basis. Junior might eat enough of Brand X to meet the requirements of a single offer, but with every crunch he could be heard to mutter, "Never again!"

Afternoon serial selection often was a matter of compatibility of dramatic vehicle, sponsor's product, and juvenile listener. Favorite-show status demanded exact triangulation, for faithfulness to hero number one was impossible without faithfulness to his product. (In the instance of *Tom Mix* the rock-bottom obligation—three bowls of Ralston a week—was set forth and sworn to under the Straight Shooter Pledge of Allegiance.) If a porridge caught in the throat, only secondary interest in that product's entertainment was ethical.

But what happened when a show switched sponsors? Youngsters who liked Ovaltine but couldn't stand Sparkies agonized when Orphan Annie changed hands. Did even a real cardboard cockpit offset victual self-torture—not to mention the desertion of Ralston or Wheaties. In such situations an only child was the greatest sufferer. In larger families a natural variety in preferences eased the strain. But then there was the battle of which show to tune at 5:30. The crises seemed never to end.

Those wise premium seekers mentioned earlier could put two of their accumulated boxtops in the mail the first night and become the first to receive the little packages addressed to J. Doe. (The first name seldom appeared, a rebuff to the ego readily mollified by what was waiting inside the packet.) To those forced to wait till the second or third day to send their orders, the early recipients of premiums appeared somewhat arrogant in their brandishing of the prizes. Moreover, the same individuals seemed always to win the race. A star-crossed child's only way of taking a lead was to send for the merchandise of a second-line serial with an offbeat sponsor. The race for membership in the Davey Adams' Shipmates Club (price: two wrappers of Lava Soap) was not as swift as that for the wares dangled by *Tom Mix, Jack Armstrong*, or the Ovaltine shows. At the same time, the reward was correspondingly slimmer.

Although premiums lent themselves to endless variation, the basic categories were few. Rings, of course, were the most common giveaways, yet rarely were they just rings. Usually they were combined with an item from a basic grouping. So rings can be considered as means of conveyance or mounting and the principal categories looked at separately.

Warning devices always were popular. Jack Armstrong sent out 6,600,000 torpedo flashlights in one of the most successful merchandising promotions. Tom Mix had flashlights, too, as well as diverse whistles and sirens. High among the torches (all quite worthwhile) was one with a tricolor mounting which allowed the carrier to flash a message in red, green, or natural light. When battery power was impossible, luminescence was the next best thing. In fact, it may have been better, because the number of glowing gadgets was extraordinary. Tom's main contribution to green gleaming was a pair of safety spurs that could be seen on dark nights. Sky King had a Signascope. The Lone Ranger, in one of his boxtop ventures, gave away a plastic belt that would protect the wearer from roadside accidents. Unfortunately, it could not be counted upon to hold up knickers.

Closely related to the warning equipment were the optical devices. In addition to the magnifying glass already mentioned, Ralston sent out a telescope and at least one periscope not attached to a ring. The telescope offer was a direct confrontation with one on *Jack Armstrong*, the Armstrong instrument long and impressive, the Mix device compact and sturdy. As always, the Ralston checkerboard symbol was on the outside, overlaid with the TM-Bar brand, and edged by the inscription "TOM MIX RALSTON STRAIGHT SHOOTERS."

One of the easier kinds of paraphernalia to insert in the plot of a thriller was that used for sending messages. Naturally, some of the articles thus far mentioned could double as visual signaling equipment. But because so many of the messages heroes had to send required secrecy, or could not be transmitted by visual methods, other equipment was enlisted. The ring with a secret compartment was a sure choice. Supposedly nobody would ever think of looking inside the small, gold-hued band, which could be adjusted to the wearer's finger size and could be relied upon to turn the finger green wherever it rested. Clickers—tinny-looking pieces of metal that went "click-click" when pressed—were tried once or twice. Presumably they were too shabby in appearance to be taken away from imprisoned champions of justice, who promptly used them to contact the Count of Monte Cristo in the next cell.

The Jack Armstrong Secret Whistle Ring was a prominent means of aural communication ("Four short whistles = We're being watched!"). More earnestly coveted, though, were two sound transmitters from Tom Mix. One was a cardboard telegraph, which when equipped with batteries did emit a message. Senders weak on Morse code found a handy rundown on the instrument itself. The second Mix communication success was an elegant variation of the tin-can phone line. Neat, checkerboard-decorated microphone-earpieces could send the human voice the length of a backyard if the connecting wire was stretched tight.

The Jack Armstrong Hike-O-Meter, mentioned earlier, proved to be an aid to 1,200,000 outdoorsmen. Other items in this line were the Tom Mix compasses and, for those who wished to know what camping clothes to take, the Lone Ranger Weather Predicter. When its owner did not need it for burning his bonds, the Tom Mix magnifier could ignite twigs—easily cut with the Tom Mix knife.

At the time Radio Orphan Annie (as she was called then) was trapped by those cannibals, she hastily made up some Orphan Annie faces, which she put in the firing openings of the stockade to fool her attackers. Through the foresight of Blackett-Sample-Hummert thousands of these masks subsequently arrived in mailboxes everywhere in the nation. Less grotesque were the Lone Ranger masks, natural premiums. Still, the ultimate facial camouflage emerged, once again, from the Ralston warehouse. The Tom Mix Movie Make-up Kit was one of the more elaborate and amusing premiums ever sent away for. Its possessor could affect a set of disguises ranging from pirate to banker by utilizing the cardboard spectacles, the eye patch, the false whiskers, and the small containers of face-coloring base. Admittedly, the colors were suitable only for portraying ghosts or Indians on the warpath, but the kits' users had little interest in subtlety.

It might be assumed that weaponry would be high on the list of offerings. Not so. About the only remembered piece of artillery was a black wooden .45 that even Straight Shooters found hard to put into their holsters in place of their Gene Autry pistols. Although the always nonlethal Lone Ranger did have a pistol premium, it was really a flashlight. We can wonder whether the munitions count might have been higher had the era of the thrillers fallen in the 1960s or 1970s.

The almost universal premium was admission to the club. It is amusing that men who pay for keys to Playboy havens once sent away inner seals of Ovaltine or tops of Ralston or Wheaties boxes to gain membership in Orphan Annie's Safety Guard or Captain Midnight's Secret Squadron. In return for their investment (which sometimes included a dime) youthful applicants received tin stars for cowboy vests, fancy wings for tunics, and brass badges for caps. Normally included in the packet was certification of membership, perhaps a wallet card or an official document suitable for framing.

The certificate, in addition to being a statement of newfound rights and privileges, normally contained a bit of moral exhortation. Members of the Supermen of America pledged to "do everything possible to increase his or her STRENGTH and COURAGE, to aid the cause of JUSTICE, to keep absolutely SECRET the SUPERMAN code . . . ." Perhaps more mercenary in origin was the last phase of the pledge: "to follow the announcements of the SUPERMEN OF AMERICA, in each month's issue of ACTION COMICS." Setting his seal and signature to all of this was Clark Kent himself.

Boys who enlisted in Don Winslow's Squadron of Peace received along with a bronze ensign's badge a copy of the creed Winslow himself was bound to uphold. Composed before World War II neared American shores, it is quaintly touching today:

> I consecrate my life to Peace and to the protection of all my Countrymen wherever they may be. My battle against Scorpia represents the battle between Good and Evil. Never will I enter into any jingoistic proposition, but will devote my entire life to protecting my Country. The whole purpose of my life is that of promoting Peace—not War. I will work in the interests of Peace and will promote the fulfillment of all things that are clean, wholesome and upright. Join me not alone in observing this creed, but likewise be patriotic. Love your country, its flag and all the things for which it stands. Follow the advice of your parents and superiors and help someone every day.

Patriotic messages were not objects of ridicule in those days, but they may or may not have been read in the haste to try on badges or wings. One part of the package was sure to be examined intently, however—the decoder. This instrument was essential to full appreciation of the daily adventures. When memberships were being proffered, there was a sudden emphasis upon secret messages within or at the end of each daily episode. To be ignorant of their meaning was maddening.

201

The codes used were never very complicated. Frequently they were simply numerical equivalents for letters: A = 7, B = 9, and so on. Captain Midnight, probably the biggest cryptographer in radio, multiplied the secrecy through an inner-dial badge which allowed the decoder to be set for any of twenty-six different codes, one for each letter in the alphabet. The captain was also bright enough not to reveal the secret message word for word on the next day's program. Orphan Annie did. With a little diligence the nonmember of Annie's new Secret Guard could keep record of the dispatches and their translations and eventually construct his own code device—thus saving the trouble of eating two packages of Sparkies while at the same time acquiring a feeling of superiority in matters of espionage.[3]

Although Tom Mix at one time supplied Straight Shooters with a codebook, his principal medium of private communication with his agents was the Tom Mix comic book. By finding clues hidden in drawings or by connecting dotted lines, his counter-intelligence men could learn keys to mysteries which noninsiders had to wait for the air adventures to disclose. Actually, except during the comic book period, Tom was involved in more predicaments than mysteries: what to do to save the TM-Bar from foreclosure; where to find water for the cattle; how to bring himself to destroy the badly injured Tony. While the far-flung *Jack Armstrong* adventures were built upon prolonged search for things lost or buried, the Tom Mix episodes drew closer to the soap-opera pattern. As it would be in *Bonanza* many years later, much of the action in this Western drama was placed in or around the ranch house. The problems were often those of the emotions instead of those of the chase. Even caricatures such as Wash or the greedy Amos Q. Snood[4] displayed feelings beyond the good-guy, bad-guy, funny-guy conventions of many other shows.

[3] Chance discovery of a misplaced code book was always a possibility, of course. One of Annie's booklets advised accidental finders that the book was for society members only (and their parents). "Anyone who finds [the book] should return it at once, *without reading,* to the owner whose name is on the back cover," the warning concluded.

[4] Some readers will recall Snood's "Pink Pills for Pale People."

Appropriately, the Tom Mix programs had what is called a solid supporting cast. The Old Wrangler was in real life the musically trained Percy Hemus, whose rich voice set the tone for the series. Sheriff Mike Shaw, who supplied much of the old West flavor when the Wrangler was written out, was played by Leo Curley—and also by the Great Gildersleeve, Harold Peary, who doubled at one time or another as Li Loo, Bertie, Foghorn, and other characters. Vance McCune handled the Wash part, with relief by Forrest Lewis, an actor whose gift for mimicry put him into many smaller roles. (Lewis' Peter Lorre voice gave Warner Brothers fits when he used it on *I Love a Mystery*.) The roles of Clamshell Pete and Amos Q. Snood were played by Sidney Ellstrom. Chris Acropolous, another Mix dabbling in dialect humor, was portrayed by Carl Kroenke. In this assemblage of accents and trick voices two were pure and unaffected: those of Jane Webb as Tom's ward, Jane, and George Goebel as Jimmy (the first *e* subsequently disappeared from the boy actor's last name).

By the 1934–35 season *Little Orphan Annie, Bobby Benson, Buck Rogers, Jack Armstrong,* and *Tom Mix* had laid claim to all five quarter-hour periods between 5:15 and 6:30 P.M., eastern standard time. From that season on, the success of a new thriller was anything but assured. Program planners had the choice of attempting to build an audience on the fringes of the prime periods or moving into direct competition with an established show. Thus a number of adventure serials came and went in a single season, sometimes without being noticed by most of the intended audience.

Og, Son of Fire and *Robinson Crusoe, Jr.,* were casualties of the 1934–35 season, though Peter Dixon's Crusoe reworking continued as a transcribed series on independent stations. The next half decade or so brought such one-year wonders or syndicated shows as *Omar the Mystic, Flash Gordon, Inspector White of Scotland Yard, Junior G-Men, Davey Adams, King Arthur, Jr., Mandrake the Magician, The Air Adventures of Jimmie Allen, Flying Patrol, Smilin' Jack,* and *Secret City.*

An on-again off-again series was *Wilderness Road*, a CBS drama which attempted to do all the good things a child's adventure should, and sometimes succeeded. It described the exciting incidents in the lives of pioneer youngsters on the trail with Daniel Boone. With an ear to child psychologists, writers Richard Stevenson and Charles Tazewell eschewed extremes of suspense in favor of appeals to curiosity. When a mountain lion suddenly attacked the principals one day, the episode did not end with the animal springing toward its victims as might have been expected. Instead, the lion was stopped by a rifle shot from a party unknown. Youngsters were left to wonder not "Will the lion kill someone?" but "Who fired the shot?" The latter question created less anxiety (and, said skeptics, less interest) in *Wilderness Road*. While writers of daily thrillers made no effort to contrive dire peril for the end of every episode, the deliberate avoidance of natural cliffhanging situations could have placed the CBS experiment at a competitive disadvantage. Nonetheless, it drew praise from both pressure groups and youngsters, no mean achievement since youngsters can smell approved entertainment a mile away. What the series did not draw was a regular sponsor. Writer Tazewell went on to create some of the thrills of *Tom Mix* in the 1940s.

Three thrillers which did break into the networks' charmed circle during the middle 1930s were borrowed from the comic pages. *Dick Tracy* started on Mutual in 1935–36, while *Don Winslow of the Navy* and *Terry and the Pirates* became NBC offerings beginning in 1937–38. The radio adventures of these pen-and-ink heroes, all of whom also were gracing movie serials at about the same time, hewed to predictable patterns. Tracy did his familiar detective work, Don Winslow persevered in his battle against Scorpia, and Terry faced the dangers of the Orient. Though perfectly capable of going it alone, Dick and Don were furnished with pals and such. Dick had Irish cop Pat Patton and his adopted Junior. Don had fellow officer Red Pennington and girl friend Mercedes Colby. Terry Lee, who needed lots of help, worked first with Pat Ryan, then with Flip Corkin and Hotshot Charlie. In addition he sported an unusual number of attractive young ladies and one of radio's noisier openings. Over a sound pattern that sounded like Shanghai at high noon, an announcer bellowed, "Terr-eee and the P-i-i-rates!" Then in chummy if tentative tone, he did a quick review of the situation:

ANNOUNCER: I wish I could give you a clearer picture of what's been happening to Terry and his friends in Calcutta, India, but things are confused by intrigue—undercover activities, spy trails that criss-cross, and many unseen dangers. But this much we do know: somewhere in Calcutta is a master spy, a Nazi enemy agent. That German operator is the evil genius who is helping the Japs in nearby Burma to improve their deadly robot bombs. That is the enemy Terry, Pat, and Flip Corkin want to catch by working with the British agents in Calcutta. But all has not gone well—nor will it. So . . . stand by!

SOUND: Gong

The action-loaded *Terry and the Pirates* scripts were enacted in broad, almost superficial, manner by performers who sometimes appeared to have seen their scripts for the first time just before the broadcasts. Cast assignments were not necessarily ideal either. Ted de Corsia, a radio heavy of the George Raft style, had to struggle to produce the élan of a Flip Corkin.

The 1940s brought three high flyers to network radio. *Captain Midnight* (Mutual, 1940–41) and *Hop Harrigan* (ABC, 1942–43) blazed through the skies in high-powered aircraft. *Superman* (Mutual, 1940–41) did it on his own, bringing in his jet stream the ultimate extension of the Green Hornet: Batman.

After eight years with *Buck Rogers*, plus a season with *Smilin' Jack*, writer Jack Johnstone had no trouble adapting the comic-book titan to broadcast form. The things Superman confronted were no more bizarre than those Buck and Wilma had faced almost a decade earlier. They too could fly alfresco, albeit with power belts. The framework of the stories in *Action Comics* served well for the radio dramas. Johnstone could have his hero perform any exploit he wished without having to worry about stunt men or special effects. He needed only a few lines of dialogue to suggest the action.

205

The change from Kent to Superman was standardized to the point of ritual:

> This looks like a job for (*voice drop*) Superman!
> Now, off with these clothes!
> Up, up, and awa-a-a-ay!
> (*swoosh*)

Called upon to deliver these staples of Kentian discourse was Clayton ("Bud") Collyer, who didn't let the memory of them affect his technique years later as master of ceremonies of television's *To Tell the Truth*. When a new cartoon version of *Superman* was prepared for TV in the mid-1960s, Collyer readily joined the radio series' narrator, Jackson Beck, and his old Lois Lane, Joan Alexander, in dubbing the voices of the animated characters.[5]

In 1945 Batman and Robin suddenly appeared in one of Superman's adventures. Although they didn't know who Kent really was, he was wise to their secret identities right away because his X-ray vision let him penetrate their disguises. This joint adventure went very well—as thousands of Batman fans could have told Superman's producers it would. Soon the Dynamic Duo were standing guest stars, with Batman almost running the show at times. The Caped Crusader, nevertheless, did not achieve broadcasting independence until his extraordinary debut on television in 1966. By that time Jack Johnstone had concluded his labors as writer-director of radio's last surviving serial drama, the cliché-ridden episodic mystery *Yours Truly, Johnny Dollar*.

Although also a comic-book character—in *All-American Comics* of the Superman-Batman chain—Hop Harrigan was a non-fantastic hero. The adventures of Hop (Chester Stratton) and his mechanic, Tank Tinker, were related to their wartime flying duties, America-based, and to normal aviation pursuits thereafter. Tank's "Jumping Jennies!" did not catch on in the manner of "Leapin Lizards!" but the Harrigan opening is remembered:

[5] A simulation of the *Superman* radio broadcasts, using the old cast and a sound-effects man, was warmly received by viewers of NBC-TV's *Johnny Carson Show* in 1969. The younger audience particularly was surprised to see what a radio production looked like in studio.

HOP: CX-4 to control tower. CX-4 to control tower.
TOWER: Go ahead, CX-4.
HOP: This is Hop Harrigan—coming in!
SOUND: *Roaring engine*

Hop Harrigan was written by former *Let's Pretender* Albert Aley, and also by one or both members of the writing team of Robert Burtt and Wilfred Moore, the developers of *Captain Midnight*. While not a transfer from comic strip or book as were the other successful thrillers of the "middle" period, *Captain Midnight*, originally a WGN, Chicago, feature, was somewhat similar to several of its network predecessors, notably *Don Winslow*. As Winslow's Squadron of Peace had skirmished regularly with a foreign menace, the Scorpion, and his organization, Midnight's Secret Squadron jousted with the forces of the Barracuda and one Ivan Shark. Both heroes had to cope with treacherous female offsprings of their adversaries—though Tasmia sounded much prettier, and far less maniacal, than Fury Shark. And both heroes had less than adequate *aides-de-combat*. Lieutenant Commander Winslow's Red Pennington and Mercedes Colby were adult at least; Captain Midnight was stuck with an upgraded Billy and Betty—Chuck Ramsey (SS-2) and Joyce ("Loopin' Loops") Ryan (SS-3). SS-1 also had to undergo the miseries attendant upon having as a mechanic and fourth-in-command the eccentric Ichabod Mudd—Ikky to his friends. If the captain hadn't had his reliable Code-o-graph, he might never have made it.

Perhaps in assigning his assistants the military was trying to tell the great aviator something. Although head of the Secret Squadron, working under Major Steele, Captain Midnight should have reflected upon his career possibilities in the service. He had gained his nickname from some midnight heroism during World War I—when he was already Captain Albright. More than twenty years later, still a captain, he was again chasing the same villain (Ivan Shark) he had captured in France in lilac time.

Promotion, of course, would have scuttled the title, if not the show. So into the television version of his adventures flew the oldest captain in time of grade in American military history. On television, as if to sprinkle salt in the wound, he was impersonated by Richard Webb, who in real life outranked him, being a lieutenant colonel in the United States Army Reserve. (The radio Captain Midnight was Ed Prentiss, a frequent performer in soap opera.)

Although unmistakably within the "Aha! Now I have you in my power!" school of adventures, *Captain Midnight* attracted a nice following in the early 1940s, despite its always formidable competition: *Tom Mix* or *Jack Armstrong*. At the war's end the program tailed off badly, as did the other war-oriented audience leader, *Terry and the Pirates*. By the 1946–47 season both were trailing a new serial called *Tennessee Jed*.

But the new quarter-hour thrillers of the immediate postwar period were few. *Cimarron Tavern* and *Sparrow and the Hawk*, both from CBS, scarcely got off the ground. A transformation was occurring in late-afternoon radio. The first evidence of it came in 1947, when *Jack Armstrong* assumed a half-hour episodic format and began alternating broadcast days with a new half-hour serial, *Sky King*—derisively called "Tom Mix with airplanes." (The description was apt, though Schuyler King, the flying ranch owner, was a purely fictional character.) Armstrong and King occupied ABC's 5:30 to 6:00 slot, Monday through Friday, while *Tom Mix, Captain Midnight, Superman*, and other thrillers continued in their quarter-hour formats.

In the 1948–49 season the movement to half-hour self-contained episodes was accelerated. *Challenge of the Yukon* and *The Green Hornet* alternated at 5:00 to 5:30 on ABC, and *Sky King* and *Jack Armstrong* continued their pairing at 5:30. Only Mutual's *Tom Mix, Captain Midnight*, and *Superman* remained of the old fifteen-minute thrillers. It was the last season of day-to-day cliffhanging on radio.

The 1940s ended with the half-hour episodic format supreme. *Tom Mix* and *Superman* survived by joining the ABC thrillers in it. New competition came in the form of a half-hour version of *Bobby Benson* (resurrected after so long a time that it appeared to be a new show) and *Straight Arrow*. Nabisco's new hero, who dressed like an Indian when he was on duty, had ridden his horse Comanche to the afternoon time period after starting as an evening avenger. In style and bearing he bore an odd resemblance to the Lone Ranger.

The early 1950s brought more half-hour thrillers—and with them the end of the old guard. Jack Armstrong, Tom Mix, and even the mighty Superman departed in favor of *Black Hawk*, *Mark Trail*, and *Clyde Beatty*, the last another drama with an impersonated hero. Also arriving at this time were three radio dramas whose titles will be recognized by those who first met dramatized adventure not on radio but on television: *Wild Bill Hickok*, *Space Patrol*, and *Tom Corbett, Space Cadet*.

Television was erasing old-time radio adventure, either by creating video rivals to radio's dramas or by transferring the dramas to visual form. Radio's afternoon thrillers dwindled to five in 1952–53, four in 1953–54, and two in 1954–55. After the next season the last two, *Challenge of the Yukon* and *Bobby Benson*, were gone.

To effect a rescue that could not be made, the Lone Ranger was summoned to a 5:30 broadcast hour, Monday through Friday. He too rode into the sunset—and silence. The afternoon air was now free for music and news. Soon the evening air would be, too. The radio serial, with radio drama, melted into the snows of yesteryear.

In an earlier chapter I described the role which a former resident of Baker Street played in the birth of the radio thriller. In his preface to *The Case Book of Sherlock Holmes* Sir Arthur Conan Doyle set down words of good-by that could be extended beyond their original meaning to include all the enduring heroes of the matchless days of radio adventure. To those who still feel guilt when a bundle of thrills sometimes pulls harder at the attention than an evening with culture or intellectual exercise, we offer these words, written on the eve of the ether's magic era:

> I have never regretted it, for I have not in actual practice found that these lighter sketches have prevented me from exploring and finding my limitations in . . . varied branches of literature. . . . Had Holmes never existed I could not have done more.

And so, reader, farewell to Sherlock Holmes. I thank you for your past constancy, and can but hope that some return has been made in that distraction from the worries of life and stimulating change of thought which only can be found in the fairy kingdom of romance.

Farewell too, Shadow and Green Hornet, Lone Ranger and Tom Mix, Jack, Doc, and Reggie. Happiness be yours in your corner of Valhalla.

THE COMIC-BOOK HEROES
AND THE RETURN TO EARTH II

What strong, mysterious links
enchain the heart
To regions where the morn of
life was spent.

JAMES GRAHAME, *The Sabbath*

During the 1960s there were more than a few indications that
Americans of the middle generation were attempting a return
to an earlier time and that many of their juniors seemed willing
to follow them there. As sophisticates struggled desperately to
define high, low, and middle camp and simple burghers raised
eyebrows at something called pop art, a game known as trivia
was spreading throughout the country, feeding on antediluvian
radio shows, singing commercials, and Flash Gordon serials.
("Tell me, who played Ming the Merciless?") Magazines from
Screen Thrills Illustrated to *Harper's* presented sunny recollections of an era marked by both depression and war. Antihero

Humphrey Bogart, dead since 1957, seemed more vital than ever, especially to the college set, which also enshrined Bonnie and Clyde.

More conventional heroes also were being recalled from the grave. Pulp idol Doc Savage was reissued in a long series of paperbacks, while worn recordings of *The Lone Ranger, The Shadow,* and *The Green Hornet* sprang forth from radio stations. So great was the interest in things past that a low-grade movie serial of 1943, renamed *An Evening with Batman and Robin,* played to capacity houses even before the debut of the television series.

The nostalgic frenzy spread even to the *New York Times,* whose reviewer of Jules Feiffer's anthology *The Great Comic Book Heroes* had only one complaint: "There isn't enough of it." Indeed, within a six-week period around the turn of 1965, the *Times* contained two articles on an unusual form of speculation, the trading in old comic books. The publications of twenty or more years earlier had acquired real value, and collecting them had become as much a test of skill and pocketbook as collecting coins or stamps. As a matter of fact, old comic books were harder to find. Great numbers of them had been donated to wartime paper drives, and not many vintage examples survived, perhaps fewer than a hundred copies of some key issues. A solemn Academy of Comic-Book Fans and Collectors was formed to watch over an unlikely hobby in which ten-cent items could bring as much as a hundred dollars on the open market. Even run-of-the-mill books from the "golden era" were listed at five or ten dollars in bulletins circulated by collectors.

Particularly valuable and significant, in 1965 and today, are issues that came from the press in 1938. That was the year in which American youngsters, almost en masse, discovered the comic book. Superman and his friends are so much with us now that it is hard to imagine children unaware of the flashy chromatic paperbacks. Yet, as the year of the Munich crisis dawned, there was no Superman. A few years earlier there were no comic books.

From time to time bound collections of *Mutt and Jeff, The*

Katzenjammer Kids, and *Foxy Grandpa* had turned up. These reprints of Sunday funnies sold well enough, despite pages the size of wallpaper samples, but they appeared sporadically. Not until 1929 did anyone try a periodical comprising original comics. In that year George Delacorte produced *The Funnies,* a tabloid-size booklet that looked like a newspaper insert and probably for that reason attracted few buyers. The project was discontinued after thirteen issues.

Several years later retreads of newspaper comics were used as premiums in stores. They had comic-book dimensions and appearance. Youthful customers took to them right away. Did they like them well enough to purchase them separately at, say, ten cents a copy? M. C. Gaines induced a few merchants to find out. Quicker than anyone could say, "Holy Moley!" youngsters grabbed up a trial batch of premium books offered for sale. An encouraged Gaines was able to persuade a once-burned Delacorte to publish a sizable run of reprint comics for sale at dime stores, where it was hoped they might be bought on impulse. They thus became companion articles to another form of ten-cent literature for children which had appeared in dime stores a few years earlier: the Big Little Books.

Whitman Publishing Company's Big Little Books—about the size of overstuffed wallets—were half words, half pictures. The narrative ran on the even-numbered pages, with related black-and-white drawings, and sometimes film stills, on the opposite pages. Protagonists ranged from Mickey Mouse and Skippy to the popular adventure heroes of radio, screen, and comic strip. Almost all the late-afternoon airwave adventurers were represented (Don Winslow, Tom Mix, Captain Midnight, Jack Armstrong) as were Hollywood cowboys Buck Jones, Tim Mc-Coy, and others. The drawings didn't always look like the real-life figures, but with comic-strip characters and radio daredevils illustration was simple. Pictures from old strips could be adapted to the Big Little Books by deleting the dialogue balloons. And who knew what Jack Armstrong looked like? Youngsters and Big Little Books were forming what might have been an enduring relationship had not comic books come along.

Not long after their appearance it became obvious that comic books had a future outside Woolworth's and Kresge's. In 1934, Eastern Color Printing produced a comics magazine for distribution to newsstands. Called *Famous Funnies*, it contained reprints of such features as *The Nebbs, Mutt and Jeff,* and *Tailspin Tommy* (which in the same year became the first adventure strip to be made into a film serial). The first issue of *Famous Funnies,* today an expensive collector's item, set no sales records. The second issue pointed to success. The funny books, as they often were called in those early days, were on their way.

In 1935, Gaines and Delacorte teamed again to publish *Popular Comics,* a mélange of *Dick Tracy, Terry and the Pirates,* and many more features taken from comic pages of earlier years. From other publishers came *Tip Top, Crackajack, King,* and *Super Comics,* all in the *Famous Funnies* mold and containing easily detectable reprinted material. A six-page feature might have the title in large letters on each page, just as it had appeared in six Sunday comic sections the first time around. Little effort was made to adapt the borrowed features to their new environment and there was almost no new material.

The break from secondhand newspaper features came in 1937. *Detective Comics* was the progenitor of a new breed whose features clearly had not come from Sunday funnies. The stories of espionage and crime detection that filled the pages of *Detective Comics* and its companion publications had the slam-bang excitement of the movie serial. The heroes were somewhat nondescript—as they were in many film serials of that time—but the foreign-looking villains might well have trained under Warner Oland in skirmishes with Pearl White. Native-born ruffians couldn't hold a candle to them.

Naturally the new kind of comic book was welcomed by young Americans, who overlooked the trifling deficiencies. What if the drawings were crude and not always in full color? What if the grammar was sometimes florid or faulty? What if Sandra of the Secret Service looked remarkably like Burma in Milton Caniff's *Terry and the Pirates* and Marg'ry Daw was Little Orphan Annie to the red dress and blank eyes? What if those few heroes with fully delineated countenances had either black wavy hair and the face of Pat Ryan or blonde wavy hair and the face of Flash Gordon? What if incidental features such as "Now You Know" seemed to be "Believe It or Not" in light disguise? These details were unimportant. Youngsters could gorge themselves on tales of secret agents, private eyes, and soldiers of the Foreign Legion. A story revolving about smuggling dope inside an Egyptian mummy might be baffling to a youngster who had not yet learned what dope was, but the genius of hiding it in a dead pharaoh's stomach he could recognize. And while the advance guard of American youth was becoming acquainted with the strange world of the *Detective Comics* group, young artists who soon would fashion the comic book's golden age were learning their trade: Sheldon Moldoff, Jerry Siegel and Joe Shuster, Bernard Baily, and a teenager who signed his *Ginger Snap,* a Little Lulu–type filler, Robert Kane.

In 1938 the Promethean fire was lighted. The June issue of *Action Comics* introduced a character who had been bouncing around the desks of comic editors for several years. Rejected time after time because he seemed too fantastic, he was that strange visitor from another planet, that mild-mannered reporter for a great metropolitan newspaper, Kal-El, alias Clark Kent, alias Superman.

He was not the first pen-and-ink hero to dash forth in leotard, swim suit, and boots. The Phantom, taking a fashion cue from Flash Gordon, had done it in newspapers in 1936. But the Ghost Who Walks, despite his bravery and aura of mystery, was mortal. Perhaps in another time the Phantom might have had the impact of Superman—even without a red cape. In the dismal transition from depression to war, however, a mortal with daring was not enough. And the Phantom's jungle seemed a long way off. Superman was a bigger-than-life hero who appeared from outer space in a year peculiarly receptive to such phenomena. (A few months later Orson Welles would confound the country with his invasion-from-Mars broadcast.) With dictators boasting of master races, how good was a hero with human limitations? It was a job for Superman.

215

And how he did perform it! Comic-book sales shot skyward as Big Little Book sales declined. The plainclothes hero of conventional ability suddenly became as dashing as a Boy Scout out of uniform. Dozens of publishers tried to come up with a star to surpass the Man of Steel. They never would. Superman's strength was limitless, his costume the one they had to copy. Rivals could wear the long underwear, but they could only be as strong as the fellow they were imitating. To offset squatter sovereignty on an extraterrestrial and superhuman scale, that wasn't enough.

Not that there weren't some noteworthy attempts at imitation —the Shield, the Blue Beetle, Captain America. These chaps were ersatz supermen who had fallen in the path of some mysterious chemical, ray, or incantation. Even fly-by-night publishers were hesitant to use another visitor from the solar system. Submariner, who came from an undersea kingdom, was the only significant natural-born powerhouse. And he was given to demolishing sections of New York City in moments of pique.

Of the many titanic rivals of Superman, Captain Marvel (introduced in Chapter 5) was by far the most successful. He isn't around any longer—he came close enough to the Superman gold (or kryptonite?) mine to cause the men behind the Man of Steel to close him down by legal persuasion—but in his heyday C. C. Beck's friendly giant commanded a host of fans and fan clubs.[1]

At first Superman's publisher, today called National Comics, seemed in no hurry to produce other characters in the likeness of the being created by writer Jerry Siegel and artist Joe Shuster. The headliner of *Adventure Comics*, for instance, was an ordinary human called the Sandman, who put crooks to sleep with a gas gun he may have borrowed from radio's Green Hornet. Only a cape and two-tone gas mask distinguished the Sandman from the average hero-on-the-street.

When rival publications flooded the market with pseudo supermen, however, National was able to match them hero for hero

---

[1] The original Captain Marvel is not to be confused with a jejune character by that name who appeared in comic books in the late 1960s, nor with a more substantial "space-born" superhero who followed.

and easily maintain the dominant position in the comic-book market it has never relinquished (despite an impressive thrust in the mid-1960s by Stan Lee and his Marvel group). National's readers of the World War II era were presented with a dazzling line of gaudily garbed fantastics they would remember with delight a quarter-century later: the Flash, the Spectre, Dr. Mid-Nite, Starman, Doctor Fate, the Hour Man, the Atom, and the Green Lantern. The sole creative, though not financial, blunder was Wonder Woman, a patent effort to lure girl readers with a female Superman.

To keep the Man of Steel just a little better than all the rest, National built some limitations into its other superheroes. The Flash was fast but not particularly strong. The Spectre could do most anything, as could Doctor Fate, but the former was dead and the latter as old as Methuselah. The Starman wasn't much good without his Gravity Rod or the Green Lantern without his lamp and power ring. The Hour Man's powers were of brief duration, while Dr. Mid-Nite was basically nocturnal. The Atom had to overcome his small size, as well as his civilian name, Al Pratt. And Wonder Woman, a true Amazon, looked like the Wicked Witch of the West in a star-spangled tutu.

Limitations and all, these characters had throngs of admirers whom the publisher surveyed continually to see if one of the heroes merited a book of his own. A few of them made it, the greatest honor that could be given a costumed crusader—a quarterly he had to share with no other avenger. Still, they were only dukes in the National kingdom. The unquestioned crown prince of the chain was unveiled in *Detective Comics* in 1939 and held his title by virtue of seniority and acclaim. Without benefit of Herculean strength or mystical force, this caped crime fighter whom Superman or Captain Marvel, or even Wonder Woman, could have dusted off with ease became the second greatest figure of comic-book history. Playboy Bruce Wayne did develop his physical skills to the utmost, and then some; yet, as Batman, he relied more upon cunning than upon brawn to defeat the villains. He put them away with style.

It is difficult to reconcile the crusading yet tongue-in-cheek

Batman of the comic book with the epigram-spouting puritan of the television series. Batman was the thinking-boy's hero. Cary Grant could have played him perfectly. The Batman élan in face of continual adversity caused many comic readers to prefer his adventures to those of Superman, whose approach seemed heavy-handed and art primitive alongside those of Bob Kane's feature.

Batman was to the manor born, and his actions reflected it. While Clark Kent, raised on a farm in the Middle West, performed the costume change that made him Superman in a dingy storeroom, Bruce Wayne retired to his stately mansion to be assisted into cape and cowl by his valet. While Superman smote a rapier-wielding alien, declaiming that "good old American fist fighting can beat fancy foreign dueling any time," Batman picked up an *épée* and fenced with his opponent. To the Batman fraternity Superman was a titanic Mr. Fixit, rescuing Lois Lane to the point of monotony and never facing a menace more serious than a hairless eccentric named Luthor. Batman, on the other hand, was vulnerable. He could expect to find himself ensnared by the most fascinating of criminals, notably the Joker. To offset his mortal limitations the Caped Crusader devised some marvelous gadgetry with Chiroptera motif, such as the Batarang, the Batsignal, and the Batmobile, thus providing merchandisers of the future with an infinite number of novelty items with which to entice young television fans.

Batman's best gadget of all, of course, was his boy assistant, Robin (Dick Grayson), whom he adopted after a year or so of going it alone. The appearance of the Boy Wonder was a memorable comic-book event of 1940. Its significance lay not in the idea of a young boy fighting beside an older hero. Bobby Thatcher had done something of the sort in the newspaper strip of that name more than a dozen years earlier. In the thirties the idea had worked well for Milton Caniff, first in *Dickie Dare*, then in *Terry and the Pirates*. Bob Kane himself had done a *Terry*-type feature for *Adventure Comics* called *Rusty and His Pals*.

Robin's distinction, the innovation that set him apart from his youthful predecessors, was his privileged place beside an already established idol. And, not incidentally, he was allowed to carry out his duties in mask and cape. Robin was the ultimate in boyish wish fulfillment. He shared the exploits of an older adventurer, who, nevertheless, remained the central figure in the stories. Batman was not Jack Armstrong's Uncle Jim or Terry Lee's friend Pat Ryan. He was no secondary hero. He was the avenger any boy in America gladly would have served beside. At the same time, Robin was more than a Baker Street Irregular, delegated only incidental duties. His assignments and risks often matched those of his older comrade. He did neither too much nor too little. Kane had balanced the Dynamic Duo in craftsmanlike fashion. Not even the camp-inspired television series could disturb their equilibrium. In games of cops and robbers, kids still were as happy to be Robin as to be Batman. Could that be said of any other pair of fictional fighters of evil?

As would be expected, the success of the Boy Wonder brought a great many hero helpers to comic books. None matched Robin, but the apprentice avengers took hold so well that the presence of one in each magazine became almost *de rigueur*. Their introduction represented perhaps the last refinement of the comic-book narrative.

Yet even before the debut of Robin the comic-book format was well defined. Readers learned it quickly. In the days when a dime bought sixty-four pages of features, the classic arrangement rarely was varied. It was something solid in a world of uncertainty. A serious modification would have been as jarring as a weather forecast at the beginning of a news program.

The leading character was given the first ten to thirteen pages of the book, depending upon his prominence. Superman and Batman always received the full thirteen. Next came a number of six-page stories with lesser heroes—men like Congo Bill, Speed Saunders, Captain Desmo, and Pep Morgan. They possessed no special powers. And, as if that were not sufficient handicap in a comic book, they had to get by without tights and cape. Their occupations ranged from soldier-of-fortuning to plain old spy and detective work. In the few stories set in the past, honest buccaneering was the leading profession. As costumed heroes became more numerous, the sleuths in the middle pages were reminders of what comic books had been like in the days before Superman. When paper costs reduced the magazines to forty-eight and then to thirty-two pages, the men in mufti disappeared forever.

The most frequently overlooked section of the comic book was the two-page short story, straight prose with a sketchy illustration or two. Occasionally in serial form, as the shorter comic features sometimes were, it was likely to be a reasonably good adventure yarn. Probably no more than one reader in a hundred dipped into it, however. There were too many distractions.

In the classic format the last nine or ten pages went to the second lead. Superman's was Zatara, the Master Magician, a character who looked amazingly like another member of the profession named Mandrake. What is more, his man Tong probably could have switched places with Mandrake's Lothar without anyone being the wiser. Zatara's powers, however, gave him a real edge over his King Features look-alike. He could send a carpet skyward by uttering, "CIGAM TEPRAC EMOC WON!" He could render weapons useless by commanding, "SNUG EMOCEB SEVOD!" The Zatara code was not so difficult as to deprive any young reader of the thrill of deciphering it. If the trick worked only for the Master Magician, what matter?

A better back-page hero was the Hawkman, who gave the Flash a good run for the reader's attention. The artwork was among the best in comic books, and it was not unusual for Sheldon Moldoff's winged champion to be on the cover of *Flash Comics*. Once in a while a supposedly secondary hero got out of hand and relegated his fading superior to the last pages and eventual oblivion. Doctor Fate did that to the Spectre. The Hour Man, with Starman's aid, did it to the Sandman. Feeling readers sensed the tragedy behind such a move. What did the deposed hero suffer when such a thing happened? What did he tell his sweetheart or boy assistant? Fortunately, most of the second leads and in-betweeners remembered their places, following the example of Dr. Mid-Nite and the Atom, who never displaced the Green Lantern.

From the beginning the back covers of comic books were repositories of a distinctive bit of advertising, the eyestraining layout of the Johnson Smith Company of Detroit. With a myriad of pictures and print almost too small to read, the mail-order company tempted readers to send for one or more items in its amazing array of gadgets. Youngsters could choose a thirty-five cent movie projector or a fifty-cent blank-cartridge pistol. More tantalizing was the World Mike, which allowed a person to talk through his own radio. I witnessed a successful demonstration of this contrivance, but I have always wondered about the efficacy of the Ventrillo, a device with which one could throw his voice "into a trunk, under the bed or anywhere." And what about the Wonderful X-Ray that sold for ten cents and made "even the flesh seem transparent," or the one-dollar pocket radio in the days before transistors, or the fifteen-cent set of telephones? Dozens of novelties were available at incredibly low prices—turtles, chameleons, swords, water wings, fencing sets. Self-helpers could try the dancing or jujitsu lessons. Probably of least interest to ordinary readers were the "Snappy Yacht Caps" and the "Beautiful Blonde Wigs to change your appearance."

Not too long ago a 1940 copy of *Action Comics* (minus the Johnson Smith ad) turned up in a box of childhood possessions. Naturally, after more than a quarter-century of mellowing on the part of both the book and its former reader, some revaluation of the literary and artistic qualities was required, but perhaps not as much as the James Bond sagas will face in the future. Agent 007's recent admirers may find their adult reading of the 1960s more difficult to explain than children's reading material of the 1940s ever could be.

In my ancient comic book Superman battled a mysterious hypnotist named Medini in a story sprinkled with some surprising three-dollar words, such as "rebuffed," "occult," and "interloper." Pep Morgan, a baseball player turned war correspondent, was up against a submarine raider with a Teutonic-looking crew. Zatara's foe was Asmodeus, a member of the mad-scientist fraternity who had given up chess tournaments for crime. (By the last panel good old Zat had transformed this nasty character into a "graven image.")

Most of the stories in that June, 1940, issue would be acceptable under today's comic-book code (adopted in 1954), even the Three Aces adventure in which a basically untalented sculptor immortalized his subjects by turning them into stone. The plots and drawings are much milder than the sex- and terror-filled crudities that brought on the code. Only the Tex Thompson caper would have trouble gaining approval today—not because of violence, but because Tex's cook was a blackface stereotype named Gargantua.

I plan to keep my old treasure, though lists being circulated among collectors suggest that it would bring a fair price. It is a good example of the comic book as it once was. And, who knows, it might provide a clue to the peculiar behavior of many adults at the outset of the space age. Certainly there is reason to wonder why mature Americans are so busily resurrecting or imitating the trivia of a somewhat dismal era. Is it a longing for the pleasures of a period that in retrospect seems to have been much happier than it really was? Is it a belated appreciation of some previously overlooked qualities? Or is it simply a fad, based in part upon the unintentional humor found in the old whizbangs?

It may be any or all of these things. Yet I wonder whether an obscure college professor, whom I shall call Kelvin Northspur, did not stumble upon an explanation more in the comic-book and thriller-serial tradition. One day while browsing at the magazine rack of a small grocery store, he happened to notice a copy of *Flash Comics*. Northspur hadn't looked at a comic book for twenty years, but something about the cover of this one troubled him. This wasn't the Flash he knew. Instead of the familiar red-and-blue costume with Mercury's helmet, he wore a skintight red uniform and cowl mask. Thinking that the old hero had been given a new look, Northspur took the magazine from the rack and began skimming the pages. It soon was obvious that more was involved than modernization of costume. This Flash was named Barry Allen, not Jay Garrick. He lived in Central City and had a girl friend named Iris West. What had happened to Keystone City and Joan Williams? Something was wrong!

For reassurance, the professor scanned the other comic magazines on display. The Baby Hueys and Donald Ducks he passed over quickly. It was the old gang of superheroes he sought. In the days of *All Star Comics* they had formed the Justice Society of America, the greatest band of crime fighters ever assembled.

The reassurance hoped for was not to be found in the magazine rack. The Hawkman's headgear wasn't right. And the Green Lantern, whose costume never did come up to those of his associates, was sporting an elegant new outfit. Closer inspection revealed that he also had a new name and reddish hair. Northspur saw a magazine called *Justice League of America*, but the delegates assembled on the cover were strangers to him.

Now the scholar's curiosity increased. He began to examine comic books on a regular basis (more accurately, each time he went to the grocery store). At last, after months of bewilderment, his diligence was rewarded. He had his answer. The heroes that he had known a generation earlier had not changed. They suddenly reappeared, with proper attire and correct names, in an issue of, once more, *Flash Comics*. Yet, happy as the good professor was to see them again, he hardly was prepared for the shock the magazine contained. The heroes were back, all right, but they were presented as inhabitants of *another world!*

To his astonishment the professor discovered that there is another planet almost identical to the one on which we live. Earth II it is called. There a graying Jay Garrick, his Flash costume stored away in a closet, lives a relatively quiet life with the girl he married, Joan Williams. With him on Earth II are the other members of the old Justice Society—also, presumably, showing the toll of the passing years—if their superpowers do not preclude aging.

A generation ago, Northspur learned, writers of comic books encountered some mysterious vibrations. These vibrations led to even more mysterious dreams, in which the writers somehow tuned in on real happenings of Earth II. Without realizing it,

223

they turned these events into narratives for their comic books. Thus, according to the *Flash Comics* explanation, the fact of one world became the fiction of another, the fiction that is at the heart of today's camp, pop art, and trivia explosion.

One more thing. Given the right conditions, Flash Jay Garrick and Flash Barry Allen can vibrate themselves from earth to earth for purposes of consultation and mutual assistance. Now, if the two Flashes can make the trip, maybe others can. Maybe others have, intentionally or unintentionally. Could that, Professor Northspur slyly asked, explain the consuming interest of some mortals in the "fictional" adventures of yesterday? Have a number of the inhabitants of this planet somehow found themselves stranded on the wrong earth? Is the unusual fascination with the recent past quite simply and quite literally nostalgia on an interplanetary level? Could the old comic books—or movie serials and radio thrillers—be the magic carpets to which the wanderers are drawn in unconscious attempt *to go home?*

THE BIRTH OF THE DAILY SERIAL

Take care not to begin anything of which you may repent.

PUBLILIUS SYRUS, SENTENTIAE

At the beginning of the 1930s the American housewife led a busy—some would say drab—life. In the eyes of historians of those times, she was chained to the hearthside by her domestic duties, with little opportunity to escape. Few jobs were open to a woman in that period of economic depression, certainly not many that offered an exciting alternative to scrubbing the kitchen floor. If her husband was working, she might have a maid to help with the household chores, but most women had to go it alone, without the assistance of the automatic devices and frozen dinners available to today's helpmates.

Still, if circumstances prevented Mrs. Average American from getting away from the tasks of homemaking, nothing prevented her from listening to the radio while she was performing them. Nothing, that is, except the programs she was likely to hear. For

225

example, the daytime offerings of WLW, Cincinnati, in the late fall of 1931 included *Beautiful Thoughts, Live Stock Reports, Our Daily Food, The Premium Man, Mrs. A. M. Goudiss* (what treasures did she unfold?), *Mouth Hygiene,* and *Edna Wallace Hopper.* These programs, presented by one of the outstanding stations in the United States, typified the daytime "entertainment" imparted by broadcasters who tended to think of programing for women as something on the order of the nonfiction features of *Good Housekeeping.* Even to a health enthusiast the escapist content of *Mouth Hygiene* was minimal. Daytime radio was a void waiting to be filled.

The process of isolating the fill material commenced in 1925, though at the time it was no more than pure research. Appropriately, like most subsequent stages of experimentation, it was carried out in Chicago, where a young vaudeville team, Jim and Marion Jordan, happened to be playing that spring. Although regular performances kept the Jordans busy enough, their agent suggested another job: a radio program. He thought it would be good publicity for the young troupers. Once again, the course of serial drama would be influenced by a promotional scheme, this one resulting in the first clear ancestor of the soap opera.

The Jordans developed a feathery series called *The Smith Family,* which WENR, Samuel Insull's fifty-thousand-watt station, presented one night a week, with a repeat broadcast on Sunday. In this open-end drama of family life, Marion Jordan became the first of the serial mothers, her sources of both delight and anxiety being two marriageable daughters, one of whom was courted by a jaunty prizefighter (Jordan). The other daughter dated a Jewish boy.

Many years later Mrs. Jordan seemed somewhat unconvinced by the suggestion of radio historian Francis Chase, Jr., that *The Smith Family* was the "great-granddaddy of the soap operas." "The humor was much too broad," she commented. Nevertheless, in the brief time it was on the air, *The Smith Family* introduced audiences to continued drama that was more like the first daytime serials than most people realize. The action, though

slapstick, concerned home and family. And most of the characters appeared regularly, affording the audience ample opportunity to get to know both them and their habits. In a way, the
listener was eavesdropping upon something happening in someone else's home at that very moment—listening to people he could
expect to meet again and again. Thus, though the relationship
was denied by one of the parents, *The Smith Family* had its place
in the soap opera's family tree, if only as a stunted root.

How much the series influenced later programing cannot be
determined. It was heard only by those listeners within the
broadcasting range of WENR. But in those prenetwork days,
when dialing faraway stations was a national hobby, WENR's
audience was widespread. It's doubtful that the program went
completely unnoticed. As for the Jordans themselves, after several more radio ventures, including another near soap opera,
Smackout, they at last found the series that would carry them
to the top of the broadcast ratings: *Fibber McGee and Molly.*

At about the time the Jordans were doing *The Smith Family,*
two young men, one from the Middle West, the other from the
South, were having their initial taste of radio. Unusually gifted
in song and chatter, they had become friends while working for
an outfit that put on home-talent shows in small towns. After
a few years on the circuit their organizational accomplishments
won them a promotion to the company's headquarters in Chicago. There, using their apartment as the booking office, the two
entertainers began to pick up some show-business engagements
in their off hours. Before long they were dabbling in radio,
mostly for the fun of it. Nevertheless, when WGN offered them
staff assignments, they jumped at the opportunity.

WGN had in mind a comic strip of the air—something on the
order of *The Gumps.* The idea was good, but the two bachelors
wondered whether they should undertake a series that would
deal with married life. Why not let them try something closer
to their experience, say a drama depicting the Negro? The older
of the two men had performed in minstrel shows. The younger
had grown up with a Negro boy his mother had taken in. To

227

the degree that it was possible for nonblacks to do so in the 1920s, they understood, and interpreted sympathetically, the rustic Negro character.

WGN liked their proposal, and on January 12, 1926, Charles Correll and Freeman Gosden introduced listeners to two young Alabamians come to Chicago to find their fortunes. At that time they were known as Sam 'n' Henry, but soon all America would know them as Amos 'n' Andy.

For two years those within range of WGN were entertained by *Sam 'n' Henry*. Each night brought a little more of the amusing, and sometimes poignant, story of the two southern lads thrust into a bustling city. Audiences were encountering a new dramatic pattern, the daily serial, and enjoying every minute of it. Soon Correll and Gosden, who played all the roles on the program and wrote the dialogue as well, were turning out phonograph records featuring the lovable characters they had created. An anthology of their scripts was printed before the show was a year old.

WGN, it should be noted, was owned by the *Chicago Tribune*, the newspaper that in 1913 had underwritten *The Adventure of Kathlyn*. It is extraordinary that an organization primarily in the business of publishing news should have brought forth both the first continued film with holdover suspense and the first daily serial of radio. But then, the *Tribune* syndicate also introduced the comic features most influential in changing the funnies from gag strips to continued stories: *The Gumps, Gasoline Alley*, and *Little Orphan Annie*—to say nothing of its other contributions to the pictorial serial: *Harold Teen, Moon Mullins, Winnie Winkle, Dick Tracy*, and later *Dondi* and *On Stage*. Several of these strips, of course, became continued dramas of film or radio, as did strips of other newspaper chains that had been active in developing the motion-picture serial. Journalism's responsibility for the creation and nurture of the serial drama should give pause to television reviewers about to undertake a piece deriding broadcasting for its sins of the *Peyton Place* or *Batman* order. Mercifully, the original sin is unknown to all but a few critics.

The Birth of the Daily Serial

The *Tribune* presented *Sam 'n' Henry* for two profitable years. Then Correll and Gosden decided to increase the size of their audience—and fatten their wallets—by transcribing the show and sending it to stations throughout the country. Standing in the path of any real profit from this move was the newspaper's ownership of the title *Sam 'n' Henry*. The characters, therefore, were transferred to a new station, and their names were left behind. On March 19, 1928, *Sam 'n' Henry* became *Amos 'n' Andy* on WMAQ, the station of the *Chicago Daily News*. The boys now came from Atlanta, instead of Birmingham, and their lodge was the Mystic Knights of the Sea, not the Jewels of the Crown, but beyond incidentals like those, *Amos 'n' Andy* was the same show that Correll and Gosden had been doing since 1926. The change did not hurt the program's popularity in the least. The *Daily News* syndicated a comic strip coinciding with the boys' on-the-air adventures. Rand McNally published a book called *All About Amos 'n' Andy*. And still better days lay ahead.

Niles Trammell, who was in charge of NBC's Chicago operations at the time, liked the new comedy serial that was playing on the network's Chicago affiliate. So did an employee at Albert Lasker's agency, Lord & Thomas, who had the Pepsodent account in mind. Both men had selling jobs to do. Trammell had to show his boss, NBC president Merlin H. Aylesworth, the merits of a daily comedy serial with Negro characters but few blackface gags. Lasker, it has been said, had to be convinced that a toothpaste stressing whitening qualities was an appropriate sponsor for a drama about persons with ebony faces, real or simulated.[1] When Pepsodent did decide to make *Amos 'n'*

[1] Undoubtedly *Amos 'n' Andy* would not be a salable program proposal today, for reasons not even considered by advertisers and network executives in 1927. Nonetheless, Correll and Gosden may have done as much (or more) to improve understanding between races in their time as did the super-Negro dramas and films of later years. To take white audiences inside black homes, albeit imaginary ones, to let them hear a black father telling a bedtime story to his little girl, was pioneering of no small order. Before *Amos 'n' Andy* audiences had seen or heard Negroes as servants, blackface comics, or drunken renegades. Fifteen years after *The Birth of a Nation,* at a time when the Ku Klux Klan was in a period of active revival, Correll and Gosden presented Negroes as heads of households, professional men, businessmen and lodge members, no better and no worse than similar characters in other dramas. It is not surprising that the

Andy its first venture in network broadcasting, nine months passed before NBC could be persuaded to sell fifteen minutes of broadcast time six days a week. The network was accustomed to selling time in units of hours or half hours. Moreover, no other advertiser was on the air six days a week. NBC was worried about setting precedents it might regret. Its misgivings not entirely offset by a promotional hullabaloo, the network at last unwrapped *Amos 'n' Andy* on August 19, 1929, at 11:00 P.M., eastern time.

The critical reaction in the New York papers was bad. The words "flop," "fiasco," and "disappointment" appeared in reviews of the heralded premiere broadcast. Critics, it seemed, were less able to adjust to character comedy in serial form than were the American people, who took to the program right away. When a pleasantly surprised NBC moved the show to 7:00 P.M., a gale of protest from the West brought about network radio's first repeat broadcast in order that listeners on the Pacific Coast and in the Rocky Mountain states could hear the program at a convenient hour.

The impact of *Amos 'n' Andy* can only be described as phenomenal. At its peak in 1930 and 1931 the series was heard regularly in more than half the homes in America with radios. And that may be a conservative estimate. During the quarter-hour the program was on the air, telephone usage dropped by 50 per cent. In warm weather, when doors and windows were left open, a person walking along the street could hear the story coming from enough homes to follow the plot without missing a line. Motion-picture houses found it necessary to put receivers in their lobbies if they expected to have patrons at broadcast

---

two actor-writers received many invitations to appear before Negro groups in the depression era.

Latter-day criticism of *Amos 'n' Andy* stemmed mainly from the television program of the early 1950s—which, ironically, provided work for many black actors. "Caricature" and "stereotype" are terms that could fairly be applied to this version, possibly because times (or people) had changed and *Amos 'n' Andy's* TV writers had not recognized that what would have passed unnoticed by social critics if their drama had portrayed white people would be interpreted as misrepresentation of a race because it was about blacks.

time. All this because of the escapades of Amos Jones (Gosden), Andrew H. Brown (Correll), and their colorful friends and associates, notably George "Kingfish" Stevens (Gosden again). When Andy found himself the defendant in a hilarious breach-of-promise suit, the whole country rallied to his defense. Selecting a name for Amos' baby girl became the problem of a million godparents. And the financial condition of the Fresh-Air Taxicab Company of America, Incorpolated, was as much a matter of public knowledge as that of Wall Street—though not one whit less stable.

Respecting neither age nor station, a contagion of periodic lightheartedness had spread through a troubled land. Even the most dignified citizens were caught saying things that sounded like "Awa, awa, awa," "Um-um, ain't dat sumpin?" and "Don't get me regusted." In the requiem of financial disaster begun in 1929, *Amos 'n' Andy* was a saving counterpoint to a leitmotif offered by the stock ticker. At dusk each day a thousand agonies abruptly slipped from mind, vanishing as if by incantation with the first strains of "A Perfect Song."

Amos 'n' Andy was the most successful radio series ever presented. It arrived when coast-to-coast broadcasting had just come of age in transmission, reception, and available audience. Advertisers, envious of the remarkable surge of sales enjoyed by Pepsodent, lost any reluctance they may have had about using network radio, while broadcasters were fascinated by the new and promising form of radio drama. NBC's Aylesworth thought Correll and Gosden were "working in a new art form," suggestive of both the magazine serial and the comic strip, yet "new and for the air exclusively."

The comedians themselves thought much of their show's success was due to the creation of character, not gags. Gosden told Ben Gross, one of the few critics who liked their network debut, that "once you establish characters, if they're likable, the public will become fond of them." Without question, a serial allowed listeners to become interested in characters as no other drama form could. *Amos 'n' Andy* would not be the only program to derive strength from the accumulating interest of listeners in the fictional individuals whom they visited each day or each week.

The first evidence of this fact was found in evening radio, where, as might be expected, continued drama was soon the dominant form of dramatic entertainment. When *Amos 'n' Andy* reached NBC, there was only one other network serial: *Real Folks*, a half-hour weekly sketch that the chain had introduced on August 6, 1928. Two years after *Amos 'n' Andy's* arrival the networks offered eight serials in the evening hours and *Little Orphan Annie* in the afternoon. 1930 brought *Uncle Abe and David, Raising Junior, Moonshine and Honeysuckle,* and *Sherlock Holmes,* all on NBC. CBS entered the competition in 1931 with *Daddy and Rollo* and *Myrt and Marge* (which it put in an unenviable period opposite *Amos 'n' Andy*). NBC that year added to its roles the droll *Clara, Lu 'n' Em* and obtained a sponsor, Pepsodent, for *The Rise of the Goldbergs,* a feature begun on WJZ, New York, in late 1929.[2]

While all this was taking place, some people in Chicago were wondering whether serial drama in the daytime would sufficiently interest housewives to sell products. They could look to nighttime radio for reassurance. Indeed, all the ingredients they needed lay before them there. *Amos 'n' Andy* offered the fifteen-minute daily format, the musical signature, and the opening and closing commercial in one successful package. *The Gold-*

---

[2] Many of the early serials of nighttime radio were folksy dramas, tied by subject matter and dialect to a particular region of the country—Down East, the Ozarks, the Deep South. The most enduring of these folksy serials was *Lum and Abner,* created by Chester Lauck and Norris Goff, and introduced on a Hot Springs radio station in 1931. With a boost from Ford dealers, it reached nationwide status in 1933 and retained it for many years. The focal point of the drama was the Jot 'Em Down Store in Pine Ridge. There was no real Pine Ridge when *Lum and Abner* began, but in 1936 Waters, Arkansas, a town whose inhabitants were typified in the series, adopted the name.

In the manner of Correll and Gosden, Lauck and Goff played several roles: Lauck portrayed Lum Edwards, Grandpappy Spears, Cedric Weehunt, and Snake Hogan; Goff portrayed Abner Peabody, Doc Miller, Squire Skimp, and Dick Huddleston (a real-life individual, the owner of the prototype of the Jot 'Em Down Store). Never high-pressured in their approach to radio or to life, Lauck and Goff entertained connoisseurs of the folksy touch through years of economic depression, war, and recovery. Having moved their show to Hollywood around 1937, they even managed a few modest films featuring their characters, assuming old-age make-up to portray them.

bergs, Clara, Lu 'n' Em, and *Myrt and Marge* contained the stuff of which daytime serials would be made—and one day they would move to a more natural daylight habitat. And if these evening programs did not hold forth enough romance to titillate housewives, the amatory effectiveness of two nonserial dramas could be studied. They were *The True Story Hour* and *True Romances*, which crossed the night sky late in the 1920s, agleam with elements no certified soap opera could be without.

With all these raw materials available to program planners it was only a matter of time before a drama for women would be presented in the morning or afternoon. One impediment was the reluctance of advertisers to invest in daytime radio. Its available audience, they pointed out, was much lower than that of the evening hours. "Who would listen to the radio in the daytime?" they asked broadcasters. (Considering the *Beautiful Thoughts* and *Mouth Hygiene* fare of the day, they had a point.) A less serious handicap facing the visionaries was the scarcity of dramatic talent in the Middle West, where daytime radio was being pushed the hardest. Neither of these factors was sufficient to discourage the small group of experimenters who in a few years would be the giants of the daytime-serial field. They went right on developing a continued drama for housewives. And when networks and advertisers beckoned, they were ready.

One of the experimenters was a quiet, scholarly-appearing man named Frank Hummert, who until 1927 was chief copywriter at Lord & Thomas. He left Lasker's firm to join the Blackett and Sample Advertising Agency of Chicago. Hummert's experience in publicity and newspaper work went back to World War I, when he coined the Liberty Bond slogan "Bonds or Bondage." When Hummert joined the new agency, his name was added to the company's title, but he was not a partner and held no stock in the firm. He received a percentage of the profits for his work as idea man and director of the production unit he organized.

In 1930, Hummert took as his assistant a young woman with a creative mind and a talent for interesting the woman listener. She was Mrs. Anne Ashenhurst, a graduate of Goucher College and a former reporter for the *Baltimore Sun* and the *Paris Herald*. With the assistance of Mrs. Ashenhurst, who in five years would be his wife, Frank Hummert set about the task of creating programs for daytime radio.

In the same year that Mrs. Ashenhurst began working for Hummert, another young woman, Irna Phillips, entered the broadcasting profession. Miss Phillips was a graduate of the University of Illinois and had done postgraduate work at the University of Wisconsin. From 1925 to 1930 she had taught school in Dayton, Ohio. Radio, however, was more fascinating to her than schoolteaching. In 1930, after a few vacation jobs for WMAQ in Chicago, she took a full-time position with WGN, the *Tribune* station. She was hired as an actress and did an extemporaneous talk program called *Thought for the Day*. Then the station asked her to use her writing talents. What resulted was the first women's serial drama of the daytime, *Painted Dreams*. (Is it unfair to note that the *Chicago Tribune* was thus involved in yet another serial first—this one, perhaps, the most embarrassing of all?)

Painted Dreams gave Chicagoans a preview of what housewives throughout the country would be hearing in a few years. To a greater degree than the serials of nighttime radio that preceded it, *Painted Dreams* was what later would be called soap opera. Moreover, with its multiplotted story of intertwined lives, it was the progenitor of a hardy strain of serials that many years later would bring forth a thriving issue called *Peyton Place*. Of course, the resemblance of *Peyton Place* to the first of its line is not really surprising. As if to keep the bloodline pure, the planners of the ABC television series, in need of a consultant, called in none other than Irna Phillips. But that is a story for a later chapter.

Painted Dreams was a tale of kindly Mother Moynihan and her grown children. Most of the action took place in their home, characters entering and leaving the drama much as they would in ABC's series of the sixties. Miss Phillips herself was in the cast, as was Ireene Wicker, the first queen of the soap opera, who later became the Singing Lady (the extra *e* in *Ireene* had something to do with numerology).

Noteworthy though it was as a pioneer, *Painted Dreams* did not trigger a rapid growth of similar programs. It failed to attract a sponsor in its early days. Nevertheless, there was a stir of interest in women's programing. Network officials, such as Frank A. Arnold, director of development at NBC, reported that for the first time advertisers were tempted to invest in daytime broadcasting. The advertisers knew that women did much of the family shopping. But did housewives have time during the day to listen to radio?

Frank Hummert thought they did—if a program could be developed that fit the housewife's daily pattern. Why he decided to try the serial he explained in a letter to me in 1958:

> As I remember it now the idea for a daytime serial was predicated upon the success of serial fiction in newspapers and magazines. It occurred to me that what people were reading might appeal to them in the form of radio drama. It was as simple as that. And results prove that my *guess* was right.
>
> I stress the word "guess" because that was all it was. Not a flash of so-called genius, but a shot in the dark. Hence I take no credit for it. Believe me, none is deserved.

We do not know how many serial dramas had reached the air at the time Frank Hummert made his guess—or whether it mattered much in his search for the right show for housewives. The long period of acceptance enjoyed by the printed serial impressed him more than anything he might have heard on radio. In truth, the rapt attention listeners gave to *Amos 'n' Andy* could have been evidence *against* using serials for the purpose Hummert had in mind. Housewives supposedly were too busy to sit glued to the radio in the daytime.

Significantly, when Hummert decided to test his guess, he turned not to a radio writer but to a young reporter who was having success as a writer of newspaper serials. His name was Charles Robert Douglas Hardy Andrews—the same writer who subsequently would devise for Hummert the upright Jack Armstrong and also do a turn as one of the early impersonators of *The Shadow*. The multitalented Andrews, able to dream up and type a page of copy as fast as the average writer could produce a sentence or two, attracted the attention of Hummert and Mrs. Ashenhurst with his *Chicago Daily News* serial *Three Girls Lost* (in 1931 turned into a film starring Loretta Young).

The radio serial Andrews was asked to write was called *The Stolen Husband*, a title suggesting that Frank Hummert needed do no more guessing as far as subject matter was concerned. He would build a career upon dramas in which husband hijacking was an ever-present threat.

From what is remembered of it, the execution of the initial Hummert domestic drama was much less accomplished than the choice of subject. At first it scarcely could have been called a drama at all. A single actor read the story, apparently trying to go Correll and Gosden one better by changing his voice and tone to suggest all the characters. When the audience reaction to one-man performance was not encouraging, additional actors were thrown into the breach to perform the final chapters.

As a program, *The Stolen Husband* was a failure. As an experiment, it was not. Hummert and his future wife learned how to produce serials while doing the Andrews story. Rarely would their later efforts go awry. They were so successful, in fact, that the several dozen soap operas of Hummert manufacture came to typify the daytime serial as a whole for many Americans.[3]

---

[3] Few radio figures were as fascinating or as widely misunderstood as the Hummerts. They would supervise writers who often produced the most banal of dialogue but at the same time would insist on the highest standards in enunciation from their actors. They would be derided by American males for a *Romance of Helen Trent* or a *Backstage Wife* but seldom thanked by those same males for a *Lorenzo Jones* or a *Jack Armstrong*. They would be careful of expenses and hold paid rehearsal time to a minimum but would be among the few major producers to resist blacklists and ignore innuendos about actors in the days when the Communist scare racked broadcasting. They would be flailed for their dramatic "horrors" but almost never praised for their more ambitious offerings. And through it all they maintained a rare personal dignity coupled with a seldom-recognized humility.

If in this book I add to the infelicity, it is with regret, and with a realization that the *Helen Trent* program I found hopelessly melodramatic brought pleasure to millions of American women. I humbly submit that I, and the body of broadcasting critics, may have missed something the Hummerts and their faithful

Yet neither the Hummerts nor Irna Phillips, despite their pioneering efforts, achieved the distinction of bringing the first daytime serial to network radio. NBC executives, seeking something different for the morning hours, decided that one of their evening programs might be just the thing. With little fanfare they relocated the pleasant *Clara, Lu 'n' Em*. On February 15, 1932, this gentle comedy became the first daytime serial to echo throughout the land.

listeners did not. This said, I shall attempt to describe the Hummert role in serial history with as much fairness as I can, trying to report or to analyze but not to condemn. If my stand is interpreted not as objectivity but as cowardice in the face of possible reprisal by all those *Helen Trent* fans, so be it.

DRAMA BY DAYLIGHT

Women like to sit down with trouble as if it were knitting.
ELLEN GLASGOW, *The Sheltered Life*

The daytime serial came to network radio in a year not noted for achievements in the arts. Few really good novels appeared in 1932, although nearly two thousand were published, including *Tobacco Road*. Ferde Grofé's melodic new *Grand Canyon Suite* resounded from east to west, but Gorney and Harburg's "Brother, Can You Spare a Dime?" was more representative of Herbert Hoover's last full year in the White House.

In Philadelphia and Chicago the opera houses remained dark. Even movie theaters were having difficulties. Average weekly attendance, which had been ninety million in 1930, dropped to sixty million. During the same period the net profit of Loew's Incorporated was cut in half. The novelty of talking pictures was no longer enough in itself to bring people to theaters. To offset the slump in attendance, a lure called "Bank Night" was being tried in the Far West. Soon it would spread throughout the country, as theaters gave away everything from money to dishes to attract customers.

Those patrons who did try to lessen their world-weariness by visiting the motion-picture theaters often were disappointed. Only the obviously escapist fare, such as *Tarzan, The Ape Man* and *Dr. Jekyll and Mr. Hyde,* seemed untouched by the pessimism of the depression's darkest year. Despite the need for laughter, there were few comedies and no memorable ones. Musicals were in a temporary decline; the first years of sound had brought too many of them. Even the lucrative gangster pictures were being temporarily shunned by Hollywood because of public outrage at such racketeer glamorizing movies as *Little Caesar* and *Public Enemy.* After months of delay, and some purification, *Scarface* was released in early 1932. It seemed out of place in a year in which the motion picture was treating the grim side of lawbreaking in *Twenty Thousand Years in Sing Sing, I Am a Fugitive from a Chain Gang,* and *The Last Mile.* Mae West and Jean Harlow brought lighthearted sex to the screen in 1932 (and tighter censorship two years later), but the accent seemed to be more upon tears than laughter, as the studios released *Back Street, One Way Passage, Grand Hotel, Broken Lullaby, A Farewell to Arms,* and *A Bill of Divorcement.*

Oddly enough, it was during the cinema's gloomiest year that the other great medium of popular entertainment began its cycle of comedy. In a sweeping raid of vaudeville halls and legitimate theaters, radio assembled a string of laugh programs that never again would be equaled. One incredible year saw the networks launch the shows of Jack Benny, Burns and Allen, Baron Munchausen, Al Jolson, Ed Wynn, Ken Murray, the Marx Brothers, and Fred Allen. Like Don Quixotes, with microphones instead of lances, the comedians of the ether rode forth on airwaves to battle the dismal reality that lay all about. Americans without the price of a theater ticket could enjoy the performances of the country's best-known entertainers without leaving their homes. Indeed, some of the new programs were amusing enough to keep people in their living rooms when money for show tickets was available. Radio rapidly was becoming the leading medium of mass entertainment.

There was a drop in over-all radio listening in 1932, but it was misleading. Broadcasters eventually discovered that it reflected primarily the diminishing of the *Amos 'n' Andy* craze. The show remained enormously popular, but no longer was everyone listening. No program could maintain such abnormally high ratings indefinitely. A leveling off was inevitable. When it came, those who could afford other diversions were the principal defectors from the program and from radio itself. Those of modest income were turning on their sets as often as ever.

Daytime radio seemed particularly promising. No one, however, suspected what was about to happen to it—certainly not the officials of NBC's Blue Network, who started the era of the daytime serial with a comedy. Yet, by borrowing *Clara, Lu 'n' Em* from nighttime radio, they employed an artful expedient that in the next few years would bring to daytime radio some of its most durable serials.

NBC's new morning program was the creation of three young women: Louise Starkey (Clara), Isobel Carothers (Lu), and Helen King (Em). At that time it was not unusual for writers to double as actors. Production aspects were much less compartmentalized than they would be a few years later. Besides, in those preunion days it saved money.

With *Clara, Lu 'n' Em* the doubling was perfectly natural, almost necessary, for the girls had improvised their lighthearted satire of small-town housewives during some idle moments at a Northwestern University sorority house. They enjoyed performing it, in one form or another, for their fellow students, who urged the creative coeds to do something with their idea. After graduation, the young ladies took their sketch to a Chicago radio station. That's right, WGN. The *Tribune* station bought it and ran the program from June, 1930, to January, 1931. Then it advanced to the Blue Network, where it was a nighttime offering for slightly more than a year before achieving its distinction as the first daytime serial on a national network. When the transfer was made, by the way, the program was aired in the fifteen-minute, Monday-through-Friday pattern that would characterize the daytime serial of radio.

In the beginning *Clara, Lu 'n' Em* had no formal scripts. After each broadcast the three actresses outlined the episode for the following day, jotting down a few notes on whatever paper was at hand. Eventually the notes grew into full scripts. Em was the pivotal character—for good reason: she had five children and an irresponsible spouse. (Her husband, though an offstage figure, thus became the first in the daytime serial drama's long line of errant males.) Lu was the widow who lived in the duplex upstairs. Clara was the housekeeper. The "girls" spent the program time chattering about the day's problems, as observers more than as participants. Suffering was at a quite decent level.

Clara, Lu 'n' Em continued on the air until 1936, when misfortune struck in the death of Isobel Carothers. To carry on without her was impossible for her old friends. Not until six years later did they agree to bring the program back to the air. When they did, they entrusted the role of Lu to Harriet Allyn, who had been their classmate at Northwestern. The characters continued to live in the familiar duplex, but *Clara, Lu 'n' Em* no longer seemed of much interest to housewives, who now had many tearful soap operas to listen to. In a short time the program disappeared forever, having attained, as things turned out, a somewhat doubtful historical distinction.

The second daytime serial of network radio, like its predecessor a domestic comedy, was the memorable *Vic and Sade*. The show, which *Time* in 1943 called the best soap opera, made its bow on the Blue Network in the summer of 1932. For some reason, perhaps its uniqueness, the program did not acquire a sponsor until late 1934. Certainly it was not ordinary entertainment, this saga of Victor Rodney Gook, chief accountant of the Consolidated Kitchenware Company, Plant Number 14. It was radio at its best, and simplest.

Gook and his good wife, Sade, puttered about the living room of "the small house halfway up in the next block," chatting about friends and neighbors, sometimes calling "Yoo-hoo" to one passing by. So entertaining was their conversation that audiences scarcely noticed that the people Vic and Sade talked about never came before the microphone. In truth, an appearance by one of the fascinating personalities described by the Gooks would surely have come as a disappointment to listeners. The inhabitants of *Vic and Sade*'s world were remarkable creatures of the imagination and were best left that way.

Mr. Buller, the president of Vic's company, pulled his own teeth. Yet what was that compared with the accomplishment of Godfrey Dimlok, the man who invented a bicycle that could say "Mama"? If *Vic and Sade* had a menace, it was not Gus Plink, the town drunk, who tottered up and down the nearby alley from time to time, or Hank Gumpox, the garbage man, who visited the alley for more creditable reasons. It is doubtful that even Cora Bucksaddle, a pretty divorcee, gave Sade any real reason for concern. For all his average-man shortcomings, Victor Gook loved—and admired—his wife. What is more, philandering would have been unthinkable to a Sky Brother of the Sacred Stars of the Milky Way (R. J. Konk, founder). Vic's pleasure lay in reminiscing about the likes of Botch Purney, L. Vogel Drum, Y.I.I.Y. Skeeber, or the unforgettable Rishigan Fishigan of Sishigan, Michigan. Sade, when not talking with her spouse, sometimes picked up the telephone to engage in some light gossip with Ruthie Stembottom and perhaps plan a little get-together at the Petite Pheasant Feather Tea Shoppe.

Early in the course of the show it was decided that a third speaking character, representing the younger generation, might be desirable. Sade, at this point, could have begun knitting tiny garments, but the laws of maturation, at least in those early years, were such that it would have taken any offspring some time to acquire the peculiar skills necessary for conversation with the Gooks. So to the house on Virginia Avenue came Rush Meadows, an adopted son. Rush, a carefree twelve-year-old who enjoyed declaiming dime novels at breakneck speed, was a perfect addition to the Gook household. And he brought his own offstage characters to enliven the proceedings, notably Smelly Clark, Freeman Scuder, and Bluetooth Johnson. Rush's dog, Mr. Albert Johnson, suffered from astigmatism and could not bark.

For most of its life *Vic and Sade* was a three-character show. Only twice was the family circle altered. After Billy Idelson, who played Rush, joined the Navy during World War II, an orphaned nephew named Russell Miller went to live with the Gooks. Not long before Rush's departure Sade's peerless Uncle Fletcher, eternally cheerful and selectively deaf, began dropping in for chats. This erstwhile straw boss from Belvidere could consume most of a program with trivialities of the kind illustrated in the following brief segment of an episode from the early 1940s.

It's almost ten o'clock at night, and in the living room of the small house halfway up the next block, we find Mrs. Victor Gook and her Uncle Fletcher contemplating an appropriate birthday present for his landlady. A four-foot length of railway track weighing 440 pounds has good possibilities as a door stop for the 360-pound Mis' Keller, but this idea is about to give way to another suggestion. Listen:

FLETCHER:	You take a good shoe scraper . . . it looks attractive screwed onto your back-porch steps, an' it's a mighty, mighty hand———.
SADE:	One of my *boys* must of got home. Heard the kitchen door open.
FLETCHER:	Fine.
SADE:	(*Calls*) You, Willie?
RUSH:	(*In kitchen*) Both of us.
SADE:	(*To Fletcher*) *Well* . . . everybody puts in an appearance simultaneous.
FLETCHER:	Fine.
SADE:	(*Raises voice*) We got lovely *company*.
VIC:	(*Approaching*) Not Addison Sweeney, the noted high diver?
SADE:	(*Raises voice*) Uncle *Fletcher's* here with me.
VIC AND RUSH:	(*Approaching*) Hi.
FLETCHER:	(*To Sade*) They been to the moving picture show, likely.
SADE:	Vic's been to lodge meeting. Rush went down to the Y.M.C.A., where the fat men play handball. (*In low, amused tones, without malice*) *Told* you that three *times.*
FLETCHER:	Fine.
RUSH:	(*Coming up*) Greetings, Uncle Fletcher.

243

FLETCHER:	Hellow, Rush.
VIC:	(*Coming up*) Essex woppum, Uncle Fletcher. Tizzy feeker yowley veep.
FLETCHER:	Uh-huh. (*Chuckles*) Dropped in on Sadie here a while ago only intendin' to stay five minutes an' been hangin' around for better'n an hour.
SADE:	I was real glad you did. Got to feelin' real lonesome.
FLETCHER:	Fine.
VIC:	Yashum tunk, Uncle Fletcher.
FLETCHER:	Uh-huh.
VIC:	(*Cordially*) Jeeler yushman vupple girp.
FLETCHER:	Yes, indeed.
VIC:	(*Cordially*) Howyah booger toko sleeb. Patch hokish uddle yickalorum goshly vex doppo . . .
SADE:	(*Low tones, giggles*) Oh, *stop* that.
VIC:	(*Innocently*) Beg pardon?
SADE:	(*Low tones, giggling*) It's *mean* to tease a person.
VIC:	(*Innocently*) I'm not teasing anybody. I'm just . . . .
SADE:	Well, *quit* it. (*Louder*) Uncle Fletcher an' me been havin' a lovely chat.
VIC:	Really?
SADE:	Tomorrow's his landlady's birthday, an' he's tryin' to think of a present to give her.
FLETCHER:	How's that, Sadie?
SADE:	I was telling Vic about tomorrow bein' Mis' Keller's birthday.
FLETCHER:	*Yes*, Vic. My landlady's *birthday* tomorrow.
VIC:	How old will she be?
FLETCHER:	Fine. (*Chuckles*) My idea was a fancy *door* stop, but Sadie here pretty much threw cold *water* on it.
SADE:	(*Giggles*) So *heavy*. He wanted to get a big hunk of railroad track from the C and A shops. Four feet long. Weight almost five hundred pounds.
VIC:	Five hundred pounds of steel outa hold a door open in good shape.
SADE:	Golly, *yes*. How's a person even get it *home* from the C and A shops?
VIC:	Put it in their vest pocket.
FLETCHER:	Moving picture show pretty good, was it, Rush?
RUSH:	I never went. Been down at the Y.M.C.A. watchin' the fat men play handball.
FLETCHER:	Uh-huh—fine.
RUSH:	(*To his folks*) Pretty fast handball game, *too*, this evening. Mr. Cunningham an' Mr. Morris almost had

a fight. I was in the society of Bluetooth Johnson, Leland Richards, an' Smelly Clark, an' the four of us——

FLETCHER: How would a *shoe* scraper be for Mis' Keller's birthday present, Sadie? (*Aside*) Excuse me for interruptin', Vic.

VIC: (*Generously*) Perfectly all right.

RUSH: (*Low tones, chuckling*) I was the party *talkin'*.

FLETCHER: (*To Vic*) I was tellin' Sadie before you got here I was turnin' a *shoe* scraper over in my mind.

VIC: Uh-huh.

FLETCHER: Shoe scraper screwed on your back-porch steps is a good-*lookin'* contraption an' a *useful* contraption. Fella can pick one up at the hardware store for three, four dollars that'll last a lifetime. I saw some the other day with fancy *grill*work. Iron *angels* an' junk flyin' around, ya know. (*Importantly*) Or . . . if ya don't want *angels* an' junk . . . they got 'em with your *initial*. (*Quotes some initials at random*) G, W, K, P, S . . . *any* of them initials you can get.

VIC: (*A few suggestions*) M, F, Y, C, J.

FLETCHER: Sure, (*A few more*) B, Q, L, E, S.

RUSH: (*Still more*) A, T, X, R, M, N, V, R . . .

SADE: (*Giggles*) Oh, *stop* that.

It is impossible with one excerpt to suggest the winsome quality of *Vic and Sade*. To say that the skits of Jonathan Winters or Bob and Ray contain some of its flavor is not enough. There was a warmth that went beyond parody and a reflection of middle-class America that added depth to each episode. Edgar Lee Masters called it the best American humor of its day. He may have been right. Responsible for the humor was a young reporter-turned-scriptwriter named Paul Rhymer. Called upon to write a program about family life, he drew upon the memories he had of the people he had known in Bloomington, Indiana. Rhymer's characters were composites of relatives and friends. Sade was inspired by Rhymer's mother. Rush undoubtedly represented the author himself and, perhaps, the typical budding teenager. On one occasion Rhymer borrowed not the personalities but the names of real-life individuals; in one episode the names of NBC's vice presidents were reeled off one by one in a list of supposed jailbirds.

Throughout the course of the program the title characters were played by Bernadine Flynn and Art Van Harvey. Clarence Hartzell played Uncle Fletcher. For twelve years the remarkable drama in which they performed was available only to those who could listen to radio during the daytime. Then, in the fall of 1944, it moved to an early-evening hour. For the first time the series could be heard by a general audience. But shortly after the move to premium time the program left the air.

Why it departed has never been satisfactorily explained. Certainly commercial factors and the more competitive atmosphere of nighttime radio were involved. Yet it may be that a simpler reason underlay the show's departure. One of Rhymer's friends told me that he noticed a change in the writer's work habits over the years. At first ideas came to him with amazing ease (often he finished the script before breakfast). But, as the years passed, the creation of the program required much greater effort. The ideas, the words, the phrases came much more slowly—and not without good reason.

The challenge Rhymer faced can be visualized more easily if one remembers that he had to turn out about 250 programs a year, each on a different theme. *Vic and Sade* was one of the few daytime serials in which each episode was complete in itself. While the average serial writer needed only four or five plot lines a year, Rhymer needed a new one every day. Moreover, he was denied the serial writer's best friend, the summary, which could consume two or three minutes of program time during any episode—two or three episodes, for that matter. After thirteen years of unusually creative writing under demanding circumstances, Paul Rhymer was entitled to lay down his pen. NBC had the wisdom not to put it in another writer's hands.

If the first two daytime serials of network radio did not suggest what was to come, the third one did. In fact, the opening installment of *Betty and Bob* (presented on October 10, 1932) may have represented the turning point in the history of daytime serial drama. It was the spearhead in the diurnal thrust of Frank and Anne Hummert. Once this astute couple had taken hold of radio's daytime serial (as their careful planning allowed them to do almost overnight), its course was fixed with little wavering by the guiding star they seemed to see shining so brightly. With a full complement of enraptured passengers, the newly launched dramatic craft would sail to Oblivion, by way of Scorn and Derision, with few side trips to the Isle of Quality and no real chance to remain there.

Without question, *Betty and Bob* was that thing soon to be called soap opera, in 99 and 44/100 per cent pure form. It would be fitting, therefore, to record that the program was underwritten by a soap company—but it was not. The sponsor was General Mills, a corporation that would become so closely associated with daytime serials that, if the programs' charm for soap makers had not been so great, they might well have become known as cereal dramas. Happily for the purists among us, network radio's first daytime serial did have a sponsor of the appropriate species: *Clara, Lu 'n' Em* was presented by Colgate.

The Hummerts' first network soap serial was written by the prolific Robert Andrews, who at the same time was toiling for them on *Just Plain Bill*, then an evening series. In fairness to its creators, it should be noted that *Betty and Bob* was a cut above many later serials in both writing and production. The Hummert unit was not yet employing assembly-line methods to grind out dozens of shows each week. *Betty and Bob* showed signs of care —at least in the beginning.

Ostensibly a love story, the drama was in fact testimony to the premise that marriage brings problems both before and after the ceremony. The Betty of the title was a pretty stenographer who fell in love with her boss. Young, handsome Bob Drake returned her affection—to the dismay of his millionaire father, who did not approve of Betty's humble origins. Their eventual marriage cut Bob from the family purse strings and forced him to go it alone, something he was not yet prepared to do.

If this much of the story seems curiously familiar to a reader not steeped in *True Romances* fiction, it may be because it had been the initial plot line of a highly popular comic strip of 1930. Two years before *Betty and Bob* went on the air, Chic Young had used exactly this situation, in a lighter vein, to begin his celebrated feature, *Blondie*.

There were other resemblances between *Blondie* and *Betty and Bob*. In both stories time moved forward naturally, the characters aging in normal fashion, an aspect which distinguished them from most comic strips and from succeeding soap operas. Too, both the Bumsteads and the Drakes were blessed in due time with baby boys, offsprings who added new facets to the common plot.

It is unlikely, of course, that the Hummert serial gained its story line from the comic strip. Moreover, the two features were utterly dissimilar in tone and treatment. *Blondie* was robust comedy, with an air of topsy-turvy optimism in which even Dagwood had his victories. *Betty and Bob* was romantic melodrama that turned into a turbid exercise in distrust and deceit—but not before it had caught millions of women in its spell.

The differences that set *Betty and Bob* apart from *Blondie* also set it apart from *Clara, Lu 'n' Em* and *Vic and Sade*. The new love story on NBC offered women something they had not heard before in the daytime. The result was instant and impressive success. The life span of *Betty and Bob* was about seven years— not long as serial lives go, but its quick acceptance by housewives showed that a serial that did not rely upon humor could be as popular in the daytime as one that did, and possibly more so. The opportunity for balance in women's programing was about to disappear. One can only wonder whether radio's daylight hours might have been a little happier in the 1930s and 1940s if *Betty and Bob* had been like *Blondie* in spirit as well as opening plot and soap opera had not reared its head before the humorous serial could gain a foothold in the daytime.

But *Betty and Bob* was not like *Blondie* in spirit. The Bumstead marriage was a frenzied but stable one, the marital crises concerning only Blondie's new hats or Dagwood's efforts to steal away for a card game with the boys. The Drake marriage was anything but stable. Bob seemed as unready for it as he was for holding a job. His attractiveness to other women provided additional problems. By late 1936 Betty and Bob had, as their announcer put it, "surmounted everything; divorce, misunderstanding, the interference of other people and, sometimes the worst of all foes, the passage of time." This was quite a lot of surmounting in less than four years. By 1940 things had become so complicated in the Drake household that even hardened soap-opera listeners no longer seemed interested. The show was replaced by a much older tale of marital difficulty: the story of Adam and Eve in a new serial based upon the Bible.

Although *Betty and Bob* died somewhat early in the daytime serial scheme of things, it was never surpassed in one regard: it gave radio its first and greatest matinee idol in the person of Don Ameche, whose mellow voice thrilled housewives as none other ever would. Before long Ameche was doing his emoting in a Hollywood film studio; yet at no time during his motion-picture career was he the romantic idol he had been on the airwaves. He was good-looking enough to play leads, but what human countenance could ever match that voice? Ameche, by the way, was not the only prominent actor to perform on *Betty and Bob*. When the program moved from Chicago to New York in 1939, the title roles were played by Arlene Francis and Van Heflin. Supporting players over the years included Shepperd Strudwick, Selena Royale, Edmond O'Brien, and Kent Smith (who would return to soap opera a quarter of a century after *Betty and Bob*'s last broadcast as Dr. Morton of *Peyton Place*).

The demise of the well-acted *Betty and Bob* in the midst of a serial boom was of interest to critics and broadcasters. For two years after its creation it had been the most popular daytime serial. Then its audience fell off sharply. Ameche's departure from the cast may have played a part in the decline, but it probably was not enough to kill the program. *Newsweek* speculated that *Betty and Bob* left the air because listeners would no longer accept a plot built upon the apparently boundless jealousies of a married couple with a child. This theory, if correct, could explain why in subsequent years children were inconspicuous in Hummert serials portraying difficult marriages. The Drakes' little Bobby had been the focal point of many episodes. He was lovable, in a syrupy way. Women would not have liked to see

249

him hurt by the inability of his father and mother to adjust to matrimony.

Perhaps, too, Bob's periodic shirking of parental responsibility struck an especially sour note during a time in which America's greatest hero was enduring the tragic loss of his son and the long investigation and trial that kept it before his mind. The Lindbergh kidnaping was the nation's dominant news story through half the life of *Betty and Bob*. Did it make listeners wonder why a father with a fine son like Bobby could stray so often from the family hearth? No one can say. One thing was certain. By the mid-1930s Robert Drake clearly was not an ideal husband and father. Daytime radio's foremost Prince Charming had feet of clay.[1]

[1] Let us not lay the children-in-the-closet syndrome solely upon the doorstep of the Hummerts. Children seldom filled their natural role in daytime radio drama. They were usually brought into a story to create difficulty for their parents or guardians. The very young served as obstacles to marriage, objects of legal contests, reasons for maternal sacrifice, and causes for parental worry. Rarely were they presented as normal children in the throes of growing up. During those periods when children were unimportant to the plot they remained virtually nonexistent. In *Our Gal Sunday* the offspring of Henry and Sunday Brinthrope did not appear in any of the more than fifty episodes to which this writer listened one spring, although they lived in the Brinthrope mansion, where most of the action took place. True, on one occasion a physician did visit the manor to treat them, but the children themselves were not heard. The physician's visit served only to further the plot and had no direct connection with the sick children.

SERIAL WORLD

Every spirit makes its house, but afterwards the house confines the spirit.

RALPH WALDO EMERSON, "Fate," *Conduct of Life*

As the first year of coast-to-coast soap opera drew to a close, there seemed not the slightest reason for apprehension about a trend toward tears in the daytime. NBC's Blue Network, the only chain presenting daytime serials in 1932, listed just three— four, if one counted *Judy and Jane*, a transcribed Hummert comedy heard in the Middle West. *Clara, Lu 'n' Em* and *Vic and Sade* were lighthearted enough to cause no concern to women's clubs, while *Betty and Bob* was merely gathering momentum for the gauntlet of miseries it would run.

Not even the program titles gave pause to critics or delight to serial scoffers. John did not have his other wife, nor Stan Burton his second. Mary Noble had not gone backstage, and Carolyn Kramer Nelson had not asserted her right to happiness. In

251

1932 life clearly was anything but beautiful. Dr. Jim Brent was not on the road of it. And Helen Trent was no farther than the verge of romance.

It was an idyllic state, obviously too good to last, and it didn't. 1933 brought seven new serials, only one a comedy. The lesson offered by *Betty and Bob* was learned quickly by daytime programers, especially those at CBS. That network unfurled all but one of the new shows. The seventh found its way to NBC's Red Network. Thus housewives could dial to a bit of tribulation on each of the three chains. The outline of the soap-opera dragon was becoming visible through the waves of air.

Perhaps no year brought as much that was memorable to daytime serial history as did 1933. For one thing, it was the year in which Irna Phillips introduced her first network serial (ironically, it was not the pioneer *Painted Dreams*). She tried to persuade WGN to sell her promising local show to a network, but the station said no. Undeterred, she turned to the courts, contending that the series was hers to do with as she wished. The ensuing action developed into a classic case of law, a case that asked the question, Did a young staff writer from the Middle West—or any staff writer—have a right to the child of her typewriter? Not if it was conceived under the direction and guidance of the station, the courts decided. The show belonged to WGN—at least, a show called *Painted Dreams* did.

But Irna Phillips was not beaten. Before the last appeal was heard, she followed the example Rudolph Dirks had set twenty years earlier when he found himself in similar legal difficulty with *The Katzenjammer Kids*. Restrained from moving the series, she began another one with almost identical characters. Just as Hans and Fritz had turned up in two places simultaneously, (the original Katzenjammer strip and a new one called *The Captain and the Kids*), the residents of the *Painted Dreams* boardinghouse began leading double lives in an NBC serial called *Today's Children*. They used assumed names, of course. The kindly Mother Moynihan, for example, became Mother Moran. Miss Phillips and Ireene Wicker continued to play two of her "children," orphan Kay and real daughter Eileen.

Miss Phillips, moreover, did not hesitate to draw upon the imagery of her former drama, especially in carrying forth the central message of the new show's early years: that marriage was a woman's finest career. When Frances, the elder daughter and an aspiring artist, complained that she did not see why a wedding ring should interfere with "the realization of the dream that I've been painting almost all my life," Mother Moran thought for a moment and then answered:

> Frances, you are paintin' your dreams, yes. And you hold the brush and must be choosin' the colors to use. But when you're paintin' your dreams, be careful of the colors you're goin' to be usin', 'cause sometimes you make a mistake, and the colors that you think are goin' to look good don't look so good in the finished picture. Now, Frances, darlin', let me be sayin' just one more thing to ya. There are three colors that have stood the test of all time. They are the colors that are the foundation of all dreams of all the men and women in the world—the colors of love—family—home.

On another day Mother Moran told feminist Bertha Manners:

> In your plan, women wouldn't be havin' time to be havin' children and keepin' a home. . . . I'm thinkin' that a country is only as strong as its weakest home. When you're after destroyin' those things which make up a home, you're destroyin' people.

Sentiments like those helped make *Today's Children* immediately popular with homemakers. Souvenir albums offered by Pillsbury, the sponsor, began appearing yearly. One was a hardcover novel. Irna Phillips needed no mere program title to achieve network success.[1]

The fate of *Painted Dreams* itself enhanced Miss Phillips' reputation as a serial writer. A short time after the debut of *Today's Children, Painted Dreams* did attain network status—though without its original author, of course. The former schoolteacher may have derived some satisfaction from seeing her former show trail far behind *Today's Children* in popularity and

---

[1] Still she continued trying to keep anyone else from using it. Not until the Illinois State Court ruled against her in 1940 (*Phillips* v. *WGN, Inc.*) did she give up the attempt to recover her brain child. By then the problem was more symbolic than real, a matter essentially of principle.

quickly disappear from the air. No doubt some of CBS's non-Chicago listeners thought it a copy of its facsimile, but Miss Phillips' easy victory in the confrontation of the two shows certainly did not damage her image as a serial maker.

In one area of serial production, however, Miss Phillips always would be in second place. Hard-working as she was, she never would be able to create as many daytime dramas as Frank and Anne Hummert. In 1933 that energetic pair produced five of the seven sponsored serials introduced on network radio. That meant that in the formative period of the daytime serial drama they controlled seven of the eleven programs on the networks. Small wonder that their influence upon soap-opera history was so great.

The first of the five new Hummert shows of 1933 was *Marie, the Little French Princess,* the story of a young woman of noble birth who found romance and happiness as an everyday American girl. Although it ran for several years on CBS, it scarcely is remembered today. Riches to rags was not as popular a theme in depression days as rags to riches was. The Hummerts themselves proved that a few years later by reversing the *Little French Princess* situation and transplanting an orphan girl named Sunday from humble mining camp to high society as the wife of a titled Englishman.[2]

Though *Marie, the Little French Princess* was only a modest success, the Hummerts could be well pleased with their other new daytime serials of 1933. Two of them were erstwhile evening dramas: *Easy Aces* and *Just Plain Bill. Easy Aces* was a domestic comedy, written by Goodman Ace and starring his wife, Jane. Legend has it that Mrs. Ace accidentally found herself on the air with her husband one night in 1930 when scheduled talent did not appear for the program he was doing on a Kansas City station. Ace, to fill time, engaged his spouse in a conversation about a bridge game they had played recently. Their chatter was so well received by listeners that a regular show with the

---

[2] Sunday Brinthrope was serialdom's most successful ex-waif. Second place probably went to Chichi, of *Life Can Be Beautiful.* Among the misplaced persons were Pretty Kitty Kelly (a countess with amnesia) and Nona from Nowhere (who quickly went back there).

Aces came into being. By 1931 they were doing the program in Chicago for CBS.

Like *Vic and Sade*, *Easy Aces* portrayed an American marriage in a gentle tone of light humor. Unlike *Vic and Sade*, however, *Easy Aces* had continuing plot lines. *New York Times* reviewer John K. Hutchens described the fictional Aces as "a couple of ordinary people set against an average background, except that something screwy is always happening to them. . . . The general atmosphere is one of pleasant existence in an amiable asylum."[3] A reviewer today would probably call the program a situation comedy. Yet that would be a somewhat inadequate appellation for *Easy Aces*, which never produced the frenzy of an *I Love Lucy* and always offered a bit of choice Goodman Ace dialogue.

The best lines, beyond doubt, went to Jane, who uttered radio's most magnificent malapropisms. *Easy Aces* listeners chuckled at: "We're insufferable friends"; "Reasons too humorous to mention"; "In words of one cylinder"; "We were playthings together"; "He's a ragged individualist"; "You could have knocked me over with a fender." Each episode had half a dozen lines like those which regular listeners picked up and repeated with amusement.

Ace liked to build toward a truly twisted closing epigram, to which his on-the-air response invariably was an amused "Isn't that awful?" One program, in which Jane asserted her rights by demanding a new car, ended with her declaration: "I'm no slave; I want a Lincoln!" Yet the solecistic masterpiece may have come when the happy-go-lucky housewife, who had gone out to adopt a child, returned with a nineteen-year-old. "Might as well get one big enough to be useful as well as Oriental," she explained.

"Radio's distinctive laugh novelty," with its familiar theme song, "Manhattan Serenade," returned to nighttime radio in 1935, but the Hummerts' other transfer from the evening hours remained a daytime feature for twenty-two years. *Just Plain Bill* (originally called *Bill the Barber*) was introduced in the fall

3 John K. Hutchens, "And Going Strong," *New York Times*, June 20, 1943.

of 1932. The story of the kindly haircutter of Hartville was so well received that CBS added a daytime broadcast a year later. This dual presentation continued until the 1935–36 season, when the philosophizing tonsorial artist was given over to the ladies exclusively and his moonlighting was brought to an end.

Although the title may have suggested otherwise, Bill Davidson was the central figure but not the protagonist of *Just Plain Bill*. He was a somewhat passive character who functioned much like a super seltzer tablet in relieving those in distress. Ordinarily the distress settled upon Bill's daughter, Nancy, and her husband, Kerry Donovan. When all seemed lost, Bill stepped in to straighten things out, much to the pleasure and satisfaction of his listeners. And enough of those listeners lived in and around New York City to fill the Roxy Theatre for ten days when Arthur Hughes, who played Bill, appeared there in the early thirties. Approximately 175,000 persons paid the unlikely admission price of ten cents and a box top to see him, according to one account of the triumph.

The fall of 1933 brought the first indication of a scheduling technique that thereafter would be associated with the daytime serial: block programing. CBS introduced it by placing several serial programs in the same general time period. Until then serials had been scattered throughout the broadcast day and were not mutually supporting. But when there were enough of them on the air to put a few together, the value of the serial block became obvious. A housewife doing the ironing might tune in one serial and then leave the set turned on to hear the dramas that followed. In one ironing session she might listen to four or more programs, depending upon her degree of addiction and the fullness of her laundry basket. After the advent of block programing, serials that were aired at odd hours and in isolation rarely were successful.

The original CBS grouping included *Marie, the Little French Princess*; *Easy Aces*; and *Painted Dreams*. In a very short time an attractive newcomer joined the assemblage. She was destined to outlive all her predecessors without revealing the slightest sign of advancing age. The background of this phenomenon was a bit clouded. She was deserted by or otherwise detached from her man, that much was certain, though the cad was around only briefly before dying. And while her actions were those of an ingenue, it was obvious that the lady had seen enough birthdays to run for president if she wished to. Her announcer let this information slip out during her first broadcast. Indeed, he repeated it so frequently as the days went on that it was evident that Mrs. Martin Trent was not just eager but hell-bent to "prove for herself what so many women long to prove—that because a woman is thirty-five (or more) romance in life need not be over —that romance can live in life at thirty-five and after."

The Romance of Helen Trent was one of the brightest stars in the Hummert crown and at the same time one of the worst dramas ever inflicted upon an American radio audience. When in 1958 it achieved the distinction of being the first daytime serial to endure for a quarter of a century, it was just as wretched a melodrama as it had been in 1933. And yet to some women it was the best of all the serials, perhaps because the Hummerts had given Helen the things that any downtrodden woman might dream of: independence, charming acquaintances, a successful career, modest wealth, and a seemingly endless string of impassioned suitors. Moreover, all these things came to Helen after she reached the threshold of middle age.

That she never was nudged across that threshold listeners did not seem to notice. Throughout the serial's twenty-seven years on the air Helen remained a widow of thirty-five. CBS explained that that age was selected because it was old enough for emotional security yet young enough for romance and a career.

There is doubt that the girl with Orphan Annie geriatric processes ever became emotionally mature, but she did rise from the position of New York dressmaker to that of successful Hollywood dress designer. And while doing so, she was pursued constantly by wealthy males. They numbered in the dozens—though Helen seldom had to deal with more than two at a time.

A more or less permanent suitor was Gil Whitney, to whom she was at intervals engaged. Gil was the square shooter personified, the perfect mate for Helen. Alas, she usually was too giddy over his rivals to put him to the test.

On the Lotharios came, one after another, chasing wildly after the pretty widow. Seldom were they untinged by some sort of villainy or avarice that Helen was invariably the last to detect. Pure and noble as she was, the Trent girl seemed drawn to men who were up to no good and did not look upon her as a sister. Inevitably their evil designs were rewarded in appropriate manner: death in a plane crash, death in a fall from a cliff, exile to South America. Kurt Bonine, who made Helen's twenty-third year on the air memorable by trapping her in a tower, found himself in prison two years later. He had, after all, shot and seriously wounded faithful Gil Whitney.

A bit of tower trapping Helen could overlook, but not the plugging of Gil. He was part of her love triangle. And upon the love triangle was built *The Romance of Helen Trent*. Even before Kurt was carted off, a new villain was introduced. At almost the same moment a Whitney-like specimen of manly probity turned up to keep the triangle balanced and Helen comfortable until her abiding admirer was up and around.

In the opinion of many critics, Helen Trent's attractive romantic situation, unusual for a woman her age, was the key to the program's popularity. Here was a heroine with whom romantically inclined women of thirty-five (or more) could identify. More than that, Helen's attainments were not impossible to them, if personality was the thing that counted. Helen Trent was the most colorless daytime serial heroine ever devised. David Gothard, the longtime portrayer of Gil Whitney, may have been ungallant, but he assuredly was truthful when he acknowledged that Helen was the object of all the romantic frenzy "for no damn good reason at all."

Except for one short period, only two actresses portrayed Helen Trent. The role was created by Virginia Clark in Chicago. When the program moved to New York City in 1944, Julie Stevens became Helen. She was still playing the role when the program came to an end sixteen years later.

The turnover in writers of the show was much higher than

Amos 'n' Andy, Freeman Gosden and Charles Correll, as portrayed by
artist Earl Christy on a fan-magazine cover of 1938.

The title characters of three pioneer serials.
ABOVE: Clara, Lu 'n' Em, as played by
Louise Starkey (Clara, center), Isobel
Caruthers (Lu, right), and Helen King
(Em, left). LEFT: The original Betty and
Bob, Beatrice Churchill and Don Ameche.
RIGHT: Myrt and Marge, Myrtle Vail and
daughter Donna Dameral.

ABOVE: The Easy Aces, Goodman Ace and wife, Jane. BELOW: Vic and Sade, Art Van Harvey and Bernadine Flynn.

Three prolific serial writers. ABOVE: Irna Phillips. BELOW LEFT: Anne Hummert. BELOW RIGHT: Robert Andrews.

ABOVE: Two Helen Trents. Julie Stevens, left, 1944–60, and her darker-haired predecessor, Virginia Clark, right, 1933–43. RIGHT: The incredibly patient Gil Whitney (played by David Gothard) for the moment enjoys being vied for by Helen and her rival of 1954, Cynthia (played by Mary Jane Higby, star of *When a Girl Marries*).

Virginia Payne as the listener may have imagined her as Ma Perkins.

Virginia Payne at the microphone.

ABOVE: From the director's booth Carlton E. Morse, right, surveys the original cast of *One Man's Family*. From left, Henry Barbour (J. Anthony Smythe), Fanny (Minetta Ellen), Paul (Michael Raffetto), Claudia (Kathleen Wilson), Jack (Page Gilman), Clifford (Barton Yarborough), and Hazel (Bernice Berwin). RIGHT: The cover of the *Today's Children* album, a popular premium offered by the sponsor, Pillsbury.

that in actors. Perhaps that was because the program's script-writers were not full-fledged writers at all, but dialoguers. Quite early the Hummerts began using for many of their shows a technique borrowed from the Alexandre Dumas writing factory of the nineteenth century. Not even the prolific Robert Andrews could write as many programs as Frank and Anne Hummert turned out over the years. The Hummerts, therefore, installed a production line. They dictated story outlines, suggesting dialogue and characterization, then distributed the outlines to the dialoguers. The latter filled in the details and returned the scripts for editing. In this way the Hummerts—Anne especially —could control the plots of many serials and still have time for other aspects of production. That is how they were able to produce 46 per cent of the daytime serials that were brought to network radio between 1932 and 1937, and 30 per cent of those introduced between 1937 and 1942.

While the use of dialoguers did increase greatly the output of the Hummerts, and that of a few others who used the technique, it did not lead to a high literary quality in the programs so manufactured. The dialoguers had little control over their writing and were bound by the outline whether they thought it right or not. One former assembly-line scribe, now a television critic, told me that he had only slight interest in what he wrote. After receiving the plot outline, he usually did a week's scripts in one day.

If a dialoguer seemed to be growing stale on one program, he easily could be switched to another. It was not difficult to effect the change, for the machine-made serials were filled with interchangeable characters and situations. To lighten the burden further, there was the hack's best friend, the narrator. While skill-ful writers were able to keep narration within reasonable bounds, letting it enhance the drama, the less talented often allowed the narrator to give the listener more information than the characters themselves provided.

Although in a few serials, notably *Life Can Be Beautiful*, the narrator preceded the opening theme with a bit of philosophy, he normally was heard for the first time after a few bars on the organ. With the music fading into the background, his mellow tones framed the words that began each episode, week after week, year after year:

> And now we present *Our Gal Sunday*, the story that asks the question, "Can this girl from a small mining town in the West find happiness as the wife of a wealthy and titled Englishman?"

After posing the topic statement (not found in all serials), the narrator might set the scene for the day's episode, provide transitions, and utter some closing remarks. He could aid the listener by reviewing the plot or adding to the dramatic impact, but more likely he would provide so much information that little was left to the imagination, as in this example from the October 26, 1936, episode of *Betty and Bob*:

> So at last Betty and Bob are truly united. Married. In love. Happy. Ideally happy. They deserve it. But people can't shut themselves up in their homes forever—and keep other people out. They have to go on living from day to day as they brush against the world. How long will this blissful state last? Will something come up to spoil it? Or have Betty and Bob learned enough to be wise when danger threatens? What does the future hold? What will happen?

By the 1950s such overuse of the narrator, though still present in a few inferior dramas, was much rarer than it had been in the two preceding decades. The daytime serial of television made almost no use of this twentieth-century manifestation of the Greek chorus. The narrator did not put in a significant appearance on video until two evening serials reanimated him in the mid-1960s; *Peyton Place*, for purposes of initial summary; *Batman*, primarily for laughs. It may be a sign of cultural advancement that narration of the kind quoted above was used only in the television adventures of a comic-book hero, with no thought that it be taken seriously except by children.

But back in the 1930s and 1940s the words of the narrator were not to be taken lightly, especially at the end of the Friday episode, when some clue might be given to the next week's developments. On other days programs could end with or without suspenseful notes. Friday's installment, however, had to build enough suspense to cause listeners to tune in on the next episode, which did not come until Monday. Through dialogue, as well as narration, serial writers stimulated listeners' curiosity in the Friday presentation, usually without resorting to out and out cliffhanging. As in other things, the less skillful writers and the dialoguers threw most of the responsibility for the Friday suspense tag to the narrator. This one was used on *Amanda of Honeymoon Hill*:

> How will Amanda, endearing, trustful but ignorant of all modern ways of life, get along with Edward's rich, sophisticated family? Is Sylvia, Edward's fiancee, jealous? What will happen if Edward discovers that Amanda means more to him than all the world?

Three burning questions that listeners could not wait to have answered that Friday a quarter-century ago.

Whatever came to pass, it probably was viewed with seriousness. Programs created in serial factories seldom contained much humor. The humorless quality was as much a consequence of their manner of creation, however, as it was of any plan to keep serials dull and dreary. Humor is hard to write and requires a reasonable degree of freedom. For dialoguers it was almost beyond reach. Their efforts to supply occasional moments of comedy relief on order were painfully apparent.

One daytime serial in which the lighter moments did come off fairly well was *Ma Perkins*, the last of the memorable serials of 1933. The story of the kindly widow who operated a lumberyard in Rushville Center and helped the folks thereabout solve their problems began as a local program of WLW, Cincinnati. After sixteen weeks of presentation under the watchful eye of its sponsor, Procter and Gamble, the program was advanced to the NBC Red Network and entrusted to the Hummerts. Except for a short vacation period, it remained a network feature for almost twenty-seven years, enduring until radio serials were no more.

Ma Perkins was popular from its first appearance. Procter and Gamble soon was investing more and more in daytime serials —so much so that the term "soap opera" was not long coming to the American language. William Ramsey, a true believer in the usefulness of daytime dramas in selling soap to housewives, saw his faith result in solid sales. His company took such pride in its tale of Rushville Center that the title became *Oxydol's Own Ma Perkins*. The association of the washing powder and the Perkins drama, like that of Jack Benny and Jello, persisted even after the firm discontinued its sponsorship many years later.

Through all the years Ma seldom ventured far from Rushville Center, though she did go to Washington during the war to straighten out a few things there. Variety of locale, as a matter of fact, was not a characteristic of the daytime serial drama. Almost every tear that fell was shed within the continental United States—and not far from home. Even when there was good reason for a serial's characters to go abroad, as in World War II, few visits were made to foreign shores. The excursion of *Backstage Wife* to Italy in the spring of 1948 stands almost alone as a departure from normal procedure. And considering the commotion the fictional characters stirred up there, the Italian Tourist Bureau could be forgiven a "Yankee, Go Home."[4]

The settings of daytime serials had a comfortable familiarity for most Americans. Not many episodes took place in the Maine woods or on the western prairie. These places were visited sometimes, but most of the action occurred in urban areas, and rarely outdoors. In fact, much of it could have taken place in the housewife's own living room.

Some of the daytime-serial cities were real ones—Chicago or New York or Los Angeles. But small or middle-sized communities with imaginary names were far more prevalent. Serial writers created the communities of Hartville (*Just Plain Bill*), Elmwood (*Pepper Young's Family*), Three Oaks (*Young Dr. Malone*), Henderson (*Search for Tomorrow*), and many more.

The locations of these fictional communities were left to the imagination, although the general-American dialects and occasional references to changes of season suggested that the towns

---

[4] Stella Dallas had a lark or two in Africa, but her late-afternoon adventures occasionally bordered on those of Jack Armstrong and gang substantively as well as horologically. Soap opera's supermother, seamstress Stella swashed as many buckles as she attached.

lay somewhere between Illinois and New York. Nothing, however, prevented a listener from placing the communities wherever she wished to. Rushville Center could be right down the
road if a housewife fancied it that way. And if she wished to believe that Elmwood was just another name for her own home
town, then Pepper Young and his family might be just around
the corner. It was not difficult to find at least one imaginary town
that seemed a lot like home.

Nevertheless, something about the fictional communities of
the serial world struck one listener, James Thurber, as unreal.
He observed that often there were no milkmen, policemen, or
neighbors. He also was unable to find the sounds of reality, such
as ticking clocks, squeaking chairs, barking dogs, or newspapers
hitting the porch. With few exceptions, Thurber discerned isolation in the daytime serial.[5] Thurber's observations were accurate. On the other hand, drama in general never has been
filled with milkmen and barking dogs unless they are important
to plot or mood. Moreover, radio writers learned quickly that
random sounds, unless explained, usually confused or annoyed
listeners. Thus, the isolation from life's sights and sounds, seldom
noticed in stage plays because of their short duration, merely
appeared to be greater in serials, which continued for years and
years. There may be reason to wonder why Helen Trent never
met the milkman. Yet serial creators well knew that adding a
touch of realism by having the deliveryman stick his head in
the door or having a chair squeak in the background also meant
hiring an additional actor or paying a sound-effects man. For
financial as well as artistic reasons they put their characters on
milk-free diets and kept them out of rickety furniture.

In over-all analysis, it was not the absence of the ordinary
that interfered most noticeably with the illusion of reality in
the daytime serial drama. Rather, it was the presence of the
extraordinary. Serials were filled with court trials, amnesia victims, lost mates, and scheming criminals far in excess of the

[5] Thurber's careful and objective analysis of the daytime serial world appeared in 1948 in a series of *New Yorker* articles and in an anthology published
that year, *The Beast in Me and Other Animals*.

271

number a normal person might expect to encounter in a similar period of years—or in a lifetime. Serial characters had unusual susceptibilities to strange diseases and afflictions, none of which the ordinary person had reason to fear. Some of these uncommon problems and afflictions struck a single individual time after time.

Why, then, did the daytime-serial world, revolving in its atmosphere of isolation, seem so real to many listeners? Probably because of one prominent feature of most of the dramas, the slow narrative. It gave time for character development and incidental action that no other dramatic form could match. And, oddly enough, that innovation came about accidentally.

Once upon a time daytime-serial narratives moved along nicely—just as critics would have wished them to had critics noticed soap operas in the formative years. But did serial listeners see things in the same way as serial critics? Of course not. Thus, in the early 1930s, serial listeners complained that the stories were moving along too rapidly. If they missed an episode or two, they could not follow the plot. To meet the objection the writers added lengthy summaries, without slowing the pace of their shows. When the complaints continued, they prolonged the action itself.

The protracted story afforded bountiful time for the delineation of character—as much as ten minutes a day, five days a week, for as long as the program remained on the air. To writers of short-lived serials that meant at least thirteen, and more likely thirty-nine, weeks. For writers of programs like *Ma Perkins* there would be a quarter-century or more to acquaint listeners with the characters. Compare that time with the three hours allowed a theatrical playwright to develop both character and plot.

The conventional three-act play, of course, is not so much ideal dramatic structure as post-Shakespearean accommodation to theater practices. *Artistically*, there is no reason why a dramatist could not produce a stage work to be taken in pieces as a novel is. *Practically*, there is every reason. The motion picture, with its mass audience and regular attendance patterns, made long dramatic narratives feasible, and almost immediately such narratives appeared. But the installment film, silent in its formative period, became lost in cliffhanging before anything significant could arise within it. Not till the broadcast serial did the crafts of playwright and novelist come together with some distinction. From *Amos 'n' Andy* in the late 1920s through *The Forsyte Saga* in the late 1960s a new dramatic medium was presenting itself for development, possibly casting its image upon other forms of drama even during its infancy.

Because it is so easy to denigrate serial drama of radio and television—soap opera especially—one is likely to overlook how this form of electronic theater expanded the walls of theater several decades ago, and not just by bringing plays to the home. Continued drama released the playwright from the constraint of the well-made play to a degree not reached in legitimate theater of the 1930s. Never did a serial writer have to raise and resolve all phases of plot between 8:30 and 11:00 P.M.; to dovetail exits and entrances so that a living-room set would always be occupied; to compress action drastically, on stage or off; to contrive departure speeches designed to carry a major character out the door amid fervid applause; and, after the few brief hours, to order a final curtain that does not drop in life.

Still, the structural modification of drama introduced in the broadcast serial is normally treated as a condition affecting only serial drama, by both traditional dramatist and critic. Perhaps that is inevitable, what with a daytime cloud cover of bathos often difficult to penetrate. One wonders, though, what secondary reading might be given to an October 14, 1969, *New York Times* review which Clive Barnes prepared for Arthur Kopit's *Indians*:

> Structurally, the play is interesting if only because it is one of the least structured yet successful plays ever to hit Broadway. Mr. Kopit has realized in greasepaint what we all have been saying in print, that nowadays a play does not have to have those old guidelines of a beginning, a middle and an end.

It is doubtful that Clive Barnes or any other Broadway critic has thought to connect the structural innovation of *Indians* and other recent plays with the serial drama of radio and television. Yet is any dramatic genre more the play of the middle (augmented by flashbacks) than is soap opera?

Probably we shall never know the extent to which serial drama has influenced the theater. The debt, if it exists, is one not likely to be acknowledged. But serial writers could, if they wished, point to a remarkable coincidence: the dash to abandon formal structure in American theater, on Broadway and off, began one generation after the broadcast serial emerged. And few American writers born after 1920 could honestly claim absence of exposure to the broadcast serial (of day or night), regardless of their attitude toward it. Was Ma Perkins, then, an unrecognized ally (or disciple) of Luigi Pirandello and Samuel Beckett? It is fascinating to speculate.

No one thought about such things in the 1930s, however—least of all serial listeners, who were becoming so deeply acquainted with the persons of the dramas that they could enjoy the satisfaction of predicting what any character would do in a given situation. It should be remembered that daytime-serial characters had a consistency of behavior that would have gratified Aristotle. When confronted with a crisis, the heroine reacted exactly as she had reacted to a similar crisis in the past and as she would react to the same crisis in the future. There was comfort in that awareness.

The extended narrative, in addition to its advantages for character development, gave opportunity for the inclusion of small details seldom found in other dramatic forms. In one episode of *Ma Perkins*, Ma's son-in-law, Willy, who had just finished painting Abby Danforth's home, complained of stiffness in his neck and shoulders. Ma suggested that it was because he hadn't used a stepladder (let's accept it: Ma had an answer for everything). Willy and Ma discussed whether the arm-weary painter should accept payment for his work. Then they worked out the price per hour, the total hours worked, and the total charge. On the same program another character gave an informal but detailed back-porch lecture on the economics of mining.

Digressions like those were not unusual. They gave an illusion of reality that it was not practical to impart in nonserial presentations, or in the adventure serial for that matter. Only the soap opera had sufficient time for the minutiae of life. Having a surplus of time and no necessity to fit a great amount of dramatic action into any episode, writers of *Ma Perkins* and her sister shows could present a drama in environmental isolation, fill it with unlikely events, and still give an impression of reality.

Some years after the slowly moving narrative had been refined to a degree that astounded critics, formal audience research supported the serial writers. It revealed that, on an average, a housewife heard between two and three episodes of a given drama each week. On other days she was presumably shopping or attending the movies or playing cards. The pace of the serials at no time bothered her as much as it did researchers and critics, who often made their analyses after listening to a number of consecutive broadcasts. Pace bothered the housewife only in one circumstance: when she missed a broadcast and something *did* happen.

Just as Bill Davidson was not the protagonist of his drama, Ma Perkins was not the protagonist of hers. She too was a helper in hour of need, rarely getting into much difficulty herself. In 1957, *Time* estimated that Ma had solved more than one hundred "real-life problems, including alcoholism, civic intrigue, and second marriage." Major dilemmas she resolved at the rate of three or four a year; minor ones, weekly or daily. The basis of her technique was a trust in people and in life itself. The philosophy behind this technique Ma explained simply, but eloquently, to Shuffle Shober following the death of the husband of her daughter Fay:

MA: Shuffle, if we'll only look around us, we'll see so much to . . . to take the sting out of our sorrows! That's what I meant when I waved my hand at *Rushville Center*. At Mr. Johnson raking his leaves. And the smell of the October leaves being burned on twenty lawns and the yellow house lights blinking on as folks like us walk home after a day's work. Living . . . I guess what I'm talking about is living. Taking the days as they come . . . the seasons . . . living for each day itself . . . just living! Putting up the screens in May and taking 'em down in September . . . doing your work, listening on an October night to the wild geese, as a mile over our heads they go on their wonderful and mysterious journey!

SHUFFLE: Yep, . . . that sure is a wonderful sound.

MA: You know, Shuffle, when I was a little girl, my father used to stand with me outside our house, of an October afternoon, and show me the wild birds going south. Looked sort of like a smoky smudge. And one year, I must have been six or so, a gray goose feather fell right at my feet. And my father laughed, and he said, "Hold on to that, young lady, the bird'll be back in the spring to get it, or maybe to drop you another feather!" And I asked my father . . . somehow it impressed me, . . . "Year after year, will that same goose be flying over our house?" He smiled sadly, and said, "If you'll be here to find the feather, the goose will drop it for you." (*A tiny pause*) I'm a woman grown, but I've never forgotten that little incident. And ever since I've *liked* the idea of year after year . . . the regularity of the seasons . . . the mysterious way of God, moving those birds across a thousand miles of day and night and empty air, and me standing there, a part of it, because I . . . well, because I'm a part of it. And that's what I'd like my children to know . . . especially Fay. . . . I'd like *her* to see that if we'll only be there to find it, the gray goose feather will always come. Telling us that the world goes on. . . .

SHUFFLE: (*Quietly; he's deeply moved*) I guess that's the story of our lives, Ma, . . . the lives of you and me and the rest of us who stay in all the forgotten little villages, and let the rest of the world go by. Except . . . *we* don't let the world go by . . . it's the folks in a hurry who let it by. Us, we got time to take it in.

MA: (*Not much volume but very earnest*) Yes, Shuffle, . . . that's it exactly! And that's the secret of peace. Let each day come, . . . take it as it comes, . . . take it for everything it has, . . . and when it goes, you've lived that day!

Despite an occasional worn phrase, this statement of the Ma Perkins outlook on life was very much the kind of reassurance a small-town listener appreciated in 1940—and could respond to today in any daytime drama. I do not mean to use the small-town context demeaningly. *Ma Perkins* was a serial for people less likely to let the world pass by than were their urban contemporaries. Through her philosophy, as well as her accomplishments as a problem solver, Ma gave encouragement to the world's little people. Her wisdom in handling difficulties was not acquired through extensive formal education. Ma's grammatical constructions and patterns of enunciation gave evidence that she was a bona fide homespun philosopher.

Curiously, the capable actress who portrayed Ma from the first episode had earned a master's degree. More surprising, perhaps, the portrayer of the great mother figure was a spinster. At first Virginia Payne's identity was not publicized. A note on an NBC file card instructed that her name was not to be released. Later, when the actress's age approached Ma's more closely, she made frequent public appearances, albeit in costume and make-up that gave her a certain resemblance to Fanny Farmer. In 1957, for example, Miss Payne was selected by the United States Church Women to narrate a shadow play at the group's Salute to Communications dinner.

At its peak *Ma Perkins* was heard on two networks: NBC and CBS, and also on stations in Hawaii, Canada, and Europe. On that day in 1960 when the radio serials died, it was the senior soap opera, *Helen Trent* having predeceased *Ma* by a few months. Rushville's lumberyard offered steady employment to actors Charles Egelston (Shuffle Shober) and Murray Forbes (Willy Fitz) for more than a quarter-century, something of a record for character actors. The end of the association with Procter and Gamble did not represent any disaffection for the program by the sponsor. Its decision to lease the series to other advertisers was simply a reflection of the trend away from single sponsorship in broadcasting. *Ma Perkins* was liked by listeners—and advertisers—until the end.

The same could not be said of the daytime serials born in 1934, a year that was as bad for launching new serials as 1933 was good. Who now remembers *Home Sweet Home, Dreams Come True, Song of the City, Peggy's Doctor, The Gumps* (as a soap opera), or *The Life of Mary Sothern?* Only the last made much stir. The 1934 serial crop is of interest primarily for bits of trivia: *Mary Sothern* was the Mutual Network's first daytime serial;

Dreams Come True was the only true soap opera—Camay sponsored, and the actors *sang*; *Home Sweet Home* featured a Dead
End Kid, Billy Halop, in the cast; *Peggy's Doctor* was the show
picked up by Blue Coal when it ceased sponsoring *The Shadow* for a while; and *The Gumps* was the first daytime serial to
be based upon a comic strip, Min being played by Agnes Moorehead. The brief life spans of the daytime serials launched in
1934 gave evidence that women were selective in their serial
listening and that not just any continued story would do. Moreover, the fate of these dramas enhanced further the position of
the Hummerts as soap-opera divines. Not one of the failures
came from their shop. Were they not the ones to emulate in
building daytime serials?

1935 was a much better year for new serials. Only six appeared, but three of them had long runs: *The Story of Mary
Marlin, The O'Neills,* and *Backstage Wife.* The first to reach the
air was *Mary Marlin.* On New Year's Day, Joseph Marlin, his
wife, Mary, and their infant son, Davey, left Cedar Springs,
Iowa, to take up new residence in Washington, D.C., where
Marlin would become a United States senator (the allegorical
significance of this is really not worth consideration; the trip by
a Joseph, Mary, and infant son to a temporary home a few days
after Christmas is more cute than meaningful). Writer Jane
Cruisinberry supposedly conceived the idea for *Mary Marlin*
while riding on a bus. It was reported that *at first* the story was
partly autobiographical. Such limitations of the statement were
essential, for by the time the program left the air in 1952, Mary
had become a senator herself and had received a marriage proposal from the president of the United States. That Miss Cruisinberry did not achieve the former distinction is obvious; that she
achieved the latter is to be doubted.

Mary Marlin, sponsored by a new product called Kleenex,
quickly became a much-talked-about serial. It was distinctive
enough to be noticed but close enough to the serial pattern that
housewives did not consider it offbeat—as, for example, they
would have regarded the short-lived musical serial *Dreams Come
True.* Mary Marlin's exploits, of a certainty, were out of the

ordinary. Not many housewives had the opportunity to mingle with the cream of Washington society. What is more, Mary constantly demonstrated how much could be accomplished by a simple homemaker left on her own. And she was left on her own quite often. Joe Marlin was one of those husbands who did things like getting lost in the vast reaches of Asia. In fact, he was missing and presumed dead an incredible amount of time.

But Mary never gave up hope. She took Joe's place in the Senate and trusted that someday the untiring Never Fail Hendricks would find her husband (the detective's name was not so extraordinary in a day that accepted *Mr. Keen, Tracer of Lost Persons*). Yet not even when Joe was at home did things go easily for Mary Marlin. At these times she had to contend with the designing Bunny Mitchell, a socialite who desired her mate. And then there was Joe's amnesia . . . . Mary might have found it all too much had not the faithful David Post been there to lean upon in time of trouble. Post never stopped loving Mary. And he seemed so solid, so much more reliable than the wandering Joe, that listeners began to think that it would be better for Mary if her senator husband didn't come back for once. Then Mary could marry David. Or, if not David, perhaps Rufus Kane. He too loved Mary. And, right in the middle of the Roosevelt administration, Kane was elected president. In an odd parallel to history, the housewife from Iowa became the confidante and inspiration of the nation's chief executive. Did any other serial heroine have such influence? Her constant listeners could be pleased with the accomplishments of Mary Marlin.

From 1937 to 1943, Mary was played by Anne Seymour, whose magnificently patrician voice was unmatched in radio. Long after she left the part for other roles, Miss Seymour remained Mary Marlin. Listeners could not forget the rich tones of the actress for whom all subsequent portrayers of Mary would be only substitutes.[6] Also indelibly associated with the Cruisinberry

---

[6] Miss Seymour's predecessor was Joan Blaine, who moved from *Mary Marlin* to rare pretitle billing as *Valiant Lady*. Miss Blaine's biographical submission to the *Variety Radio Directory* placed her as great-great-granddaughter of Secretary of State James G. Blaine, with degrees in law, arts, and speech from Northwestern University. Before performing in soap opera she was a "prac-

drama was its theme song—played on a piano instead of an organ, as most soap-opera themes were. To this day the strains of "Clair de Lune" recall *The Story of Mary Marlin* to thousands of women.

The Hummerts tried four new serials in 1935. One, *Mrs. Wiggs of the Cabbage Patch,* was the first network soap opera adapted from a novel. As happened so often in daytime radio, the lightness of its early episodes gave way to melodrama. Minor Hummert dramas of 1935 were *Five Star Jones* and *Molly of the Movies.* They were overshadowed by the unforgettable *Backstage Wife.*

The long-running story of Mary Noble and her matinee-idol husband was introduced by the Mutual Network on August 5, 1935, and moved to NBC in March, 1936. To its last broadcast the program depended upon a recurring situation that was present from the beginning. Larry Noble was attractive to women and not too able to spurn their advances. Mary Noble, the perfectly named serial heroine, was attractive to men, especially mentally unbalanced ones. Through the years "other men" and "other women" regularly brought the Nobles to the verge of divorce. Only Mary's steadiness in the face of Larry's jealousy and instability prevented the ultimate from happening. Time after time the couple was reunited, only to be driven apart a short while later. I remember a Monday episode in which Mary and Larry swore that they never again would part. Three days later Larry was torn by jealousy.

For Larry's suspicions, of course, there was no cause. Mary would ever be true to him. She just could not avoid lunatics. No doubt about it, *Backstage Wife* had daytime radio's best selection of deranged villains. Helen Trent, it is true, had to fend off some obsessed schemers, but Mary Noble's pursuers were much more desperately in need of medical attention. They seemed mild enough at first, but sooner or later they made things most

---

ticing lawyer, school superintendent, concert singer and harpist, film and legit actress." She was also reported as having served as head of the legal department of a Tiger, Colorado, gold mine. No wonder Mary Marlin (and Valiant Lady Joan Barrett) were cut to such heroic mold!

unpleasant for Mary. They threatened her life, drugged her Ovaltine, left her to die in lonely places, and even threw acid in her face. They were not very nice chaps, those Rupert Barlows and Philip Tomkins.

The men of *Backstage Wife* served as constant reminders of which sex was the superior one. If they were not unbalanced, they were weak. In this serial the male was denied the one bone usually thrown to soap-opera leading men, professional preeminence. With no training or interest in acting whatsoever, Mary Noble actually surpassed her husband in his principal talent. Persuaded to appear with him in a film, she so far outshone her spouse that she tried to destroy the print in order not to disgrace him (and, it is to be assumed, lose her status as a backstage wife). Perhaps in this instance Larry could have been excused his inferior performance. In the middle of the filming he was accused of murdering the producer's wife. But did someone extricate him from this difficulty and then turn in a magnificent performance in *Twilight Symphony*? You bet your daytime serial formula she did!

1 2 3 4 5 6 7 8 9 10 11 12 **13** 14 15 16 17 18 19 20 21 22 23 24

SERIAL ANCESTORS

Our ancestors are very good kind of folks; but they are the last people I should choose to have a visiting acquaintance with.

RICHARD BRINSLEY SHERIDAN, *The Rivals*

The fabled daytime-serial formula was a subject for discussion (and, of course, derision) almost from the time the shows were introduced. In 1938, Frank Hummert called the formula "simple and time tested." What he undoubtedly meant we shall see a few pages later. In the meantime, let us acknowledge that there was a discernible set of conventions for serial making, though not all writers drew upon it to the same degree, and some scarcely at all. Actually, there may have been several formulas, the Hummert formula, the Irna Phillips formula, and so on.

Frank Hummert, telling a *New York Times* reporter about his recipe in 1938, stressed the importance of consistency of character. He spoke of characters human and lovable, logical and believable in their actions, "painted against the canvas of everyday American life." His good people had to be "uniformly consistent and high principled" because they were "so close to the audience and so much a part of their daily lives."

That was an understatement of the serial formula, at least as compounded by the Hummerts. It did not reflect the extremes to which these rules were applied. High-principled women did not have to be given the impossibly pure character of Helen Trent. Consistency did not demand that heroines always should be stronger and nobler than their husbands in almost any situation. The canvas of American life was not filled with so many crimes, trials, strange diseases, lost mates, and causes for extended suffering as was the canvas of the daytime serial, especially as painted by Frank and Anne Hummert. Their canvas was drawn not from everyday American life but from an entirely different source. And to that source they and most other serial makers were as faithful in reproduction as they were astigmatic in the representation of American life.

The prolonged plot evolved after the serials had been on the air for a time. But what about the other ingredients of the serial formula? How did they happen to be present in the dramas from the very beginning? Why was the pioneer serial *Painted Dreams* so much like Irna Phillips' later efforts? Why was *Betty and Bob*, the Hummerts' first network daytime serial, a typical soap opera, and *The Romance of Helen Trent* even more so?

It is possible that the creators of the daytime-serial form developed their ideas from some as yet unrevealed data concerning the preferences of women listeners in the early 1930s, but there is no evidence to support such a theory. And it should be emphasized that Frank Hummert called his attempt to end the doldrums of daytime radio through serial drama a "shot in the dark," a "guess" that proved correct. His hope, as he recalled it more than a quarter-century later, was that the serial fiction that people were reading in newspapers and magazines might appeal to them on radio. The success of *Amos 'n' Andy* apparently was not foremost in his thinking.

Yet to relate the daytime serial drama only to the printed serial of the late 1920s and early 1930s is merely to relate the serial to an unspectacular older sister, not to name the formidable ancestor it resembled much more closely. The daytime serial owes its form and features to a now-forgotten genre that in the second half of the last century entertained the housewife in the same manner that the soap opera would in later years. If the writers of the first daytime serials wished to find an example of home amusement that enthralled women and proved highly lucrative to its creators, a form of fiction far more influential than the printed serial was in an era of radio and film, they had only to look back a few years to the most popular commercial entertainment for women up to the early 1900s: the domestic novel.

This precursor of the soap opera reached Victorian Age maidens and matriarchs in hard-cover editions and in weekly installments appearing in magazines called story papers. The inexpensive weeklies were awaited eagerly by women readers who had no radios or motion-picture theaters to carry them away from their unexciting environments. From the stories in the *New York Ledger* or *Saturday Night* they derived the evanescent escape that their granddaughters would one day obtain from daytime serials.

The flowery tales of the domestic novel came from the pens of a group of matrons whose names once were as familiar as they now are forgotten: Augusta Evans Wilson, Mary Jane Holmes, Caroline Lee Hentz, Mrs. E. D. E. N. Southworth, and a few others. Their books, *The Wide Wide World, Self Made, The Curse of Clifton, Queechy, The Hidden Hand, The Lost Heiress, St. Elmo,* could be found in almost every home. Mrs. Wilson's classic, *St. Elmo,* was such a sensation a hundred years ago that its title (the name of the brooding hero) was given to plantations, steamboats, schools, hotels, articles of merchandise, a punch drink, American towns and avenues, and a number of unfortunate little boys. The story, an account of the rise of a poor but honest damsel, sold at least a million copies. Mrs. Wilson loaded it with florid passages such as this one describing the Murray mansion, the principal setting of the narrative:

The parlors and sitting-room opened on a long, arched veran-
dah, which extended around two sides of the building, and was
paved with variegated tiles; while the stained-glass doors of the
dining-room, with its lofty frescoed ceiling and deep bow-win-
dows, led by two white marble steps out on the terrace, whence
two more steps showed the beginning of a serpentine gravel walk
winding down to an octagonal hothouse, surmounted by a richly
carved pagoda-roof, two sentinel statues—a Bacchus and Bac-
chante—placed on the terrace, guarded the entrance to the dining
room; and in front of the house, where a sculptured Triton threw
jets of water into a gleaming circular basin, a pair of crouching
monsters glared from the steps.

That is the *first* sentence of the description. Now let us see
what Mrs. Wilson had to say about the crouching monsters:

When Edna first found herself before these grim doorkeepers,
she started back in unfeigned terror, and could scarcely repress a
cry of alarm, for the howling rage and despair of the distorted,
hideous heads seemed fearfully real, and years elapsed before she
comprehended their significance, or the sombre mood which im-
pelled their creation. They were imitations of that monumental
lion's head, raised on the battle-field of Chaeroneia, to com-
memorate the Boeotians slain.

Now back to the house itself, as Mrs. Wilson introduces a
touch of mystery:

In the rear of and adjoining the library, a narrow, vaulted passage
with high Gothic windows of stained glass, opened into a beau-
tifully proportioned rotunda; and beyond this circular apartment,
with its ruby-tinted skylight and Moresque frescoes, extended two
other rooms, of whose shape and contents Edna knew nothing,
save the tall arched windows that looked down on the terrace.
The door of the rotunda was generally closed, but accidentally it
stood open one morning, and she caught a glimpse of the circular
form and the springing dome. Evidently this portion of the mansion had been recently built, while the remainder of the house
had been constructed many years earlier; but all desire to see it
was extinguished when Mrs. Murray remarked one day:
"That passage leads to my son's apartments, and he dislikes
noise or intrusion."
Thenceforth Edna avoided it as if the plagues of Pharaoh were
pent therein. To her dazzled eyes this luxurious home was a fairy

palace, an enchanted region, and, with eager curiosity and boundless admiration, she gazed upon beautiful articles whose use she could not conjecture.

It is no wonder that the eyes of heroine Edna were "dazzled." The Murray home was both a museum and a menagerie:

> The furniture throughout the mansion was elegant and costly; pictures, statues, bronzes, marble, silver, rosewood, ebony, mosaics, satin, velvet—naught that the most fastidious and cultivated taste or dilettantism could suggest, or lavish expenditure supply, was wanting; while the elaborate and beautiful arrangement of the extensive grounds showed with how prodigal a hand the owner squandered a princely fortune. The flower garden and lawn comprised fifteen acres, and the subdivisions were formed entirely by hedges, save that portion of the park, surrounded by a tall iron railing, where congregated a motley menagerie of deer, bison, a Lapland reindeer, a Peruvian llama, some Cashmere goats, a chamois, wounded and caught on the Jungfrau, and a large white cow from Ava.

And there we have the Murray house and grounds. If literary allusions to Bacchus and Chaeronea seem out of place in a novel intended for the nineteenth-century housewife, remember that the American women of that time had discovered higher education. Mrs. Wilson and other writers of the domestic novel were well aware of that discovery and made the most of it in their novels.

Although today few recall the domestic novels, their characteristics (rhapsodies about education excepted) are familiar to most of us. They found their way into the theater and early motion pictures and then, after vanishing from those media, reappeared, almost undiluted, in the daytime serial.[1]

The parallels in structure between the domestic novel and the daytime serial are striking. Yet the relationship is not surprising when one remembers that both forms were intended primarily for women and were to be enjoyed at home. Men encountered

[1] The reader may have found in the *St. Elmo* passages overtones of the Gothic novel, which appeared in the eighteenth century and influenced many of the domestic novelists. The Gothic influence on the radio soap opera, however, was twice removed and too slight to be considered. Gothic appeal did not truly emerge in the daytime serial until the days of television with *Dark Shadows* (1966).

these genres, written for women by women, at their own risk.

So close are the two forms that a description of the distinguishing features of the domestic novel easily could be applied to the soap opera. The books of Holmes, Southworth, Wilson, and others were set in the present, with most of the action occurring in the home. While the subjects were commonplace, the plots were filled with strange diseases, lost mates, deserted wives, and marriages in name only. Current events received no more attention than they did in the radio serials. Few figures of history appeared. The illustrious characters of the domestic novel were the heroines. This is Edna Earl, heroine of *St. Elmo,* as the reader first meets her:

> Her large black eyes held a singular fascination in their mild sparkling depths, now full of tender loving light and childish gladness; and the flexible red lips curled in lines of orthodox Greek perfection, showing remarkable versatility of expression; while the broad, full, polished forehead, with its prominent, swelling brows, could not fail to recall, to even casual observers, the calm, powerful face of Lorenzo de' Medicis, which, if once looked on, fastens itself upon heart and brain, to be forgotten no more. Her hair, black, straight, waveless as an Indian's, hung about her shoulders and glistened. Edna loved trees and flowers, stars and clouds, with a warm, clinging affection, as she loved those of her own race; and that solace and amusement which most children find in the society of children and the sports of childhood, this girl derived from the solitude and serenity of nature. To her, woods and fields were indeed vocal, and every flitting bird and gurgling brook, every passing cloud and whispering breeze, brought messages of God's eternal love and wisdom, and drew her tender, yearning heart more closely to Jehovah, the Lord God Omnipotent.

Heroines of such purity and character were bound to go about exerting moral influence. In the domestic novel, as in the daytime serial, they exerted it upon the male principals, who could be admired for their professional talents but were possessed of faults—especially a tendency to wander out of the story so that the heroine could operate alone.

The men of women's domestic fiction all too often were manifestly weak either in body or in spirit, and sometimes in both.

The whole man of vital years was a rarity. Let us compare the colorful St. Elmo Murray with the young Edna Earl:

> A stranger looking upon St. Elmo Murray for the first time would have found it difficult to realize that only thirty-four years had plowed those deep, rugged lines in his swarthy and colorless [*sic*] but still handsome face; where midnight orgies and habitual excesses had left their unmistakable plague-spot, and Mephistopheles had stamped his signet. Blasé, cynical, scoffing, and hopeless, he had stranded his life, and was recklessly striding to his grave, trampling upon the feelings of all with whom he associated, and at war with a world, in which his lordly, brilliant intellect would have lifted him to any eminence he desired, and which, properly directed, would have made him the benefactor and ornament of the society he snubbed and derided.

Does a man with the faults of St. Elmo begin to look like a worthy subject for the missionary zeal of a good woman—an Edna Earl or one of her soap opera successors? Mrs. Wilson continues:

> Like all strong though misguided natures, the power and activity of his mind enhanced his wretchedness, and drove him farther and farther from the path of rectitude while the consciousness that he was originally capable of loftier, purer aims, and nobler pursuits than those that now engrossed his perverted thoughts, rendered him savagely morose.

That was St. Elmo, a handsome, brilliant man gone astray, the prototype of dozens of daytime serial males, give or take a few deep, rugged lines, midnight orgies, and habitual excesses.

Hewing closely to the precepts of the Protestant ethic, the authors of domestic novels provided homely little object lessons for life's situations, always mindful that eventually virtue should be rewarded and vice punished. Their fictional world was one that Helen Trent would have found comfortable. There was little outright sex, only implication. Neither was there humor—of an intentional kind. The nineteenth-century counterpart to the soap-opera critic, of course, found humor in abundance on every page.[2]

---

[2] An *Atlantic* reviewer disposed of a Southworth tale in this manner: "*The Fatal Marriage* is one of forty-three novels by this writer, every one of which is

Familiar characterizations, situations, and plots were used and reused, as the domestic novelists set patterns for their radio-serial heirs in the use of stereotyped characters. For them, as for those who would follow, the emphasis was upon suffering. Of little importance were the actions that brought it about. The same could be said for mystery or strong suspense. The domestic novel was concerned with duties and decisions, not events. Nevertheless, countless episodes were employed to tell the meandering story.

I could continue this description of the women's fiction of the last century, but the reader probably needs no further evidence of the origin of the daytime-serial formula. The prescription for entertaining women of the 1930s which Frank Hummert called "simple and time-tested" was exactly that. It was working successfully long before radio was even dreamed of.

From a purely literary standpoint, did time bring any improvement? Of course it did. For all their limitations, real and alleged, the soap operas were a step forward in the evolution of women's popular literature. Stated negatively, they were not as bad as the books which preceded them, and they were often considerably better. I cite one more passage from *St. Elmo* to close the case. Douglass Manning is speaking:

> "There is a singular magnetism about you, Edna Earl, which makes me wish to see your face always at my hearthstone; and for the first time in my life I want to say to the world, 'This woman wears my name, and belongs to me forever!' You are inordinately ambitious; I can lift you to a position that will fully satisfy you, and place you above the necessity of daily labor—a position of happiness and ease, where your genius can properly develope itself. Can you consent to be Douglass Manning's wife?"
>
> There was no more tremor in his voice than in the measured beat of a base [*sic*] drum; and in his granite face not a feature moved, not a muscle twitched, not a nerve quivered.
>
> So entirely unexpected was this proposal that Edna could not

a separate astonishment." John Greenleaf Whittier had some appreciation for Mrs. Southworth's talents, and male theatergoers, critics included, applauded some of the dramatizations of the story-paper tales, but formal literary criticism recognized the domestic-novel genre as significant only in its bulk and popular impact. As a phenomenon it merited consideration.

utter a word. The idea that he could ever wish to marry anybody seemed incredible, and that he should need her society appeared utterly absurd. For an instant she wondered if she had fallen asleep in the soft, luxurious corner of the carriage, and dreamed it all.

Completely bewildered, she sat looking wonderingly at him.

"Miss Earl, you do not seem to comprehend me, and yet my words are certainly very explicit. Once more I ask you, can you put your hand in mine and be my wife?"

He laid one hand on hers, and with the other pushed back his glasses.

Withdrawing her hands, she covered her face with them and answered almost inaudibly:

"Let me think—for you astonish me."

"Take a day, or a week, if necessary, for consideration, and then give me your answer."

Mr. Manning leaned back in the carriage, folded his hands, and looked quietly out of the window; and for a half hour silence reigned.

While the thirty-minute silence reigns, Edna reflects upon this turn of events, a "brief, but sharp struggle" raging in her heart. After thirteen paragraphs of romantic analysis, the heroine, with a "rigid paleness in her face and a mournful hollowness in her voice," makes reply:

"No, Mr. Manning! We do not love each other, and I can never be your wife."

A simple, straightforward statement, but Edna does not leave it at that:

"It is useless for me to assure you that I am flattered by your preference; that I am inexpressibly proud of the distinction you have generously offered to confer upon me. Sir, you can not doubt that I do most fully and gratefully appreciate this honor, which I had neither the right to expect nor the presumption to dream of. My reverence and admiration are, I confess, almost boundless, but I feel not one atom of love; and an examination of my feelings satisfies me that I could never yield you that homage of heart, that devoted affection which God demands that every wife should pay her husband."

There is more:

"You have quite as little love for me. We enjoy each other's society because our pursuits are similar, our tastes congenial, our aspirations identical. In pleasant and profitable companionship we can certainly indulge as heretofore, and it would greatly pain me to be deprived of it in future; but this can be ours without the sinful mockery of a marriage—for such I hold a loveless union. I feel that I must have your esteem and your society, but your love I neither desire nor ever expect to possess; for the sentiments you cherish for me are precisely similar to those which I entertain toward you."

And now the line many a soap-opera heroine would borrow:

"Mr. Manning, we shall always be firm friends, but nothing more."

After an expression of surprise drifts across, but does not settle on Manning's quiet countenance, he asks whether Edna is not being too hasty. Is her decision mature and final?

"Yes, Mr. Manning—final, unchangeable. But do not throw me from you! I am very, very lonely, and you surely will not forsake me?"

Would Douglass Manning forsake Edna Earl? A million or more American women could have answered that question. But that was another century, another genre. We must return now to the 1930s and the "new" fiction that is fascinating the fairer sex.

1234567891011121314151617181920212223324

SETTLING IN

Father, Mother and Me,
Sister and Auntie say
All the people like us are We,
And everyone else is They.

RUDYARD KIPLING, *We and They*

By 1936 network radio programing had taken on the character it would maintain until the days of television. The *Variety* year-book called it "eclectic conglomerate." No longer was any form of program dominant. The comedy, variety, and light-music shows of earlier years still were present (even the fading A&P Gypsies and Cliquot Club Eskimos), but they were sharing the broadcast hours with an increasing number of prestige dramas, crime and mystery shows, quiz programs, and amateur hours (the rage at the time). The absence of any program trend was revealed by the diversity of the features introduced in the mid-thirties: *Fibber McGee and Molly, Hollywood Hotel, The Co-*

292

lumbia Workshop, Major Bowes' Amateur Hour, The Lux Radio Theatre, Cavalcade of America, Lum and Abner, Gang Busters, Gabriel Heatter, Between the Bookends, Uncle Jim's Question Bee, Renfrew of the Mounted, Professor Quiz, and *Famous Jury Trials.* No single program type occupied more than 15 per cent of the evening hours. Radio had achieved some sort of balance—after 6:00 P.M.

In daytime radio the battle was all but over. More than half the commercial network time was devoted to what was then called "adult serial drama." A poor second was the talk program, consuming about one-sixth of the sponsored hours. Third (one sponsored hour in ten) was the juvenile group, which included the thriller serials. After only four years the soap opera was in an unchallenged position during the daylight hours. And though twelve new serials appeared in 1936—as many as had appeared in the two preceding years—it had yet to experience its period of greatest growth. In a sense, daytime serial planners were consolidating their forces and gathering a few reinforcements for the push that lay ahead.

It was at this time that the daytime serial and the family saga achieved a perfect union, though it could be said that the marriage was somewhat forced and the bride stolen. In earlier seasons radio programers had looked to the nighttime for possible transplants to summer patches, and in 1935–36 they did so again, with excellent results. They appropriated three chronicles of family life that often would be found among the leaders in daytime-rating reports of the years ahead.

First came *The O'Neills,* transferred from the evening hours on October 8, 1935. The writer was Jane West, who also played Mrs. Bailey, a family friend. Kate McComb was Ma O'Neill, responsible for a fatherless brood that included two adopted children in addition to her own offspring. Always there to give assistance was Mr. Levy, played by Jack Rubin. *The O'Neills* enjoyed high daytime ratings until 1942, when it was taken off the air for a short time, given a new emphasis by the Ted Bates Agency, and returned to the daytime wars. As a drama given over to the problems of youth, with Ma O'Neill in the back-

293

ground too often, the program was not well received. It was heard last in 1943.

In January, 1936, three months after *The O'Neills* came to daytime radio, two other nighttime dramas did the same thing. They were *The Goldbergs* and *Pepper Young's Family.* In the way of good politicians, the broadcasters had established attractive and comfortable daytime hearthsides for Catholic, Jew, and Protestant. In no way, however, were these programs constructed along parochial lines. They could be, and were, enjoyed by listeners of all backgrounds.

The Rise of the Goldbergs, one of radio's first serials, began as a weekly nighttime drama on WJZ, November 20, 1929, moving to the full Blue Network of NBC a short time later. The writer was Mrs. Gertrude Berg, who also played Molly (Mrs. Jake) Goldberg, the central figure of the series. Aided by recommendations from radio producer Hyman Brown and Ben Bernie (or his brother, Herman), the thirty-year-old Mrs. Berg persuaded NBC executives to try her stories of Jewish life in the Bronx. At the time the endeavor was something of a gamble, programs about minority groups having appeared infrequently. *Amos 'n' Andy*, in fact, had come to NBC only three months earlier.[1]

Possibly Anne Nichols' farcical *Abie's Irish Rose*, which had concluded its long Broadway run just two years before, could be considered the precedent for Mrs. Berg's drama, yet *The Goldbergs* was a clear test of whether radio audiences would accept a relatively straightforward treatment of Jewish family life. Gertrude Berg's characters were not stereotypes, just colorful, and fallible, human beings. As such they were welcomed in homes across the nation, where soon there was a familiar ring to Molly's "Yoo-hoo, Mrs. Bloom," "Enter, whoever," and "If it's nobody, I'll call back."

---

[1] There is evidence that a sketch of Jewish life in America, "The Night Message," appeared on WJZ's *Little Drama Movement*, August 26, 1929, a short time before the debut of *The Goldbergs*. The play, by Lawrence Grattan, was about a family named Goldberg, including a father named Jake and a daughter named Rosie. The coincidence in names did not extend to the Jewish mother, who was Rebecca, not Molly.

Mrs. Berg's efforts to maintain a realistic quality in her drama have been cited frequently. To keep the dialogue true, and to gain story ideas, she made regular visits to New York's Lower East Side, believing that the program could not retain its character unless she maintained contact with the people about whom she was writing. Her idea of realism included frying eggs in the studio when the script called for Molly to do so, or hanging a microphone outside the window to get traffic noises. Once she administered an on-the-air shampoo.

Some well-known performers acted in *The Goldbergs* at one time or another: Everett Sloane, Van Heflin, Joseph Cotten, Marjorie Main, and Keenan Wynn. Their appearances came early in their careers and probably provided good training for their later endeavors, as soap-opera work often did. Coming to the program with established reputations, two outstanding singers added stature to Mrs. Berg's drama. In 1933, Mme Schumann-Heink, appearing as a social worker, sang Brahms's "Lullaby." Jan Peerce performed in holy-day seasons each year. Not many serial dramas had such distinguished alumni.

The Goldbergs left radio shortly after the close of World War II. Mrs. Berg turned the story into a Broadway play, *Me and Molly*, which ran for 156 performances. Later on, she introduced the series to television. In these nighttime presentations the family had moved to a new home in the suburbs. Gone were the cross-courtyard chats that had endeared many listeners to the old radio show, and—in the opinion of the *New York Times* reviewer—gone was the charm of the drama as it once was. *The Goldbergs* became another casualty of suburbia, its author moving on to acting triumphs in other roles.

Gertrude Berg's over-all success as a writer and actress is remarkable in that she came to radio as an amateur, with no intention of playing in the sketches she submitted. She was forced to read her sample scripts aloud because she had presented them in an undecipherable longhand. Perhaps if her submission to NBC had been more orthodox, her auditioner never would have discovered that Mrs. Berg herself was the best possible Molly.

The Goldbergs with another principal actress would be difficult to imagine.

Unlike Gertrude Berg, the author of another famed serial entered as an established professional. Elaine Sterne Carrington had written stories for *Harper's, Good Houskeeping, Woman's Home Companion, Redbook, Saturday Evening Post, Collier's,* and other magazines. Her move to broadcasting was noted by the *New York Times* in 1932:

> *"Red Adams"* *Appears*—Elaine Sterne Carrington, whose stories have hitherto found their way between magazine covers and into celluloid, now turns to a new medium, the microphone. Beginning tomorrow, her sketch, "Red Adams," will be presented for WJZ's audience at 10:30 P.M.

The title *Red Adams* may not be recognized by the reader, but the program used it for only three months. When Beech-Nut Gum began sponsoring the happy drama of a teenager and his family, it had no intention of reminding listeners of a prominent chewing-gum rival each time the title was mentioned. The teenager suddenly became *Red Davis*, making everyone, except perhaps the Adams makers, happy.

But young Red Adams' search for identity was not over. Through several seasons Curtis (Buck Rogers) Arnall and then Burgess Meredith gave him life as he faced the minor trials of youth in a way that led *Radioland*, a fan magazine, to call his dilemmas a "riot of laughs and dramatic episodes." While that description scarcely made the show a candidate for daytime-serial status on the eve of the great era of gloom, Procter and Gamble called it to the afternoon on January 13, 1936. For both practical and artistic reasons the title again was changed, to *Forever Young*. This time the teenage principal lost both first name and last. The other characters started calling him Pepper. Finally in one last change of title, he was identified as the central figure of *Pepper Young's Family*.

As a daytime drama Mrs. Carrington's story placed greater emphasis upon serious elements. The Henry Aldrich–like escapades of Red/Pepper were de-emphasized, while the other members of the family were given greater attention. Despite the modifications, however, the program achieved a literary level a bit higher than that of most other daytime serials. Mrs. Carrington's concept of soap opera evolved from her experiences with the slick magazines. This background put her one step away from the domestic novels that provided the frame of reference for some of her associates. The Youngs faced many difficulties, it is true. Yet the listener could feel that they were troubles which might come to a family living on this planet and that characters resembling real people were facing them. It is not surprising that Max Wylie selected an episode of *Pepper Young's Family* as the first daytime serial to be included in his yearly anthology of *Best Broadcasts.*

The popularity of Mrs. Carrington's drama must have been reassuring to those who held to slick-magazine standards for the soap opera. In 1938, for example, it was presented at three different hours each day and was carried by both NBC and CBS. *Pepper Young's Family* was not a literary masterpiece—no drama heard five days a week every week could be—but if a wild rush to daytime serials had not occurred in the second half of the 1930s, and if one serial factory had not been in such a dominant position, a few more Carringtons, or Bergs, might have begun writing daytime serials. As it happened, the genre had little attraction for good writers because of the relatively narrow opportunity to place worthwhile dramas on the air and the necessity, if one was successful in doing so, of protecting them from the tampering of those who "knew what women liked to hear."

Another discouragement was the enormous work load. By 1938, when Mrs. Carrington was also writing *When a Girl Marries* and *Rosemary,* her weekly output was estimated at 38,000 words. Surprisingly, the addition of the two shows did not appear to dilute the quality of her product, for, as James Thurber put it, "her dialogue was frequent and facile." She dictated her scripts to a machine, "standing usually," said Thurber; "lying down," said Max Wylie; "plopped down on a seven-foot bed," said the writer of her *New York Times* obituary in 1958.

Mrs. Carrington, apparently, had not given away all her secrets. But standing, lying, or plopped, she turned out scripts that earned her many thousands of dollars each week. Furthermore, she was wise enough to retain ownership of her shows, receiving writing credit at the beginning and end of each day's episodes. Elaine Carrington, accordingly, was one of the few daytime-serial writers whose name was readily recognized by listeners. She used this prestige to strengthen the position of less prosperous radio authors as one of the founders of the Radio Writers Guild. After her death the writing of *Pepper Young's Family* was carried on by her children, Patricia and Robert.

Lest it seem that writing of the quality found in *The Goldbergs* or *Pepper Young's Family* was heard in all new daytimers of 1936, it must be reported that *John's Other Wife* was also born that year. Frank and Anne Hummert launched it, along with three other shows, *Rich Man's Darling, Love Song,* and *David Harum. John's Other Wife* was known to millions who never heard it simply because of its title. It lent itself magnificently to parody. Actually, the drama was a potboiler which never enjoyed good ratings and vanished in 1941. Comedians continued to make sport of it for many years after its demise, undoubtedly unaware that it was gone.

David Harum cannot be mentioned without a comment upon the commercial technique so strongly associated with it: the premium offer. Premiums were by no means confined to serials for children. From the earliest days of soap opera, listeners were tendered gifts in exchange for labels, box tops, and, perhaps, a coin. Advertising man Duane Jones, who claimed to have been the first person to apply the premium technique to a nationally advertised product on a radio network, made his first experiment on *Clara, Lu 'n' Em* in 1933. It led to similar presentations on other serial programs. Procter and Gamble dangled a photograph of Ma Perkins. Pillsbury introduced the first of its *Today's Children* albums. Both sponsors considered the efforts successful.

Less satisfied was the sponsor of *The Gumps* in 1935. When a sack of 5,800 letters, each containing a dime, was stolen from the company safe, the advertiser promised to send the proffered article to listeners whose letters were lost. They had only to send their names and addresses. In response to this tempting invitation came post cards from twelve thousand listeners, more than half of whom received prizes that were not their due.

Until the coming of *David Harum*, the premium was a peripheral device, employed mainly to demonstrate the number of listener-customers drawn to a serial program. When Duane Jones withdrew from Blackett-Sample-Hummert to establish his own firm, the premium took on new dimension. Jones acquired the account of the Benjamin Talbot Babbitt Corporation, a soap manufacturer long associated with giveaways. In the middle of the nineteenth century the company had overcome women's suspicion of wrapped soap by offering panel pictures in exchange for soap wrappers. It may have been the first significant use of premium advertising, and it was one of the many schemes used by Babbitt, a friend of P. T. Barnum, to sell Babbitt's Best Soap. In another ploy the promotion-minded soap manufacturer astounded the press by purchasing in one deal almost $70,000 worth of Percherons. Soon his horse-drawn trucks were meeting ferryboats to distribute free samples of the soap that Babbitt proclaimed was "For All Nations." His immense soap kettles, allegedly filled with $250,000 worth of costly ingredients, were a New York tourist attraction.

In 1936, when Duane Jones took charge of the advertising, Babbitt's fortunes were low. Its best-known product, Bab-O, a scouring powder, was seventh in its field. Jones decided to employ daytime radio as a means of spurring sales, concentrating his efforts initially upon the densely populated East and Northeast. He acquired the rights to *David Harum*, a best-selling novel of 1898 that had been turned into a film starring Will Rogers in 1934, and asked the Hummerts to produce the radio version for him.

When the program had been on the air a few months, Jones initiated his first test of listener response. A contest was announced in which listeners were invited to rename David's horse. (The characters in the drama, conveniently for the contest, had decided that Xanthippe was not a suitable name for the steed.) In a short time 400,000 suggestions had arrived on the backs of Bab-O labels. Recognizing a good play on words when they saw it, the judges voted for a modernization of the name of Socrates' gossipy wife. Xanthippe became Town Talk.

Not long after that contest came *David Harum's* first premium offer. More than 275,000 dimes and accompanying labels were mailed by listeners in response to an offer of flower seeds. The nineteen stations carrying the program at the time—under a method called PI ("per inquiry") advertising—received from Jones the sum of 3.9 cents for each letter. Bursting with success, Babbitt began announcing premiums at the rate of three or four a year. Sales grew. More important, many of the first-time Bab-O users continued to buy the product. Soon the easygoing story of Homeville's horse-trading banker was carried by ninety-three stations. The usefulness of premiums had been well established.

Naturally, the example set by *David Harum* was followed by other serials. Only a few producers, however, allowed their programs to serve primarily as vehicles for giveaways in the manner of the Jones-Hummert combination for *Harum*, or for their later joint efforts, *Lora Lawton* and *Nona from Nowhere*. At one time a horse was given away each week on *David Harum*, but most of the offers were of small objects. In the spring of 1940, for example, flower seeds were the lure on *Ellen Randolph, Woman in White, Ma Perkins, Myrt and Marge*, and *Aunt Jenny's True Life Stories*. Other offerings that spring were Libby glasses, recipe books, and jewelry.

Jewelry was used often because brooches and pins could so easily be worked into the stories themselves, thereby increasing response. One day shortly before an offer was to be announced, the heroine could be expected to exhibit the item proudly. Then her acquaintances would admire it ad nauseum for several episodes, one of them, perhaps, becoming so enamored of the object as to filch it, precipitating an extended search until it was returned to the bosom of its rightful owner. When the moment was right, the announcer asked the listeners whether they would not like to have a pin or brooch just like the one in the story. The dimes and labels poured in.

Somehow, in dramas intended for adults, schemes of this sort seemed out of place. Many serial makers never employed them, keeping premium pitches, if any, outside the story. In the juvenile thrillers the integrated offers could be regarded as good fun. The telescopes, periscopes, and decoders fit naturally into the stories—which, of course, were for boys and girls, not adults, anyway. But when the characters of daytime serials rattled on about the beauty and artisanship of dime-store articles crudely jammed into the narratives, not only was the writing of questionable quality but a general contempt for the intelligence of the audience seemed to be revealed.

Such a disregard for the serial listener's acumen can readily be explained. No one knew who really listened to daytime dramas or why. In the formative period between 1932 and 1937 no formal research study of the daytime serial drama or its audience was made. Not until 1935 did researchers even begin gathering material for such a study, and not until 1939 did a significant report of the findings appear. Soap-opera research in the early years was confined to program ratings (sketchy in the daytime until 1936) and analysis of listener mail. Ratings and letters resulting from premium offers were primarily quantitative measures. They provided little more than names and numbers. Only the letters that came in without solicitation, the so-called fan mail, offered much in the way of qualitative information. But measures of this sort have little validity. A letter may tell quite a bit about the individual writer, but not whether that writer is representative of the whole, or even the majority. As an indication of the over-all daytime serial audience, fan mail proved seriously misleading.

Too much attention was given in those early days to naïve responses. Letters warning the heroine of impending danger, or revealing the identity of a murderer "heard in the act," did not paint an elevating picture of the serial audience. Nonetheless, such letters were encouraging to those producers who designed their programs for listeners of the lowest social and educational levels. Disregarding the device of sampling, these producers accepted the ingenuous letters as proof of their unflattering concept of the daytime-serial audience. Proper evidence, alas, came too late.

In the 1940s formal research revealed no typical soap-opera listener. The serial audience, though mostly made up of women, was not of a single educational, psychological, or sociological level. Rather, it came reasonably close to the statistical profile of American women in general. The female population was about equally divided between listeners and nonlisteners, with no significant differences discernible between or within the two groups.[2]

The "typical soap-opera listener" was—and is—a convenient fiction. By the time research findings came along to dispel it, the world of the radio serial and its critics was too fixed to be easily altered. Uninspired dramas were camped on too many corners and imaginative writers were giving up trying to dislodge them. A comfortable status quo made adjusting to research data seem like tampering. Was any study sufficient basis for meddling with or replacing a long-running show, no matter how artistically absurd the critics considered it? Not many producers or advertisers thought so.

Only the serial giants had much opportunity to work with unfamiliar ideas. Even they were not immune to stumbling. In 1936, nine months after *Pepper Young's Family* moved to the daytime, Elaine Carrington entered into a venture called the *Heinz Magazine of the Air*. Her serial, *Trouble House*, was part

[2] The first generally published research regarding the daytime serial was the Princeton Radio Project, supervised by H. M. Beville; *Social Stratification of the Radio Audience* (1939). In 1943 appeared Leda P. Summers' *Daytime Serials and Iowa Women*, the Blue Network's *A Survey of Daytime Radio Listening Habits*, and the Herta Herzog–Helen Kaufman–Rudolf Arnheim analyses in Paul Lazarsfeld's *Radio Research 1942–1943*. Francis Wilder's compilation of Elmo Roper's data, *Radio's Daytime Serial*, appeared in 1945.

Collectively, the studies detected no significant difference between serial listeners and nonlisteners in age, attitude toward family, residence, concern with public affairs, income, education, cultural attainments, personality, social participation, range of intellectual interests, or extent of worrying. Serials tended to be more popular with women of lower income and education, and among farm women, but not significantly so.

While preferences for certain serials among different groups were shown, the Beville and Summers studies suggested that those preferences were not linked to the sex or age of the leading character, the comedy relief, the amount of suspense, the socioeconomic level of the principals, or the age and literary level of the dramas. Incidentally, the Roper survey indicated that 75 per cent of the respondents who regularly listened to the daytime serials thought that they were true to life.

of a larger program containing music and interviews that was heard for half an hour, three days a week. Celebrities of the stature of Theodore Dreiser, Amelia Earhart, and Lillian Gish appeared as guests. B. A. Rolfe was there with his orchestra, and Delmar Edmondson served as "editor."

Within five months of its initial appearance, the radio magazine was voted the best women's program in a Scripps-Howard poll of 252 radio editors. Audiences were meeting the renowned of many fields at the rate of two a broadcast: Emily Post, Walter Hampden, Lawrence Stallings, Faith Baldwin, Fannie Hurst, Christopher Morley, Osa Johnson, Dale Carnegie, the Grand Duchess Marie, Cholly Knickerbocker, Alexander Woollcott, William Lyon Phelps, Lou Little, Dorothy Canfield Fisher, Beatrice Fairfax, John Mason Brown, Angelo Patri, Gelett Burgess, and Stephen Vincent Benét. The guest list seemed endless. The program was not. It was off the air about a year after the editors' poll.

Perhaps it was all too much for the housewife, who had too many things to do between 11:00 and 11:30 in the morning to sit down and digest the remarks of William Lyon Phelps. Moreover, the interviews were not spontaneous. The guests, many of whom had books to plug, worked from full scripts, and sometimes were confounded by last-minute deletions (Dreiser merely ignored them). A few personalities were terrified by the microphone, and yet had to undergo a rebroadcast for the West Coast. One of these double sufferers became so confused that he read his quivering script backwards, starting at the third page and working back to the first. Another dignitary forgot about the second broadcast and was on board a train for home when the show came along. John Reed King did a masterful emergency impersonation of the absent-minded notable (a professor, naturally).

Somewhere in the middle of the music and talk came Mrs. Carrington's serial, which was supposed to keep the women listening from broadcast to broadcast. The task was not enviable. The opposition programing on NBC included *David Harum*, *Backstage Wife*, *The O'Neills*, and later *Road of Life*. Each of these programs was on the rise at the time. Moreover they were presented each weekday, not just on Mondays, Wednesdays, and Fridays. In sustaining a daytime audience, the daily-broadcast pattern was almost essential. Habit was part of it, but even if a listener did not or could not tune in each day, she preferred not to have to stop and think: "It is Wednesday or Thursday? If it's Wednesday, I can hear a good show on CBS now. If it's Thursday, they'll have that awful cooking talk. . . . Or is the cooking show on Wednesday and the one I like on Thursday?" Experienced daytime planners rarely required this kind of decision making of the housewife. They knew that, "Tune in tomorrow, same time, same station," was more than a catchy tag line.

The *Heinz Magazine of the Air* did not need additional difficulties to overcome, but it had them. The program inherited only a modest audience from the broadcast that preceded it (a news commentary), while *David Harum* was picking up many listeners who stayed tuned following the popular *Today's Children*. And, most telling of all, *David Harum* and the other competing serials cost much less to produce than the Heinz show. The food company was underwriting a program expensive by daytime standards, yet, by its nature, presumably of greatest appeal to the smallest segment of the available audience (those on higher socioeconomic levels). The return, apparently, was not worth the price—at least for a sponsor who was not catering to a select group of customers. After *Trouble House* came to an end and was replaced by a new story, the omnibus concept was abandoned. Only the serial remained. What had begun as the *Heinz Magazine of the Air* passed its last months as *Carol Kennedy's Romance*. It had tried to satisfy a wide range of tastes and in the end pleased no one. Yet neither it nor the magazine format had been given a fair test.

In later years the magazine-of-the-air idea did meet success. Kate Smith made it work on radio and television. The early morning *Today* program, the shorter-lived *Home* show, and even the *Mickey Mouse Club* were close to the Heinz pattern. While neither *Today* nor *Home* used drama, Disney was successful in blending the adventure serial with the music, dancing, variety acts, cartoons, and educational features of his five-day-a-week series. Miss Smith, on the other hand, found the domestic serial not too compatible with the magazine approach.

Somehow the daytime serial always has done best without encumbrance, in the simplest of production settings. It never has survived as a hybrid, nor when it has been set in a fancy garden. But those are minor limitations, for it needs no special nourishment and, once rooted, will bring forth blossom year after year with a minimum of care and expense. Only once has the daytime serial shown the effects of blight. And then the fault, as we are about to see, lay not in the seed but in the sowing.

TOO MANY SERIALS

He who desires only what is enough, is troubled neither by raging seas, nor hail-smitten vineyards, nor an unproductive farm.

HORACE, *Odes*

Early in 1937 another durable veteran of evening radio, *Myrt and Marge*, turned up in the afternoon. It was a transfusion daytime radio no longer really needed, for veteran vaudevillian Myrtle Vail's saga of an older showgirl (Myrt) and her daughter-protégée (Marge) was followed in the next five years by seventy-three new soap operas, all of them sponsored and all on network radio. Swelling the ranks of these dramas was an indeterminate number of sustaining, local, regional, and syndicated serial productions.

Soon casual listeners were wondering whether network radio offered anything but soap operas while the sun shone. In the spring of 1941, between ten in the morning and six in the evening, eastern standard time, a woman's serial could be heard during all but a single quarter-hour (from 5:30 to 5:45—*Jack Armstrong's* time period—was the time of grace). In twenty-six of the thirty-two quarter-hour periods at least two serials were available. In six time periods there were three serials. What is more, because each network gave way to local programing at various hours, there were times when the only network offerings were soap operas—sixteen such times, as a matter of fact. To that extent, the casual listener's wonderment had foundation. For the equivalent of four hours a day it was serial drama or nothing on the networks.

Figures regarding sponsorship were equally one-sided. The 135 quarter-hour segments devoted to sponsored daytime serials in January, 1937, rose to 285 in January, 1940, and to 290 in January, 1941. In 1940 and 1941 nine of every ten sponsored network programs in the daytime were serial dramas.

Naturally, this phenomenal increase in soap operas did not go unchallenged, even in the trade magazines. In April, 1939, *Broadcasting*, though not antiserial, suggested that networks were playing follow-the-leader, making every day washday. Still, it expressed confidence that poise, more subtle selling, and diversity would come to daytime radio as they had come to nighttime broadcasting. In the following December, *Broadcasting* continued to hold strong hope for diversification in daytime programing and noted, in an editorial titled "Frankenstein," that there now were signs of listener dissatisfaction.

The signs that *Broadcasting* perceived were coming mainly from New Rochelle, New York, where, in November, 1939, six hundred women at a woman's club forum had voted to urge the networks to broadcast fewer "love dramas." The note had come after home economist Ida Bailey Allen complained that, of the 378 broadcasting hours on the three major chains, only 45 minutes were spent on what she called problems of the home.

Soon the New Rochelle women had begun mobilizing for action. They announced an "I'm Not Listening" campaign, hoping that the movement would spread throughout Westchester County and New York and across the United States. By March, 1940, the movement had gained sufficient strength to merit a broadcasting symposium in Westchester County, at which the campaign chairman, Mrs. Everett L. Barnard, proudly reported that women in thirty-nine states were not listening (skeptics suggested that they may not have been listening even before the campaign began).

The broadcasting industry took enough note of the ladies' protest to send an executive to face them at their symposium. Donald S. Shaw, principal vice-president of WMCA, New York, made the trip to New Rochelle. Softening his audience by referring to daytime serials as "dripping love dramas," he reminded them that broadcasters had to make a profit and that serials brought in money to pay for worthwhile sustaining programs. Then, somewhat embarrassed, Shaw mentioned a research study conducted by a leading soap company which had found that (1) the radio public listened to serials and (2) serials sold soap.

On seeing the group's reaction to that news, a lesser man might have withdrawn, but Shaw attempted to divert the concern of the group to something that could cause it to forget about serials. Comic books, the radio executive suggested, were far more offensive than soap operas could possibly be. And, as everyone knew, comic books were read by *children*. . . . The broadcaster returned to New York confident of a job well done.

Broadcasting's response to the "I'm Not Listening" campaign was a statement that it was foolish to charge broadcasters of foisting upon the public programs it did not like. After all, it commented, the criticism came from an audience "substantially above average." Clubwomen were not representative serial listeners, the magazine continued, and they did not constitute buyers of the products advertised in soap operas. One thing was certain, observed *Broadcasting*: soap companies were not spending their money foolishly.

Not everything said about the daytime serial in the land-rush period was negative in tone. Stuart Metz, the announcer of *Pepper Young's Family*, defended the programs against radio writer Arch Oboler's charge that serial actors could not live their parts. In a letter to the *New York Times*, Metz countered that the unhurried serial gait allowed actors to live their roles as they could in no other medium.

Another defender, serial heroine Bess Johnson, acknowledged that it was smart to laugh at washboard weepers. Nevertheless, she considered them healthy forms of escape (a conclusion which research studies later supported). Miss Johnson assumed that women never would be able to resist backyard gossip and wondered whether soap operas did not provide a harmless alternative, meanwhile allowing the housewife an escape from household trials.

Variety offered a limited defense of the daytime serial in 1941. In what may have been interpreted as damning with faint praise, it commented that serials were better in script, directing, and acting than they had been "a year or two back." The improvements noted by *Variety* actually were refinements in production techniques. For example, in 1936 actors commonly rehearsed for two hours in preparation for a single episode. Two or three years later the rehearsal time had been cut in half, without loss of quality—in fact, the performance was likely to be better.

Gordon Hughes, who directed *The Story of Mary Marlin, The Guiding Light,* and many other serials, has recalled that in the early days it was difficult to obtain enough competent actors. The inexperience of many performers made the long rehearsal time necessary. Too, scripts often needed last-minute revision— and sometimes turned out to be too short, in which case the harried actors were forced to ad-lib to fill in the time. In one instance a lost script was rewritten while the program was on the air and brought into the studio a page at a time.

As the actors' skills developed, less time was needed to polish an episode. Before long a small group of veteran serial performers gathered, first in Chicago and then in New York. They moved from studio to studio, often shifting character types with each move. To them the telephone was almost as important as the microphone, for it brought urgent calls to new roles.

Although the full schedules of the veteran actors allowed little time for rehearsal, producers were willing to sacrifice rehearsal time in order to benefit from the talents of the seasoned performers, most of whom could move into their parts almost instantly. In serials the actors knew their characters so well that they needed only a brief run-through.

Another reason for production streamlining was the establishment in 1937 of the American Federation of Radio Artists. Before AFRA was formed, it was common for actors to receive less than ten dollars for a serial performance. Some actors were willing to work without any pay in order to establish themselves. In addition, kickbacks in exchange for roles were common. By 1939 the AFRA regulations were requiring that an actor be paid fifteen dollars for a single serial appearance, plus five to six dollars for the first hour of rehearsal. Additional rehearsal brought the performer three dollars an hour. Although producers could receive slight discounts on the basic fee if they employed an actor for thirteen weeks, the rehearsal fees encouraged them to minimize the amount of time used for practicing and further encouraged the use of experienced performers.

The Hummert production agency is said to have been the principal cause of the union's creation; certainly it battled AFRA until 1939. In point of fact, however, the agency's costs did not rise appreciably under AFRA rules, for the regular Hummert performers always had been reasonably well paid for performance. The Hummerts saved on rehearsal costs by careful casting.

Union problems and all, the Hummerts brought twenty-two new serials to the networks between 1937 and 1942. Although their entire 1939 crop—six programs—failed, in each of the other years they introduced one or more long-lasting shows: *Our Gal Sunday, Lorenzo Jones,* and *Arnold Grimm's Daughter* in 1937; *Valiant Lady, Young Widder Brown, Stella Dallas,* and *Houseboat Hannah* in 1938; *Amanda of Honeymoon Hill, Light of the World,* and *Lone Journey* in 1940; and *Front Page Farrell* in 1941.

Many years before all this—in 1904, as a matter of fact—Ethel Barrymore had improvised a curtain line for a popular play in which she was appearing: "That's all there is, there isn't any more." As far as the play, *Sunday*, was concerned, Miss Barrymore was correct; there wasn't any more. But in *Our Gal Sunday* the Hummerts continued the story from the point at which the play left off. First, however, they retraced the familiar story of the orphan girl named Sunday, who was reared by two miners in Cripple Creek, Colorado, and then married a titled Englishman, Lord Henry Brinthrope. Each weekday for more than twenty years the strains of "Red River Valley" introduced another episode in Sunday's struggle to find happiness as the wife of a handsome aristocrat—a jealous one at that. Somehow she found herself in the same veil of suspicion more times than anyone can remember (or would wish to).

For the most part *Our Gal Sunday* was written in somewhat routine fashion by someone on the Hummert staff. At times, however, it rose distinctly above its usual level. One such time was the Christmas broadcast of 1941, in which Sunday read a fairy story to her two adopted children. *Variety* called the episode "a memorable example of how impressive commercial drama can be, but rarely is."

Variety's praise for the episode suggests that Frank and Anne Hummert were quite capable of producing serials of quality—and indeed they were. Their *Lone Journey*, written by the most honored of all daytime serial writers, Sandra Michael, was one of those distinguished failures that are called artistic successes. Collaborating with Miss Michael in the writing of *Lone Journey* were her sister, Gerda, and her brother, Peter. The quality of the drama was apparent from beginning to end. The closing narration was not a curiosity-baiting catchall, but something that rounded off the day's drama in exquisite manner:

> Henry's voice echoed happily in the still, cold air. Sydney left her baking and came hurrying out of the house, and together they stood listening for the faraway sound of Mel's car. Soon from the direction of the Double Spear T came the signal of several short, cheerful blasts of the car horn.
>
> Sydney and her Uncle Henry smiled and nodded quickly. Wolfe had come home. In a bare tree just beyond the porch, Mr. Olsen, the magpie, scolded in jealous annoyance at not being noticed. Sydney ran into the house and came back to give him an

outrageously big helping of his favorite feed. Holiday warmth and excitement spread in great waves, from the oven within doors, to include the yard, the ranch, and the whole valley under the peaceful sky of a November afternoon.

Another atypical Hummert serial was *Lorenzo Jones* (1937), one of their few comedies. In its earlier years it did, as it claimed, contain more smiles than tears. Lorenzo was an impractical inventor who dreamed his way through life while his understanding wife, Belle, struggled with the problems of everyday life he seldom noticed. Lorenzo's thoughts rested upon more important things—the three-spouted teapot, for instance. One spout was for strong tea, one for medium, and one for weak. Like most of Jones's ideas, it did not work out, but the happy-go-lucky inventor was not dismayed. He went on to a new gadget, a perpetual foot warmer. That one he managed to sell, only to misplace the money in a vase in his living room.

In its later years *Lorenzo Jones* lost its humorous touch and became melodrama. Troubles more typical of the serial world came to the once-happy tinkerer in Jim Barker's garage. In the fall of 1952, Lorenzo, kidnaped and wounded by confederates of some jewel thieves he had helped capture, awoke in a New York hospital with the classic amnesia. Soon he was wandering here and there taking odd jobs, a sad circumstance for an undiscovered genius who a few years earlier had hoped to interest a movie studio in his life story, *Lorenzo Jones the Man*. For two years the amnesia persisted, as Lorenzo almost went to the altar with Gail Maddox, a deed that would have made him soap opera's first bigamist. Only intervention from on high could save him from further woe, and it came in 1955, when NBC cut back on the number of its serials, bringing Lorenzo's agonies to a merciful end.

The alteration of the Jones image may have been the unavoidable consequence of following *Stella Dallas* around for his last seventeen years. After that much time melodrama was bound to creep across the 4:30 station break and engulf Lorenzo. Assuredly Olive Higgins Prouty's old tearjerker, refurbished for radio, had melodrama to spare. Picking up the plot where it had ended in the successful Barbara Stanwyck film of 1937, the Hummert's made *Stella Dallas* a tribute to both the sacrificial nature and the sheer resourcefulness of the all-American mother. The new Stella could, while bound, escape entrapment in a skyscraper by dangling darning thread she had extracted from her purse until it attracted the attention of a passer-by far below. This bit of ingenuity preceded a rescue from gangsters of her daughter, Laurel, a damsel also prone to abduction by lustful sheiks. (Stella, it may be recalled, stunned Ahmed the lecherous by reaching his seraglio via submarine.)

Differing from Ma Perkins in her approach to problem solving as Superman would from Sherlock Holmes, Mrs. Dallas used a go-get-'em attack that defied resistance. She could help an injured pilot nurse an airliner to the ground against one-hundred-to-one odds or escape enchainment to a tree in "darkest Africa" and continue her hunt for rare orchids. Stella's protection was not restricted to the addlepated Laurel but embraced all little people, as well as rich ones she thought might see the light. Son-in-law Richard Grosvenor was in the latter group, especially when "wealthy but insane" Ada Dexter was on the prowl. In her book *Tune In Tomorrow* serial veteran Mary Jane Higby has recalled the day Mad Ada and her chauffeur raced to the golf links to drop the unsuspecting Dick with her elephant gun. It looked as though not even Stella Dallas could get a warning to him in time—that is, until she appropriated a sound truck and rolled over the greens thundering, "Dick Grosvenor, take cover!"

Stella Dallas was afternoon drama for the poor and forgotten —and for anyone else who could accept the Amazonian heroics. Harder to accept, though, was the ceaseless maternal involvement by one who had (in the daily words of announcer Ford Bond) "decided to go out of her [daughter's] life forever." The sacrificial involvement seemed to boil over when Stella huskily breathed her name of endearment for her grown offspring. "Lolly-Baby," as crooned by actress Anne Elstner in her Stella Dallas voice, was a thing not easily expunged from memory. The delivery could have been matched only by the mature Tallulah Bankhead, or, perhaps, Tex Ritter.[1]

Much in contrast to the plebeian Stella and Lorenzo Jones were the leading characters introduced in the late 1930s by Irna Phillips. *Today's Children* had gone, replaced by Miss Phillips in 1938 when the death of her mother left her without inspiration for Mother Moran. The year before, with the unpublicized aid of assistant writers, she had begun *Road of Life* and *The Guiding Light* (from which *The Right to Happiness* evolved in 1939). In these serials Irna Phillips presented a new soap-opera protagonist: the professional person. Originally most serial principals had been simple people with little higher education. Although frequently involved in the most romantic of situations or married to people of wealth or importance, they remained plain folk whose business or personal success came not from special advantage but from inherent ability. Naturally, attorneys and physicians appeared at one time or another, but their professions remained secondary to the home-centered plots.

Irna Phillips, who had always seemed to be leaning in that direction, brought the professional life to the fore. Dr. Rutledge of *The Guiding Light* was a highly trained minister whose pastoral study became a focal point of the drama. Dr. Jim Brent of *Road of Life* brought with him to the serial world the crises and intrigues of the hospital milieu. Rutledge and Brent soon were followed by a flock of trained and dedicated men and women with whom they could be professionally and socially comfortable. There were doctors (*Joyce Jordan: Girl Interne*— later *M.D.*; *Young Dr. Malone*; *The Life and Loves of Dr. Su-*

[1] Although Miss Elstner coarsened her voice and enunciation for the role of Stella Dallas, she has several times expressed the conviction that she won the part because she sounded more like Barbara Stanwyck of the film version than did any of her two-dozen competitors. The actress first achieved radio prominence with a much different characterization, that of Cracker Gaddis in the evening serial of the 1930s *Moonshine and Honeysuckle*. In the years since 1955, when the wild melodrama of Stella Dallas was brought to an end by NBC, Miss Elstner has enjoyed meeting thousands of former listeners at the restaurant she and her husband (Jack Matthews) operate in an old mill at the edge of the Delaware River. On special request she will resurrect the Dallas voice to say, "Lolly-Baby, I ain't got no time for nothin' but trouble!"

san), nurses (*Kate Hopkins: Angel of Mercy* and Miss Phillips' own *Woman in White*), lawyers (*Portia Faces Life*; *Terry Regan: Attorney of Law*; and *Her Honor, Nancy James*), social workers (*Hilltop House* and *The Story of Bess Johnson*), educators (*Against the Storm* and *We the Abbotts*). All these dramas had appeared by 1941, seven of them by the end of 1938.

The professional person gave some plausibility to the unusual doings of soap operas. What was more natural than for physicians or attorneys to become involved in one interesting situation after another? At the same time, nothing prevented these characters from encountering the problems of private life that befell the nonprofessional principals of other serials. The latter set of problems lay within a housewife's range of experience, the former she could now encounter by surrogate.

The rise of the new heroes and heroines did not lead to the extinction of the already established types. Writers continued to introduce serials about everyday families, problem husbands, and simple but resourceful women. Allowing for a bit more erudition, there were even some new homemade philosophers in the daytime serial's second five years. Scattergood Baines, distrustful of city slickers and the overeducated, was closest to the old school, but Clarence Budington Kelland's familiar Vermonter of magazine fiction was not a radio fixture as long as was Parson Rutledge—or the kindliest of all daytime sages, Papa David Solomon of *Life Can Be Beautiful* (known in the industry as "Elsie Beebe").

The difficulties untangled by the gentle proprietor of the Slightly Read Book Shop generally had fallen upon his word, Chichi, who stumbled into his tiny island of serenity within the city one day and never really departed. Papa David's optimistic philosophy, warmly set forth by Carl Bixby and Don Becker and spoken by Ralph Locke, helped Chichi believe, though not immutably, that life indeed could be beautiful.[2]

As Scattergood Baines was the conscience of a village and

---

[2] Occasionally the Bixby-Becker philosophy went awry because of a script-reading lapse. On January 20, 1943, Papa David advised, "Love ain't something you can throw out of your heart like bucket from a water."

Papa David that of a metropolis, Dr. Rutledge represented the spiritual strength of suburbia. *The Guiding Light* was enacted in the city of Five Points, where the pastor's charge was a neighborhood church, on whose organ the show's musical backgrounds supposedly were played by the parson's daughter. On important holidays there were special programs, the traditional Good Friday message, "Seven Last Words," being repeated year after year, even after the drama became a television series. By that time, however, most of the original characters, including Dr. Rutledge, had disappeared. Only the organ music remained from the old days—maddeningly so. No program in heaven or earth could match *The Guiding Light* in ominous chords, stings, and cadences.

The market in family sagas had been so well cornered by *Pepper Young's Family*, *The Goldbergs*, and *The O'Neills* that prewar introductions in this area never caught on. One, *The Andersons*, was characterized by *Variety* as "a first class example of a vacuum wedded to static." Other forgotten family dramas were *Those Happy Gilmans* and *Your Family and Mine* of 1938, *The Carters of Elm Street* of 1939, *We the Abbotts* of 1940, and *The Bartons* and *The Johnson Family*, two comedy serials of 1941. Of these, *The Johnson Family* was clearly the most novel. A single actor, Jimmy Scribner, played all twenty-one characters. Less novel, yet still interesting as an idea, was *Margo of Castlewood* (1938). Margo was a seventy-nine-year-old matriarch of the Carver family. Playing opposite Barbara Luddy in the title role was Francis X. Bushman, making a comeback on radio. Margo never made eighty.

In display of marital difficulties *Our Gal Sunday* was, of course, the unchallenged drama of the period. Others in the *Betty and Bob* tradition were *When a Girl Marries* (written by Elaine Carrington), *Midstream*, *The Man I Married* (a Bixby-Becker show starring Van Heflin), and *The Trouble with Marriage*, all of 1939; *Amanda of Honeymoon Hill*, of 1940; and *Helpmate*, of 1941. Two serials of 1938 whose titles precisely indicated the source of the nuptial discord were *Stepmother* and

Mother-in-Law. The mother-in-law—not surprisingly in a program intended for women—was treated sympathetically.

After the appearance of Helen Trent, no serial motif was more in evidence than that featuring a woman alone against the world, be she married, single, divorced, or widowed. Three young unmarried heroines of 1937–38 were *Pretty Kitty Kelly, Jane Arden,* and *Kitty Keene.* Miss Arden, it may be remembered, was a comic-strip character created by Monte Barrett. The girl reporter with the trim and frequently displayed figure was also the subject of a motion picture in 1939. The microphone, however, was insensitive to trim figures. Jane Arden's soap-opera career was fleeting. The two Kittys—measurements unknown—were gone before 1942.

Three other single girls were part of the Mutual Network's attempt to break into the daytime-serial market in 1941 with shows beamed from affiliated stations. The girls were heard in *Edith Adams' Future; Helen Holden: Government Girl;* and *I'll find My Way.* Neither the programs nor Mutual's attempt succeeded. The never-married heroine was simply a poor risk as a daytime-serial protagonist. But then, there were not many of them. *Girl Alone* and *Big Sister,* two of the handful who made it, managed to do so by marrying shortly after their 1936 debuts.

If the leading lady of a soap opera was single at a given time, one could assume that she was a widow. It was most unlikely that she was divorced or never had wed. Perhaps the most difficult thing to reconcile with the sweet-sixteen behavior of many a serial heroine was her earlier romantic involvement with at least one man. From a biological standpoint, the virginal heroine was rarely to be found in the daytime serial. From a behavioral standpoint, she was ever present. Although once she had been married, perhaps to a less than admirable male, nothing in her actions suggested she had known even puppy love. (Helen Trent wilted one fiancé pro tem by telling him that an engagement ring did not give him the right to hold her hand.) Too often the unattached soap-opera heroine displayed the innocence of a maiden when it was clearly absurd, and possibly dishonest, for her to do so.

317

The number of widowed heroines, by the way, was startling. Twenty-five years after the introduction of Helen Trent, each of the unmarried leading ladies of her network (CBS) had lost one or more husbands. Often the widowhood was discernible only after patient listening. But sometimes the serial had as its foundation the problems that face a widow, particularly a widow with children. There were advantages in having a widowed heroine. She had once faced the problems of marriage—just as the housewife listeners were doing at the moment—yet she was free to follow a career or find romance as a single woman.

Not all the serial females had the clear path of the young widow, of course. Some were trapped by circumstances or drawn by duty. Stella Dallas was one of these noble souls. Others of her age or older were found in *Hilltop House, Woman of Courage, Mother o' Mine,* and *Houseboat Hannah.* Hannah O'Leary's husband had lost his arm in a cannery accident, and so the O'Leary's home became a houseboat in San Francisco's Shanty-Fish Row. There the good woman tried to find happiness and security for her family.

Houseboat Hannah was first heard coast to coast in 1936 by means of electrical transcriptions distributed to local stations, a procedure used with such programs as *Linda's First Love* and *Mary Foster, the Editor's Daughter.* Transcribed dramas could be popular in some areas and completely unknown in others. Rarely did they receive publicity on a national level, and few of them were elevated as *Houseboat Hannah* was by NBC in 1938.

Hilltop House, written originally by Addy Richton and Lynn Stone, was the story of an orphanage directress. Edward Wolf, who packaged the program for Palmolive, freed the writers from many of the conventions of the daytime serial, and they responded with a drama of better-than-average literary quality. The program was a vehicle for actress Bess Johnson, whose name was used for the character she played. Miss Johnson, a convincing impersonator of Lady Esther in cosmetics commercials, had played one of the daytime serial's first career women, Fran Moran of *Today's Children*.

This warm-voiced actress and *Hilltop House* were involved in an odd bit of maneuvering in 1941, when Palmolive changed advertising firms. The new agency preferred low production cost to quality drama, yet did not wish to lose the commercial appeal of Bess Johnson. Wolf, to his credit, had no intention to let *Hilltop House* become a cut-rate show. Instead, he chose to remove it from the air. Thus, on Friday, March 28, 1941, Bess Johnson left her beloved orphanage. The next Monday, same time, same network, same sponsor, she was driving down the road from Hilltop House toward new adventure as a character in a new daytime serial drama. In the soap opera's ultimate example of character identification, an actress named Bess Johnson was starring in a series entitled *The Story of Bess Johnson*.

More in the good old descriptive tradition were the titles of two dramas about women who, though married, were still alone. The shows were *Valiant Lady* and *The Right to Happiness*. Joan Barrett Scott of *Valiant Lady* faced sufficient adversity to deserve her title. In 1941 her husband, Dr. Truman (Tubby) Scott, was suffering from brain damage. Nevertheless, as *Movie-Radio Guide* faithfully reported, Joan, "a devoted wife, a valiant lady," was determined to stay with her husband and "try to right the wrongs he is doing." The news was reassuring.

Carolyn of *The Right to Happiness*, the most-married heroine of soap-opera land, faced similar difficulties with husband after husband. In 1952, while exhausting husband number three, Governor Miles Nelson, she made herself an inmate of a women's prison. It was her way of saving her mate from political ruin. The governor, understandably, did not immediately comprehend her sacrifice.

This woman's earlier way of life was less than wholesome and had to be improved to promote listener identification. Max Wylie, who once plotted the program, remembered that she killed one husband, divorced another, and gave birth to a child in the state penitentiary. She spent most of her later serial days worry-

319

ing about the behavior of her teenage offspring, while picking up a husband or lover here and there. Somehow, Victor Moore stumbled into the series late in 1957, playing a whimsical artist. Carolyn let him get away.

More often than not, a daytime serial woman alone was a good business manager. Ellen Brown, of the durable drama *Young Widder Brown* (1938), ran a tearoom. What is more, she ran it despite a distracting love life in which every conceivable obstacle prevented her from marrying the ever-patient Dr. Anthony Loring.

Jenny Peabody (1937) was versatility personified. She was the proprietor of a small hotel, owner of a general store, and postmistress of Hillsdale. The heroine of *Caroline's Golden Store* (1939) was another small-town merchant. Connie Vance of *My Son and I*, the young widow of her vaudeville partner, had to account for every penny as she struggled to make a living for herself and her young son.

The peak of feminine resourcefulness during this period may have been reached by Connie Tremaine of *Arnold Grimm's Daughter* (1937). When her husband died, she opened a lingerie shop. Nothing extraordinary there. But when her father was taken ill, Connie came through, like the heroine of a Red Chinese movie, stepping into Daddy's place at the factory. Moreover, with true spirit she designed a new stove that put the factory back on its feet.

In mentioning resourceful women, we must not forget Portia Blake of *Portia Faces Life* (1940), the most successful female attorney of the daytime serial. She was married to, but did not get much help from, Walter Manning, whose main functions were to create problems for Portia to solve and simply to go away, leaving the lady more or less a widow.

To tell the truth, Walter probably went away in discouragement. Portia, like many a serial heroine, was too much for even a strong male. And strong males did not appear too often during the first quarter-century of the daytime serial drama. Although the men of the soap opera were successful (most of the time) in their businesses or professions, they usually lagged a step or two behind their women in strength of personality. The heroines were largely perfect, with the exception of a few pleasantly feminine characteristics; the men, not really heroes, nearly always lacked some virtue or desirable attribute. They were excessively jealous or unduly attracted to other women or unstable or indecisive. The resulting impression was one of masculine weakness—or, at least, one of feminine superiority.

Often the male principal was placed in a position of weakness by a crippling disease or injury. Thus, in the spring of 1958, Gil Whitney lay seriously wounded in a hospital bed while Helen Trent sought his assailant. That was ten years after James Thurber had called the man in the wheel chair the standard daytime serial "symbol of the American male's subordination to the female and his dependence on her great strength of heart and soul."

Indeed, in the golden days of the radio serial it was difficult to find a program in which one husband or lover had not suffered some affliction of the lower extremities. Stephen Hamilton of *Life Can Be Beautiful* was a classic case. A man unable to walk, he was given a job in the bookshop by Papa David. The novice bookseller was resigned to life in a wheel chair until Chichi appeared. She gave him the incentive to try an operation that restored his mobility. Ah, but he was not to be a walking male long. While saving Chichi in an accident, he was crippled once more. Emasculation and impotency were the words critics and researchers used in commenting upon the symbolic meaning of injuries such as Hamilton's.

About all that can be said for the unfortunate male of the soap opera is that his lot improved over the years. Women achieved a great amount of independence during World War II. That independence was reflected in the serials, albeit at glacier pace. Julie Stevens (Helen Trent for sixteen years) commented in 1954 that daytime dramas were adapting to the times. This star of perhaps the most backward of all serials noted that women were better informed and more active in world affairs than they had been when serials began. Disappearing, she thought, were the "gumptionless" men who always needed help from women. Alas, they never quite disappeared from *The Romance of Helen Trent,* mad schemers excepted.[3]

This comment leads one to the inevitable exceptions to the generalization. Throughout the radio serial era two groups of male characters did exhibit strength: the villains and the patriarchs. The villains, it must be admitted, had moral deficiencies. And seldom were they three-dimensional characters. Nevertheless, they were far more interesting than most of the male leads, who did not have much to recommend them except mellow voices and, from what the listener was told, good looks.

The elderly patriarchs, such as Papa David, Bill Davidson, and David Harum, heading consanguineous or adopted clans, dispensed wisdom and advice that even heroines needed on occasion. It is interesting to note that these men had feminine counterparts of equal ability, Ma Perkins in particular. In truth, it is difficult to decide whether Bill Davidson was a male Ma Perkins or Ma Perkins was a female Bill Davidson. The actions of the patriarchs and matriarchs were largely neuter in gender.

Despite the general male weakness in soap land, a surprising number of male protagonists turned up during the five years before World War II, largely, it would seem, because of their occupational status. Physicians Brent and Malone and attorney Terry Regan were joined by the cub reporter of *The Affairs of Anthony* (1939), by a rancher-architect in *Lone Journey* (1940), by a serious composer working as a cab driver in Mutual's *We Are Always Young* (1941), by an army recruit in *Buck Private and His Girl* (1941), and by a vagabond singer in *Bright Horizon* (1941).

And we must not forget that prime specimen of masculine strength and resolve in America at the time, *Li'l Abner.* He came along in 1940 but departed almost as soon as he arrived. The

---

[3] Fifteen years after Miss Stevens made her statement, a new television serial introduced just the kind of weak male that could have been expected in the days of the radio serial but was rarer in television. Roy in CBS-TV's *Where the Heart Is* admitted to the program's good woman, Kate, that he was "an alcoholic, a weakling, and a coward." On October 20, 1969, Kate reviewed Roy's admission while trying to comfort him, praised him for confessing his faults, and patiently began her efforts to reconstruct him. Roy thanked Kate for her assurances that he could make a new start but cautioned, "Don't count on it."

ladies could not tolerate a male with Abner Yokum's independence for very long. In fact, they did not have much to do with most of the male protagonists, save for those of *Road of Life* and *Young Dr. Malone* and possibly *Bright Horizon*. The last-named program was a companion to the older *Big Sister*, borrowing as its lead character a young man named Michael West. Ruth Wayne (Big Sister) was woven into the new drama for a short time to help it get started. Later, a number of well-known individuals appeared playing themselves, among them Burl Ives and Risë Stevens.

The five years preceding World War II were years not only of accelerated serial growth but also of modest experimentation. That was the time when soap-opera makers explored the possibilities in the Bible, in the mystery story, and in tales that actually came to an end. No new trend resulted from this exploration, but a touch of variety came to daytime drama.

An example was *Aunt Jenny's True Life Stories*, introduced in 1937. In this series a different story was dramatized each week, providing work for a host of free-lance writers and many rising performers, including Orson Welles. Although the stories usually changed weekly, a strong link between them was the narrator—more accurately, the storyteller—Aunt Jenny. Each program opened in her cheery kitchen in Littleton, the town in which the stories themselves took place. With the sounds of teakettle or skillet in the background, the folksy yarn spinner chatted with the show's announcer, Dan Seymour, as her thoughts turned to signs of spring; to the doings of her husband Calvin, editor of the Littleton paper; and assuredly to matters of cuisine. The cooking chatter led to mention of the sponsor's product, Spry, which Aunt Jenny would be using at that moment to whip up some confection or other. Seymour, who subsequently became an important advertising executive, offered assorted sounds of approval and anticipation as the delicacies he was certain to sample sizzled in the background.

In 1940 an ultimate-conclusion format, minus the braising and frying, was used for the only biblical soap opera. Forsaking

Betty and Bob, General Mills added *Light of the World* to its afternoon block of serials known as The Gold Medal Hour. These biblical dramatizations were supervised by the Hummerts, who set aside their formula to present sincere and simply worded episodes of the Old Testament. In the first one Albert Hayes and Eleanor Phelps were heard as Adam and Eve. Among the more popular sequences of later years were the tales of Samson, David, and, of course, Jezebel. Serving as consultant to the program was Dr. James H. Moffat, of the Union Theological Seminary. Authorities of other faiths also were consulted by the writers, who, in true daytime-serial fashion, managed to make a single verse of scripture suffice for many episodes. In fact, the program lasted until 1952.

With the exception of *Light of the World,* whose sequences came to an end for obvious reasons, *Aunt Jenny's True Life Stories* was the only daytime serial with changing stories to survive more than a few years. I should, however, mention some of the other closed-end serials, if only because of their content. *Wheatena Playhouse* is one. In 1940 the makers of the well-known breakfast food tried a transcription series featuring moderately prominent actors in dramatizations of novels such as *Wuthering Heights, Alice Adams, Of Human Bondage,* and *The Citadel.* The second season brought *The Rains Came, My Man Godfrey,* and *Jane Eyre.* Wheatena's project was worthwhile and ambitious, though not as daring as it might appear, for almost all the novels had proved themselves dramatically as motion pictures.

Taking a slightly less classical approach to the task of bringing literary works to housewives, in 1941 General Mills began a series quite similar to that of its rival grain company. Even the commercials of *Stories America Loves* seemed to be directed against Wheatena specifically. Edna Ferber's *So Big* was one of the early dramatizations in the series, as was Owen Wister's *The Virginian,* which would become a nighttime television serial two decades later. Faced with unimpressive ratings, the producers of *Stories America Loves* projected a longer run for *Kitty Foyle,* which began during the summer of 1942 (eighteen

324

months after the release of the film version starring Ginger Rogers). It was planned that *Kitty Foyle* would finish out the year. As 1943 approached, however, it was evident that Christopher Morley's portrayal of the white-collar girl confronting Philadelphia's Main Line society was achieving higher ratings than had the earlier dramas of shorter duration. It was no surprise, then, that the rotating-story concept was abandoned and that *Stories America Loves* dissolved into *Kitty Foyle*. The across-the-tracks romance of Pop Foyle's daughter and the vacillating Wynn Strafford was spun out until 1944, when Kitty gave way to *Light of the World* in a shuffling of General Mills programs.

A lesser ultimate-conclusion program of this time was *By Kathleen Norris*, presenting Miss Norris' novels as dramatized by Phillips H. Lord, Inc., makers of *Gang Busters*. In typical Lord technique, Miss Norris, like *Gang Busters'* policemen-narrators, appeared "by proxy." Not for long, though. *By Kathleen Norris* suffered the fate of all closed-end serials save *Aunt Jenny's True Life Stories* and *Light of the World*: short life and sudden death.

In 1937, the year of Aunt Jenny's first appearance, a mystery-and-adventure program called *Follow the Moon* joined the ranks of the daytime serial. It starred radio's only true thriller serial team, Elsie Hitz and Nick Dawson, whose greatest success was the nighttime episoder, *Dangerous Paradise*. This attempt to bring action to the ladies, revolving about a good-bad man called the Parson, was short-lived, as was another mystery and adventure series, *Thunder Over Paradise* (1939).

In the spring of 1941, General Mills tried dramatizations of popular suspense novels on *The Mystery Man*. First was Mary Roberts Rinehart's *Window at the White Cat*. Using a surprisingly effective theme from *Swan Lake* and an impressive narrator, Jay Jostyn (*Mr. District Attorney*), *The Mystery Man* was a good escapist series, inserted in a favorable position within The Gold Medal Hour. It failed, nevertheless. Respectable but not spectacular ratings were not enough for a prime broadcasting spot when Irna Phillips stood ready with a new, and open-end, drama needing a home.

The closest thing to a crime thriller among the successful daytime shows of the period was *Front Page Farrell*, which began on the Mutual Network in 1941. It was that network's first live-serial origination from New York City and represented the first business given to Mutual by Blackett-Sample-Hummert. Despite initial dialogue that *Variety* compared to that of *The Drunkard*, the program soon advanced to NBC, where for fourteen years reporter David Farrell (played by Richard Widmark and later by Staats Cotsworth) and his wife, Sally, pursued one big story after another, most of them related to crime and criminals. A significant asset of the program was a late-afternoon program time that brought it within range of male listeners.

The difficulties of the mystery serials were evidence not so much that housewives did not enjoy a bit of spine tingling as that women preferred to have their chills or crime mixed with the ordinary elements of the serial world—as in *Front Page Farrell*, which always remained the narrative of an excitement-filled marriage. Familiar characters caught up in melodrama that invaded their homes or their professional lives were much more appealing to daytime serial listeners than a new set of individuals introduced to unfold a standard mystery story.

Certainly crime was nothing new to the daytime serial. It had been worked into most of the shows by the late 1930s and became ever more prominent as the years went by. In the fall of 1952, twenty years after the debut of *Betty and Bob*, at least half the serials were concerned with crime or litigation of some sort. In *The Right to Happiness, Helen Trent,* and *When a Girl Marries* it was merely slander that was before the house, but in other shows things were much more serious. Murder had been committed in *Front Page Farrell, Rosemary, Stella Dallas,* and *This Is Nora Drake. Our Gal Sunday* focused upon a hit-and-run killing, while *Backstage Wife* was concerned with narcotics traffic. Even *Lorenzo Jones*, till then one of the happier serials, was employing a plot line built upon kidnaping, assault, and jewel theft.

This reign of larceny and violence continued into the television era. On Christmas Eve, 1957, crime was at the forefront of seven of the nine television soap operas.

I use the word crime instead of mystery because seldom was there much of the latter in the daytime serial. The identity of a culprit almost always was known to listeners or viewers. The criminal acts served primarily to bring a good person under suspicion—or, better yet, to trial. The number of criminal actions brought against the characters of soap operas is beyond count and still growing. But then, experience had early proved that nothing could boost audience interest as a good trial could. Many weeks of courtroom sensations became customary fare before acquittal broke off a long period of mental torture for the innocent man or woman. Sometimes only a posttrial confession ended the innocent's agony. That was how Helen Trent escaped the gas chamber in 1950.

In mentioning the failure of mystery shows per se to obtain a foothold in the daytime I do not wish to leave the impression that they were the only unsuccessful serials of the prewar period. The reader who has been keeping score in this chapter is aware that in the expansion years a good many "conventional" serials vanished almost as soon as they appeared. They were the inevitable result of overplanting. Most well-rooted shows managed to hold on, and often thrive, showing that the fault was not in the serial form itself. New plantings, however, were as likely to wither as they were to grow. And when one failed, there were many others waiting to take its place.

Even seemingly sure transplants such as *Myrt and Marge* could have difficult going. Unlike *Pepper Young's Family* and *The Goldbergs*, which had a year's head start, *Myrt and Marge* did not find the transfer to the daytime particularly fortuitous. It held its own for a time against its already established soap-opera rivals, but it was ebbing seriously by 1941, when Myrtle Vail's daughter (real as well as fictional), Donna Damerel, died only minutes after childbirth. Actress Vail kept the show on the air, with Helen Mack in the role of Marge, but Miss Damerel's

327

stilled voice had been a vital asset to a drama that was being called old-fashioned in the 1940s and was enduring partly through listener sentiment. The program soon disappeared.[4]

With so many dramas on the air, it was not easy to develop the daytime audience necessary to convince a sponsor that his money was being well spent, particularly with so many potential soap operas around the corner awaiting their turn. As the day filled with serials, the available audience was spread thinner and thinner, sometimes being divided among three networks. It was too much even for a hearty form. With a weeding out a near certainty, some executives began thinking about good substitutes, notably Tom Brenneman's *Breakfast in Hollywood*. But before any thinning occurred, the daytime serial had to undergo the evils of quick success: high attrition in new programs and heavy criticism. It also had to face its first and only confrontation with the real world, beginning in December, 1941.

[4] Names like Myrtle *Spear* and Marge *Minter* helped sell *Myrt and Marge* to P. K. Wrigley in 1931, but were as awkward as the name of another character, Clarence Tiffingtuffer, in the daytime-serial milieu. Myrtle Vail had to remodel her drama for the afternoon and for Colgate, something as unsettling for her as the change in her writing habits necessitated by the earlier hour of presentation. Other writers assumed the duties. When the girls ceased being carefree globe-trotters, however, and domestic crises took over, the program moved to a position between fish and fowl. The old *Myrt and Marge* would not serve, least of all in its new habitat, and a satisfactory restyling was never quite achieved.

IN TIME OF WAR

Nothing she does, or seems,
But smacks of something
greater than herself,
Too noble for this place.

WILLIAM SHAKESPEARE, *The Winter's Tale*

It was a coincidence worthy of the soap opera that the time of greatest critical trial for the daytime serial approximated its finest hour. For a few busy years in the 1940s the world of women's drama neared contact with the real world it had thus far avoided. This circumstance, nevertheless, brought scant praise from cynics. After all, they challenged, had not many things changed because of the war? Was it not logical that the daytime serial at least acknowledge it?

Over all, motion pictures and radio reacted to the national crisis in a manner that at best could be called praiseworthy, at worst shrewdly commercial. Excellent films and programs brought inspiration, information, and needed humorous relief to a nation rebounding from sudden attack. With both broadcast and film media enlisted in special instructional and morale-building efforts, it was natural for the serial genre to follow the patriotic pattern—invited to or not.

The movie serial, of course, was involved symbolically in the struggle before it began. As World War II approached, those foreign powers bent on stealing the destructive ray gun or ultra-powered explosive began to look more and more like Axis nations. When hostilities began, it was necessary only to identify the spies or aliens of the "steal-the-secret" serials as Germans or Japanese (characters of Italian origin or nationality, frequently villains of crime dramas, seldom appeared as enemy agents in serial or feature films).

Quicker than they could have anticipated, the Axis schemers were being battered cinematically by the likes of the Spider, Batman, Spy Smasher, the Masked Marvel, and Secret Agent X-9, not to mention the miscellaneous senior and junior G-men who rapidly took up the chase. Not even across the Atlantic were they safe, for Rex Bennett pursued them all the way to Gestapo headquarters. And while he left Africa unguarded, Ruth Roman, as the Jungle Queen, gave the Germans difficulty on the Dark Continent. The hunt was actually extended back to the 1860s. In the Civil War Western serial *Raiders of Ghost City* a North-South struggle over gold shipments became the camouflage for a power play by Prussian conspirators Lionel Atwill and Virginia Christine.

No doubt about it, in jungle, prairie, or metropolis, the cliff-hanging heroes and heroines did their part in the war effort—though one must overlook their apparent aversion to ordinary service in the armed forces. Scenes of battle action were no more than inserts in tales of spy fighting or fifth-column activity.

The thrillers of radio were companion settings for anti-espionage activity. In fact, one of the new wartime dramas of the evening hours was called *Counterspy*. It was a logical extension by Phillips H. Lord of his earlier success, *Gang Busters*. Other nighttime shows which owed their presence on the airwaves to the global struggle were *Bulldog Drummond,* the *FBI in Peace and War,* and a tongue-in-cheek Herbert Marshall vehicle, *The Man Called X.* Naturally, the large corps of private eyes who plied their trade on radio in the war years occasionally came up against enemy machinations. At other times, however, only reference to rationing or shortages gave indication that a war was in progress.

Around the dinner hour the ether reverberated with the sounds of endless skirmishes, but it had ever been thus, at least since the early 1930s. Ironically, Don Winslow of the Navy, a career serviceman, had vanished from the air before the war broke out. Perhaps he had moved on to duty in the theaters of war. In any event, his polished oxfords were capably filled by such worthies as Captain Midnight and Hop Harrigan. Even the children came to the fore, from Terry Lee and Jack Armstrong to tiny ageless herself, Little Orphan Annie, who by that time was playing a secondary role to the Captain Midnight imitation called Captain Sparks.

Many males over forty recall the sudden impact of the war upon the juvenile serial. Possibly the most conspicuous adjustment occurred in *Jack Armstrong.* On the Friday night before Pearl Harbor, Jack was pursuing a typical high adventure in the Philippines. The Japanese invasion of those islands caused his writers to yank him quickly from that area of hostilities so that he could fight Axis representatives on less precarious ground. As soon as things were comfortable with Jack and friends, his sponsor settled down to the most flagrant capitalization upon the national emergency that one could find on radio. In warm but meaningful tones announcer Franklyn McCormick advised Armstrong fans that not keeping in shape by eating Wheaties was nothing less than treasonous.

Somehow even Tom Mix got into some brushes with the Japanese, without leaving the TM-Bar Ranch. One of his memorable story lines involved a giant as big as King Kong who was terrifying the western countryside. At length Tom unmasked it as a huge balloon manipulated by Japanese agents for not-too-well-explained reasons.

In face of all this diligent anti-Axis labor in its serial brothers and sisters, it was no more than proper than the soap opera make some sacrifices for the duration. Actually, and to its favor, it must be stated that one part of the daytime-serial world had acknowledged the Axis menace before the United States entered the conflict. In the fall of 1939, as Hitler's forces were overrunning their hapless victims, a writer named Sandra Michael was given opportunity by William Ramsey of Procter and Gamble to bring to the air the most honored daytime serial of all: *Against the Storm.*

Miss Michael's drama, unfolded in prose that James Thurber called "often sensitive, occasionally poetic," portrayed the family and friends of Dr. Allen, an American college professor who tried to alert the world to the Fascist danger. In the *New York Times* John K. Hutchens observed that, in relation to the level of the average serial, *Against the Storm* was "practically stratospheric." He found in the characters recognizable human beings who could think and who could talk about poetry, art, and politics. Hutchens compared the program to a lengthy novel of the old school which, although not steadily interesting, was steadily of high standard.[1]

Several important guests appeared on *Against the Storm* in testimony of the esteem in which it was held by them. On April 24, 1941, Edgar Lee Masters read from his *Spoon River Anthology.* On November 3, 1941, John Masefield was heard from England by short wave. No commercials intruded upon this episode, in which Mr. Masefield lectured and read his poetry to Professor Allen's class. Ironically, a scheduled appearance by President Roosevelt was canceled because of the strike upon Pearl Harbor.

In the spring of 1942, *Against the Storm* received a Peabody Award, the only daytime serial ever to be so honored. By December of that year the drama had disappeared. The agency which supervised the program suggested that it had reached the end of its story line. Miss Michael and her sister Gerda, who had joined her in writing the program in July, countered that they had been forced to resist attempts to make the program more like other

[1] John K. Hutchens, "This One is Good," *New York Times*, October 9, 1941.

332

serials. For whatever reason, the numbers of listeners declined in the program's last months. Possibly the story really had run its course. If so, it was one serial that was not stretched interminably.

During the months in which *Against the Storm* approached its demise, elements of war began to appear in the plots of many serials. Although the focus of the dramas remained on the home, the tragedies of war were recognized. In the fall of 1942, CBS examined its serials for incidents concerning death in military action and found that during August and September of that year such incidents had been included in *Big Sister, Young Dr. Malone, Pepper Young's Family, Aunt Jenny's True Life Stories*, and *David Harum*. The only nonservice death of that period occurred in *We Love and Learn*.

As the war progressed, many of the serial males, for real or fictional reasons, were put into uniform. In some instances that meant taking the characters out of the plot—regrettable, certainly, for actors who lost work when their roles evaporated, flattering, no doubt, to actors such as Billy Idelson of *Vic and Sade*, whose fictional service coincided with actual military duty. Another actor not replaced for the duration was Alfred Ryder of *The Goldbergs*. When Ryder departed for service from Pennsylvania Station, Sammy Goldberg did so simultaneously on the air. The broadcast was presented from the railway station itself.

When real events did not dictate complete removal of a man in uniform, he was likely to be kept close to home and plot line, getting involved in much the same kind of difficulties he had faced as a civilian. Those who went abroad on military or special missions were generally men who had had a tendency to wander in peacetime as well. It was inevitable that the peripatetic Joe Marlin would be missing in action for a near eternity before being found in North Africa, his eyes swathed in bandages. Roving newspaperman and special agent Walter Manning of *Portia Faces Life* had many hard weeks in Germany before returning to the comforting embrace of attorney Portia Blake (his wife-to-be), who had to defend him in court against charges that he was a Nazi. Later on, the sorely tried Manning underwent the added humiliation of receiving psychiatric care from another man in love with Portia.[2]

As I have indicated, most of the war-associated action in daytime serials concerned the characters who were left at home. In rare parallel with the thriller serials, little action took place in the battle areas. For example, on NBC in the fall of 1943 Front Page Farrell did his bit by covering wartime problems for his paper—problems selected by the show's writers on special advice of the Office of War Information. David Harum, having given up horse trading, was managing a war plant, as was Sam Young, Pepper's father (Stella Dallas, of humbler station, merely worked in one). In the general rush toward industrial mobilization, the breadwinner of *When A Girl Marries*, legal counsel for still another fictional factory, was delivering patriotic speeches about sticking to the job when he could find a likely group of slackers. NBC's highest-level wartime tycoon was probably *Lora Lawton*'s gentleman friend, who owned a shipbuilding concern.

While not industry-minded, the heroines of NBC's *Brave Tomorrow, Backstage Wife, The Guiding Light*, and *Young Widder Brown* were proud to be wives or sweethearts of servicemen, though Mrs. Brown tended to rotate hers. Prouder yet were the leading ladies of *Right to Happiness* and *Helpmate*; their husbands had been wounded. And I must not overlook a female character in *Lonely Women* who, in the most fascinating wartime alliance of them all, wed a reformed Nazi agent. Meanwhile, in the courtroom, Portia Blake faced life defending democracy. Of the twenty NBC serials with contemporary settings in the autumn of 1943, only five had plots that were not concerned with the war.

Although Young Dr. Malone's presumed death in action (which allowed his wife an affair with a navy flier) and Young Widder Brown's compulsive flirtations with medical officers of

---

[2] One of the few male characters virtually to begin and end his fictional career as an ordinary soldier overseas was Neil Bishop (played by Lawson Zerbe) of CBS's short-lived *This Changing World*. Despite periodic flashes to Bishop in France, the drama focused upon his wife, Martha, and her problems of adjustment in the absence of her mate.

the armed services were plot devices that brought little elucidation to the problems of women during a war, there were moments in which meaning and comfort did come through. At times the meaningful or informative content of the wartime serials resulted from the inspiration of the writers; at other times it was owed to outside stimulation. Because of the strong sales results which the daytime serial had demonstrated through the years, welfare groups and governmental agencies were eager to have their policies or campaigns outlined through the dramas.

For the most part, serial writers were pleased to co-operate—and not at all reticent to admit their co-operation. Elaine Carrington was proud of the praise she received from the surgeon general of the United States for the informative material on emergency medical treatment which she worked into installments of *Pepper Young's Family*. Irna Phillips, however, outdid Mrs. Carrington in name dropping when she told a college conference in 1944 that her stories emerged from consultation with (in alphabetical order) the American Legion, the American Medical Association, the Association for Family Living, the Federal Council of Churches of Christ in America, the National Education Association, the Navy Department, the Office of War Information, the Red Cross, the Veterans Administration, and the War Department.

Miss Phillips no doubt was telling the truth. Certainly the Office of War Information was eager to enlist radio writers in its efforts. It supplied them with a series of pamphlets on matters of importance. The rush of serial characters to war work was one result of the OWI's urgings. So were the several series using familiar serial characters in special week-long serializations devoted to wartime problems. NBC offered *Victory Volunteers*, with Clifton Fadiman as moderator; CBS presented *Victory Front*. Talent and crews for these programs donated their services.

Augmenting the special dramas were frequent informational messages on the ongoing programs themselves. If Ma Perkins, who had lost a son in the fighting, asked the housewives of America to save fat or tinfoil, the results could be expected to be good. To add impact, soap operas brought many wartime personalities to their fictional communities. For instance, Lieutenant Thomas M. Reardon, the first marine to land on Guadalcanal, visited *Bright Horizon's* Riverfield on a war-bond tour. Waves commander Mildred H. McAyer was heard one day on *Aunt Jenny's True Life Stories*, as was Mrs. Theodore Roosevelt, Jr. Another Roosevelt, Eleanor, chatted with the heroine on *The Story of Bess Johnson*.

During the war the daytime serial performed its own kind of overseas service. The co-ordinator of Inter-American Affairs requested permission to broadcast *Bachelor's Children* in Spanish to Latin America in order to increase hemispheric solidarity.[3] The British Broadcasting Corporation borrowed the serial format for the war-centered series *Frontline Family*, which portrayed forthrightly the effects of the war in Britain on the "Blitzed Family Robinson."

Thus far I have been describing changes in serials that were on the air when the war began. But some daytime dramas came into being largely as a result of the war. One was *The Open Door*, Sandra Michael's well-written story of Erik Hansen, dean of Vernon University, a man who had experienced life in Nazi-occupied Denmark. Dean Hansen, who tried to make the struggle meaningful to the young, was played by Miss Michael's friend of many years, Dr. Alfred Dorf, pastor of Our Savior's Church in Brooklyn.

The program's theme was set forth each day in its opening lines:

HANSEN: Come in, come in! The door is open.
NARRATOR: There is an Open Door
           To a Good Way of life for all men.
           This Open Door is called brotherhood
           And over its portals are these simple words:
           "I *am* my brother's keeper."

[3] The usefulness of soap opera in carrying messages to Latin America was well demonstrated at this time. A quarter-century later the United States Information Agency was producing counterparts of the radio dramas: *Nuestro Barrio* portrayed problems of urban neighborhoods, and *Emilio Espina* emphasized self-help through the Alliance for Progress.

Billboard regarded *The Open Door,* which was sponsored by Chase and Sanborn Coffee, as literate daytime fare that might lead to a new term for daytime serials: "coffee operas" (the suggested appellation was never adopted). *The Open Door,* like *Against the Storm,* became a point of dispute when its producer (Miss Michael's husband, John Gibbs) balked at the attempts of its supervising agency to make the series conform more closely to the pattern for daytime serials. The urging by the agency caused Miss Michael to request release from the program in January, 1944, and again in March. A month later she collapsed and refused to continue writing the program. For a short time a substitute writer carried on, but—to paraphrase *Variety*—the battle between Gibbs and the agency finally closed *The Open Door.*

Two less-troubled wartime serials were *Green Valley U.S.A.* and *Sweet River.* Both sought to present the problems of American life in typical communities. *Green Valley U.S.A.* was an unsponsored serial with different stories each week. *Sweet River* told of the problems faced by a community in wartime, when new factory workers came to town, disturbing the status quo. It was created by Charles Jackson, who at the same time was writing a novel, *The Lost Weekend.*

Just as the titles of *Sweet River* and *Green Valley U.S.A.* conveyed Americana, those of *American Women* and *Woman of America* appealed to feminine pride, while titles such as *This Changing World, Lonely Women,* and *Brave Tomorrow* reflected uncertainty and dislocation.[4] *Lonely Women,* Irna Phillips' wartime drama, looked at the women who lived in the Towers, a New York hotel for women. Contrasted to this metropolitan setting was that of *Woman of America,* the daytime serial drama's venture into historical romance. Prudence Dane's

---

[4] *Brave Tomorrow* was without a tomorrow. Reportedly called by a Procter and Gamble representative "the most ghastly dismal failure you ever saw," it followed a soldier and his bride from army camp to army camp as he awaited impending overseas orders that somehow never came. Meanwhile, the drama explored in depth the most mundane of problems, notably the little woman's inability to obtain a set of dishes. When the search had gone on beyond reason, the man from Procter and Gamble wired his advertising agency, "For God's sake, tell her there is still Sears and Roebuck!"

trek along the Oregon Trail, narrated by great-granddaughter Margaret, recalled the heritage of the American woman and related it to the contemporary scene. Anne Seymour, no longer Mary Marlin, portrayed the two Dane women, whose saga ended as the war which generated it drew to a close.

In the final months of the war the specific problems of servicemen and veterans were presented in several serials. Big Sister's husband, Dr. John Wayne, returned from a Japanese prison, the subsequent action leading Colonel Robert C. Cook, director of the Veterans Administration hospital in the Bronx, to congratulate the program for its help to returnees. The War Department itself employed the serial technique in an NBC Blue Network program of short duration, *Chaplain Jim, U.S.A.* And, just as in 1941 the problems of the draftee had been presented in *Buck Private and His Girl*, the problems of the veteran provided the framework for NBC's *Barry Cameron* in 1945.

The end of hostilities brought an end to the intrusion of outside events into the world of the daytime serial. Soon things were just about as they had been before. And, except for minor acknowledgment of the Korean or Vietnam actions in a few programs, the daytime serial drama has continued in its remarkably isolated environment since 1946. The serial characters live their lives in apparent oblivion to all external events—except traditional holidays.

Yet those who worked in the production of daytime serials during the wartime era can in some cases feel genuine pride for their contribution to the over-all effort to defeat the Axis. If all the writers were not Sandra Michaels, at least many of them made a sincere effort to integrate themes or messages of merit into their series. And who is to say that Ma Perkins' patriotic suggestions did not influence some women who otherwise might not have been reached at all?

Certainly it can be acknowledged that a previously untapped potential of the daytime serial drama was at least partly realized during World War II. As audiences grow more sophisticated through the years, as serial writers move more and more toward subjects that are of greater significance than those currently providing the bases for serial plots, that potential may be tapped again. A second Peabody Award for the daytime serial is not beyond possibility—or at least hope.

CRITICS, ARISE!

Plays make mankind no better,
and no worse.
LORD BYRON, *Hints from Horace,* l. 370

The antiserial movement that was started by women's clubs in 1939 lost momentum when the United States' entry into the war provided more important outlets for such energy. Moreover, a natural reduction in the number of serials tended to weaken the argument that soap operas were too numerous. For alarmists a new basis of criticism was needed, preferably one associated with the war effort. That would make them patriotic alarmists. Rising to the challenge was the well-known psychiatrist Louis Berg.

Dr. Berg had achieved a certain fame as a writer. He was the author of the novels *Prison Doctor, Devil's Circus,* and *Prison Nurse* (made into a motion picture by Republic Pictures, the thriller studio). Dr. Berg had also written several plays. In 1942 he presented a report on the daytime serial drama which was filled with serious adverse criticism. James Thurber's fancy was caught by this comment:

> Pandering to perversity and playing out destructive conflicts, these serials furnish the same release for the emotionally distorted that is supplied to those who desire satisfaction from a lynching bee, lick their lips at the salacious scandals of the *crime passionnel*, who in the unregretted past cried out in ecstasy at a witch burning.[1]

Dr. Berg concluded that the daytime serial was a devitalizing drain upon many Americans, his patients particularly. In a time of war, he believed, such an effect was "little short of treason."

So shocking a charge naturally received attention in the nation's press. Dr. Berg became the champion of the antiserial movement and went on to another study—based principally upon his own blood-pressure and pulse readings before and after serial listening. He discovered, in addition to acute anxiety state, the following terrifying symptoms: "tachycardia, arithmias, increase in blood pressure, profuse perspiration, tremors, vasomotor instability, nocturnal frights, vertigo, and gastro-intestinal disturbances."[2]

Although Dr. Berg's studies purported to be scientific investigations, they were poorly and inadequately constructed. Careful examinations of his work by broadcasters, critics, and fellow physicians caused serious doubts about his findings. Max Wylie pointed out that Dr. Berg's subjects were essentially his assistant and the psychiatrist himself. Using irony to attack Berg's stand against the more violent elements of daytime serial, Wylie listed the chapter titles of the psychiatrist's own book, *Prison Doctor*. Among them were: "Madhouse," "Hypo," "Prison Riots," "A Man Dies," "World Without Women," "The Easiest Way," and "Bug Tests."[3]

James Thurber also took a sharp look at the doctor's reports. His curiosity was particularly aroused by one of Dr. Berg's state-

[1] James Thurber, *The Beast in Me and Other Animals*, 251–52.
[2] Louis Berg, "Radio and Civilian Morale," quoted in Max Wylie, "Dusting Off Dr. Berg," *Printers' Ink*, February 12, 1943, 44.
[3] *Ibid.*

ments in the first paper. Thurber wondered why the psychiatrist remarked, "There are several excellent [serials]. Naturally, an analysis of them has no place in a study of this kind."[4]

A former colleague of Dr. Berg's provided the most embarrassing observation, however. Dr. Matthew Chappell noticed that the symptoms of serial listening described by Dr. Berg were identical to those which attend anger. He suggested, somewhat devastatingly, that Dr. Berg had merely recorded the irritation which soap opera itself aroused in him.[5]

Still more trouble awaited the would-be serial slayer. A committee of doctors headed by Dr. Morris Fishbein criticized the use of blood-pressure apparatus, which focused upon single serial incidents. Did not the slow pace of the daytime serial drama, the medical committee asked, make attention to the whole more appropriate than attention to small parts? Fishbein's committee decided that the psychological problems featured in daytime serials were not presented in "undue proportions." Agreeing that daytime serials were much in need of improvement, the physicians saw the dramas as tending "toward helpfulness more than harm" in that their plots arrived at ethically acceptable solutions to human problems.[6]

For a while Dr. Berg's reports spurred antiserial groups to further action, but in time the weight of criticism against his studies resulted in his disappearance as an important critic of the serials. His efforts, however, did lead to examination and research of the daytime dramas by opponents and defenders alike.

Dr. Matthew Chappell, through several articles and reports, presented the opinion that the daytime serial drama needed a new formula to combat some 1942 rating drops. While doubting that the reading level of the general public had risen much since the days of the Horatio Alger tales, he noted that in contrast with the dime novel—a genre which had exalted the ability of the common folk to overcome obstacles—the daytime serial rational-

---

[4] Thurber, *The Beast in Me,* 252.
[5] Wylie, "Dusting Off Dr. Berg," *Printers' Ink,* February 12, 1943, 44.
[6] "Say Virtues of Daytime Serials Outweigh Shortcomings," *Printers' Ink,* February 12, 1943, 20.

ized the frustrations and failures of the humble man. Serial problems, he thought, were just too much for the characters.

To explain this theory Chappell connected daytime serials with the era in which they were spawned, suggesting that depression literature had characteristically attempted to make palatable the failures of the period in which Hamlet was a national model. To Chappell, the positive thought of wartime necessitated a more dynamic approach. Serial characters, he proposed, needed to fight, not wallow in, the sea of troubles if the daytime serial was to regain its former popularity. Chappell could not foresee, of course, that the nonhero, as typified by Humphrey Bogart, was yet to enjoy his greatest vogue.

Apropos the Chappell argument, John K. Hutchens, in the *New York Times*, reported a feeling among some people that the influence of the war and the special nighttime serials of the Office of War Information would start a trend toward more aggressive characters and a greater social awareness in daytime serials.[7] *Time*, commenting on Chappell's theory, observed that CBS was presenting daytime programs on Monday evenings in an effort to acquire new listeners.[8] Another network, nevertheless, was not going to bother. The executives of the newly independent Blue Network Company (the American Broadcasting Company) were so certain that daytime serial dramas had lost their appeal that in 1943 they eliminated them from their schedule and planned an aggressive campaign based upon variety and audience-participation programs.

There was in all this seeming evidence that soap opera was in danger. But pessimists (or were they optimists?) were looking at the wrong data. While a drop in the average ratings of serials could be shown in the early years of the war, the ratings of the more popular serials scarcely wavered. Furthermore, sales results were more important than the ratings of many serials. Only the weaker serials, in this context, were in possible need of a new formula.

[7] John K. Hutchens, "Are the Soap Operas Only Suds?" *New York Times Magazine*, March 28, 1943, 19.
[8] "Daytime Classics," *Time*, November 12, 1942, 45.

With the arguments of those who considered serials danger-ous blunted by the attacks on Dr. Berg's studies—and by research studies which indicated that Dr. Berg's findings were inaccurate —a new basis for criticizing serials was needed. Coming forward to provide it was Charles Siepmann, an Englishman who had been in the United States only a few years. Before reaching American shores, Siepmann had, as Jack Gould put it, "prowled the mystifying corridors" of the BBC.

Siepmann's position was founded upon the old idea that there were too many serials. To that concept he added the jarring theory that most women really did not like soap operas. In his book *Radio's Second Chance* he pointed to a study of the 1944–45 season, which indicated that only 10 per cent of the audience available for any given serial listened to it. Why, then, did soap operas dominate daytime radio? Siepmann held that it was be-cause of the low production costs, the convenience of the format for the placement of commercials, and great sales achievements.

In 1945, Siepmann served as a consultant to the Federal Com-munications Commission. It can be no coincidence that in 1946 his views on the daytime serial appeared in the important FCC publication popularly known as *The Blue Book*. This report—which has been wrongly represented by one critic as causing broadcasters to hunt for "fiendish communists under every studio couch"—became something of a standard for radio criticism. Siepmann's opinion, whether or not identified as his own, soon became popular with other critics of the daytime serials.

In a sense Siepmann was correct in stating that only a minority listened to individual serials. But that minority was larger, on the whole, than the audience of any other form of daytime en-tertainment. Siepmann simply stated the popularity of the day-time serial in a negative manner without relating it to the popu-larity of other daytime program forms. His description of the "morbid frame of mind," the "low IQ," and the "pitiable creduli-ty" of the serial "addicts" was more in line with Dr. Berg's pic-ture of the daytime serial listener than it was with the findings of the valid research studies which were available to him. Siep-mann's direct knowledge of the serials themselves apparently was slight. The only serials he described specifically in *Radio's Second Chance* were those of Irna Phillips (whom he called Jean Phillips). His only acknowledgment of differences in quality among serials was that "they vary in subject and treatment."

In his enthusiasm to reduce the number of serials on the air (not an unreasonable goal considering the overcrowding), Siepmann exaggerated his presentation in such a manner as to give a false impression to those who were not acquainted with the daytime serial. At the same time, he did not win the support of many critics, broadcasters, and others who might have supported a fairer presentation.

Gilbert Seldes, for example, analyzing the daytime serial drama in *The Great Audience*, called it radio's "single notable contribution to the art of fiction." He praised the way in which the serial had adjusted itself to the listening pattern of housewives and developed "a technique of narration as skillful as that of Joseph Conrad and, in its way, as complex." Seldes did, however, express regret that a form with such great promise had been sorely abused and that it had been neglected by serious writers of other media.

In analyzing the male-female relationship of the serial, Seldes had this to say about masculine bloodlessness:

> The weak man required by the structure of daytime serial is peculiarly useful because he is, obviously, impotent, and although a woman may weep at suspected infidelities, she is never deceived; her long self-examinations to decide whether she loves him conceal what she knows, that he cannot make love to her.[9]

The observation that male impotency was important to the structure of many daytime serials possibly was an acute one, but it still awaits scholarly investigation. Impotency, manifested in the general weakness of many male characters, in their tendency to be absent in times of need and in the strange illnesses and crippling accidents that struck them, perhaps was more than literary happenstance. It could be inferred from Seldes' suggestion that housewives derived certain satisfaction and compensation from the impotency of male characters and that to a woman con-

9 Gilbert Seldes, *The Great Audience*, 117.

fined to the home the symbol of her domination by men was the symbol of manhood itself. In order for all things to be equal, then—in order for female domination to be exerted—that symbol had to be erased. It is an interesting theory, to say the least.

A study of serial listeners which Gilbert Seldes and others considered worthy of attention was the 1948 symbolic analysis executed by Lloyd Warner and William Henry for the Office for the Study of Social Communication in Chicago.[10] Using *Big Sister* as a serial in point and middle western urban housewives as subjects, the researchers administered a ten-picture Thematic Apperception Test (TAT) and the Verbal Projective (a story technique arranged upon the drama's plots). They also conducted interviews, some while the serial was on the air.

What did *Big Sister* do for or to the contemporary social structure? The program strengthened and stabilized it, concluded Warner and Henry. For instance, housewives who might have felt that their achievements were less significant than those of their career-girl acquaintances were offered a resourceful fictional homemaker making demonstrable contributions to day-to-day living. Warner and Henry described *Big Sister* as a minor (and secularized) morality play employing idealized symbols of good and evil to express the feelings and beliefs of the audience. The drama raised normal and adaptive anxiety, treated it constructively, and at the same time condemned neurotic anxiety. Problems, the investigators noted, had logical bases of solution.

Warner and Henry found almost nothing to confirm the theory that serials had harmful effects. They held them to be much like folk tales, expressing the hopes and fears of their female audiences and contributing to "the integration of their lives into the world in which they lived."

Although in many ways the daytime serial was an easy target for the barbs of critics and amateur researchers, there was one area in which the daytime serials could not be seriously challenged: cost per listener. Low production costs had been one of

[10] Lloyd Warner and William Henry, "The Radio Daytime Serial: A Symbolic Analysis," *Genetic Psychology Monographs*, February, 1948, 3–71.

the principal factors which had attracted sponsors to the serial in its early years. When low production cost was combined with high ratings, the outlay required to reach each listener seemed most attractive to sponsors. In December, 1943, *Billboard* began a series of reports on the relationship between ratings and costs. The first report showed that, while it cost $609.76 in production expense for each rating point of the highest-rated program, *Kate Smith Speaks*, the production cost for each rating point of the second-rated *When A Girl Marries* was only $287.50. *Ma Perkins* cost only $164.56 per point, and its rating almost equaled that of Kate Smith's program. The noticeable differences in cost per listener resulted from the fact that it cost $5,000 a week to produce the Kate Smith program. The cost of a week's install-ments of *Ma Perkins*, on the other hand, was a mere $1,300. Low cost per listener and favorable sales results helped daytime serials remain attractive to many sponsors, whatever the critics had to say.

Some advertisers were so enthusiastic that they bought whole blocks of serials at discount—and sometimes received a lagniappe with their purchase. For instance, during the 1943–44 season three Irna Phillips serials appeared next to each other in the General Mills Hour: *The Guiding Light*, *Woman in White*, and *Today's Children*. (On December 13, 1943, Miss Phillips had reactivated the *Today's Children* title to replace that of *Lonely Women*.) The proximity of three programs by the same writer made possible an experiment which, though repeated, would never again work so dramatically. In what is now known as a crossover, Miss Phillips used interchanging characters. Captain Midnight's impersonator, Ed Prentiss, as host-narrator, intro-duced all three General Mills programs, in which characters from one drama played small roles in others. Thus, when Eileen Holmes of *Woman in White* entered Municipal Hospital, her path was crossed by Dr. Jonathan McNeill of *The Guiding Light*. She also encountered Dr. Paul Burton of *Today's Chil-dren*. During this period some highly interesting plot sequences occurred, including a spectacular murder trial in which the lis-tening audience served as the jury.

In 1946, it should be mentioned, the General Mills Hour was involved in another experiment. During the late 1930s and early 1940s the production headquarters of the daytime serial drama, which was largely under the control of advertising agencies, gradually had been moved from Chicago to New York City. But in 1946 it was decided that the General Mills serials would be presented from Hollywood, which had become an active broadcasting center. The transfer of programs was begun in July, 1946, when Irna Phillips' new serial *Masquerade* (which told of a triangle involving a war widow) moved across the country. It was soon followed by *Woman in White* and *Today's Children*.

The Guiding Light was left behind because it was the subject of a lawsuit by Emmons Carlson, who eventually proved to the satisfaction of an appeals court that he had helped Irna Phillips originate the serial. General Mills, meanwhile, dropped the program, prompting the legally vexed but never nonplused Miss Phillips to sell it to Procter and Gamble (as she did *Road of Life* and *The Right to Happiness*). With or without the *Guiding Light* complication, however, the move to Hollywood was not especially successful. New York City, indisputably the business center for the daytime serial drama, remained the production center as well.

Among the daytime dramas introduced in this transitional period—not discussed in the preceding chapter because they were not associated with the war—were Elaine Carrington's *Rosemary* and two mystery programs, the successful *Perry Mason* and the unsuccessful *Two on a Clue*. *We Love and Learn* and the amusing *Tena and Tim*, which had been syndicated offerings, were also added to network daytime logs in the early 1940s, as was *Snow Village*, a former nighttime program written by the author of the old *Soconyland Sketches*, William Ford Manly.

One more war-era addition to the daytime log was *Second Husband*, which for five years had been a Hummert evening feature starring Helen Menken. *Variety* acknowledged the new daytime status of the program in this manner: "Nobody ever accused the program of understatement or subtlety, and no scene or situation ever passed until milked dry. As a daily quar-ter-hour it comes more into the idiom of which it was an arch example, daytime grief in open valve falsetto."[11]

A relatively low output of three new serials by Blackett-Sample-Hummert during World War II was the natural conse-quence of the agency's dissolution at the end of 1943, when Frank Hummert, who had never been a formal partner, with-drew his services. Although most of the agency's business had come through Hummert, through half-owner John G. Sample, or through the agency's president, H. M. Dancer, the other half-owner, Hill Blackett, would not sell his interest to Sample. As a result the old firm disappeared, and two new agencies were formed: Hill Blackett and Dancer-Fitzgerald-Sample. The Hum-merts continued to produce serials, domestic and thriller, through Hummert Radio Productions (formerly Air Features). Playing no favorites, they made their productions available to both the new agencies.

The last Blackett-Sample-Hummert serial was an ultimate-conclusion program, *Dreft Star Playhouse*. Under the title *Hol-lywood Theatre of the Air* it replaced *Lone Journey* on June 28, 1943. Initially the program presented week-long adaptations of popular motion pictures, using well-known film stars such as Jane Wyman and Martha Scott in leading roles. After eight months the adaptations were extended to two weeks each, then to four weeks each, then to six weeks. The last adaptation ran almost ten months—without the famous actors. The adaptations had been extended to the point that the ultimate-conclusion program essentially became a new, almost open-end, serial: *An American Tragedy*, based on Theodore Dreiser's novel.

This transformation demonstrated again the importance of the long narrative to the daytime serial drama. Listeners appar-ently preferred to become well acquainted with at least one serial character, something that was impossible when the story changed each week. Even the use of well-known stars and stories could not compensate for the lack of opportunity to iden-tify with specific serial characters during a substantial period

[11] "Second Husband," *Variety*, April 29, 1942, 36.

of time. That had been shown earlier in the Wheatena transcription series—and in *Stories America Loves,* which had evolved into *Kitty Foyle.*

Joyce Jordan, which replaced the *Dreft Star Playhouse,* did present somewhat unrelated cases initially, in the fashion of the successful mysteries *Front Page Farrell* and *Perry Mason.* Yet in these series there was always one or more connecting characters with whom the listener could become well acquainted and possibly identify.

But enough of this line of thought for the moment. This chapter began with the musings of one serial critic, and it ends with those of another. In the spirit of fairness let me present the viewpoint of radio historian E. P. J. Shurick, whose remarks in *The First Quarter-Century of American Broadcasting* might have startled Dr. Berg—and serial writers too:

> . . . no one could deny that here was a potent force which could wield a tremendous influence upon the education and enlightenment of social living. The listeners, in most part, little realized the effect that the daytime radio drama had upon them in their everyday affairs. But the effect has been great, and by an almost fervent devotion to the responsibilities placed in their writings the authors have contributed much to countless worthwhile causes.[12]

What say you to that, serial critics?

[12] E. P. J. Shurick, *The First Quarter-Century of American Broadcasting,* 77–78.

COMPETITION COMES TO
THE LIVING ROOM

*Here's talk of the Turk and the Pope, but it's my next door neigh-
bour that does me harm.*

THOMAS FULLER, *Gnomologia* (after George Herbert)

In 1946 the daytime serial was involved in an experiment which,
though in itself of little consequence, gave a clue of what was
to come. When a single episode of the radio serial *Big Sister* was
brought into a television studio for a one broadcast test, the no-
longer-precocious child of the depression was not only heard
but seen.

During the postwar period television developed rapidly in the
United States, and by 1951 its growth was having a serious
effect upon the radio industry. Until then, however, network
radio enjoyed a prosperous business. The daytime serial continued to thrive. After a decrease in the number of serials in late
1946, the average number remained at about thirty-three a day

351

until the fall of 1951, when television forced a reduction of 20 per cent.

Ratings of serials remained high. When the death of Tom Brenneman sharply reduced the popularity of *Breakfast in Hollywood*, the only serious network competition of the daytime serials was provided by the daily programs of Arthur Godfrey. On the other hand, only three of the new radio serials of the late 1940s were successful: CBS Radio's *Wendy Warren* and *This Is Nora Drake* (introduced in 1947) and NBC's *The Brighter Day* (1948).

The creation of *Wendy Warren* is worth mention. When the popular Kate Smith noontime program was about to leave the air in 1947, CBS executives began looking for a replacement. Miss Smith's show, the focal point of her phenomenal sale of war bonds a few years earlier, included a short news report each day. It also presented features of special interest to women. The programers hesitated to eliminate these features, but they were drawn to the idea of using a serial in the time slot. Somehow they came up with, of all things, a soap opera containing news reports.

Wendy Warren, lady broadcaster, after a brief newscast by Douglas Edwards, read some bits of news for the girls. At the end of her report Wendy (played by Florence Freeman) said, "Broadcast's over," and whisked herself into a fictional atmosphere which entertained listeners for eleven years. A behind-the-mike story line undoubtedly added to the drama's appeal.

This Is Nora Drake also had a long run (and, like *Wendy Warren*, a widowed heroine). Nurse Nora, at one time assistant to the chief of a large mental clinic, never was at a loss for problems to solve, both professional and personal. In fact, there was enough material for a hard-cover novel that was published by Duell, Sloan and Pearce in 1950. This put the drama one up on *Wendy Warren*, which made it into print with only its theme song, "My Home Town," published, it was said, because of many requests from listeners.

The third successful postwar radio serial, *The Brighter Day*, was the story of Liz Dennis and her widowed father, a clergyman. In a well-calculated maneuver the program was launched through the device of having the about-to-be-replaced Joyce Jordan introduce the members of the Dennis family in the concluding episodes of her program. By the first installment of *The Brighter Day* the characters had become so familiar to the listeners that the transition was extraordinarily smooth. *The Brighter Day* was presented on radio until December 19, 1952. It later became a television serial.

Aside from the *Big Sister* experiment, the first daytime serial of television was *A Woman to Remember*. A 1947 sustaining program of the Du Mont Television Network, its life was very short. Sponsored daytime drama came to television in December, 1950, when CBS introduced *The First Hundred Years*. As the title suggests, the program described the problems of newlyweds, one of whom was played by former child actor James Lydon. The sponsor, Procter and Gamble, was one of the half dozen companies which had dominated the sponsorship of daytime serials on radio.

After examining this first significant television serial, critic John Crosby decided that its title was well selected, not because it made reference to the difficult first hundred years of marriage but because daytime serials were supposed to last at least a century. Crosby also decided that the new drama met the slow-pace standard expected of its genre: it took the young couple eleven days to get to a country-club dance. Noticing less sustained anxiety in *The First Hundred Years* than was found in most serials of radio, Crosby wondered how long this relative euphoria would continue.

Not long, as it turned out. *The First Hundred Years* was followed in 1951 by *Miss Susan* and *Hawkins Falls* on NBC Television and by *The Egg and I*, *Search for Tomorrow*, and *Love of Life* on CBS. *Miss Susan* and the last two CBS shows had their full share of anxiety.

At the time of this writing *Search for Tomorrow* was television's oldest daytime serial. The story of an American family, it introduced the first queen of the television serial, Mary Stuart, in the role of a widow who remarried (widowhood, almost *de rigueur* in radio heroines, was not long in becoming required of the heroines of television). This durable drama soon drew the kind of criticism which its radio predecessors had so often received. Of the program *TV Guide* had this to say in May, 1954:

> The only difference between CBS-TV's *Search for Tomorrow* and other soap operas is the fact that it can be seen daily at 12:30–12:45 P.M. (EDT). No other soap opera can make that statement, which is a very good thing.
>
> Frankly, "tomorrow" had better come soon for the characters on this show, before they all lose their minds. . . .
>
> The people . . . are never very happy. They keep searching for happiness, . . . but they keep winding up in a hospital or a lawyer's office. . . .
>
> The plot? Well, there's this widow who is in love with this man who either has a wife or hasn't, he isn't sure, and there is this other woman, in a hospital, who keeps saying she is so his wife. Whether she will ever walk again has not yet been disclosed. One thing, though—she can still see. Most times they go blind.

Love of Life, television's second-oldest soap opera, was introduced by CBS only a few weeks after *Search for Tomorrow.* At its beginning in 1951 it told the story of two sisters, Meg and Vanessa Dale. Vanessa married but became a widow, while Meg married and had a child. In 1958, in a typical plot complication Meg began a divorce action against her husband, by whom she was pregnant. The husband had been blackmailing Meg's new lover and was currently attempting to implicate him as the cause of Meg's "condition." Things didn't get any better in the years that followed. A decade after the preceding complications a *Love of Life* writer complained about the problem of finding predicaments in which his characters had not already discovered themselves.

Hawkins Falls, a somewhat happier drama, took place in a community patterned after Woodstock, Illinois, which had been selected as a typical middle-western town by the State Department. Background films for the serial were shot in Woodstock, and several of the program's sets were replicas of the real town's landmarks. The program, begun on nighttime television as something of a variety program, reached the daytime hours as a "novel for television." Anticipating *Peyton Place* in one aspect, *Hawkins Falls* brought into its story many more characters than were found in the average serial. Its four-year run ended in July, 1955.

Producing a television serial such as *Hawkins Falls* was far more complicated than producing one for radio, and the expense was correspondingly greater. *Sponsor*, the broadcast-advertising magazine, in January, 1951, reported that it required a crew of twenty-seven to produce *The First Hundred Years*, not counting actors, product demonstrators, organist, and announcer. Four and a half hours of rehearsal preceded each day's show. In addition to the large crew needed to produce a television serial, sets, props, and costumes were required. The weekly cost of a typical quarter-hour daytime serial in the year 1951 was $8,650, in contrast to $3,500 for a typical radio serial, according to an estimate by *Sponsor*. Within a few years that $8,650 for a week's worth of television serials was approximately the cost of a single episode.

The high cost of presentation opened the possibility that, for economic reasons alone, the serial form might not achieve the success in television that it had in radio. To push back over-all expense, CBS in 1956 tried two serials of half-hour length, production expenses for one half-hour serial being less than those for two quarter-hour dramas. This more economical program length caught on and by 1968 became universal; but television's daytime dramas remained costly, especially when compared to panel and game shows or film reruns.

In the face of imposing financial risks, packagers of television serials stayed close to proven and prevailing success formulas in creating new programs. As a result television brought forth no daytime serials reminiscent of *Vic and Sade* or *The Goldbergs* or *Against the Storm*. At the same time it produced nothing resembling the romantic pulp fiction of *Helen Trent* or *Backstage Wife*. Daytime television's unique retrogression to the literary and dramatic style of an earlier era would be *Dark Shadows* (1966), a derivative of the Gothic novel and the horror film.

The soap opera of television mirrored the middle-of-the-road radio serial. Critic Ben Gross found that it "brought before the cameras the same collection of woes which benumbed the radio listener." From the first there was unusual emphasis upon the aural portion of the drama. A housewife could follow most of an episode without having to look at the television screen—and thus could keep on with her chores. Jean Holloway was criticized almost immediately for writing *The First Hundred Years* with radio in mind. But, dramatic considerations aside, that was exactly her intent and that of her successors on other dramas. When *The Guiding Light* came to television, the radio and video versions were identical. Indeed, the announcer of one television serial in the late 1950s regularly reminded the audience to "be sure and *listen* every day."

Irna Phillips, dean of daytime-serial authors, once told me that, from a writer's standpoint, the techniques of writing television serials were much like those employed in writing for radio, although the producer and director played more important roles in preparing television dramas. Easily observable, nevertheless, were stylistic differences between the aural and the visual soap operas. The narrator, the mainstay of the radio dramas, was conspicuously absent on television. Substantially reduced was that notorious device for reviewing or prolonging action, the soliloquy. Writers of television serials would repeat whole scenes and turn frequently to dream sequences, but never would they produce the kind of purely expository soliloquy that Dr. Julian Abbott uttered in an episode of *Our Gal Sunday*: "Christopher Lane, whom I asked to help Lord Henry to rid himself of the obsession that Sunday was untrue to him . . . could I know he would fall in love with Sunday?"[1]

---

[1] Broadcast, CBS Radio, March 4, 1958. Television, incidentally, is not without its expository moments. In the introductory installment of NBC's *Bright Promise* on September 29, 1969, a fleeting conversation between the president of Bancroft College and the dean of women revealed that (1) President Boswell had lost his wife six months earlier, (2) her name was Phoebe, (3) Boswell no longer could communicate with his son, Jerry, (4) the lad was a recent Harvard dropout, (5) Bancroft College had ten thousand male students and five thousand coeds, (6) Professor of English Bill Ferguson and his wife, Martha, had been married twelve years, and (7) the dean of women had never married. Writers Frank and Doris Hursley made actors Dana Andrews and Coleen Gray ambulatory books of facts, spouting information that two long-term friends would

In repeating scenes television authors had problems not presented to radio writers. Because audiences had both heard and seen the situations portrayed in flashback, few liberties could be taken in reconstructing the past action. On occasion writers of radio serials showed such blissful disregard of what had been aired previously that repeated sequences were altered in both action and dialogue, with the effect that the narrative seemed to be progressing. Hummert staff writers especially liked to rearrange the past, as illustrated by this example from radio's *The Romance of Helen Trent*:

In early 1958 the ageless heroine, the prime suspect in a shooting incident, was attempting to absolve herself of the crime. One Monday in March she went to see Inspector Mullin, hoping that he could help her. The moment Helen passed through the door to his waiting room, she came face to face with May Getz, the "girl in red," a mysterious female who earlier had offered the innocent widow information that would clear her name. Startled at seeing Helen in police headquarters, the young woman fled immediately. With our heroine vainly exhorting the others in the waiting room, "Stop her!" the episode came to an end.

On Tuesday the incident of the day before was repeated, but with variation. Mrs. Trent did not call upon others to detain the girl—after all, they had failed the first time around. Instead she tried to persuade Miss Getz not to leave. But to no avail—once more the girl bounded out of sight. Now enter Inspector Mullin, emerging from his inner office to learn the cause of the commotion (he had had much more reason to do so on Monday, when Helen was clamoring). After being told of the incident, the day's drama concluded as he commented on the unreliability of a lady in red.

On Wednesday the fast exit was again enacted. This time, however, no time was spent in telling Inspector Mullin of the sprint. In this episode he was an observer of the scene from beginning to end. A brief confrontation had thus been presented in three different ways on successive days, consuming a good bit

have possessed before the conversation began. Later episodes were less fact-crammed.

of time and giving the illusion of plot progression to those who did not think too deeply about the whole business. In analyzing such flagrant disregard of earlier action, one must keep in mind that many listeners did not hear all three broadcasts—and none saw them, which may or may not excuse the practice of rearranging sequences, as writers of radio serials sometimes did, but does explain how they could get away with it.

To turn from stylistic to sociological considerations, a comparison of the daytime serials of radio and television in the 1950s reveals that possibly even fewer characters of the video dramas represented a cross section of American society than did those of radio. When the principal character of a TV serial was made, invariably he was a lawyer, a doctor, or a member of some other profession. Few, if any, Just Plain Bills and Lorenzo Joneses could be found to represent the barbers, garage mechanics, farmers, and miners of America. No important character was an unskilled laborer. Even as late as the beginning of the 1970s, Ernie Downs, the understanding garage owner of *Another World*, would have found it difficult to find a fellow character in any daytime drama with hands soiled by labor.

There were, of course, housewives among the principals. But just as marriage had not prevented Mary Noble of *Backstage Wife* from having a successful fling at motion-picture acting or Mary Marlin from coming close to running the country, the marital state did not keep the homemakers of television from side adventures beyond the hope of Mrs. Average American. It must be noted, however, that the television housewife was more recognizable as such than was her radio counterpart (possibly because puttering around a kitchen provided good stage business). And never did the nonhousehold achievements reach the level of fancy of radio's golden days.

Beyond question the economic level of television's serial society was higher than average. The settings alone demonstrated this fact. Yet great wealth was not common to the main characters, most of whom worked for their money. Some serial principals employed servants, but not nearly as many as in the radio era of the 1930s, when help was less expensive. If servants appeared, they tended, as in radio days, to be related closely to the lives of their employers, almost becoming members of the family. They could be called upon for advice, and sometimes they had problems of their own. Television, however, produced no dignified gentleman's gentleman to match Peterson of *Helen Trent*, who helped Helen carry out her amateur criminal investigations.

It was as servants—Gardenia of *Betty and Bob* and Lily of *When A Girl Marries*—that Negroes appeared in daytime serials in the earlier years. By the 1950s even this station was largely denied them—perhaps to avoid offense. Most of the characters of the daytime serial drama of television, employers and employees, were Caucasian American Protestants. Although minority characters were portrayed sympathetically, television had no Goldbergs, no kindly Papa Davids. Strong pressures did finally result in the introduction of some Negro principals in 1968, but, considering the dominant strata of serial society, it was a most difficult integration. One trick was to make blacks patients or physicians in hospitals. But only *One Life to Live* (introduced in 1968) could be said to have carried things beyond tokenism at the threshold of the 1970s.

In moral tone the television serial was less severe than its parent. The radio serial was weighed down with the Puritan ethic it had borrowed from the domestic novel. In an atmosphere of perfect justice its villains were unmistakably destined to lose in the end—even if that end did not come until after the rascals had caused difficulties for months or, as was more likely, for years.

Although justice normally came as a matter of course, with no necessity for divine intervention, a troubled character of radio days occasionally might ask for help from above. The request, nevertheless, came close to being a reminder that justice should be served. In episode 2,119 of *Portia Faces Life* a man on trial for a murder he did not commit gave an excellent précis of soap-opera philosophy not so readily found in television dramas: "The God whom I love is a just God and merciful. He will not let Carl Hubbard go free while I pay with my life for a crime of which I'm innocent. Bill and Kathy will get here in time. Joan will be able to tell the truth on the witness stand."

While crime was emphasized in the daytime radio serial, sex was not. The occasional love scenes would have been approved by Underwriters' Laboratories. The ultimate in radio soap-opera passion, the kiss, often was merely suggested—by a pause and a sigh. In television things had to be more explicit. Initially, moments of real ardor were reserved for wayward husbands and "other women." (And to balance the fact that the audience could see what was going on during the pause, television directors deleted the sigh—or cut quickly to a commercial.) As the years went by, however, the contrast between radio and television romance became enormous.

The interpretation of sex in the radio dramas of the Hummerts was absurdly naïve, of course, even by radio standards. I think immediately of the time Helen Trent reminded her fiance that an engagement ring did not give him the privilege to hold her hand. Helen and her kind had a way of making a kiss seem like sexual excess. Once, when she was not herself, Helen threw caution aside and asked Gil Whitney, her oldest suitor in point of service, to put his arms around her and press his face to hers. It was a shocking thing for Helen Trent to do. To set matters right, she took the only course open to a good girl of thirty-five or more: she asked Gil to marry her—right away. The patient lover, clearly overcome by the face pressing, ecstatic after fifteen years of waiting, and moved to the point of eloquence, exclaimed, "You bet!"

Timeworn scenes of attempted seduction appeared frequently in the factory-made radio serials, even in the late 1950s. A 1957 episode of *Backstage Wife* contained this bit of melodrama from the Gay Nineties:

VILLAIN: I'll kiss that hatred out of you!
MARY: No, you wouldn't!
MUSIC: Organ theme to end episode.

Three months later Helen Trent was again in the same kind of fix. Villain Kurt Bonine had trapped her in an empty house. As he approached lustfully, Helen cried, "Kurt, you're mad!" A commercial message saved Helen for sixty seconds, after which listeners were returned to the empty house, where Helen faced a "desperate unmasked devil." The desperate unmasked devil was discoursing upon his revenge. Helen had repulsed him long enough; his vengeance would begin. As the end of the episode approached, Kurt declared, "When I'm through with you . . . ." He never finished the line. Helen, her back to the wall, broke in with the injunction sacred to Hummert heroines: "Kurt, Kurt, you wouldn't!"

It was not true that Kurt wouldn't—most of the thrill from a scene like that came from knowing that Kurt very well would if given the time. But in the radio serial it was certain that Kurt and his fellow villains *didn't*. Something or someone always spoiled their fun. Then, too, there always was an element of doubt about what the villain had in mind. Sometimes what sounded like attempted seduction turned out to be an act less heinous to a Hummert heroine: attempted murder.

Toward the end of the radio serial era naïveté about sex began to disappear. Television's soap operas—and the later ones of radio—seemed more in touch with life. On the same day that Helen Trent was resisting the advances of Kurt Bonine, Vicky Harcourt, in TV's *Love of Life*, was teasing a producer into giving her a part by touching the top button of her blouse and laughingly threatening to "call for help and say you were molesting me." The scene, played for humor, made the *Helen Trent* installment of the same day seem even more out of step with the times. By the mid-sixties, when soap-opera love scenes were unquestionably the hottest things on television, the radio serials, which had been gone only a few years, seemed of another century.

The portrayal of minor vice, by the way, also moved closer to social mores in the late 1950s. Good characters were allowed to smoke or drink occasionally in almost all serials, radio and television. Helen Trent—whose only excess was donning "glamorous" evening gowns—remained a nonsmoker, of course, as did several other principals. But abstinence as a means of showing the moral superiority of one character over another was vanishing. A vestige of the old soap-opera attitude could be found only rarely, as in a 1958 episode of *Helen Trent* in which the villainess, Lisa Voltner, offered the archangel a cigarette. "No, thank you," Helen responded with forced tolerance. "But *you* go ahead."

Perhaps, when literary and sociological aspects are set aside, the essential difference between the daytime serials of the two media was that for obvious reason much less was left to the imagination of the viewer than was left to that of the listener. Despite the lack of stress upon visual action, the television serial, including people and things, was there to be seen. Characters were not as a viewer imagined them; they were as they were. The living room in which the action was unfolded had furniture and draperies and accessories—even a view out the window which told what season it was or, perhaps, the geographical setting. Even more important than the furnishings were the wardrobes of the women in the cast, which of necessity had to undergo the scrutiny of the women watching at home. A good girl in the wrong dress was a calamity in television soap opera.

With great care and astute judgment the packager of a daytime serial for television could put together the visual aspects in a manner that might approach the way an individual viewer would have arranged things in her mind if the program had been on radio. But the risk was great, and the result was never as satisfactory as one left to the imagination. Surely that in part explains why the television serial could not and cannot impress its audience (and thus upset its critics) in the same manner as did the continued dramas of early radio.

Admittedly, those who encountered the serial drama in the mid-1950s and later were more sophisticated, knew more of the world, than their counterparts of depression days. But in its few years of glory radio drama was a special medium allowing freer rein to the fantasy zone of the mind than any that had preceded it. When molded into serial form, it afforded an opportunity for identification with characters and use of the imagination that may never be seen again. The gain or loss that has resulted from its disappearance I leave to the reader. Anyone captured by a radio serial drama is bound to be prejudiced in his answer.

AFTER NOON TV

ON THE SET WITH DARK SHADOWS

EXCLUSIVE STORIES!

Jonathan Frid
Joan Bennett
Peter Hansen
Macdonald Carey

"HAPPY BIRTHDAY, GENERAL HOSPITAL"

PHOTOS! BIOS!

FABULOUS TV CONTEST
(See page 33)

Barnabas Collins (played by Jonathan Frid), the vampire of *Dark Shadows*, eyes a possible victim on the cover of *Afternoon TV*, a magazine devoted entirely to daytime serials.

Nancy Hughes (played by Helen Wagner) and a pensive Grandpa Hughes (Santos Ortega), of *As the World Turns.*

The original cast of *As the World Turns*. ABOVE, FROM LEFT: Chris Hughes (Don McLaughlin), Claire Lowell (Anne Burr), Nancy Hughes (Helen Wagner), Edith Hughes (Ruth Warrick), Penny Hughes (Rosemary Prinz), Ellen Lowell (Wendy Drew), and Jim Lowell (Les Damon). BELOW: Ellen and Penny share a secret.

Three of the many paperback books based upon daytime serials in the late 1960s and early 1970s.

Mary Stuart, who in 1951 began her long tenure as the heroine of
Search for Tomorrow, television's oldest daytime serial.

The principal characters of *Peyton Place* beam from the cover of a souvenir magazine published by Ideal Publishing Corporation.

GOLD EDITION

a new novel of
suspense based on ABC-TV'S

DARK SHADOWS

Mysterious footsteps in the night terrify
Victoria Winters at Collins House—a mansion
haunted by legends of murder, madness and evil.

Marilyn Ross

The first in a long series of paperbacks built upon *Dark Shadows*.

A GENEALOGY OF THE FORSYTE FAMILY

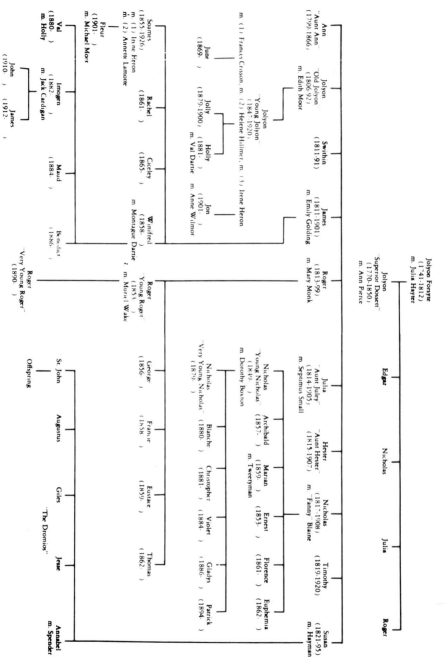

INCONSTANCY

The old sailor said this to Neptune in a great storm: "O god, thou shalt save me if thou please; if not, thou shalt lose me; yet will I keep my rudder true."

MONTAIGNE, *Essays*

When television supplemented radio as the major broadcast medium, the history of the daytime serial drama became more than ever a reflection of the attitudes and fortunes of the three leading networks. Neither Mutual's large radio system nor the short-lived Du Mont television chain offered much daytime programing. Further, the transcribed domestic dramas of the radio syndicators were almost gone, one of the last being *Ruby Valentine*, created for the Negro market in 1953, and featuring *South Pacific*'s Juanita Hall as the operator of a metropolitan beauty shop. By the middle of the 1950s only ABC, NBC, and CBS were carrying soap opera to the whole nation, with different degrees of success and interest.

371

The American Broadcasting Company had pointedly abandoned the daytime serial during World War II and made no
use of it on television until the 1960s. But in the 1951–52 season
ABC's policy makers decided to make a strong bid for radio's
daytime audience with about a dozen serial dramas. One, *When
a Girl Marries*, was transferred from NBC. The rest were revivals
—shows such as *Mary Marlin, Valiant Lady, Lone Journey,
Joyce Jordan*, and, curiously, *Against the Storm*. ABC had been
without serials for too long, however, to draw listeners away
from the established soap operas of radio or the budding ones of
television. In 1953 the popular *When a Girl Marries* was ABC's
sole survivor. Linked to its glorious past by the voice of Mary
Jane Higby (who played Joan), it survived until ABC adopted a
music and news format for its radio network in 1957.

Despite its past success with the genre, the National Broadcasting Company demonstrated an inconsistent attitude toward
the daytime serial in both its radio and its television networks.
Serials had long been the bulwark of NBC's radio programing,
and the network had a strong block of them in the afternoon.
But in the fall of 1955, NBC began to eliminate some of its oldest
and most successful continued dramas to make room for a conglomerate multihour program called *Weekday*. By the time the
network had completed its program reorientation, it had eliminated in less-than-tender fashion such long-running features as
Just Plain Bill, Lorenzo Jones, Stella Dallas, and *Young Widder
Brown*.

In the face of all this carnage—and the attendant wailing—it
must have embarrassed NBC executives when Weekday, a vir-
tual repudiation of the "same time tomorrow" concept on which
daytime radio was built, failed dismally. In the summer of 1956
the network struggled to rebuild its daytime programing, with
self-contained dramas—and daytime serials.

NBC's changeability, coupled with CBS Radio's loss in serial
sponsorship in 1955, placed daytime serial drama in a critical
position. To some, the death of radio soap opera seemed imminent. Yet CBS Radio held firm, presenting its serials in an
unbroken two-and-a-half-hour block, whether sponsored or not,

in the expectation that the regular listening patterns which always had sustained daytime drama would overcome the attractiveness of television. The network's trust was well placed. Not only did CBS Radio's serial sponsors return, but the network gained new daytime listeners. In the spring of 1956 a CBS vice-president, John Karol, told the Wisconsin Broadcasters' Association that the preservation of the serial block had resulted in an 8 per cent increase in the daytime audience of his chain. At the same time, the major competitor, NBC, had lost more than half its daytime listeners, making the CBS daytime audience twice that of any other network. Karol pointed to the new $1.5 million contract with Colgate as an indication of the appeal of the daytime serial.

The television wing of CBS also gave importance to the daytime serial drama, again to the company's advantage. CBS kept *Search for Tomorrow* and *Love of Life* on the air and steadily added new serials. Most of them thrived. For its part NBC Television made a series of sweeping changes in its serial programs. In 1953 a small morning block of daytime serials was developed, only to be replaced in a matter of months by the *Home* program. In 1954 a two-hour afternoon block of daytime serials was developed. The next year the serial period was cut in half to make room for *Matinee Theatre*, an hour-long drama program hailed as the answer to the daytime serial. The remaining serials survived for a while, because of their favorable positions in the broadcast schedule, but they dwindled until, by the summer of 1956, NBC Television had only one daytime serial drama.

The NBC serials of the early and mid-1950s appeared and disappeared rapidly. *The House in the Garden* (also called *Fairmeadows, U.S.A.*) lasted just three months in late 1952. A woman alone was the predominating character in most of the NBC failures. She was a Philadelphia society girl in Elaine Carrington's *Follow Your Heart* (1953–54), a New York model named Poco in *Three Steps to Heaven* (1953–54), a girl reporter in *A Time to Live* (1954), a widowed physician in *The Greatest Gift* (1954–55), an aspiring singer in *Golden Windows* (1954–55), and a famous but over-forty actress in *Concerning Miss*

Marlowe (1954–55). None of these ladies became serious rivals to the memorable heroines of radio, largely because of NBC's erratic policy. But it must be noted that four of them had not married by the time their shows left the air. This fact suggests another weakness of the serials: housewives could not identify with the heroines as they could with those of such serials as CBS Television's *Valiant Lady*, who acquired the necessary scars of connubiality and hung on a little longer.

Not even matrimonial disorder, however, could keep the NBC ax from *The Bennetts* (July 6, 1953–January 8, 1954) and the slightly longer running *First Love* (1954–55). The most nearly successful NBC-TV daytime serial during this period was *The World of Mr. Sweeney*, starring Charlie Ruggles as Cicero P. Sweeney, the widowed proprietor of a general store. Ironically, this drama, which ran from October, 1953, to December, 1955, was the farthest from the formula serial of any daytime drama of television.[1]

The World of Mr. Sweeney, once part of the *Kate Smith* program, was episodic in format, one of daytime's few self-contained serials since *Vic and Sade*. The slightly more common closed-end format of *Aunt Jenny's True Life Stories* cropped up in three NBC-TV soap operas of the mid-1950s. Of the three only a one-time radio feature, *Modern Romances*, was of any consequence. From 1954 to 1958 the program unfolded week-long confession stories in a third-person style which exchanged secret sharing for keyhole peeping.

In this time of near disaster for the daytime serial on NBC, that network's chief television rival introduced several of its better daytime investments. One was the near crime drama, *The Edge of Night*, which first appeared on CBS-TV in 1956 and has survived into the 1970s. Here was soap opera with a strong male lead: detective (and later attorney) Mike Karr, first played in virile manner by the late John Larkin, radio's Perry Mason. An-

---

[1] By coincidence NBC had an offbeat serial on its radio network at the same time, also with a film veteran in the lead. Frank McHugh played Mr. Jolly in *Hotel for Pets* until the kindly former postman's animal shelter was demolished in the NBC serial cutback of 1955–56.

other CBS success built upon a male character, less virile, was *The Secret Storm*, depicting widower Peter Ames. Surprisingly, *Road of Life* ("Dr. Brent, call Sur-ger-ee!") in no way matched its radio tenure. A second CBS failure anchored to a male psysician was *The Seeking Heart.* Its exit was less noteworthy, however, than that of Portia Blake, who, as a radio retread, faced life only briefly on television.

Irna Phillips, always handy with family dramas, brought two serials to CBS-TV as she began her mastery of a new medium. One, *The Guiding Light*, duplicated the concurrent radio adventures of the Bauer family, daughter Meta being the prominent clan member in 1952, when the telecast was introduced. A wholly new Irna Phillips family drama was the highly popular *As the World Turns* (1956). It and *Edge of Night* were television's first half-hour daytime serials.

At what pace did these longer dramas move? The question can perhaps be answered through a synopsis of seven days' events in *As the World Turns* during midsummer, 1957, when a well-extended plot strain of illicit romance was being replaced by new narrative turns. *ATWT* then, as now, was a tale of two families, the Lowells and the Hugheses, residents of the exclusive Oakdale area (presumably near Chicago). The household of attorney Chris Hughes comprised his wife, Nancy; children Penny, Don, and Bob; and his elderly father, known as Grandpa. An important figure in the drama in 1957 was Chris's attractive spinster sister, Edith. She was the paramour of Jim Lowell, Chris's partner in the law firm founded by his father, white-haired Judge Lowell. The authorized Lowell women were Jim's wife, Claire, and his teenage daughter, Ellen (Penny Hughes's best friend).

As we begin our story, Jim Lowell has been killed in a boating accident in Florida—a fate that might be considered serial justice, in that he had gone south for less than noble reasons. Lowell was in Florida to wait out a divorce from Claire, who had discovered his affair with Edith Hughes. Until the fatal accident young Ellen Lowell had tried earnestly to keep her parents from divorce. Now the Lowells and the Hugheses face the problem of recovering from sorrow as well as scandal. The synopsis follows:

Wednesday, July 24, 1957: Penny Hughes asks to go to Cornell instead of the local university. Her parents try to dissuade Penny, knowing that it is not Cornell but Cornell man Chuck Henderson who really interests her. Later, at the local coke bar, Chuck is not properly impressed by Penny's announcement of a change in her college plans.

Thursday, July 25, 1957: Over coffee Judge Lowell tells Claire that he has spent enough time at her house recovering from the loss of his son. In the next scene Edith Hughes examines the offices of Dr. Doug Cassen, whom she will assist for two weeks as a receptionist. That night Dr. Cassen has dinner with Claire Lowell and her father and agrees that the old gentleman is well enough to go home. ("It is time to break the Cord," he says. "Cord?" asks Claire, and Dr. Cassen explains the Silver Cord to the apparently well-educated woman. He concludes by saying, "It's psychological." Claire replies, "Oh.") After Judge Lowell retires, Dr. Cassen casually asks Claire to dinner the next week.

Friday, July 26, 1957: Ellen Lowell criticizes her mother for putting away her father's picture. The next morning Edith begins her new job. After her first day's work she dines with Dr. Cassen. She tells him that her temporary work in a doctor's office has already helped her to see that others have problems.

Monday, July 29, 1957: Ellen visits Penny in her bedroom. Their conversation recapitulates events of preceding months. While they are discussing Chuck Henderson, Penny receives a call from him. Ellen does not approve of their romance, and says so. She also announces that she will study law so that she can take the place of the father she idolized. Meanwhile, at the Lowells', Claire and Emma, the maid, agree that Judge Lowell looks good but express concern over Ellen. When the girl returns from the Hughes home and discovers that her mother plans to dine with Dr. Cassen, she is hurt and horrified.

Tuesday, July 30, 1957: The story resumes immediately following the preceding episode. Ellen apologizes for her behavior. In the Lowell garden Judge Lowell and Grandfather Hughes chat. Ellen joins them and pointedly asks how Edith is getting along in Dr. Cassen's office. After Grandpa Hughes leaves, Judge Lowell asks Ellen why she brought up a subject that hurt the old man. Ellen replies that Edith is a bad woman, that she does not think Judge Lowell should have asked Edith's brother to be a senior partner in the law firm. When Judge Lowell reminds his granddaughter that nothing can change the fact that Edith and Jim loved each other, she turns her attack to the dinner date her mother is currently having with Dr. Cassen. In a parallel scene, Dr. Cassen, echoing Judge Lowell, tells his dinner partner that Edith and Jim loved each other.

Wednesday, July 31, 1957: In the Hughes living room Chris Hughes tells his wife of his concern over Penny's interest in Chuck Henderson. Nancy is not worried. Meanwhile, in the living room of the wealthy Baker family, young Jeff Baker, who likes Penny, tries unsuccessfully to interest his father in his plans for college. At a country-club dance Penny and Chuck discuss materialism briefly, but soon are kissing. Back at the Hughes home, Jeff Baker is a visitor. In Penny's parents he has found two people who will listen to his plans for the future. His own parents are not interested.

Thursday, August 1, 1957 (the same day which began with the Monday, July 29, episode): Grandfather Hughes has returned from the Lowells'. In the Lowell living room the judge is worried about Ellen's attitude toward her mother. Ellen, on the other hand, prefers to discuss her plans for a law career and *her* concern about Penny. Then the action returns to the Hughes home. It is late and Chris is worried. At last his daughter and Chuck return from the dance. They kiss, and Penny arranges another date. After Chuck leaves, Chris tells his daughter that she might be hurt. He feels that she wants marriage too much. Penny asks him to have a little faith in her.

As the World Turns continued at the same leisurely pace. On Friday, August 15, 1957, the situation was about the same as it had been seventeen episodes earlier. Ellen Lowell was still mourning the loss of her father (as she would be more than nine months later in the Memorial Day episode of May 30, 1958), Penny was seeking marriage, and Jeff Baker was seeking Penny. After almost a year the problems brought on by Jim Lowell's death had not been solved. In the meantime there was an annulled marriage (Penny and Jeff) and, in April, 1958, a murder trial, with Jeff the defendant and Chris his attorney. Both of these complications resulted from conditions which were known to the viewers at least as early as July, 1957; Penny's desire for an early marriage and the lack of understanding demonstrated by Jeff's parents. Serial events seldom took viewers by surprise.

Yet as slow as events might seem to move in an Irna Phillips serial, strange accelerations could occur chronologically. Selected individuals could age in miraculous fashion. Jeff Baker, a teenager at the time of the happenings described above was a successful man in his thirties just six years later. Married a second time to Penny, Jeff became one of the more popular male characters of afternoon television. Only the desperation of his impersonator, Mark Rydell, to escape the confinement of the series ended the tortures inflicted upon this matinee victim of annulment, trial for murder, alcoholism, and pericarditis. Jeff Baker, who could not conceivably be represented by another actor, met death on a rain-soaked roadway, thus bequeathing to his loved ones agonies enough for years of analysis and reconciling. Meanwhile other boys of *As the World Turns* shot forward in age in startling manner to fill the romantic-male gap left by Baker's death. Through a biological miracle these youths were explaining the facts of life to their offsprings at a time they themselves should only have been emerging from puberty.

The production studio of *As the World Turns*, incidentally, was a veritable Valhalla of former radio stars. Grandfathers Lowell and Hughes were played by, respectively, William Johnstone, The Shadow for many years, and Santos Ortega, enactor of numerous character roles, including that of *The Shadow's* Commissioner Weston. The part of Chris Hughes was assigned to Don McLaughlin, known on radio as Dr. Jim Brent (also as David Harding: Counterspy and, briefly, as Batman). These actors held their roles into the 1970s. Three others in the original cast—Anne Burr (who played Claire), Les Damon (James Lowell), and Wendy Drew (Ellen)—at one time occupied the title roles in radio's *Big Sister*, *The Thin Man*, and *Young Widder Brown*, respectively.

One Hughes family member came not from radio but from television stardom—of a sort. Don Hastings (Bob Hughes) was the Video Ranger on Du Mont's quaint serial adventure *Captain Video*. Rounding out the strong original cast were Helen Wagner (portraying Nancy Hughes), Rosemary Prinz (Penny), and Ruth Warrick (Edith). Miss Warrick, as Hannah Cord, would later become a conspicuous member of the *Peyton Place* entourage. In January, 1970, she was reunited with Miss Prinz, possibly the most popular of all daytime serial performers, for the bow of ABC's *All My Children*. That title, by the way, offered extraordinary promise in that it was obvious from the first episode that Amy Tyler, the principal character, had borne at least one child out of wedlock. *All My Children*, if it lives up to its beginning, could become television's most comprehensive family drama.

FAMILY SAGA

The security and elevation of the family and of family life are the prime objects of civilization, and the ultimate end of all industry and trade.

CHARLES W. ELIOT, *The Happy Life*

The attention given in this book to the family-centered serials of the daytime, from *The Goldbergs* to *As the World Turns*, is not meant to imply that after the families of Molly Goldberg and Pepper Young moved to afternoon radio in 1936 the nighttime air was devoid of household dramas. Most of the situation comedies in prime broadcasting hours revolved about domestic problems of one kind or another. The early serial *Raising Junior* (1930) portrayed the problems of parents with young children, as did several other radio (and later, television) comedies, such as *Blondie* (1939), *The Adventures of Ozzie and Harriet* (1944), and *Beulah* (1945). The long-running series *The Aldrich Family*, with its familiar "Hen-ree! Hen-ree Aldrich!" emphasized the dilemmas of a teenage boy, played brilliantly by Ezra Stone. *That Brewster Boy* (1941) was of the same pattern. Female counterparts of the Aldrich scion (but lacking his colorful "Coming, Mother!" catch line) were the principals of *Meet Corliss Archer* and *A Date with Judy*, two series begun in the 1943–44 season.

None of these dramas, however, could be called family sagas. A little closer to that classification were *Father Knows Best* (which was introduced to radio in 1949 and to television in 1954) and *Mama*, the 1949–57 television adaptation of the play *I Remember Mama* (which itself was based upon the book *Mama's Bank Account*). Other television shows depicting a whole family with approximately equal emphasis on each member were *The Life of Riley* (introduced on radio in 1943 and on television in 1949), *Life With Father* (1953), and *The Real McCoys* (1957).

But of all the American-produced family series of radio and television only one approached the chronological span of John Galsworthy's novels known as *The Forsyte Saga*, which perhaps not incidentally served as its inspiration. In the spring of 1932 radio listeners all over the United States began to notice a weekly continued story that careful after-dark tuning could bring in from its point of origin at KGO San Francisco (and shortly thereafter the Pacific regional stations of NBC). By the next spring *One Man's Family* was a national program, something it would continue to be for more than a quarter-century, as listening to it became in the 1930s and 1940s a Sunday-night ritual. The saga of the Barbours did not end until 1959, just four days before its twenty-seventh anniversary.

One Man's Family was a profitable labor of love for its creator, Carlton E. Morse, the author of *I Love a Mystery*. Indeed, he employed the same actors in both dramas, though he called the mystery a drama of plot and the family series one of characterization. Morse, who drew the characters for both series with care, always associated the fictional persons with the actors who played them. He wrote his scripts with the performers in mind, even when creating new characters. So closely did Morse asso-

381

ciate his characters with his actors that he eliminated the important role of Clifford Barbour from the *One Man's Family* radio series on the death of Barton Yarborough, the actor who had played him for many years.[1] Clifford moved to Scotland and was heard from only by letter.

The tenure of Morse's actors was extraordinary. When *One Man's Family* left the air in 1959, many of the roles of the radio version were being played by performers who had originated them in 1932. Long-time bachelor J. Anthony Smythe, in his eighties, still held forth as Henry Barbour, and Minetta Ellen, the original Fanny Barbour, had given up her role to Mary Adams of the television version only two years earlier. Page Gilman (Jack) and Bernice Berwin (Hazel) were veterans of the first broadcast. And only after many seasons had Michael Raffeto (Paul—and Jack Packard of *I Love a Mystery*) been replaced by Russell Thorson, the Paul of television.

Through casual bits of dialogue, occasional moments of recollection by the drama's characters, and printed materials such as *Jack's Camera Scrapbook*, a popular premium, it was possible for the regular listener to trace the Barbour saga as far back as San Francisco in the 1890s, when Henry Barbour (born in 1875) began courting Fanny Martin (born in 1878 of New England stock). Fanny had two other suitors: Glenn Hunter, a promising young lawyer, and Fred Thompson, a horse-and-buggy doctor. Henry Barbour had worked his way from grocery clerk to stockbroker's aide, but it appeared that his rivals would soon leave him behind financially.

Fanny chose Henry, however, and married him in her home in 1896. Future Judge Hunter, she explained later, was surrounded too often by female admirers, and young Dr. Thompson always smelled of antiseptic. Both rejected suitors, nevertheless, remained close friends of the Barbours over the years

---

[1] Yarborough, who had played Doc on *I Love a Mystery*, was also written out of *Dragnet* at the time. Rather than put another actor in the Ben Romero role, Jack Webb gave Sergeant Friday a new assistant, played by Ben Alexander. Incidentally, the third of the original leads of *I Love a Mystery*, Walter Paterson (Reggie), was also in *One Man's Family*, playing Nicholas Lacey. He too died, but his role could not be eliminated from the family drama and was continued by other actors.

and offered them financial assistance in the formation of the Barbour Stock and Bond Company. Henry stolidly refused the help.

In 1897, Paul, the tragedy-marked oldest child of the Barbours, was born. Hazel came along in 1900. The financial struggle of the fledgling stockbroker was in no way improved by the San Francisco earthquake of 1906, but by 1912, the year twins Claudia and Clifford were born, the new firm was on solid footing. The Barbour residence at Sea Cliff was built in 1916, the year before youngest child, Jack, was born—and twenty-year-old Paul went off to war as an aviator. When the radio series began in 1932, Jack was a teenager and Paul, a somewhat disillusioned veteran whose bride, nurse Elaine Hunter, had died in 1918.

Paul never married again, though he fell in love with one of Clifford's companions, widow Beth Holly (played by Barbara Jo Allen, who on the Bob Hope radio show changed personality to become the man-crazy Vera Vague). The oldest Barbour son moved through the series as a philosopher/counselor who presented what often must have been the Carlton Morse viewpoint. Father Barbour, though he loved young children, tended toward conservatism in his outlook, and after a joust with Paul or another of his offspring he was likely to retire to his gardening, a mild deprecation rumbling around somewhere between his larynx and his lips.

The high-spirited Claudia (originally played by Kathleen Wilson) often fell into melancholy, but used long walks along the sea cliffs or chats with Paul as therapy. The mercurial Clifford suffered the deaths of wives Ann Waite (in childbirth) and Irene Franklin (in an auto accident) before finding offstage happiness in Scotland with Mary McLeod. Steady Hazel (Father Barbour's favorite) had a happy marriage to Bill Herbert and after his death married Dan Murray. As everyone expected he would, Jack married his childhood sweetheart, Betty Carter.

Long before *One Man's Family* reached television for the first time in 1949, the Barbour children had children, making the clan a bit large for transfer to a new medium. So, for the home screen, Morse, as he would do for a daytime-television run in 1954, began the saga again, leaving the radio characters as they were. An interesting aspect of this time trick was that Anne Whitfield, who played granddaughter Penelope in the nighttime radio version became her mother, Claudia, on daytime TV (the Claudia of the earlier television run was Eva Marie Saint). The Father Barbours of television were Bert Lytell and Theodore von Eltz.[2]

Though often associated with daytime serials, even before it became one, *One Man's Family* always seemed to have a little extra stature. Its many years as a Sunday night radio feature made it something of an institution in American homes, a veritable paean to family life. The long summaries that followed the announcer's designation of "Book ——, Chapter ——" were almost like letters from a favorite relative recounting recent experiences of friends or loved ones. As the years went by, Bill Andrews, Ken Carpenter, and other announcers reviewed events in the lives of the Barbours: Claudia's wild romance with Johnny Roberts (and her stabilizing marriage to Englishman Nicholas Lacey), young Jack's boyish fancies, Paul's tragic romance with the lovely Beth Holly, Cliff's continual stumblings, granddaughter Joan's infatuations with older men. Somehow the events did not seem maudlin; there was an underlying spirit of optimism and warmth and sometimes quiet humor. Morse and his actors were able to turn long chats between characters—almost moribund exchanges in the daytime serials—into realistic vignettes of middle-class Americana. The warm relationship of Mother Barbour and daughter-in-law Betty came forth vividly when they talked upstairs while folding laundry or hanging curtains. Paul's wartime conversations with his foster daughter, Teddy, a girl driven as if by the wind from one attachment or consum-

[2] In making *One Man's Family* a daytime serial in 1954, NBC Television put what had been for most of its life a half-hour series into a fifteen-minute, Monday through Friday, format not too propitious for a story with so many characters (the earlier television series had presented hour-long weekly episodes). The daytime version was among the dramas pushed off television in 1955 to make room for *Matinee Theatre*. In this daytime run, incidentally, Johnny Roberts was killed in action, not in China of the mid-1930s, but in Indo-China of the mid-1950s.

ing passion to another, became models of communication between generations.

The "Destiny Waltz," by Sydney Barnes, introduced the program, dedicated by the announcer to "the mothers and fathers of the younger generation and to their bewildering offspring." (After 1941 the theme was organist Paul Carson's "Patricia.") Morse's characters and format eventually became so familiar that they lent themselves splendidly to parody. Bob and Ray obliged with "One Feller's Family, the Story of the Butchers"— an exercise, incidentally, much more respectful of the original than was their "Mary Backstage, Noble Wife," which slapped at both soap opera and McCarthyism.

Before parody, though, came imitation, principally in the form of *Those We Love* (1938–45) the story of the Marshalls and Dr. Leslie Foster. *Those We Love's* performers, most of them film actors, included Donald Woods (Dr. Foster), Francis X. Bushman (John Marshall), and Nan Grey and Richard Cromwell as the Marshall twins, Kathy and Kit. Jean Rogers, of the *Flash Gordon* chapter plays, and Robert Cummings also were heard at times in the drama. The writer was the capable Agnes Ridgway. While always supported by a respectable audience (generally a touch smaller than that of *Dr. Christian*, actor Jean Hersholt's quiet, long-running nighttime series, which also emphasized the virtues of American life), *Those We Love* posed no threat to *One Man's Family's* role as radio's family drama of prestige. Only the changing fortunes of broadcasting were able to diminish and finally end Morse's drama.

When it was necessary to close the final book in the Barbour saga, listeners of almost three decades were entitled to lament the departure from public life of this distinguished family. Americans who could not have named the secretary of commerce in 1959 had no trouble rattling off the lineage of the Barbours, from Henry and Fanny to the grandchildren: Hazel's Margaret and twins Hank and Pinky; Clifford's J. D.; Jack's Elizabeth Ann, Janie, Mary Lou, and triplets Abigail, Deborah, and Constance; Paul's Teddy; and Claudia's Penny, Nicky, and

Joan—whose own "bewildering offspring" began the fourth generation.

Just as the Barbour people had become real to many listeners, so had the Barbour places: the residence at Sea Cliff and the Sky Ranch retreat. Sky Ranch was actually the author's King's Mountain hideaway. Its characteristics often were worked into the dramas, adding to the realistic tone for which Carlton Morse's drama is remembered.

After filing away the 14 million words and 150 book-length volumes that had been *One Man's Family*, Morse wrote in the *Los Angeles Times* on June 6, 1959:

> Always the philosophy and the story line have been devoted to the idea that "so long as the integrity of the American family remained intact no great harm could come to this nation. . . .
>
> My own sorrow is not so much in the cessation of the show as such as in the thought that one more happy, sober beacon to light the way has been put out. One more marker has been torn down. . . . The signposts for sound family life are now few, and I feel the loss of *One Man's Family* is just another abandoned lighthouse.

Millions of disappointed listeners—and a few critics too—agreed with him.

LEAVE-TAKING

> *A thousand thrills and quivering sounds*
> *In airy circles o'er us fly.*
> *Till, wafted by a gentle breeze,*
> *They faint and languish by degrees,*
> *And at a distance die.*

JOSEPH ADDISON, *Ode for Saint Cecilia's Day*

As the end approached, the daytime serial seemed still to have a place in network radio. 1958 drew to a close with sixteen continued dramas listed in program logs of the radio chains (television had ten). Seven of the sound dramas were twenty or more years old, a sign of good health. Audience ratings were large, an even better sign. And all the radio serials were at least partly sponsored.

Commercials were so evident, as a matter of fact, that the leisurely pace of the old radio soap opera seemed utterly lost. Here is the outline for the episode of *Helen Trent* on December 23, 1957:

ANNOUNCER: Statement of program's sponsors
MUSIC: Chords played on guitar
TRANSCRIPTION: Commercial for Spry
MUSIC: "Juanita" played on guitar and hummed
ANNOUNCER: Standard opening with music in background
DIALOGUE: (One minute, twenty seconds)
TRANSCRIPTION: Commercial for Breeze
MUSIC: "Juanita"
ANNOUNCER: Returns listeners to the program
DIALOGUE: (Four minutes, forty seconds)
MUSIC: "Juanita"
ANNOUNCER: Returns listeners to the program
DIALOGUE: (Fifty-seven seconds)
ANNOUNCER: Urges audience to listen the next day
TRANSCRIPTION: Commercial for Scott Waldorf tissue
MUSIC: "Juanita"
ANNOUNCER: Standard closing with music in background.

The dialogue of the Helen Trent program totaled six minutes, fifty-seven seconds. That was about one minute less than the average amount of dialogue on the CBS Radio serials of that day —eight minutes, eleven seconds. The many interruptions of the dramatic portions undoubtedly made serial plots appear less static than they really were.[1]

During the last days of the radio serial it was possible to draw some fairly sharp distinctions among basic types. Easiest to isolate were the overly melodramatic formula serials best represented by *The Romance of Helen Trent*. This group once contained the greatest number of daytime dramas because of the assembly-line methods of the Hummerts; but as the years went by, the number of such buskins noticeably decreased. The decline in number did not mean, however, that old-style serials had become unpopular. The ratings of *The Romance of Helen Trent*, *Backstage Wife*, and *Our Gal Sunday* were of substantial size until the end. But were the audiences of these programs made up largely of women who had listened to them for many

---

[1] Such precision in timing could be achieved more conveniently through pre-taping. Gone were the days of live drama where serial actors waited desperately for the next page of the script while the drama was on the air. Similarly, most television serials were taped, usually on the day before the broadcast after extensive rehearsal.

years, or did the shows also attract younger women? Programs
of this sort did not appear on television, though Frank Hummert, writing in the summer of 1958, did not believe that the
serial audience in general had changed much:

> Running in the daytime the appeal was primarily to women. As
> much so, let's say, as the big women's magazines. And from what
> I am told, . . . this same appeal is the basis of them today.
> I do not believe the audiences have changed, or their [the
> serials'] appeal for that matter. The audiences are not so large
> now because of television. But reports show they still appeal to a
> fairly large audience. And to the same type of listener. . . .
> From the great number of letters—fantastic in fact—that listen-
> ers write to these shows over the years, they seemed to fill a void
> in the lives of many people in all walks of life. So they are prob-
> ably not as horrible as they have been said to be.[2]

A second group of serials of the late 1950s displayed literary
quality beyond that turned out by "dialoguers." Though overlaid with many problems and much suffering, these dramas were
closer to the artistic standards of women's glossy magazines than
to those of the old-time story papers. Not that this fact necessarily made them more palatable than a quaint *Helen Trent*
(*Young Dr. Malone* was dreadfully morbid in outlook). But the
stylistic distinctions of this group, which included most of the
daytime serials of radio and television, were readily recognizable.
Irna Phillips, principal creator of the dominant serial form, expressed her philosophy of writing as follows:

> The underlying principle of the serial will always remain the
> same, whether it be a serial that runs in a magazine, on the radio
> or television, or even many of the strips that are so popular in the
> newspapers—Rex Morgan being one of the better strips and closer,
> I believe, to the daytime serial than any of the others. . . .
> The important factor as far as I'm concerned in the serial is that
> the story grow out of characters rather than story superimposed
> upon characters. This I have found to be most successful, realistic
> and believable. We do what we do because we are what we
> are. . . .
> As to how one creates a daytime serial—who are the people you
> want to tell a story, what is their story? What they are, who they

[2] Letter to the author from Frank Hummert, August 23, 1958.

are, how identifiable they are—and in this case to the woman viewer—again is a deciding factor in what you create.

Painted Dreams of the 1930's and As The World Turns of the 1950's are alike in many respects. They're about people. The times have changed, the tensions are greater, life is more complex, but the emotions are the same—the hopes, the frustrations and the dreams are the same. People have been and always will be people.[3]

The thoughts of Miss Phillips regarding the importance of characters were similar to statements by serial writer Elaine Carrington which had appeared in 1945:

I would say that the secret of successful serial writing for radio is not so much the story line—not even the "cliff-hanging," which means the climax at the end of each episode in order to make listeners tune in again the next day. I have found that the establishment of character is far more important than plot. The story must be written about people you come to know and like and believe in. What happens to them is of secondary importance. Once characters are firmly established and entrenched in the hearts of listeners, the latter will have to tune in to find out what becomes of the characters because of what they feel for them.

It has been my experience that stories about middle class families have the widest appeal. People can identify the characters with their own friends and relatives. Simple, homely little episodes are those which happen in the listeners' homes, too, and they understand them and love them.[4]

The remark that Irna Phillips made about the relationship of certain comic strips to the daytime-serial form needs some comment. Over the years a transformation had taken place in the comic pages of the United States in that most of the strips were no longer comic. Many were either stories of crime or stories that were very similar to those of the formula daytime serial. Perhaps the best example of the transformation was found in the change of a light and humorous strip about a simple street-corner merchant (Apple Mary) to a strip about a well-dressed kindly philosopher. Apple Mary became Mary Worth, and her

---

[3] Letter to the author from Irna Phillips, July 30, 1958.
[4] Elaine Carrington, "Writing the Radio Serial," in Margaret Cuthbert (ed.), Adventure in Radio, 111.

story changed from comedy to romantic drama. The dialogue for the March 24, 1958, installment of the strip ran as follows:

WOMAN: I've always thought you felt I was a . . . an anchor, dragging behind your car! . . . stalling your career, Frank!
FRANK: Let me say it again, darling . . . It was the business I wrote the month you helped me that won the award! If the judges had known the truth, this citation would read . . . "To the insurance WOMAN of the year!"
WOMAN: The trip abroad could be . . . sort of a second honeymoon, couldn't it?
FRANK: Right! And I promise it'll not be *exactly* like the first one! . . . I'll carry a *guide* book this time! . . . Not a *rate* book![5]

On the same day the following dialogue appeared in the strip *Judge Parker*:

DORIA: I'm suddenly frightened, Alan . . . terribly frightened!
ALAN: It'll be all right, Doria! I'm sure it'll turn out all right!
DORIA: But you don't really believe that, do you Alan?
ALAN: I believe that an innocent person will be proven innocent, Doria.[6]

Comic-strip lines that could have been moved to most of that era's daytime serial scripts without alteration.

Where would they have jarred, as radio dramas gave way to those of television? Perhaps they would not have fit such non-formula serials as *The Verdict Is Yours* (a simulated courtroom drama of CBS-TV), *The Second Mrs. Burton*, and *The Couple Next Door*. The last two, far from being washboard weepers, were carefree comedies.

The Second Mrs. Burton had an especially interesting history. In the mid-1940s it was written in a skillful and intelligent manner by Martha Alexander. In 1947 she asked to leave the show because of difficulties with the agency. After her departure *Burton* became a formula serial. It was in that state when Hector Chevigny became the writer in 1952 (inheriting an amnesia sequence). Late in 1954, when CBS Radio assumed control of the serial from the advertising agency, Chevigny was given permis-

[5] Allen Saunders and Ken Ernst, *Mary Worth*, March 24, 1958.
[6] Paul Nichols, *Judge Parker*, March 24, 1958. Note the resemblance to the *Portia Faces Life* quotation on pages 359–60.

sion to write the program in whatever manner he saw fit. The result was a light drama far removed from the formula serial it had been. In a letter Chevigny described his program:

> What Burton is can, I think, be best described by what it is not. It is not "sick," within the psychiatric meaning of that word. My two principal couples, Terry and Stan and Marcia and Lew, are well married, sexually satisfied. They are not preoccupied with sexual misadventures or even with vague hints that these can threaten them. This I have done consciously, not out of any religious or moral bias in that direction, but entirely practically, because I decided that the great majority of people wish for strong marital unions even if they themselves have been unable to attain them. So Mother Burton and her perennially-unfruitful attempts to dominate wash unsuccessfully against the foundations of the marriages of her daughter and son to stable personalities.
>
> I treat all this lightly, of course, and as you appear to have observed. But much of the lightness lies in our actors more than in my writing. Ethel Owen, who plays Mother, was primarily a comedienne, as is Alice Frost, who plays Marcia. And Teri Keane and Dwight Weist, who play Terry and Stan, are pretty good comedians too.
>
> This much of the show has been borrowed from the tradition of comedy writing. I write what in show business we call "routines." That is, I write for personalities. . . . I do *not* write lines, as part of a story, into which any actor is then cast. . . . What's on the Burton show is an unending series of similar personal reactions to changing story lines. And, you may have noticed, my storylines are never much.
>
> My most successful sequence was the courtship of Marcia by Lew, against Mother's bitter opposition. My least successful revolved around child adoption.[7]

Chevigny's intelligent attitude toward the daytime serial drama led to what was probably the first presentation of a drama classic in a daytime serial. On November 26, 1957, a seven-part dramatization of Oscar Wilde's *The Importance of Being Earnest* was begun. The drama was worked into the story as a production of a little-theater group which was formed by the serial's characters. Chevigny noted with pleasure that the ratings of the program went up, not down, during this sequence, a point made

[7] Letter to the author from Hector Chevigny, June 12, 1958.

too late, unfortunately, to be of significance to daytime radio drama. Cold winds were arising in all parts of the land, and they brought with them no good for Ma Perkins and friends.

Yet even as the form was being pushed from radio by external factors, the sales appeal of the daytime serial remained strong. The nation's press observed this fact and CBS Radio emphasized it through a series of trade advertisements stressing the economy of frequent contact with housewives through daytime dramas. The cost per thousand impressions could be as low as forty-nine cents. And as had long been known, the impressions made within the soap opera setting were strong ones.

But the belief of a network and its advertisers in daytime serials mattered little to local affiliates, which in the days of television competition gained little from network programing. The fees stations received for carrying the network's offerings were much less than those they could obtain by selling the same time locally. Accordingly, CBS Radio's affiliates asked, then demanded, that network offerings be reduced substantially to free more hours for local sales. That, at last, was the death sentence for radio's serials. It was not that they as a form were not wanted. Listeners as well as advertisers still loved them—as they probably would tomorrow if the dramas miraculously reappeared. No, network radio itself, at least as it survived from the golden days, was the entertaining, but now unwelcome, guest.

During December, 1958, CBS Radio announced that in January, 1959, it would cut its network programing from sixty-three to thirty hours a week. In January, 1959, four of its ten quarter-hour serials, *Backstage Wife*, *Our Gal Sunday*, *Road of Life*, and *This Is Nora Drake*, were discontinued. At the same time the network's daily half-hour self-contained drama, *Whispering Streets*, was converted into a daytime serial of ultimate conclusion.

While the network reduced its over-all programing by more than half, the reduction in the programing of serials was proportionately much less: from two and a half hours to two hours each day. Serials actually represented a greater fraction of network hours *after* the CBS cutback. (In December, 1958, approximately one-fifth of the programing of CBS Radio was devoted to daytime serial dramas; after the reduction, one-third.) The network to the end gave great importance to daytime serials. John Karol, vice-president in charge of sales, called the two hours of serials "the biggest audience-attracting block of programing in all network radio." An expensive promotional piece of 1959 showed that serials were audience leaders in their time slots in most major cities.

It was all to no purpose, however. Daytime serials, successful or not, stood in the way of local progress, and daytime serials had to go. Arthur Hull Hayes, president of CBS Radio, said something about network radio having to move away from entertainment forms "which can be presented more effectively by other media" and then scheduled the public execution for the week of November 21–25, 1960.

Possibly in deference to her eternal modesty—or her age—Helen Trent was permitted to slip away quietly several weeks before the end. In a frothy climax bathed in rose-petal cologne Madame Trent gazed into the sunset with the last of her panting Romeos, senatorial candidate John Cole. Resisting the tongue-in-cheek urgings of cast and crew that Helen's affairs be ended in spectacular fashion (by slow poisoning at the hands of a chuckling Ma Perkins, for example), Helen's writer, Margo Brooks, moved her toward what appeared would be a consummated romance—though it could be expected that after leaving the wedding service Helen would make a quick call for advice to Doris Day.

To preserve those final moments, with Helen "standing on the terrace, the wide expanse of sea behind her," here is her last love scene:

MUSIC: *Romantic strings underlying scene*
JOHN: Helen, . . . I love you.
HELEN: (Laughing) Oh, John, you say it like a campaign slogan.
JOHN: I've got to. Helen, you drive me crazy. I'm as sure as that I stand here that as long as I know you I'll be fighting the men off—men you insist on being nice to without *any* idea that everyone of them has an ulterior motive.
HELEN: John, that's absurd!
JOHN: It's the truth, Helen. You're *dynamite!* But you won't

face it. You've got a little girl attitude that you can walk
through life with men making passes all around you
but nothing can ever happen. Well you've got to grow
up someday. Maybe I'm the guy to show you how.

HELEN: Maybe you are, John.

JOHN: But if I do, I'll be tough. I'll knock the first man down
who looks at you!

HELEN: (Ecstatically) Oh, will you!

JOHN: (Chuckling) Well, you scrappy little wench you.
(Change of tone) Helen, . . . will you marry me?

HELEN: (Startled) Oh, John?

JOHN: Now don't say it's a surprise. You've had your hooks into
me for months. I won't ask you to set a date; I'm going
to win this election bare knuckled first.

HELEN: Oh, you *will* win it, John. You'll win it because you have
everything it takes . . . courage and honesty, toughness
and ideals. (Hushed) Oh, John, I love you so much.

JOHN: Will you wait . . . six months?

HELEN: Oh yes. I'll wait six months. Darling I'll wait . . .

JOHN: (Interrupting) Not *forever*, Helen. (Whispering) Not
unless you're sure.

HELEN: I'm sure now, John, . . . very sure.

MUSIC: *"Love, Here Is My Heart"* up full, then under for

ANNOUNCER: With this broadcast we bring to an end the present
series in *The Romance of Helen Trent. The Couple Next
Door* will be heard every weekday, Monday through
Friday at this same time.

Helen was gone, and there was little left to poke fun at in daytime radio.

The final hour, when it came at last, brought surprisingly few
cheers, even from critics, and more than a few moments of sad-
ness. Struggling pridefully to bring to a tidy close dramas that
had begun compounding problems as much as twenty-seven
years earlier, the writers of the old-guard serials let them disappear with grace.

The vestiges of unseen romance and melodrama were *The
Right to Happiness, Ma Perkins, Young Dr. Malone,* and *The
Second Mrs. Burton.* They became only memories following the
broadcast day of November 25, 1960 (three closed-end dramas
hung on until November 29 but vanished unnoticed). What happened during those last episodes? The answer is found below:

PROGRAM HIGHLIGHTS FROM CBS RADIO

Press Information Department,
6121 Sunset Blvd., Hollywood 28, Calif.
Phone: HOllywood 9-1212

Nov. 22, 1960

<u>MONDAY-FRIDAY NOV. 21-25</u>

Following are the concluding story lines of CBS Radio's "The
Right to Happiness," "Ma Perkins," "Young Dr. Malone" and "The Second
Mrs. Burton" for the week of November 21-25.

<u>"RIGHT TO HAPPINESS"</u>

Now that Dick Braden has been paroled from prison and his parents have become reconciled, the Braden family is united again. Grace
has assured Skip that he is the only boy in her life, and Lee's court
case has come to a satisfactory close, even though the missing witness
has not been found. Carolyn and Lee now face the future with assurance,
the events of the past few weeks having brought them closer than ever
together.

<u>"MA PERKINS"</u>

Charlie Lindstrom has accepted a job in the East. He and Mary
are taking leave of Ma Perkins and Rushville Center. On Thanksgiving
Day, the entire family is gathered at Ma's house. Ma Perkins herself
sees happiness ahead, primarily because Anushka and her grandson,
Junior, will be married next month.

(MORE)

"YOUNG DR. MALONE"

During a hospital board meeting, Judge Allen attempts to force Dr. Ted Mason to resign as director of the clinic, a post formerly held by Dr. Jerry Malone. The latter refuses to accept the Board's offer to reinstate him. Ted's first reaction is that of relief, but, after Molly West makes him see the truth about his untenable position, he calls on Jerry, asking him to go back to his old job. When Mason tells him that he is leaving immediately for a destination somewhere out West where he can think out his many problems, Jerry agrees to return as head of the clinic.

Meanwhile, plans for the wedding between Scotty and Jill proceed, despite the open antagonism of his possessive mother. In a last effort to effect a reconciliation, Dr. Malone calls upon Mrs. Scott and makes her realize that her son's love must be shared. Finally, she tells her son and future daughter-in-law that she will attend the wedding after all.

"SECOND MRS. BURTON"

Terry realizes that Mother has gotten herself into a trap by agreeing to take her young artist-protege, Fenno, to Paris. Arranging to send Fenno abroad with a young friend in her place, Terry gets Mother out of that predicament, much to the relief of the rest of the family.

As for Mother Burton, she now concentrates all her energies into preparing for an ambitious Christmas bazaar. Thanksgiving Day Dinner at her house is highlighted by the return of Lew and Marcia from their Carribean vacation.

The press release described conclusions which, had broadcast economy been different, might never have been reached.

Just as the press release made only casual note of what was happening, CBS Radio stations throughout the land proceeded with the November 29 broadcast day as though business were as usual. Ma Perkins' brave "Goodbye, and may God bless you" was all but lost in the hurry to put on another spot announcement. Serial enthusiasts were left with a vacant feeling and disbelief that it could all end like that.

Yet if radio did little to note the passing, the press did. Newspapers from New York to Los Angeles recognized the end of an era and commented upon it respectfully. It was as if only after it had gone did serial listeners and nonlisteners realize how much fun it had been to have the form around, how oddly precious was even this maligned remnant of radio drama. In the *New York Times* it was: "Dear radio soap operas, come back. There is a real need for you for the stay-at-homes." But the editorial in the *Los Angeles Times* portrayed the cold facts of commercial survival more realistically: "Organ music, up and out."

REPRISE

The fire which seems extinguished often slumbers beneath the ashes.

PIERRE CORNEILLE, *Rodogune*

In the fall of 1962, fifty years after the birth of the serial drama, the future of the form looked dark to many experts. The Hollywood film factories had not turned out a cliffhanger since 1956, and there were no signs of chapter-play revival anywhere. At about the time serials vanished from motion-picture lots, the last of their counterparts, the children's thrillers of radio, disappeared from the late-afternoon air. And, of course, the breadwinners of daytime radio for almost three decades, the soap operas, had uttered their last sighs.

Except for a solitary, and imperiled, soaper on NBC (*Young Dr. Malone*) the final stronghold of the open-end serial was CBS-TV. And this network, which never gave up on the daytime

399

serial, had been forced to cluster its six surviving operas in the afternoon hours because housewives seemed too busy to settle down to serious worrying until after lunch.

A *New York Times* critic, writing in September, 1962, of the events that left CBS with six serials and NBC with only one, called the cancellations of the former's *The Brighter Day* and the latter's *Our Five Daughters* "further indication that daytime serials do not stimulate interest on television as widely as they did on radio." He went on to observe that "the only real home they have found in television—a somewhat mortgaged one at that—is on CBS."

But appearances were misleading. The daytime serials of television were healthier than they may have looked in 1962. Although not the sensations (or irritants) their radio precursors had been, the CBS serials were doing quite well, with between three and seven million viewers each day, enough to place them in the upper half of daytime ratings for programs of all networks. In fact, 1962 marked the midpoint of an audience-building period so satisfactory to CBS that on December 16, 1965, the network took a full-page ad in the *New York Times* to boast of it. Under a large photo of Chris and Nancy Hughes in a pose suggesting one of their many man-and-wife chats of *As The World Turns* appeared this tongue-in-cheek copy:

(THE LIVING ROOM OF CHRIS AND NANCY HUGHES.
THEY HAVE JUST FINISHED DINNER.)

NANCY: You seem distracted, dear. Is anything troubling you?

CHRIS: Not really. (Pausing) Nancy, wouldn't you say we've been pretty honest with each other all these years?

NANCY: As honest as the day is long.

CHRIS: There's something I've been wanting to tell you for a long time, but I haven't known exactly how. It's pretty complicated.

NANCY: Just say it, dear... I'll understand.

CHRIS: Nancy, we're on the most popular daytime program in all television.

NANCY: How marvelous!

CHRIS: There's even more to it than that. CBS daytime programs are now delivering 64 per cent larger average audiences than the next closest network, and 119 per cent larger audiences

400

than the third network. And in each case it's a bigger lead than a year ago.

NANCY: (Excitedly) It's too good to be true!

CHRIS: It *is* true. CBS daytime programs reach almost as many households as the other two networks combined. As a matter of fact, our programs have averaged the biggest daytime audiences for 8 years. We've been first in every one of Art Nielsen's last 74 reports.

NANCY: He must be a very busy man!

CHRIS: Yes, and there's even more: CBS has 5 of the Top Five daytime programs, 10 of the Top Ten, and 13 of the Top Fifteen.

NANCY: Why, Chris, we have just about everything!

CHRIS: You can say that again. In fact, that's the reason why the nation's leading daytime advertisers spend almost as much money on the CBS Television Network alone as on the other two networks combined. And they've been doing it for years.

NANCY: (Drawing close) They've been wonderful years, Chris, haven't they?

CHRIS: The best—and there are many more to come.

And there were good years to come, though with the aid of some daytime serials of their own the other networks began to give chase to CBS as the 1960s moved along. ABC introduced a successful daytime drama, *General Hospital*, on April 1, 1963, and in 1966 struck gold with *Dark Shadows*, a Gothic novel in soap-opera form. Two years later came the interracial *One Life to Live*. Meanwhile, NBC, recognizing a sure way to attack CBS's near monopoly of daytime drama, asked Irna Phillips to create a serial for its stations. The result was *Another World*, sold to a dozen participating sponsors six weeks before the program went on the air in May, 1964, and a strong feature from its first appearance. Although failing to establish a prenoon beachhead with *Paradise Bay* and the aptly titled *Morning Star*, NBC also developed two solid afternoon features: *The Doctors* (a good blending of seriousness and humor) and *Days of Our Lives*, a Macdonald Carey vehicle about a physician and his family.

Despite these incursions by other networks, CBS maintained its dominant position throughout the 1960s by holding six strong cards (*Search for Tomorrow, Love of Life, The Guiding Light,*

401

The Secret Storm, Edge of Night, and *As the World Turns*) and by adding in 1967 a new series, *Love Is a Many-Splendored Thing.* The shaper of this updating of the 1955 motion picture? Irna Phillips, whose thirteen-year-old *As the World Turns* easily withstood a 1969 assault by NBC's *Hidden Faces.*

If the daytime serial of television was stronger than might have been supposed at the beginning of the 1960s, the serial form had subtly taken over nighttime television as well. Although seldom recognized as such, the prevailing dramas of the 1960s, the *Bonanzas,* the *Gunsmokes,* the situation comedies, were nothing more than episodic serials. The once dominant live-anthology dramas of earlier television—*Studio One, Robert Montgomery Presents, Playhouse 90*—and their filmed successors—*Twilight Zone, Alfred Hitchcock Presents, Zane Grey Theatre*—had been supplanted almost entirely by dramas in which the same characters appeared each week in a continuing environment. Normally each episode in these serials offered resolution short of absolute conclusion. Audiences knew that, network willing, new or slightly used problems would await the principals the next week—unless, as sometimes happened, a single problem was spread over two, three, or even five installments.

At such times echoes of old-fashioned cliffhanging and situational endings could be expected until the dramas reverted smoothly to the episodic format, very much as it had been in Universal's *The Indians Are Coming* (1930), the first significant chapter play of the talking film. Several installments of that Tim McCoy covered-wagon thriller came to minor resolution, just as would episodes of television's *Wagon Train* many years later. It is rarely noted, of course, that the first dramatized serial (*What Happened to Mary*), as well as the most famous one ever filmed (*The Perils of Pauline*), pioneered the episodic technique; cliffhanging chapter endings did not become the vogue until after the motion-picture serial had become an established form. By birthright, if not by investiture, *Bonanza* was as much a serial drama as *Jack Armstrong, Ma Perkins*—or *The Fugitive.*

The Fugitive is a conspicuous example of how serial formats could be alternated—or, more precisely, blended—with spectacular success. In 1962, when continued drama was being given up for dead on the fiftieth anniversary of its birth, television producer Roy Huggins was telling ABC executives about an idea he had for a modern-day version of *Les Miserables* with overtones of *The Wandering Jew*. Reportedly without even a look at a finished script, the network representatives accepted Huggins' proposal, and *The Fugitive* went into planning.

When it reached the air in 1963 (with Quinn Martin in charge, replacing Huggins, who had other commitments), each hour-long episode recalled in flashback the circumstances which had caused Dr. Richard Kimble (played by David Janssen) to flee punishment for a murder he had not committed. Then Kimble moved into his current environment, as he searched the country for the one-armed man who had run from his home the night his wife was slain. Doggedly pursuing Kimble was Lieutenant Gerard (Barry Morse), from whom the fugitive had escaped during a derailment of the train taking him to prison. In each installment the pursued physician brought some good to someone—often at the risk of capture—but unless it was a two-part segment, Kimble was forced to take wing at episode end because Gerard was in close pursuit or because Kimble had found a new clue to the one-armed man's whereabouts.

The attractions of the series were many. The natural curiosity and suspense factor of the serial genre, of course, was one. But that aspect was enhanced by sympathy for a good man hounded for a crime that was not his, yet still willing to risk his life or his vindication to help others. Then, too, there was the attraction for males of a hero who could kiss and run with complete justification—or at least comfortable rationalization. Adding dimension to the series were the capable characterizations of Janssen and Morse, playing two strong men who respected each other but were determined to reach their individual goals.

In the end both did—before one of the largest audiences ever assembled for a television series. During the 1966–67 season Martin and his associates reached the decision that, after four years, the best fruits of the enterprise had been harvested and that it would be wise to quit before interest waned sharply. Thus, in the summer of 1967, after announcements to that effect, they released in two parts the denouement they had long before prepared for *The Fugitive*.

On Tuesday, August 22, the first segment brought Kimble close to the mysterious one-armed man but also revealed that Kimble's brother-in-law was somehow involved and possibly was the actual murderer. On August 29 almost three-quarters of those persons watching television in the New York area tuned in to see the mystery unraveled. *The Fugitive's* audience figures throughout the country were equally high, and they carried over to the late-night *Joey Bishop Show*, which received its highest rating to that date because actor Janssen was a guest.

The one-armed man (Bill Raish) was the killer after all. And though the final episode drew the kind of criticism that chapter-play followers often directed at slightly synthetic closing installments, the farewell of *The Fugitive* was the greatest evocation of the wonderful anguish of cliffhanging since the days of glory at Republic. It would be interesting to know how many of the millions who witnessed Dr. Kimble's vindication had also been with Pearl White in 1916 when she learned the identity of the Laughing Mask. And would that we had data to tell us how many of *The Fugitive's* last audience had been seasoned in measured waiting by training over the trying courses of *The Fighting Devil Dogs* and similar ventures.

Long before the thread of *The Fugitive* was spun out, the program had imitators. One, *Run for Your Life* (1965–66), was certainly a legitimate variation: it was created by Roy Huggins. Instead of a doctor trying to find a murderer, Paul Bryan (portrayed by Ben Gazzara) was a lawyer racing to spend his last days in meaningful living, while a medical center labored to find a cure for the disease that otherwise would soon take his life. The next season a Quinn Martin character, David Vincent (Roy Thinnes), began his thankless battle to save the world from alien beings he alone recognized as *The Invaders*. Other serials emphasizing a search or race of one kind or another were *Hank* (1965), *Run, Buddy, Run* (1966), *Coronet Blue* (1967),

The Guns of Will Sonnett (1967), and *The Prisoner* (1968). In the 1969–70 season the roving-protagonist format appeared in *Then Came Bronson* (reminiscent also of *Route 66*) and in a pilot film of feature length, *The Immortal*.

Other episodic serials of *The Fugitive* era conveyed an impression of continuing narrative stronger than that found in like dramas of earlier day on both radio and television. The European air war seemed to progress with the successive episodes of *Twelve O'Clock High* (a Quinn Martin production), just as the ground war seemingly advanced on *Combat, Garrison's Gorillas,* and *The Rat Patrol*. Moreover, such shows as *High Chaparral, Julia,* and the amusing musical drama *That's Life* were clearly sequential in their introductory installments, something of a departure for episodic drama. While enjoyable independently, each unit of these programs carried added meaning for those who had seen what had happened before.

A possible interpretation of these developments of the later 1960s was that the episodic format was moving into conjunction with the serial format most effective for developing meanings beyond meanings, the one which permits writers to minimize resolutions of individual episodes while adding layers of characterization and interaction. Not without significance, this format—that of the open-end serial—had brought its presence to nighttime television in dramatic fashion in the autumn of 1964. For reasons beyond those mentioned, it was an auspicious moment for a serial sensation. Clear-cut experiments with the continued-story form were being carried out on several levels. On October 5, NBC unveiled a nighttime throwback to the overlapping dramas of the *General Mills Hour* in the 1940s. A ninety-minute episodic series called *90 Bristol Court* brought together three individually titled half-hour dramas whose major characters lived in the same apartment motel in California. The idea was clever, but the scripts were not. *90 Bristol Court* was torn down to make room for the headquarters of U.N.C.L.E.

The other prominent autumnal explorations of serial drama in 1964 came within the two big medical shows: *Dr. Kildare* and *Ben Casey*. Both shows, suddenly finding the going more diffi-

405

cult as they approached their fourth seasons, needed partial transfusions. Young Kildare's pattern of quick romances was broken, therefore, with a three-part series entitled "Rome Will Never Leave You." A Sally Benson script allowed Kildare (Richard Chamberlain) to visit Italy, fall in love with a titled signorina (Daniela Bianchi) in the very garden set Leslie Howard and Norma Shearer had used in *Romeo and Juliet* (1936), and then step out of the girl's life so that she could carry out the wish of her dying father (Ramon Novarro) and marry a nobleman. Ben Casey, meanwhile, helped a lovely patient played by Stella Stevens come out of a fifteen-year coma and mature from the psychological age of thirteen to her real age of twenty-eight. Casey (Vince Edwards) achieved this goal in the first five episodes of the season, concurrently attending to other problems. The next year Dr. Casey was involved regularly in subplot serialization of this kind, while Kildare's shows became twice-a-week ultimate-conclusion serials, with story sequences sometimes running almost a month.

The memorable serial event of nighttime television in the fall of 1964, however, was *Peyton Place*. Loosely derived by way of two feature films from Grace Metalious' once-scandalous novel, it was a twice-a-week open-end drama *on film*, something without counterpart in American television. Having noted the success of a two-night-a-week evening series on British television, *Coronation Street*, officials of 20th Century Fox decided to put such a series before motion-picture cameras, even though cost-reducing reruns could not be counted upon for some time, if ever. Fox officials entrusted executive producer Paul Monash with developing this idea exactly fifty years after the first film serial, *What Happened to Mary*, was conceived in 1912.

Monash, who had helped develop *The Untouchables*, set to work preparing a pilot. For a time the project used the title *Eden Hill* because of the unattractive overtones of the book. When Monash's promising pilot appeared, however—with the salacious angle reduced—conservative opinion was set aside in order to capitalize on a presold title.

Still, the hour-long pilot underwent some heavy examination

when ABC entered the project. The Cross family, a not-too-nice element, was eliminated completely—despite the fact that Stephanie Cross had been played brilliantly by Monash's young daughter. And Michael Rossi was changed from high-school principal to newly arrived physician, while old Doc Swain became a small-town editor doubling as a Greek chorus.

Involved to an undetermined degree in this predebut shuffling was a special consultant ABC executives called upon for insurance purposes after Monash completed the pilot film. The consultant was the soap opera queen, Irna Phillips—a fact that may indicate the way some persons at ABC and Fox regarded the show.

Miss Phillips' actual contribution to the series is clouded in the pushing and pulling that preceded the first telecast. Monash continued at the helm when the show went on the air, and it can therefore be assumed that his was the dominant voice. But no doubt the program profited to some degree from the Phillips touch. The switch of Rossi from principal to physician to put him at the center of village action certainly smacks of the emphasis upon the professional person which Miss Phillips brought to the daytime serial in the 1930s. So does the plot line with which the series began: Betty Anderson (pretty and poor) pregnant by Rodney Harrington (handsome and rich)—a hasty marriage to preserve her honor—a secret miscarriage—an annulment of a marriage in name only—a together/apart relationship between Betty and Rod that would go on for years despite other men (even husbands) and other women.

Was the miscarriage, we might wonder, the way Miss Phillips avoided the suspected cause of the demise of the Hummerts' once-popular soap opera, *Betty and Bob*: hubby's continued romantic and matrimonial instability after the baby came along? In *Peyton Place*, after five years and, between them, five marriages, it could at least be said that neither Rod nor Betty was an irresponsible parent. Their romantic dabblings were not indulged in at the expense of innocent babes.

To pursue Miss Phillips' possible influence, young Harrington was involved in a long murder trial which added interest to

Peyton Place, just as trials had always done to daytime serials. And in the autumn of 1968 Rod (what latent symbolism there is in that name!) was in a wheelchair, paralyzed from the waist down, bewailing his inability to be a full man to his wife. And wife (Betty) was embarked on her third marriage, the second to Rodney. Consultant Phillips may have been gone by that time, but her notes had not been burned.

Let us not overstate Miss Phillips' influence, however. Chief responsibility for the long *Peyton Place* story line (1964–69) always rested with Paul Monash, who trained a team of highly paid writers to work from a story board that might have been the Hummerts'. Although the show normally maintained a thirty-episode backlog, Monash was ever sensitive to audience reaction and current events. The unexpected warmth generated by Tim O'Connor as ex-convict Elliot Carson (Allison "McKenzie's" real father) resulted in his remaining in the series as the husband of Allison's mother (Dorothy Malone) instead of meeting violent death as a near villain. Actress Mia Farrow's romance with Frank Sinatra, on the other hand, put the innocent Allison into a coma and eventually out of the drama as a runaway daughter—a departure for which Monash could not compensate, despite several replacement virgins.

Peyton Place never escaped classification as "nighttime soap opera"—a pejorative which, accurate or not, was a simplification. In plain fact, if those who used the term even before the first broadcast had taken a real look at the program, they would have seen a carefully mounted series, with skillful writing, capable direction (by Ted Post and Walter Doniger), realistic and expensive scenic work, well-arranged cinematography, and highly competent acting. Its juveniles—Barbara Parkins, Ryan O'Neal, Chris Connelly, Mia Farrow, and Patricia Morrow—were always miles above their counterparts in typical Hollywood movies about reckless youth—in part, I suspect, because the extended narrative allowed them to develop their skills and characterization as they could in no other setting but a repertory company. The character actors of *Peyton Place*—George

408

Macready, Dan Duryea, Lee Grant, and Erin O'Brien-Moore—
were performers of stature long before entering the cast of
Monash's drama. And almost all of them commented on the
unexpectedly high level of production they encountered. A
domestic serial it was, with all that means, good or bad; but
when looked at fairly, *Peyton Place* was a drama produced with
care and taste exceeding that found in at least half the nighttime entertainment fashioned for the home set. It should be
given no more than its due, but it should be given that.

The skill that went into *Peyton Place* was best revealed when
other shows were conceived in the hope of matching it or playing on its success. Scarcely was it in production when another
film studio, aware of the money that was being lavished upon
an untried evening serial, hired a noted writer to prepare a continued film narrative about a married couple— just in case. When
Peyton Place became an instant audience leader two nights a
week, announcements of other serials spilled forth. In January,
1965, NBC indicated that it was working on something called
The Duffield Story, which, though a twice-a-week evening
serial, would definitely not be a copy of *Peyton Place*. Someone
just happened to think of it one day. Warner Brothers, meanwhile, was trying to get a nibble for a serial tentatively called
Jack and Jill. There was also talk of a running story based upon
The Chapman Report. And, to keep daytime serial drama from
falling behind, writer Sterling Silliphant planned to uplift it
with a proposed series called *The Bitter and the Sweet*.

The world still awaits these projects, partly because they
never got put together correctly and partly because, for once,
Irna Phillips made a false step in connection with a serial drama.
At the outset her idea did not look unpromising. As things went
in television, a cycle of continued domestic drama seemed in
the offing for the nighttime hours. There would be an advantage
in being the first "noncopy" of *Peyton Place*. Moreover, the nature of the medium was such that a program using video-tape
techniques and made in a television studio could be mounted
faster than the product of a Hollywood film studio. Certainly it

would be less expensive to produce and thus easier to sell, particularly in light of the logical necessity to set aside thoughts of reruns.

What Miss Phillips proposed was, in the language of television, a spin-off. She would take a central character from her *As the World Turns*, the most popular serial of the daytime, and build a twice-a-week evening serial around her. Interestingly, the character chosen was not one of the good people. Instead it was a girl housewives loved to hate, one of the best-received vamps since the days vamps became obsolete. Her name was Lisa, and not even marriage to as good a catch as Dr. Bob Hughes could keep her from dropping handkerchiefs in the paths of men susceptible to flirtatious females.

To get *Our Private World* underway on May 5, 1965, Lisa (played by Eileen Fulton) left behind former husband and little boy in Oakdale to find a new life—and assuredly new loves —in Chicago. There, pretending to be a single girl, she took up residence in the household of a kindly but watchful landlady and soon was encountering attractive males, a few girls in one trouble or another, and a society matron (Geraldine Fitzgerald) whom she hoped to make her mother-in-law. There were references to people and incidents of *As the World Turns*, just as on the afternoon show the wandering Lisa was a topic of conversation. Action in *Our Private World* took place after the cocktail hour more frequently than it did on the source program, and, of course, Lisa was the pivotal figure, but beyond that the shows were similar.

That, perhaps, was one difficulty. Despite orchestral backgrounds in place of organ improvisations and some exterior shots on film, *Our Private World* was daytime drama at 9:00 P.M., with little of the polish of competing film dramas. Its inspiration, *Peyton Place*, in addition to artful production, had subject matter that could hold the male viewer—or at least keep him from sulking in the living room while his wife watched. *Our Private World* was unmistakably a drama for women, just as Eileen Fulton's Lisa was a woman's idea of a seductress. Miss Fulton, small and slender, was not the corporeal threat to female ego that full-bodied Barbara Parkins of *Peyton Place* was. She was closer in appearance to Mia Farrow, whose innocence on the Monash show was the perfect counterpoint to the Parkins bedroom eyes. While the *Peyton Place* smoothness, coupled with the balanced Parkins-Farrow tandem, offered a little something for the boys (who could feel lustful or protective, depending on which girl was on camera), two nights a week of women's drama, with a woman's femme fatale, were more than a one-TV-set family could possibly tolerate—particularly during baseball season.[1]

The ratings of *Our Private World*, though not the lowest of evening television, were not sufficiently impressive to Procter and Gamble to justify the expense of nighttime air. The company could reach a female audience for much less money in the afternoon. Lisa's new romance, therefore, was a May-to-September affair. Soon she was back in Oakdale, to the delirious joy of *As The World Turns* watchers, who had had no one to hate (or secretly envy) while Lisa was away.

The misfortune that befell *Our Private World* was not encouraging to the cultivation of the domestic serial in the evening. But coming as it did in the summer, it had no real influence on the 1965–66 season that was largely outlined before Miss Phillips' serial went on the air. A stronger indication that *Peyton Place*, with a newly added third segment, would be enough to meet the demand for its kind of entertainment was the cancellation of a projected spin-off with Barbara Parkins, to be called *The Girl from Peyton Place*. *Peyton Place* did not

---

[1] Lest my suggestion of the conflict between baseball and nighttime domestic drama be considered rhetorical flippancy, I must point out that the problem is most ticklish for a network station which happens to carry both baseball games and serials, day or night. There is no winning in such a situation. A reduction in the number of games carried to avoid interference with serial continuity can bring howls of outrage from sports fans; failure to present an episode results in the same kind of crisis with serial lovers. The ABC outlet in Philadelphia hit upon a technique of taping any lost installment of *Peyton Place* and holding it for later presentation. That did not assuage all viewer grief, but it did allow serial adherents to follow the narrative without missing an episode. Such changes in schedule were carefully announced in advertisements, one of which began, "*Peyton Place* fans take heart, . . ." and ended, "You realize, of course, that tonight there are only *two* hours between episodes!"

411

enjoy the long period in a regular time slot that a serial needs to develop fully. One segment would have a high rating, another a low one, in the same week. Yet despite the network's fast and loose scheduling of the program, during its lifetime it brooked no imitations. The nearest competitor was an hour-long series based upon the work of an author more distinguished than Grace Metalious. William Faulkner's 1940 novel, *The Hamlet*, which Fox had put on the motion-picture screen as *The Long Hot Summer*, had moderate television success under that title during the 1965–66 season.

Not until *Peyton Place* concluded in 1969 an impressive run of 514 episodes—enough for almost twenty years at the rate of 26 new programs a year of other nighttime dramas—did patent efforts to play upon its success appear among TV dramas. That fall ABC launched the expensive television "novel" by Harold Robbins, *The Survivors*, featuring a host of well-known actors, including Ralph Bellamy, Lana Turner, and George Hamilton. Heralded as a *Peyton Place* of the Jet Set, it may have been just that: people in fancy trappings with very little character underneath. If nothing else, it showed *Peyton Place* deriders the difference between good and bad after-dark soap opera. It lasted not even one season.[2]

Another bow to the success of Peyton Place in the fall of 1969 was *Bracken's World*, a multicharacter peek inside the motion-picture industry. It was filmed at 20th Century Fox with the old *Peyton Place* sets rising ghostlike in the background of studio scenes to remind the producers that gloss cannot cover vapidity.

More prestigious, however, was the British-made serial *The Forsyte Saga*, released to educational channels in the United States. The program had been incredibly popular in England, where social functions and church services reportedly had to be rescheduled so as not to interfere with the broadcast, and was

[2] Even parody of *Peyton Place* had to wait until its subject had gone away. On January 14, 1970, a hilarious spoof, *The Shameful Secrets of Hastings Corners*, appeared on NBC. It was a pilot film for a series that did not catch the brass ring. The mirth and originality of the trial program probably would have worn away quickly in a series framework.

almost equally well received on the Continent, even in the Soviet Union.

This series, based on the John Galsworthy works, had an extraordinary cast, headed by Kenneth More, who played Young Jolyon, a genial nonconformist in a world of conformity. The magnetic character of both the novels and the dramatic version, however, was the often acerbic Soames Forsyte, who grew in both wisdom and warmth as the series progressed. Eric Porter impersonated him magnificently through twenty-six episodes in what has to be considered a theatrical tour de force. Soames's first wife, the cold and imperious Irene, was given exactly that quality by a New Zealand actress, Nyree Dawn Porter (no relation to Eric Porter). Susan Hampshire, known earlier for her ingenue roles, brought the reckless Fleur to life and won an Emmy award for her efforts.

Yet every actor in *The Forsyte Saga* performed admirably—Joseph O'Connor, as the understanding Old Jolyon, John Welsh, as Soames's taciturn father; Margaret Tyzack, as the uncomplaining wife of the worthless Montague Dartie. To mention all the good performances of *The Forsyte Saga* would be to name the entire cast. And approval could not end there. The costuming and set decoration were painstaking; the adaptation was in excellent taste.

If awed critics praised the twenty-six-part drama—and they did—they also found it difficult to reconcile quality with soap opera. *The Forsyte Saga* was a milestone in the direction of charitable treatment of serials. Critics examined it with a tenderness that a domestic product of plainer label would not have enjoyed. James Michener, writing for *TV Guide* (May 30, 1970), called the series "one of the significant cultural events of this century." A panel of judges for *Saturday Review* cited *The Forsyte Saga* for a sustained level of excellence "demonstrating that the lowly art of soap opera can be elevated to new heights." The British novelist Anthony Burgess, however, put the praise in perspective. For the *New York Times Magazine* of November 16, 1969, he wrote:

The Forsyte Saga is a great television triumph, since the Galsworthian conception has the near-coarseness, the near-melodramatic simplicity of superior soap opera; it has been waiting all these years to slide into its true medium—the leisurely, middlebrow television serial.

All of which might suggest that while a surprising number of critics liked the dramatization of *The Forsyte Saga*, and not without reason, English critics were not awed by Victorian elegance—or British accents.

It must at least be acknowledged that the rich dialogue and the brilliant acting and staging that enhanced the dramatization of *The Forsyte Saga* disguised plot elements which, if placed within a daytime, or nighttime, serial of contemporary setting and Hollywood or Manhattan origin, would have drawn the expected derision of critics. One can construct typical critical comment. Would the almost weekly demises have escaped such criticism as:

> The characters die in a variety of places—in fourposter beds, in wicker chairs on the verandah, under the wheels of onrushing carriages. The principal figure expires after an expensive painting falls out of a window onto his head?

Assuredly, critics could have found a rich variety of typical soap-opera males in *The Forsyte Saga*:

> A cuckold whose sexual frustration leads him to rape his own wife, a bohemian architect who seduces that same wife, a gambling wastrel who steals his wife's jewels, and a pleasant-enough fellow who runs off with his children's governess. The truly admirable men are those over sixty—the harmless ones, in other words.

And no American critic could have overlooked the women or the plot progression of *The Forsyte Saga* had it been homegrown:

> Though restrained by the conventions of the highly structured Victorian society, there are sufficient strong (or willful) women to keep the Forsyte men in agony, or in line, by virtue of their patience, their frigidity, their wailing, or their seductiveness. Alas, there is no Ma Perkins to straighten things out from time to time.

The narrative's principal path to resolution of knotty problems is an abrupt jump forward to another decade. And the further the drama moves from its comfortable, well-organized, Victorian setting, the more it looks like soap opera.

That *The Forsyte Saga* escaped such typical serial criticism should not cause envy in those who create or support the American-produced serial. Instead, it should encourage them to think that, just as James Fenimore Cooper broke through the aura surrounding English literature and led the way to a native craft that could bring praise, an American writer in the 1970s might (in the manner of radio's Sandra Michael) bring respect to television serial drama produced in New York or California for NBC or CBS or ABC. Such a writer may come to the television serial, drawn by the success of *The Forsyte Saga*, or he may already be toiling in the daytime-serial vinyards, waiting for a kind word from a critic about a present effort to upgrade his milieu. Yet as long as the moments of literary or performing quality in daytime dramas—and there are more than might be supposed—pass unnoticed by critics, who thus far have reviewed them only occasionally and with a view to derision, the genre will be slow to improve. That is why *The Forsyte Saga* brings hope to serial drama. It has demonstrated that a serial drama can please critics as well as audiences. If creative broadcasters and their financial supporters harken to the *Forsyte* lesson, the Galsworthy dramatization will not remain unique in its distinction.

OF BATS AND VAMPIRES

St. Francis and St. Benedight,
Bless this house from wicked wight,
From the nightmare and the Goblin
That is hight Good Fellow Robin.
Keep it from all evil spiretes,
Fairies, Wezles, Bats, and Ferrytes
From Curfew Time to the next Prime.

WILLIAM CARTWRIGHT, a house blessing

One last serial eruption of the 1960s awaits our notice. It was presaged not by *The Fugitive* or *Peyton Place* but by *Jonny Quest* and *Voyage to the Bottom of the Sea. Quest*, an animated half-hour thriller, had characters and backgrounds close to the comic-book mold, in contrast to earlier nighttime cartoons such as *The Flintstones.* Jonny and his scientist-father met witch doctors, mummies, and headhunters while prowling exotic locales in vehicles once favored by Tim Tyler and Jack Armstrong's Uncle Jim.

416

Matching *Jonny Quest* in hairbreadth escapes was *Voyage*. On a military mission against shadowy powers, the Jules Verne–inspired submarine *Seaview* was more likely to bump against grisly creatures of the 1916 chapter-play or *Lost World* variety than it was to encounter normal enemies. Richard Basehart as the admiral gave the series the semblance of reality which Orson Welles had once lent *The Shadow*. Otherwise the adventure was pure chapter-play material, though normally in episodic format.

The producer of *Voyage to the Bottom of the Sea* was Irwin Allen, who in the autumn of 1965 added a second far-out series to his growing stable. Almost called *Space Family Robinson*, it portrayed interplanetary doings of the near future, as *Voyage* had concerned itself with undersea happenings in an era yet to be. Unlike the tales of the *Seaview*, though, *Lost in Space* was a fully qualified cliffhanger—or craterhanger, as one wit termed it. The pacing, the presummary, the what-will-happen endings of these tales of a space researcher's family and associates stranded on an unknown planet all suggested the film serial of the 1930s. Even the thrill music was in the *Flash Gordon* mode, being a masterful reworking of the score of an adventure feature.

Youngsters familiar with classic cliffhangers through Saturday reruns on television immediately took to *Lost in Space*. It followed paths charted by the Flash Gordon films, by *Hawk of the Wilderness*, and by silent cliffhangers such as Joe Bonomo's *Perils of the Wild*. *Lost in Space* was also the television counterpart of the old *Buck Rogers* series of radio, complete with ray guns, marvelous transportation, and sterile romance.

In its first season *Lost in Space* had the misfortune to encounter extraordinary cliffhanging competition which it managed to combat but not outlive. In the middle of the 1965–66 broadcast year ABC introduced a television phenomenon. Setting January as the start of its "second season," the network devoted enormous publicity to one of its new shows, conceived in secrecy that only added to the advance interest in it. Described by a prominent critic as "a magnificent triumph for the Medici of

417

1966, the press agents," Episode 1 of *Batman* appeared on Wednesday, January 12, 1966.

It was apparent from the first broadcast that producer William Dozier of 20th Century Fox—who had once guided the prestigious *Playhouse 90, You Are There*, and *Studio One*—had fashioned an enormous put-on. The camp-influenced style of presentation could be laid most precisely to Lorenzo Semple, Jr., who wrote the initial episodes. On the heels of animated opening titles, a narrator set the seal on the undertaking with a "gee-whiz" delivery of auguries such as, "Hissable enemy number one is about to strike!" In this kind of setting the actors had no choice but to intone solemnly the preposterous dialogue or walk off the set. But how would the public receive such a series?

Obviously the intention of Dozier and company was to offer adults something to laugh at while giving youngsters a fast-moving thriller. And for a while it appeared that the dual approach might work. Beyond any doubt, the youngsters, possibly introduced to the show by curious adults, embraced Batman and Robin immediately. Adult reaction was harder to gauge. Comic-book aficionados of the Dynamic Duo in the 1940s naturally were disappointed at the desecration of their former idols. Humorist Russell Baker called it "subversive." But iconoclasm and all, there was potential for entertainment in *Batman*. The one-liners were fun, though too numerous, and the guest villains, noted actors all, were obviously having the times of their lives. Cinematography, settings, costumes, and titles were in a comic-book mode that was instant pop art, but not necessarily the harder to define or attain camp.

The critics were dumbfounded. The *Batman* program received the most cagily worded reviews one could find anywhere. Pointing to both its strengths and its weaknesses, Rex Polier of the *Philadelphia Evening Bulletin* wondered how long the cuteness would last. He also suggested that ABC, which had hit it big with another serial, *Peyton Place*, the year before, "may have the grand slam of the season with *Batman*." In the *New York Times* Jack Gould, who clearly enjoyed the premier episode, suggested that for the nostalgic adult viewer it "was probably the best therapy since Lawrence Welk's Champagne Music." But Gould too saw weak spots in what he recognized would be at the least a season's sensation. "The true test for Batman," he pointed out, "won't be this week or next, but in a couple of months when the novelty of his cape and expertise begin to wear off."

And so *Batman* enjoyed the time in the pop-art sun which Gould had predicted for it. Children raced around backyards with blue or yellow towels around their necks. A merchandising campaign of Batman products was launched with expectations of seventy-five million dollars in first-year sales. Batman (Adam West) and Robin (Burt Ward) filled theaters and parks in personal appearances. Silent star Neil Hamilton was working regularly again as Commissioner Gordon. And—as proof that all was right with the world—mothers, counselors, and *Pravda* started to worry. *Pravda* claimed that *Batman* brainwashed Americans into being "willing murderers in the Vietnam jungle." The Reverend R. E. Terwilliger, an Episcopal priest, while stating that *Batman* "provided a much-needed emotional and almost religious outlet for many television viewers," also indicated his dislike for "this cultish worship of Batman" because, as he put it, "it is worship without commitment." And though Dr. Benjamin Spock reassured parents in a television interview that *Batman* would do the kiddies no harm, Eda L. LeShan, consulting psychologist of the Pengilly County School, announced to her school's parents, and to the *New York Times Magazine*, that her institution was "At War with Batman." The drama's conspicuously lighthearted approach to the absurd crimes of its bizarre villains produced a ban at Pengilly against "costumes, posters, books, comics, and bubble gum cards"—almost everything the merchandisers needed to reap their seventy-five million dollars. If Pengilly children were to watch *Batman*, their parents should watch too, "as guardians of civilized values." The pro-Batman, anti-Batman argument was never resolved, but it is comforting historically to observe that the Pengilly school is located in New Rochelle, New York, the headquarters community for the "We're Not Listening" campaign against soap operas in 1939.

The quick success of the *Batman* program, which put it among the top ten programs, greatly encouraged those planning adventure programs for the 1966–67 season nine months away. The *Tarzan* series, a project that seemed on the verge of introduction several times, was locked in for Friday nights on NBC. Also set for that network was a science-fiction series directed at adults and older children: *Star Trek*. Both were hour-long episodic serials in color. (To help it meet the *Batman* competition, *Lost in Space* was also given color in that season.)

Expectedly, ABC tried to capitalize strongly on the audience boost *Batman* had given it. The most obvious duplication was *The Green Hornet*, which had been in the planning stages when Batman went on the air. Ironically, the old fictional character of radio that had inspired the *Batman* comic feature was immediately looked upon by many viewers as a watered down imitation of *Batman*. This adventure, by the way, was played straight, a technique that might have worked if *The Green Hornet* had reached television first but had no chance of succeeding once *Batman* had carried the masked-crusader-in-fast-car framework to absurdity and beyond. Even old-time radio buffs found it difficult to generate enthusiasm for the series, which had some amateurish acting to help sink it if nothing else did. No doubt to modernize the drama, the producers scrapped one of its best assets, the exciting "Flight of the Bumblebee" theme, and substituted Al Hirt playing trumpet trills distantly related to the original melody.

Irwin Allen, in this period of high adventure, brought to ABC the third of his major fantasy serials, *Time Tunnel*.[1] His two heroes, lost in the void of time, bounced from era to era, momentous event to momentous event, while the scientists who created the time tunnel into which they had entered tried desperately to recover them. The wanderers thus stepped into and out of fateful moments of history, science fiction being confined mainly to Time Center scenes at random points in the episodes. In contrast, NBC's *Star Trek* presented a giant internationally manned space ship moving through galaxies in some future time

[1] Allen's fourth, *The Land of the Giants*, appeared in the 1968–69 season.

and testing the imagination of Gene Roddenberry's writers as well as those of the audience. An unexpected attraction of *Star Trek* was Leonard Nimoy as the almost emotionless Mr. Spock, the scientific leader of the Enterprise. This supposed second lead became one of the more interesting figures of television drama, despite his seeming coldness and pointed ears. Nimoy will long be remembered as one of television's two not-quite-human idols of the late 1960s. The other, as we shall see, was Jonathan Frid, of the afternoon serial *Dark Shadows.*

Batman's exclusive hold on network television's cape-and-cowl market lasted less than a year. With no thought of amusing adults or poking fun at the superhero, a group of animation studios broke it with a cycle of Saturday-morning excitement far removed from the gentleness of *Casper, the Friendly Ghost.* Though preceded by some grotesque Japanese-made syndicated adventures seen on independent stations, *Space Ghost* was one of the first of the animated avengers to make a real impression on the network level. Alongside it, or coming not far behind, were the animated adventures of Superman (with the old radio cast supplying the voices) plus those of Birdman, Spider Man, the Fantastic Four, and, of all things, Super President. Spider Man and the Fantastic Four were creatures of the Marvel Comics group, chief rival of National Comics in the 1960s. Other Marvel figures, notably Captain America, Submariner, and the Mighty Thor, were put into animation for syndicated series which achieved some prominence.

The superheroes took possession of Saturday morning, forcing most of the comic cartoons off the air. Producing kinetic comic-book adventure became extremely lucrative business, leading, of course, to the inevitable views of alarm. Mothers who had no idea what was inside comic books were quite able to see (and hear) the incessant, uninspired furor their offspring were witnessing hour after hour. Though there was little to defend artistically in these distortions of both comic-book and chapter-play entertainment, Dr. Wilbur Schramm did produce a study which suggested that psychologically the shows were harmless in themselves and could do no more than "feed the malignant impulses that already exist." Opposing his position was Dr. Frederic Wertham, for many years an opponent of Batman and his associates and the principal mover in the generation of a comic-book code that drove out the grotesque horror comics of the 1950s.

The events of history brought for once, if not a conclusion, at least a momentary resolution to a harmful-effects argument. The American self-analysis which followed the assassinations of Martin Luther King and Robert Kennedy put Dr. Wertham's argument in the ascendancy. Most of the animated superheroes were gone from the networks by the 1968–69 season, though they remained on independent stations and were not necessarily gone beyond recall.[2] Of a certainty their supposedly comic replacements were sorry stuff. (One, called *The Banana Splits*, blended comedy with a crude cliffhanging serial containing more brutality than could be found in the animated shows.)

Shortly after the *Batman* premiere Jack Gould wrote: "A year from now, the nation could be looking back on the premiere of 'Batman' as one of its golden nights." It was not that Gould saw *Batman* as one of television's magnificent dramas. Instead, he regarded it as a glorification of the nonevents that might kill such things by at last destroying their shield against the perils of overexposure. His conclusion? ". . . the secret answer to camp is exhaustion not protest. 'Batman' promises to be a real help."

Gould, as it turned out, had read the signs correctly. When his year was up, Batman was facing *real* difficulty. He was being outcamped by a couple of absurd superhero parodies which arrived just twelve months after his television debut. And he was losing much of the audience he had captured from *Lost in Space*.

A half hour apart on January 9, 1967, NBC and CBS introduced their answer to ABC's Caped Crusader. It was almost as though they agreed to save money by using the same idea for two programs—that of an ordinary mortal who acquired great physical strength but had no idea how to use it without being the buffoon. Imagine Dagwood Bumstead suddenly achieving

[2] NBC, by removing *Birdman* and *Super President* before the end of their contracted runs, lost approximately $750,000, according to one report.

Superman's powers and haberdasher, and the reader has pictured NBC's *Captain Nice* and CBS's *Mr. Terrific*. To decide which was worse would be difficult. As George Gent put it in the *New York Times*: ". . . both networks should be ashamed for further trivializing their medium with excursions into comic-book fantasy."

The parodies came at a bad time for Batman. The avenger was having sufficient trouble without having to associate with a pair of fools. For approximately a year *Batman* had followed a serialization pattern in which two-part stories began on Wednesday and ended on Thursday. The first installment closed on a ridiculously exaggerated cliffhanging note that was capped by the narrator's exhortation to tune in the next day, "same Bat-time, same Bat-channel." Whether there truly was suspense in the old chapter-play mode was questionable. In any event, by the middle of the 1966–67 season when the novelty of *Batman* had worn away, producer Dozier observed a significant difference between his program's Wednesday and Thursday ratings. The Thursday shows did better, Dozier thought, because the audience—and by that time it was solely juvenile—had discovered that there was enough summary before the concluding installments to follow the action easily. That permitted alternate serial entertainment on Wednesday nights—*Lost in Space*. To offset the loss, Dozier broke the Wednesday-Thursday pattern by moving to three-part stories which might end on Wednesday.

Clever as it was, the maneuvering was academic by the 1967–68 season, because the comic-book-inspired series, which had once walked with the top ten, had been cut back to a once-a-week basis and given an episodic format. The addition of an alluringly clad Batgirl may have attracted a few new viewers to the series—though not necessarily the young girls reportedly aimed for in this change—but the course plainly had been run. Two years after the dramatic premiere came the announcement that *Batman* would not be back in 1968–69.

To mourn the series might be unwise, however. Reruns began as soon as legally possible. A new crop of youngsters started to move into the fold as older brothers and sisters peeked over their shoulders, experiencing the first breezes of reminiscence. The vagaries of nostalgia are too untraceable to predict where the Batman of television will stand a generation later.

Surely it is foolhardy to foretell what programs will one day be remembered affectionately, since contemporary entertainment taste is so resistant to divination. Who would have foreseen that the daytime-serial sensation of the late 1960s would smack of the low-budget horror film of the 1940s? On June 27, 1966, Dan Curtis, inspired, he said, by a mysterious dream, introduced an afternoon drama which seemed at the outset to have as its principal attraction former screen star Joan Bennett, who portrayed the mistress of Collins House, a brooding manor on the Maine coast. To this locale, where frequently "all the elements of nature seemed at war with each other," came a young governess, Victoria Winters (played by Alexandra von Moltke). Before long what appeared at first to be an updated *Jane Eyre* became a daytime *Dracula.*

Section by section the cover was removed from the skeleton in the Collinses' spacious closet. Barnabas Collins, the cousin living on an adjoining estate, was revealed to be a full-fledged (if reluctant) vampire two centuries old. As occasional viewers stared in disbelief, the drama drew upon every cliché ever used in a Universal horror film, plus a few more. Rare was the episode that did not bring to view a Karlovian laboratory or ghostly crypt complete with feeble-minded attendant, intense scientist, Frankenstein monster, and werewolf. One season the drama, actors and all, moved back to the 1700s to show how a sorceress scorned made Barnabas what he is today. From then on expeditions to the past became common.

Although *Dark Shadows'* actors admitted that at times they had no idea what was going on, past or present, the Gothic moods were somehow achieved. The program soon attracted to itself an odd mixture of escape-minded housewives, children home from school, and cherishers of camp. To serious watchers —who, according to one report, included Mrs. Jackie Onassis— the chief attraction, assorted terrors notwithstanding, was the vampire, played by Jonathan Frid. In a break with Transylvanian tradition, this night creature was portrayed sympathetically. Barnabas Collins yearned to be an ordinary man, if necessary at the cost of his eternal life. Actor Frid, trained for Shakespeare, joined the *Dark Shadows* company on April 14, 1967, with no thought that by playing a creature from beyond the grave he would become the most popular male performer in soap opera. His fan mail grew to extraordinary volume—as many as fifteen hundred letters a day. The stunned Frid soon was the subject of many magazine articles, not to mention a ghoulish photo album, and was much sought after for personal appearances. When visiting children's television shows, he good naturedly slipped into his artificial fangs upon request.

By January, 1969, *Dark Shadows* had spawned six paperback books based upon the Collins saga, with more following. They were written for Paperback Library by W. E. Dan Ross under the pen name Marilyn Ross (female authorship being a convention of Gothic publishing). Thus the daytime serial form, which owed much of its original character to melodramatic (though not quite Gothic) fiction for women, was returning to the print medium something of what it had borrowed. Frid and his vehicle were, quite appropriately, "part shadow, part substance."[3]

[3] Despite its success, which led to an MGM film version, *Dark Shadows* remained daytime television's unique Gothic horror at the time of this writing—on a network level at least. In 1969, Krantz Films unleashed a video-taped syndication product: *Strange Paradise.* Produced by Jerry Layton and written by Ian Martin, it substituted the voodoo and reincarnation of West Indian lore for the witchcraft and vampirism of New England. The program's derivation was so apparent that it well could have been called *Dark Shadows of the Caribbean.*

CODA

*In the characters there are four points to aim at. First and fore-
most, that they shall be good. . . . The second point is to make
them appropriate. . . . The third is to make them like the reality.
. . . , The fourth is to make them consistent.*

ARISTOTLE, Poetics

The attention directed to *Dark Shadows* as the 1960s passed
into the 1970s—it even spawned a cookbook— was one of many
signs that after four decades the daytime serial form was very
much alive. In its Sunday edition of summer, 1968, the *New
York Times,* which in 1962 had speculated that the genre faced
imminent demise, thought fit to print four extended articles on
soap-opera matters. Once more the daytime serial was the subject of analysis—and with much more compassion than had been
its lot in the early 1940s. In January, 1968, Rick DuBrow, television critic for United Press-International, had gone so far as
to write, "Everything is relative, and in the world of television

Coda

I honestly believe that the daily soap operas are among the better regularly scheduled shows."

DuBrow further observed that daytime serial production was one of the few areas in video entertainment where both creators and viewers cared about what they were doing or watching. He believed that, because of the unassuming honesty with which the staffs of soap operas approached their product, they were "more real, more sophisticated, and more civilized to talk with than some of the strictly mercenary sharks of the more publicized and highpower series." Continued DuBrow, "They are what they are: professional people doing a professional job."

I agree with that evaluation. Those persons of the daytime-serial world whom I have encountered and with whom I have corresponded—Frank Hummert, Irna Phillips, and later arrivals such as Hector Chevigny and producer Joseph Hardy—have been sincerely interested in their work, without pretending to be working in the realm of the literary or dramatic masterpiece. When Agnes Eckhardt Nixon, a protégée of Irna Phillips and creator of *One Life to Live*, mentioned the accomplishments of serials in bringing to the attention of the viewers the Pap smear, a test for uterine cancer, and the work of the Children's Aid Society, it was with genuine satisfaction in service to American women, not with pretentious claims of aesthetic uplift—or apology for association with a shoddy genre. Miss Nixon wrote, "We are doing a job we like, getting a satisfying response from the audience we are trying to entertain and even have the feeling, at times, of accomplishing something truly worthwhile along the way."[1]

In mentioning signs of daytime-serial vitality, I should not overlook a bimonthly magazine which first appeared in 1968. The magazine was titled *Afternoon TV*, as though to fire back the allegation that the settling of soap operas in the post meridian was an indication of senility. A fan publication devoted exclusively to daytime drama, it was a significant advance upon the amount of printed space devoted to the continued stories of radio in such magazines as *Radioland* and *Radio Mirror*.

[1] Agnes Nixon, "They're Happy to Be Hooked," *New York Times*, July 7, 1968.

427

Afternoon TV, whose advertising and layout were slanted toward younger women, may also have reflected the serial preferences of the newest generation of housewives. Although still audience leaders, long-running dramas such as *As the World Turns, Guiding Light,* and *Search for Tomorrow* received conspicuously less coverage in early issues than some of the newer dramas, notably *Dark Shadows, Another World,* and *The Doctors.* Undoubtedly enough time had passed since the appearance of television's first serials to allow the development of different audience groups. Women who were young mothers when first they saw Mary Stuart as Joanne Tate on *Search for Tomorrow* could well have been young grandmothers when the series entered its twentieth year in September, 1970. Their tastes and those of their daughters may not have been exactly alike.

Fortunately, if tastes did differ, some variety could be found in daytime serials, as well as new degrees of competition. On September 9, 1968, there was for the first time a three-way battle for the serial audience of the daytime. Viewers at 3:00 P.M., eastern daylight time, could choose from ABC's *General Hospital,* CBS's *Secret Storm,* and NBC's *Another World.* A year later CBS began challenging the morning schedule by advancing *Love of Life* to 11:30 and inserting a new program, *Where the Heart Is,* in the vacated spot.[2] Concurrently, NBC's *Bright Promise* extended the three network struggle to the 3:30 P.M. time slot. At the beginning of the 1970s the network-serial day spanned five consecutive hours (11:30 A.M. to 4:30 P.M.), included nineteen half-hour dramas, and showed signs of the devastating competition that had characterized daytime radio.[3]

[2] CBS's invasion of the morning hours was shrewdly conceived and executed. *Love of Life* was strong enough to take the move to the morning in stride and also to deliver a large tryout audience to *Where the Heart Is.* Robert D. Wood, president of CBS-TV, advised me that the new drama (supported on the other side by *Search for Tomorrow*) had an exceptionally good start, fortifying the already strong daytime position of the network. CBS entered the 1970s maintaining the lead it had held over the other networks in daytime audience for fifteen years.

[3] Chronologically, shows numbered 17, 18, and 19 were three dramas introduced on March 30, 1970. ABC entered the noon-hour competition with *The Best of Everything* (inspired by the novel-based movie) and *A World Apart* (a generation-gap drama). Giving daytime television yet another "world," NBC added

428

Coda

As a footnote to the contention for viewers, it should be recorded that in late October, 1968, one of the individual participants was the distinguished film actress Joan Crawford. When surgery forced her daughter Christine to take a leave of absence from the cast of *The Secret Storm*, the senior Crawford took over the young woman's role for four episodes, ostensibly to prevent it from going permanently to another actress. The publicity value of a serial fling by an Academy Award winner scarcely can have been overlooked, however. While Joan Crawford was not the first film actress to attempt soap opera—Joan Bennett, Ann Sheridan, Coleen Gray, Gloria DeHaven, and others had done so earlier—her guest appearance carried no suggestion of an ebbing career's bitter pill. Joan Crawford was a celebrity gracing *The Secret Storm* set, as Jan Peerce and Mme Schumann-Heink had once graced the studio of *The Goldbergs*. Logical or not, the temporary casting captured attention for a show facing two strong competitors. Surely that was why an on-camera announcer proclaimed the cast change before each fifteen-minute segment of the program.

Whatever the outcome of the "battle of three o'clock," the daytime-serial form gave every appearance of good health as the 1970s began. Even if episodic and open-end serials were to lose their firm hold on the portion of nighttime air not turned over to feature films, it appears safe to assume that continued dramas of one kind or another will be in view at the turn of the next century, perhaps some of the very programs that exist today.

The seemingly incongruous aspect of this conjecture is the present, and quite likely future, diminution of the ingredient so often associated with serial drama: the highly suspenseful chapter ending. While no research study ever supported the assumption, few adults could be found to dispute a statement that it was cliffhanging which brought audiences back to theaters week

a second half hour's worth of *Another World,* calling it *Another World—Somerset* (the original serial was renamed *Another World—Bay City*). The new series (aired at 4:00 P.M., eastern standard time) contained a nucleus of popular characters from the older drama who had moved to a new town or visited there occasionally. If *Bright Promise* had not intervened between the two shows, they could have been considered daytime's first hour-long serial.

after week in the chapter-play era. Most journalists espouse this theory, despite the awkward historical presence of *The Perils of Pauline* and several other early film serials which did not use physical predicaments at episode end. Captivating as cliffhanging may have been, however, it is impossible to ascertain the extent of its value, even in juvenile entertainment. It may have intensified the serial experience when superimposed upon a good basic product. It may have helped disguise the weaknesses of shoddy merchandise. It may also, as serial pioneer Frank Leon Smith has suggested, have sealed the doom of the chapter-play species.

One thing we know: when the device was leaned upon less strongly in the daily children's thrillers of radio and almost completely eliminated in the episodic dramas and soap operas, no damage seemed to be done to serial appeal. Writers of the open-end serials for children recognized that they could not produce the direct threat of death at the end of each program and turned frequently to the situational ending with the emphasis, perhaps, on mystery:

ANNOUNCER: What is in the strange packet that Spider Morley managed to hide in that hollow trunk before Von Sturgeon's men carried him away? Don saw him conceal it and is going to try to get to the packet without being seen. Will it at last unlock the secret of the Inca cave? Be sure to be with us tomorrow . . . same time, same station!

As effective as the mystery break-off—and easier to produce on a day-to-day basis—was the tactical/strategical review:

ANNOUNCER: Well, rangers, what will Tex do? Do you think he'll accept Rain Cloud's invitation to meet him at the Mountain of the Skulls? All of a sudden the strong-willed redman is willing to talk about releasing the captives. Utah Jack is sure it's a trick, and the way Rain Cloud has acted in the past, I can't say I blame him. So keep listening, fellas and gals, as we continue the exciting adventure of the Golden Saddle!

Thus, in the radio thriller, the holdover question of the film

430

serial—"Will X escape death?"—evolved to a more cerebral "What will happen?" And despite this change in focus, the youngsters kept listening. Today, with probably no recollection of any of the pure cliffhanging crises that did, of course, end some installments of *Jack Armstrong, Captain Midnight,* and *Tom Mix,* adults retain warm and vivid memories of the vanished heroes and their milieu. They came to know them as well as they knew the contents of the treasure box hidden from prying eyes in the recesses of the bedroom closet. They would recognize the former champions instantly if the earnest voices were to spring once more from the ether.

Still, one serial form outdistanced the juvenile thrillers in establishment of familiar characters. In the soap opera the dramatis personae came for luncheon and stayed a day, a fortnight, and sometimes for decades. Early in their visit the chapter ending of the nonepisodic serial took what seems to have been the ultimate step. For obvious reasons a drama intended primarily for women required the stimulus of physical danger less frequently than did a *Jack Armstrong,* but it soon was discovered that not even mental dilemmas were needed each day to keep the audience listening. A bit of quandary posing often was enough to carry an established program through the most critical interval, the weekend. Moreover, the rise of soap opera to near monopoly of daytime radio coincided with the time critics began to complain that *nothing* was happening. The women's dramas of the 1930s brought nonepisodic serial dramatization to the point that the holdover question could be discarded, leaving only a simple promise: to be continued.

And so the dramatic form that in its embryonic stage was characterized by chapter endings which threatened dissolution survives and grows on a covenant of continuity. The open-end serial makes this pledge candidly; the episodic serial, by an implication that seeps through the overlay of individual-program resolution. Cliffhanging, though not entirely vanished with the chapter play, no longer is transcendent, which means that we must look elsewhere for the amulet that keeps the serial drama alive, the hook that catches and holds the viewer. To do so, we must turn again to the daytime serial, the continued-drama form that lies farthest from the cliffhanger—and the only serial medium which has been the subject of significant research.

At first thought it might seem easy to explain the attraction of soap opera. One can mention the frequent appearance of such elements as strong and virtuous heroines, weak and floundering males, strange diseases, recurring crises—the stuff of the formula serial. But such elements cannot be considered essential to daytime serial success, any more than they can be considered insurance therefor. Those who remember not just *Portia Faces Life* and *Backstage Wife* but also *Vic and Sade, Lorenzo Jones, The Second Mrs. Burton,* and *The Goldbergs* know that serial programs have enjoyed impressive runs in the daytime with and without noble heroines, frequent crises, unending suffering, exotic illnesses, lost mates, court trials, contemporary domestic settings, literary merit—and even scripts. Research studies have further suggested that four elements of structure did not affect audience composition: the sex of the leading character, comedy relief, amount of suspense, and the age or socioeconomic level of the leading characters.

When the variables are eliminated, there is only one characteristic that is common to every successful daytime serial—a set of characters in a continuing narrative. So if a secret is to be found, it is to be found in the essence of the form itself. And if one takes his eyes from the conspicuous, yet nonessential, accouterments of soap opera, the significance of characters in a continuing narrative can be seen. In fact, the history of daytime dramas has shown that the most popular programs have been those that exploited this characteristic to the fullest extent, while the ultimate-conclusion serials, which by design changed characters and stories frequently, were singularly unsuccessful.

Let us make a quick comparison. By our count 155 open-end (and episodic) serials achieved sponsorship on daytime radio and television before 1959, the last full year of the radio soap opera. Of the 155 dramas, 55 (35 per cent) survived for five years, and 15 of them were on the air in December, 1958. In

definite contrast, of the 18 sponsored serials of ultimate conclusion during the same period, only 2 (11 per cent) reached an
age of five years, and neither was being broadcast at the end of
1958. Moreover, the two ultimate-conclusion dramas which did
last several years despite their changing stories and characters
had special characteristics to aid them. *Light of the World* had
the familiar figures of the Bible, while *Aunt Jenny's True Life
Stories* had Aunt Jenny and her always-hungry announcer, who
chatted in her cheery kitchen each day, giving the series a feeling of continuity overriding that of the changing stories.

Because collectively the daytime's open and closed-end serials
had only duration of characters and story to mark them as separate forms, the general failure of the ultimate-conclusion
dramas over the years points to a positive relationship between
serial durability and the use of characters in an extended narrative (to be technically accurate, one should say the use of continuing dramatic agents in prolonged actions—Helen Trent and
her eternal quest of love after thirty-five, for example). Plot, as
we have seen, is unstressed. Writers can make a single plot last
for months, weaving in a new thread now and then to keep the
action going—to keep Helen on the trail of love, as it were. At
the same time, the extended action, considering the lightness of
plot, throws extraordinary emphasis upon the characters of the
drama—who, because of the meandering narrative structure,
appear to be living at the pace of real life.

The daytime serial, today as in the radio era, benefits from a
cumulative factor. With each episode watched, the viewer in-
vests more deeply in the undertaking. The continuing characters, expanded by the illusion of reality that accompanies the
extended action, become as real as neighbors. More real, perhaps, because the viewer knows every secret—the child a mother
cannot acknowledge, the disease that will destroy a young surgeon's sight, the marriage that is in name only. This detailed
knowledge adds nuance to each piece of action, and it adds
meaning that critics (who watch only occasionally, and clin-
ically) cannot detect or appraise. Those who do not follow a
particular serial regularly are like those who enter a church dur-

ing a rainstorm and witness a wedding. They see what takes place, but not through the eyes of the bride's mother or family doctor or disappointed suitor. It is not through coincidence, I believe, that of all the critics of the daytime-serial form, the most sympathetic was James Thurber, who, having been captured by one or two of the dramas during a long illness, followed the normal audience pattern more closely than did the occasional examiner of the form.

The feeling-out period for a serial and its follower is indeterminate, though networks allow a new daytime drama many months to develop an audience. At some point, however, the program, new or old, is either embraced or discarded. If it is embraced, the cumulative appeal has probably already set in. Like one reading a compelling novel, the viewer may at odd hours contemplate the situation of her electromagnetic acquaintances. She turns to their imaginary households—who are always there at the same place and time each day—as she might telephone or visit someone of the real world: out of interest and curiosity or to enjoy a bit of companionship. The extent to which a serial viewer calls upon her "friends," as well as the character with which she may choose to identify, will differ from that of the serial viewer down the street, just as one person differs from another in personality, self-reliance, degree of loneliness, or interest in others. As mentioned earlier, while soap-opera audiences reflect those at home in the daytime, research studies have failed to disclose a typical daytime serial listener or viewer.

It is likely that the oft-cited elements of content enhance the appeal of given programs for some viewers and strengthen the identification with long-continuing characters. Although there are today no paragons of productive feminine virtue like Mary Noble and Portia Blake, talented and useful women such as the look-alike blonde physicians of *The Doctors* and *Days of Our Lives* or the demure dean of women on *Bright Promise* may have a part in holding one set of women viewers. Others may prefer the steady, supportive, homemaker image projected by Nancy Hughes in *As the World Turns*. The crimes and litigations that dot several daytime serials bring experiences anyone might wish to observe from a safe distance (though it does not seem accidental that these elements appear most frequently in late-afternoon dramas, which may have audiences of males and youngsters higher than the 30 per cent reported by *Newsweek* as the mean for the whole day). Medically oriented dramas also offer a safe kind of observation for those whose interests are so inclined.

While elements of sex and romance can be found in almost any program if the daytime serial viewer waits for them, fields of specialization exist here also. Diluted miscegenation has always been in the offing in *Love Is a Many-Splendored Thing*, with its Eurasian-American heroine, and more serious stuff was promised in a long sequence on *One Life to Live*, until the supposedly white Carla Benari (played by Ellen Holly) turned out to be of the same race as black physician Price Trainor. (Some viewers claimed a cop-out; others sighed in relief.) Even incest crawled from its dark corner in *Days of Our Lives* when amnesia-racked Dr. Mark "Brooks" came to the brink of marriage with Marie Horton, who did not recognize him as the older brother she thought had died years earlier in Korea. This sequence gave way to the problems that arose when a second Horton brother "raped" a third brother's wife, producing a child the sterile cuckold thought to be his own.

The plot patterns and aberrations of individual programs make colorful copy and may well provide the basis for selection —or rejection—of daytime-serial entertainment. Once an affirmative decision is made, however, these elements become the seasoning in a broth whose stock is a group of characters in an extended narrative, brought to fullness by the cumulative factor, the catalyst of daytime serial drama.

Does the catalytic function of the extended narrative in the daytime serial carry over to the continued dramas of the nighttime? Yes, though for several reasons not to the same degree. *Peyton Place* profited from it, naturally. Its open-end story moved at a pace that, while faster than that of a daytime serial, gave an impression of life's pattern. As the characters and their problems became familiar, regular viewers saw all kinds of things the casual observer missed.

The complexities of broadcast programing, however, make nightly open-end serials unlikely, at least in any significant number, for several reasons: the time slots are not available, there are too many pre-emptions for special programs, and reruns are somewhat illogical while the original program is still running. *Peyton Place* was unique in reaching three evening presentations a week; yet even that program was never kept at the same broadcast hour or on the same days long enough to enjoy the advantages of regularity given the humblest serial of the daytime. Nightly serialization also represents a large financial risk if the program is to be allotted the comparatively lengthy tryout period afforded in the daytime. A thirteen-week trial—not long as serial tryouts go—means sixty-five programs, enough to last a weekly drama almost two years.

Thus the cumulative factor must prevail at night in the one-broadcast-a-week pattern that has become standard. For it to come into effect a new serial drama must withstand the brutal rating race that marks a new season, an especially difficult task if the competition includes a well-established evening program or two. Nevertheless, if the early crisis is passed, an episodic or open-end drama of the night can benefit from accumulated knowledge of and interest in a set of characters in a continuing action.

The illusion of reality found in the day-in, day-out pattern of the soap opera is not to be expected, of course. Evening programs move from one night to another as networks attempt to outwit each other. Special programs interrupt the pattern. Reruns in the summer work counter to the thread of reality. And the very presence in the average home of most of its occupants in the evening is a barrier to the absorption of characters by viewer (or viewer by characters) possible to soap opera.

Still, though the writers of nighttime serials must work harder than their daytime counterparts to produce believability, they have a gift of time not accorded writers of single-unit dramas.

They can develop their characters over months or years, and although they are forced to work with plots of short duration, they can introduce episodes intended primarily for character definition. Accordingly, on several Sundays *Bonanza* turned from the problems of the Ponderosa to tell the bittersweet stories of Ben Cartwright's short and tragic marriages to the women who bore his sons. Other Sunday episodes became essays in personality: Hoss's gentleness within a massive frame, Little Joe's desire to prove himself mature and capable. And always in the *Bonanza* frame of reference were the interrelationships of father and sons, set against the western atmosphere but portraying situations that could occur in any patriarchal home.

In hailing the longevity of *Bonanza* at the beginning of its eleventh season in 1969, Jack Gould pointed to the Cartwrights as individuals of characterization "engaged in a narrative to which gunplay has always been incidental." His observation of the program's emphasis upon people could be extended to that other durable Western drama, *Gunsmoke*, to which Matt, Kitty, Doc, and deputies Chester and Festus have been much greater assets than .45's or thundering hoofs. Complementing each other in rich fashion, the continuing *Gunsmoke* characters display mutual affection, irritation at each others' minor foibles, and loyalty to the point of risking life itself. These facets of character operate independently of the momentary plot, or inside it, with equal frequency. Can it be coincidence that of all the "adult" Westerns that flooded the television market in the late 1950s, the only survivors in the early 1970s were the two dramas that alone put character above action or gimmick? Writers have called *Bonanza* and *Gunsmoke* more soap opera than horse opera. For once, "soap opera" may not have been a pejorative.

Other nighttime programs can be mentioned as examples of the importance of well-drawn characters in a continuing action: the home-centered *Mama, Father Knows Best, My Three Sons,* and *The Farmer's Daughter*; the profession-centered *Marcus Welby, M.D., Ben Casey,* and *The Defenders*; and the school-centered *Mr. Peepers, Mr. Novak,* and *Room 222.* Though not of uniform quality, these dramas portrayed indi-

437

viduals as opposed to caricatures. And with each passing month the layers of character grew, the pieces of enriching biography accumulated.

Even the situation comedies, whose writers never could be accused of probing depths of character, derive distinct gain from the compensations of continuing dramatic action. In fact, the debt of the writer of a successful situation show to the logrolling effect of serial drama might be the greatest of all. Rarely does he attempt to go beyond surface characterization, and yet his characters are not merely tolerated by the audience as stereotypes but are delighted in for their predictability of behavior or reaction. The long-anticipated maternity sequence of *I Love Lucy* was a triumph of farce based solidly upon the audience's enjoyment of seeing the Ricardos and the Mertzes behave in exactly the chaotic manner viewers well knew they would when the crisis arrived. *Bewitched* built its long run on situations in which audience foreknowledge of the mixed blessings of wifely witchcraft heightened the pleasure. And can we overlook the reward Jack Benny reaped during decades of broadcasting from a gradually amassed interest in the half-real, half-fictional people of his programs? Many of his sketches would not be amusing if his audiences were not steeped in the peculiar traits Benny gave himself and his associates—stinginess, attraction to the bottle, gluttony, momism, and so on. What the comedian really began on CBS Radio in 1932 was, in one framework or another, the longest permanent floating episodic serial of broadcasting. The successive additions to the legend gave each new Jack Benny offering a head start, just as it sometimes has extended the lives of other comedies or dramas when the original inspiration or ingenuity has begun to disappear.

But if interest in the figures of a drama ends—as it will through creative carelessness or indifference or because of a change in the times—the cumulative effect can change from one of increased interest to one of growing distaste. Serial writers cannot ignore their special obligation to the characters they are creating or to the people for whom they are creating them. Knowledgeable serial makers recognize that television audiences are a changing lot. A program's clientele may remain mostly women, or mostly young moderns, or mostly middle-class forty-year-olds for season after season; but what happens within those groups as time passes? A glance at the history of popular fiction or drama of the past one hundred years suggests that the mass audience—youngsters included—has been growing in sophistication, albeit slowly. The course of serial drama from the days of the chapter play is marked by failure to recognize this fact—or if it is recognized, to make appropriate adjustments for fear of rocking a boat.

Thus a *Bracken's World*, in the planning stage in 1962 (before *Peyton Place*) belatedly arrives on television in 1969, looking like *Peyton Place West* but lacking the depth and characterization of the program universally compared with it in the reviews. The situation becomes one of replacing the film *Grand Hotel* of 1932 with *Our Dancing Daughters* of 1928.

Then there is *Perry Mason*, which for years has entertained large audiences despite a near-ritualistic closing-act format and a preordained loser in prosecutor Ham Burger. One autumn, by decree of CBS network programers, the show is placed beside a sophisticated legal drama, *The Defenders* (in which the good guys sometimes lose). Alas, the toy does not seem as shiny any more. A line is drawn that was not there before, and some viewers are ready to cross it, without the possibility of easy return. While affection for the old characters continues, the efforts of Raymond Burr and fellow actors cannot make the Mason people as three-dimensional as are the new ones in the *Defenders'* cast, headed by E. G. Marshall. Young adults, those who have grown from childhood to maturity while *Perry Mason* is on the air, are not turning up in the ratings, leaving the original viewers, like the Old Guard at Waterloo, too few to prevail. Esteemed but no longer wanted, attorney Mason moves to the exile of reruns, while Burr's vigor is resurrected in *Ironside*, a crime drama more predictable than *The Defenders* yet less hackneyed than *Perry Mason* became in its twilight years.

What if the Burr resurrection had been tried at an earlier level of sophistication? It may have succeeded, but the odds,

The Serials

I think, would have been against it. Within each tent of serial drama—mystery, soap opera, melodrama, situation comedy—accommodations must be made to life's changes as they are reflected in those sought as viewers. The Craig Kennedy who fascinated adults in *The Exploits of Elaine* could prosper in the late 1960s and early 1970s only in the multiple bodies of those doing the scientific tricks on *Mission: Impossible*. Within a few years it is doubtful that even such diversification could cover the absence of an enduring character in the mold of say, Sherlock Holmes.

Pauline of the perils, Helen Trent, Jack Armstrong, The Shadow are creatures of their eras, acceptable only in their eras. There is always a place in the public's heart for such creations, provided they are at least at the periphery of fictional acceptance. In a world of rapid change this periphery recedes at an ever-faster pace. To keep within it, serial writers, particularly those of soap opera, will continue to move farther from *St. Elmo* and *East Lynne* and closer to the Forsyte novels and *Our Town*. They will not reach a *Don Quixote* or *Madame Bovary*—and should not be expected to in their medium—but they can produce an electronic *Vanity Fair* or *Tale of Two Cities*. Of a certainty serial writers have in large measure learned the importance of careful characterization. *Amos 'n' Andy*'s Correll and Gosden stressed it in analyzing their technique, as did daytime serial pioneers Irna Phillips and Elaine Carrington. The writers of *Bonanza* and *Gunsmoke* have demonstrated their reliance on character before millions of viewers each week. And in 1968, Agnes Nixon, one of the more active daytime-serial writers of the second generation, wrote as follows for the *New York Times* in 1968:

> Perhaps it is not mere coincidence that Charles Dickens, one of the greatest creators of immortal literary characters, started his career as a writer of serialized stories. He knew, and demonstrated with genius, that for a public to stay with a story they had to care about the characters in it.

Given characters worth savoring, care about them serial followers do. They love them, loathe them, admire them, feel su-

440

perior to them, laugh with them, worry about them, but never do they ignore them. Captured by the special magic of the serial narrative, they come to the world of continued drama (in the afternoon especially) with arms open, senses honed. Amid critics and skeptics they await the next tantalizing development in the American-made dramatic genre that seems destined by its very nature *to be continued.*

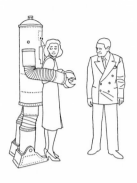

APPENDIX A

The Daytime Network Serials of Radio

The sponsored daytime serials of the radio chains are grouped below by year in the order of network premiere. An asterisk following the title indicates a program which was presented locally, regionally, by syndication, or at night before it moved to daytime network presentation. Advertising agencies and sponsors are mentioned when they are closely related to the program's development.

The principal sources of this data were the program files of the national networks, the yearbooks of *Variety* and *Broadcasting*, Harrison B. Summers' *A Thirty-Year History of Programs Carried on National Radio Networks in the United States, 1926–1956*, and published newspaper and magazine program logs. Where data were contradictory, an effort was made to determine the most reliable information. The occasional inconsistencies of network records, unreliability of memory, and difficulty of distinguishing between program and network premiere have produced some gray areas, though none extend beyond periods of more than a few months.

The Daytime Network Serials of Radio

*Clara, Lu,'n' Em**

Benton and Bowles supervised for Colgate on NBC Blue beginning on February 15, 1932. (Introduced on WGN, Chicago, in June, 1930; became an NBC evening feature on January 27, 1931.)

Writers: Initially, the actresses themselves
Actresses: Louise Starkey (Clara), Isobel Caruthers (Lu), Helen King (Em)

The show left the air in 1936, when Miss Caruthers died, and returned briefly in 1942, with Harriet Allyn as Lu.

Vic and Sade

Sustained from June 29, 1932, through November 3, 1934; several sponsors thereafter, notably Procter and Gamble. On NBC Blue.

Writer: Paul Rhymer
Actors: Art Van Harvey (Vic), Bernadine Flynn (Sade), Billy Idelson (Rush), Clarence Hartzell (Uncle Fletcher)
Theme: "Chanson Bohémienne" (Boldi)

Judy and Jane

Blackett-Sample-Hummert supervised for J. A. Folger on NBC Blue (Middle West) beginning on October 10, 1932.

Writer: Robert Andrews
Actors: Ireene Wicker, Margaret Evans (Jane Lee); Joan Kay (Judy), Walter Wicker (Jim Sargent)

Presented by transcription.

Betty and Bob

Blackett-Sample-Hummert supervised for General Mills on NBC Blue beginning on October 10, 1932.

Writer: Robert Andrews
Actors: Beatrice Churchill, Alice Hill, Arlene Francis (Betty); Don Ameche, Les Tremayne, Van Heflin, Onslow Stevens (Bob); Edith Davis (Mrs. Drake, Gardenia)
Theme: "Salut d'Amour" (Elgar)

Replaced by *Light of the World* on March 18, 1940.

The Serials

Marie, the Little French Princess

Blackett-Sample-Hummert supervised for Louis Phillippe on CBS beginning on March 7, 1933. (The first daytime serial of CBS.)

Actors: Ruth Yorke (Marie), James Meighan (Richard Collins), Allyn Joslyn

Discontinued in 1935.

Today's Children

Hutchinson Advertising supervised for Pillsbury on NBC beginning on September 11, 1933.

Writer: Irna Phillips
Actors: Ireene Wicker (Eileen Moran), Walter Wicker (Bob Crane), Bess Johnson (Frances Moran), Lucy Gilman (Lucy Moran), Irna Phillips (Kay Norton, Mother Moran)
Announcer: Louis Roen
Epigraph: "And today's children with their hopes and dreams, their laughter and tears, shall be the builders of a brighter world tomorrow."

Miss Phillips discontinued the program in 1938, revived the title for NBC's *Lonely Women* in 1943.

Easy Aces*

Blackett-Sample-Hummert supervised for American Home Products on CBS beginning on October 10, 1933. (Began on KMBC, Kansas City, 1930; CBS evening show for Lavoris, March 1, 1932.)

Writer: Goodman Ace
Actors: Jane and Goodman Ace (themselves), Mary Hunter (Marge)
Theme: "Manhattan Serenade"

Returned to nighttime radio (NBC) in 1935. Discontinued in 1944.

Painted Dreams*

Erwin, Wasey supervised for Battle Creek health foods on CBS beginning on October 10, 1933. (Irna Phillips had originated the drama three years earlier for WGN.)

Writers: Bess Flynn, Kay Chase

Actors: Bess Flynn (Mother Moynihan), Mary Afflick, Kay Chase, Alice Hill

This drama, from which *Today's Children* had sprung, format and cast, appeared sporadically on network radio during the balance of the 1930s.

*Just Plain Bill**

Blackett-Sample-Hummert supervised for American Home Products (Kolynos) on CBS beginning on October 16, 1933. (First presented in the evening, beginning on September 19, 1932.)

Writer: Robert Andrews

Actors: Arthur Hughes (Bill Davidson), James Meighan (Kerry Donovan), Ruth Russell (Nancy Davidson Donovan)

Theme: "Polly-Wolly-Doodle" (Hal Brown on harmonica and banjo)

Epigraph: "The real life story of a man who might be your next door neighbor . . . a story of people we all know."

Moved to NBC in 1936 and continued there until 1955.

The Romance of Helen Trent

First presented on July 24, 1933. Blackett-Sample-Hummert supervised for Edna Hopper on CBS beginning on October 30, 1933.

Actors: Virginia Clark (1933–43), Julie Stevens (1944–60) (Helen), David Gothard (Gil Whitney, Philip King)

Theme: "Juanita" (Stanley Davis humming)

Discontinued in 1960.

Ma Perkins

Blackett-Sample-Hummert supervised for Procter and Gamble (Oxydol) on NBC Red beginning on December 4, 1933. (Introduced on WLW, Cincinnati, on August 14, 1933.)

Writer: Orin Tovrov

Actors: Virginia Payne (Ma), Murray Forbes (Willy Fitz), Charles Egleston (Shuffle Shober)

Theme: Original melodies by Larry Larsen and Don Marcotte

Discontinued in 1960.

1934

Dreams Come True

Pedlar and Ryan supervised for Procter and Gamble (Camay) on

NBC Red beginning on July 16, 1934. Musical drama about Barry McKinley, baritone, and his novelist-sweetheart. Ray Sinatra's orchestra.

Last broadcast on April 11, 1935.

Home Sweet Home

Blackman Advertising supervised for Procter and Gamble (Chipso) on NBC Red beginning on July 23, 1934.

Writer: Burr Cook
Actors: Cecil Secrest (Fred Kent), Harriet MacGibbon (Lucy Kent), Billy Halop (Dick Kent), Joe Latham (Uncle Will)

Last broadcast on November 16, 1936.

Song of the City

H. W. Kastor supervised for Procter and Gamble (Dreft) on NBC Red beginning on August 14, 1934.

Writer: Walter Wicker
Actors: Ireene and Walter Wicker, Irna Phillips, Lucy Gilman

Known first as *Rainbow Court*, the story of a crippled girl and her doctor. Discontinued in 1935.

Peggy's Doctor

Ruthrauff and Ryan supervised for Delaware L & W Coal on NBC Red beginning on October 1, 1934.

Actors: James Meighan (Dr. John McKeever), Rosaline Greene (Peggy Dale), Allyn Joslyn

Northern doctor in Kentucky village woos daughter of penniless horse breeder. Discontinued in 1935.

*The Gumps**

E. W. Hellwig supervised for Corn Products Refining on CBS beginning on November 5, 1934.

Producer-director Himan Brown supervised various writers, including Irwin Shaw.
Actors: Agnes Moorehead (Min), Walter Wilmer (Andy), Jackie Kelk (Chester)

Based upon the comic strip by Sidney Smith. An earlier series had appeared on WGN (1931) with different cast, including Bess Flynn and son Charles (Jack Armstrong).

Life of Mary Sothern
McCord supervised for Sterling (Cal-Aspirin on Mutual).

Writer: Don Becker
Actors: Minabelle Abbott (Mary), Jay Jostyn (Max Tilley)
Theme: "Just a Little Love, a Little Kiss"

Originated by WLW, Cincinnati, the program became Mutual's first daytime serial. Discontinued in 1938.

1935

The Story of Mary Marlin

Lord and Thomas supervised for Kleenex on NBC Red beginning on January 1, 1935. (Introduced on WMAQ on October 3, 1934.)

Writer: Jane Cruisinberry
Actors: Joan Blaine, Anne Seymour, Muriel Kirkland (Mary); Robert Griffin (Joe Marlin); Carlton Brickert (David Post); Fran Carlon (Bunny Mitchell); Frank Dane (Never Fail Hendricks); Rupert La Belle (Rufus Kane)
Theme: "Clair de Lune" (Debussy)

Discontinued in 1945. Revived by ABC in 1951–52.

Mrs. Wiggs of the Cabbage Patch

Blackett-Sample-Hummert supervised for American Home Products on CBS beginning on February 4, 1935.

Actors: Betty Garde (Mrs. Wiggs); Robert Strauss, Jay Jostyn (Mr. Wiggs); Agnes Young, Alice Frost (Miss Hazy); Joe Latham (Stubbins)

Hummert reworking of a story by Alice Hegan Rice about life in Kentucky shanty town. Last broadcast on December 23, 1938.

Five Star Jones

Blackett-Sample-Hummert supervised for Mohawk Rugs on CBS beginning on February 4, 1935.
Actors: Johnny Kane (Tom Jones), Elizabeth Day (Sally Jones)

A Hummert story about an ace reporter. Last broadcast on February 5, 1937.

Backstage Wife

Blackett-Sample-Hummert supervised for Sterling (Dr. Lyons) on Mutual beginning on August 5, 1935. (Moved to NBC on March 30, 1936.)

Actors: Vivian Fridell, Claire Niesen (Mary Noble); Ken Griffin, James Meighan, Guy Sorel (Larry Noble)

Themes: "Stay as Sweet as You Are," "The Rose of Tralee"

Epigraph: "The story of Mary Noble, a little Iowa girl, who married Larry Noble, handsome matinee idol, dream sweetheart of a million other women, and her struggle to keep his love in the complicated atmosphere of backstage life."

Discontinued in 1959.

The O'Neills *

Blackman Advertising supervised for Procter and Gamble on NBC Red beginning October 8, 1935. (Started as evening feature, December 10, 1934.)

Writer: Jane West

Actors: Kate McComb (Ma O'Neill), James Tansey (Danny O'Neill), Jack Rubin (Mr. Levy), Jane West (Mrs. Bailey)

Theme: "Danny Boy"

Discontinued in 1943.

Molly of the Movies

Blackett-Sample-Hummert supervised for Wander Company (Ovaltine) on Mutual beginning October 10, 1935.

Writer: Thompson Buchanan

Actors: Gene Byron ("Molly"), Ray Jones

Last broadcast on April 23, 1937.

1936

The Goldbergs *

Introduced by WJZ as a sustaining feature on November 20, 1929. On NBC for Pepsodent on July 13, 1931. Daytime for Colgate on January 13, 1936.

Writer: Gertrude Berg
Actors: Gertrude Berg (Molly Goldberg); James Waters (Jake); Roslyn Silber (Rosalie); Alfred Ryder, Everett Sloane (Sammy)
Theme: "Serenade" (Toselli)
Discontinued in 1945.

Pepper Young's Family
First presented in daytime by NBC on January 13, 1936. (Introduced as evening feature in 1932 under title *Red Adams*. Later called *Red Davis, Forever Young*.)
Writer: Elaine Carrington
Actors: Curtis Arnall, Lawson Zerbe, Mason Adams (Pepper), Marion Barney (Mrs. Young); Jack Roseleigh, Thomas Chalmers (Sam Young); Elizabeth Wragge (Peggy Young); Eunice Howard (Linda Benton)
Theme: "Au Matin"
Discontinued in 1959.

Dan Harding's Wife
Introduced as sustaining feature by NBC Red on January 20, 1936. Acquired sponsor (Nabisco) on January 3, 1938.
Writer: Ken Robinson
Actress: Isabel Randolph (Rhoda Harding)
Discontinued in 1939.

*David Harum**
Supervised by Blackett-Sample-Hummert and Duane Jones for Babbitt on NBC Blue beginning on January 27, 1936. (Earlier on WOR.)
Actors: Wilmer Walter, Craig McDonnell, Cameron Prud'homme (David); Eva Condon, Charme Allen (Aunt Polly); Peggy Allenby (Susan); Arthur Maitland (Zeke Swinney)
Theme: "Sunbonnet Sue" (Stanley Davis humming with guitar)
Discontinued in 1950.

Rich Man's Darling
Blackett-Sample-Hummert supervised for American Home Products on CBS, beginning on February 17, 1936.
Writers: Addy Richton, Anne Hummert

Actors: Karl Swenson (Packy O'Farrell), Peggy Allenby (Peggy O'Farrell)

Replaced by *Our Gal Sunday* on March 29, 1937.

Modern Cinderella

Blackett-Sample-Hummert supervised for General Mills (Gold Medal) on CBS beginning on June 1, 1936. (On WGN earlier.)

Actors: Rosemary Dillon, Luise Barklie, Larry Burton, Eddie Dean, Jimmy Gale, Ben Gage

Broadcast in 1936–37 as part of the *General Mills Program.*

*Girl Alone**

N. W. Ayer supervised for Kellogg on NBC Red beginning on July 13, 1936. (First broadcast in 1935.)

Writer: Fayette Krum

Actors: Betty Winkler (Pat Rogers); Pat Murphy (Scoop Curtis); Les Damon, Karl Weber (John Knight); June Travis (Stormy)

Theme: "The Girl Alone Suite" by Don Marcotte

Discontinued in 1941.

Love Song

Blackett-Sample-Hummert supervised for General Mills on Mutual beginning August 31, 1936.

A two-station feature (WGN and WLW). Last broadcast on March 5, 1937.

Heinz Magazine of the Air

Maxon supervised for Heinz on CBS beginning on September 2, 1936.

The serial *Trouble House* was written by Elaine Carrington and starred Carleton Young as Bill Mears, with Anne Elstner as Martha Booth and Elliott Reid as Ted Booth.

The second serial of this radio magazine, *Carol Kennedy's Romance,* was all that survived of the series in August, 1937. It too departed, on July 30, 1938. The performers included Gretchen Davidson (Carol) and Mitzi Gould (Kathy).

John's Other Wife

Blackett-Sample-Hummert supervised for American Home Products on NBC Red beginning September 14, 1936.

Actors: Matt Crowley, William Post, Jr. (John Perry); Adele Ronson, Erin O'Brien-Moore (Elizabeth Perry); Phyllis Welch (Martha); Irene Hubbard (Molly); Elaine Kent (Carlie)

Theme: "The Sweetest Story Ever Told" (Stanley Davis singing with guitar)

Department store owner John Perry's other wife was his secretary. His romantic dichotomy ended in 1942.

Big Sister

Ruthrauff and Ryan supervised for Lever on CBS beginning on September 14, 1936.

Writer: Lillian Lauferty (the drama's creator) and others

Actors: Alice Frost (Ruth Evans Wayne, big sister); Martin Gabel (Dr. John Wayne); Haila Stoddard, Dorothy McGuire (Sue Evans, little sister)

Theme: "Valse Bluette"

Opening: (After tolling of bells) "Yes, there's the clock in Glen Falls' town hall telling us it's time for Rinso's story of *Big Sister.*"

Discontinued in 1952.

Bachelor's Children

Roche, Williams, and Cunningham supervised for Cudahy (Old Dutch) on CBS beginning on September 28, 1936.

Writer: Bess Flynn

Actors: Hugh Studebaker (Dr. Bob Graham), Marjorie Hannan (Ruth), Patricia Dunlap (Janet, Ruth's twin), Olan Soule (Sam Ryder), Marie Nelson (Ellen, the housekeeper)

Theme: "Ah, Sweet Mystery of Life" (Herbert)

Graham's promise to his wartime sergeant to take care of his daughters brings him twin eighteen-year-olds. One, Ruth, eventually marries Dr. Bob.

Discontinued in 1946.

1937

*Myrt and Marge**

First presented in daytime by CBS on January 4, 1937. (Introduced as an evening feature on November 2, 1931.)

Writer: Myrtle Vail

451

Actors: Myrtle Vail (Myrt Spear), Donna Dameral (Marge Minter), Vinton Hayworth (Jack Arnold), Ray Hedge (Clarence Tiffingtuffer)

Theme: "Poor Butterfly"

Epigraph: "*Myrt and Marge* is a story of Broadway, a story that goes beyond the lights of the gay white way into the lives of two chorus girls."

Discontinued in 1942.

Follow the Moon

Lennen and Mitchell supervised for Jergens on NBC Red beginning on January 4, 1937. This Elsie Hitz–Nick Dawson mystery, written by John Tucker Battle, was discontinued in 1938.

Aunt Jenny's True Life Stories

Ruthrauff and Ryan supervised for Lever (Spry) on CBS beginning January 18, 1937.

Actors: Edith Spencer, Agnes Young (Aunt Jenny, the storyteller); Dan Seymour (Danny, the announcer)

Theme: "Believe Me, If All Those Endearing Young Charms"

Discontinued in 1956.

The Guiding Light

Compton supervised for Procter and Gamble on NBC Red beginning on January 25, 1937.

Writer: Irna Phillips

Actors: Arthur Peterson (Dr. Rutledge); Ruth Bailey (Rose Kransky); Mercedes McCambridge, Sarajane Wells (Mary Rutledge); Ed Prentiss, John Hodiak (Ned Holden); Gladys Heen (Torchy); Jone Allison (Meta Bauer); Raymond Edward Johnson (Mr. Nobody from Nowhere)

Theme: "Aphrodite" (Goetzl)

The longest narrative of daytime drama moved from radio to television. Discontinued in 1956 as radio feature.

We Are Four*

J. Walter Thompson supervised for Libby on Mutual (WGN and WOR) beginning on March 1, 1937. Bess Flynn wrote this drama originated by WGN in 1936. The performers included Marjorie Hannan, Charles Flynn, Alice Hill, and Sallie Smith.

Pretty Kitty Kelly

Benton and Bowles supervised for Continental Baking on CBS beginning on July 19, 1937.

Writer: Frank Dahm

Actors: Arline Blackburn (Kitty), Clayton Collyer (Michael Conway)

Theme: "Kerry Dance"

Discontinued in 1940.

Our Gal Sunday

Blackett-Sample-Hummert supervised for American Home Products (Anacin) on CBS beginning on March 29, 1937.

Actors: Dorothy Lowell, Vivian Smolen (Sunday); Karl Swenson, Alistair Duncan (Lord Henry Brinthrope); Jay Jostyn, Robert Strauss (Jackie and Lively)

Theme: "Red River Valley"

Epigraph: "The story of an orphan girl named Sunday, from the little mining town of Silver Creek, Colorado, who in young womanhood married England's richest, most handsome lord, Lord Henry Brinthrope. The story asks the question: Can this girl from a mining town in the West find happiness as the wife of a wealthy and titled Englishman?"

Discontinued in 1959.

The Couple Next Door

Blackett-Sample-Hummert supervised for Procter and Gamble on Mutual beginning on April 12, 1937. Performers at one time or another included Olan Soule and Donna Creed, Harold Vermilyea and Dorothy Gish, Alan Bunce and Peg Lynch (in the 1957 revival). Last broadcast (on CBS) in 1960.

Lorenzo Jones

Blackett-Sample-Hummert supervised for Sterling drugs on NBC Red beginning April 26, 1937.

Actors: Karl Swenson (Lorenzo); Betty Garde, Lucille Wall (Belle)

Theme: "Funiculi, Funicula"
Epigraph: "We all know couples like lovable, impractical Lorenzo and his wife, Belle. Their struggle for security is anybody's story, but somehow with Lorenzo, it has more smiles than tears."

Discontinued in 1955.

The Road of Life

Compton supervised for Procter and Gamble on NBC Blue and Red from June, 1937.

Writer: Irna Phillips and others, including Howard Teichman
Actors: Matt Crowley, Ken Griffin, Don McLaughlin (Dr. Jim Brent); Lesley Woods (Carole); Charlotte Manson (Dr. Carson McVicker); Virginia Dwyer (Jocelyn McLeod); Julie Stevens (Maggie Lowell)
Theme: "Pathetique Symphony" (first movement) (Tchaikovsky)

Last broadcast on radio in 1959.

Arnold Grimm's Daughter

Blackett-Sample-Hummert supervised for General Mills on CBS beginning on July 5, 1937.

Actors: Don Merrifield (Arnold), Betty Lou Gerson (daughter)
Theme: "Modern Cinderella"

Discontinued in 1942.

Kitty Keene, Inc.

Blackett-Sample-Hummert supervised for Procter and Gamble on NBC Red beginning on September 13, 1937.

Writer: Lenton Huntley
Actors: Fran Carlon, Gail Henshaw, Beverly Younger (Kitty)
Theme: "None but the Lonely Heart" (Tchaikovsky)

Discontinued in 1941.

Jenny Peabody

Mento Everitt supervised and starred for F & F on CBS beginning on October 18, 1937. The story of Hillsdale's postmistress and general store proprietor. Discontinued in 1938.

Hilltop House
Benton and Bowles supervised for Colgate in CBS beginning November 1, 1937.
Writers: Addy Richton, Lynn Stone (Adelaide Marstone)
Actors: Bess Johnson (Bess Johnson); Jackie Kelk (Marny); Carleton Young, Spencer Bentley (Dr. Robbie Clark); Ronald Liss (Tiny Tim); Gee Gee James (Tulip)
Theme: Brahms's "Lullaby"
Epigraph: "A child crying in the night; a child crying for light."

1938

Terry Regan: Attorney at Law
Needham, Louis and Brorby supervised for Johnson Wax on NBC Blue from January 3 to June 29, 1938.
Actors: Jim Ameche (Regan), Fran Carlon (Sally Dunlap, his secretary)

Margo of Castlewood
Lord and Thomas supervised for Quaker on NBC Blue during show's brief run. Barbara Luddy played Margo, the seventy-nine-year-old matriarch of the Carver family.

Woman in White
Hutchinson supervised for Pillsbury on NBC Red beginning on January 3, 1938.

Writer: Irna Phillips
Actors: Luise Barclay, Betty Lou Gerson (nurse Karen Adams); Karl Weber (Dr. Kirk Harding, who married Karen); Macdonald Carey, Marvin Miller (Dr. Markham); Sarajane Wells (Eileen Holmes); Ken Griffin (Dr. Paul Burton)
Theme: "Interlude" (Lucas)
Discontinued in 1948.

Stepmother
Benton and Bowles supervised for Colgate on CBS beginning on January 17, 1938.
Actors: Sunda Love (Kay, second wife of John Fairchild), Francis X. Bushman (Fairchild), Peggy Wall (stepdaughter)

Theme: "Impromptu" (Chopin)

Discontinued in 1942.

Your Family and Mine

McKee and Albright supervised for Sealtest on NBC Red beginning on April 25, 1938.

Actors: Bill Adams (Matthew Wilbur), Lucille Wall (Winifred), Joan Tompkins (Judy, the "Redheaded Angel"), Parker Fennelly (Lem Stacy)

About the time this drama vanished, in 1940, Miss Wall transferred her wifely sympathy to another dreamer, Lorenzo Jones. Discontinued in 1940.

Joyce Jordan, Girl Interne (Joyce Jordan, M.D.)

Brown and Tarcher supervised for General Mills on CBS beginning May 30, 1938.

Writer: Julian Funt

Actors: Elspeth Eric, Ann Shepherd, Betty Winkler (Joyce); Myron McCormick (Paul); Erik Rolf (Dr. Hans Simons); Richard Widmark; Frank Lovejoy; Ed Begley

Discontinued in 1948. Revived by ABC in 1951–52.

Valiant Lady

Blackett-Sample-Hummert and Knox-Reeves supervised for General Mills on NBC Red beginning on May 30, 1938. (Started on CBS March 7 as part of Gold Medal Hour.)

Actors: Joan Blaine (Joan Barrett); Bill Johnstone (Joan's father, Jim); Charles Carroll, Bartlett Robinson (Dr. Truman "Tubby" Scott)

Theme: "Estrelita"

Opening (following the date): "Time for *Valiant Lady*. General Mills presents Joan Blaine in *Valiant Lady*—the story of a brave woman and her brilliant, but unstable husband—the story of her struggle to keep his feet planted firmly upon the pathway to success.

Discontinued in 1946. Revived by ABC in 1951–52.

Young Widder Brown

Begun on June 6, 1938. Blackett-Sample-Hummert supervised for Sterling on NBC Red beginning September 26.

Actors: Florence Freeman (Ellen Brown); Clayton Collyer (Peter Turner); Marilyn Erskine, Tommy Donnelly (Janey and Mark); Ned Wever (Dr. Anthony Loring)
Theme: "In the Gloaming"
Discontinued in 1956.

Stella Dallas*
Blackett-Sample-Hummert supervised for Phillips on NBC Red begining on June 6, 1938. (Started on WEAF, New York, on October 25, 1937, for Tetley Tea.)
Actors: Anne Elstner (Stella), Vivian Smolen (Laurel), Macdonald Carey (Dick Grosvenor), Arthur Hughes (Stephen Dallas)
Themes: "Memories" and "How Can I Leave Thee?"
Opening: "And now Stella Dallas, the true to life sequel—as written by us—to the world famous drama of mother love and sacrifice." (Later, and longer, openings credited Olive Higgins Prouty.)
Discontinued in 1955.

Those Happy Gilmans
Blackett-Sample-Hummert supervised for General Mills on NBC Red from August 22, 1938, to May 19, 1939.
Actors: Bill Bouchey, Edith Adams, John Hench, and Joan Kay as the Gilmans.

Life Can Be Beautiful
Compton supervised for Procter and Gamble on NBC Red beginning on September 5, 1938.
Writers: Carl Bixby and Don Becker
Actors: Ralph Locke (Papa David Solomon); Alice Reinheart, Teri Keane (Chichi Conrad Gerard); John Holbrook, Earle Larimore (Stephen Hamilton)
Theme: Original composition by Don Becker
Epigraph: "*Life Can Be Beautiful* is an inspiring message of faith drawn from life. . . ."
Discontinued in 1954.

Madame Courageous
C. Wendell Muench supervised for Durkee on NBC Blue from September 26 to December 23, 1938.

Writer: Howard McKent Barnes
Actress: Sarah Brayden (Betty Craine)
The story of a divorcee with a family to raise.

Houseboat Hannah*

Blackett-Sample-Hummert supervised for Procter and Gamble on
NBC Red beginning on September 26, 1938. (A syndicated tran-
scription series from October, 1936.)
Writer: Irving Vendig
Actors: Doris Rich (Hannah), Norman Gottschalk (Dan O'Leary)
Theme: "The Last Rose of Summer."

Network broadcasts discontinued in 1941.

Jane Arden

Sherman K. Ellis supervised for Ward Baking from September 26,
1938, to June 23, 1939. William Hodapp adapted the Monte Barrett
comic strip stories for radio.
Actress: Ruth Yorke (Jane)

Her Honor, Nancy James

Lord and Thomas supervised for Kleenex on CBS from October 3,
1938, to July 28, 1939.
Actors: Barbara Weeks (Nancy James), Ned Wever (district attorney), Joseph Curtin (mayor).
Theme: "Song of Youth"

Scattergood Baines*

Niesser-Myerhoff supervised for Wrigley on CBS beginning October
31, 1938. (On CBS Pacific Network from February 22, 1937.)
Actor: Jess Pugh (Scattergood)
Discontinued in 1942.

This Day Is Ours

Compton supervised for Procter and Gamble on CBS from November
7, 1938, to January 20, 1940. (On NBC Blue until March 29, 1940.)
Writers: Carl Bixby, Don Becker
Actors: Jay Jostyn (Curt Curtis); Templeton Fox, Joan Banks (Elea-

nor MacDonald); Alan Devitt (Wong); Santos Ortega (General Ming)

Central City

Blackett-Sample-Hummert supervised for Procter and Gamble on NBC Red beginning on November 21, 1938.

Narrator: Tom Powers
Actors: Eric Dressler, Elspeth Eric, Van Heflin, Kent Smith, Shirley Booth, Arlene Francis

A *Grand Hotel*–type story of intertwined lives which foreshadowed *Peyton Place*. Last broadcast on April 25, 1941.

1939

*Doc Barclay's Daughters**

Blackett-Sample-Hummert supervised for Personal Finance on CBS from January 23, 1939, to January 19, 1940.

Actors: Bennett Kilpack (Doc Barclay), Mildred Robin (Mimi), Elizabeth Reller (Connie), Vivian Smolen (Marge)

The Life and Loves of Dr. Susan

J. Walter Thompson supervised for Lever on CBS from February 13 to December 29, 1939.

Writer: Edith Meiser
Actress: Eleanor Phelps (Susan Chandler)

The Carters of Elm Street

Blackett-Sample-Hummert supervised for Wander (Ovaltine) on NBC Red beginning on February 13, 1939.

Writer: Mona Kent
Actors: Virginia Payne (Mrs. Carter), Vic Smith (Mr. Carter)
Theme: "My Heart at Thy Sweet Voice" (Saint-Saëns)

Discontinued in 1940.

Manhattan Mother

Pedlar and Ryan supervised for Procter and Gamble on CBS from March 6, 1939, to April 5, 1940.

Writer: Orin Tovrov
Actresses: Margaret Hillas, Kay Brinker (Patricia Locke)

The Serials

*Midstream**

H. W. Kastor supervised for Procter and Gamble (Teel) on NBC Red beginning on May 1, 1939. (Began on WLW, Cincinnati, in 1938.)

Writer: Pauline Hopkins

Actors: Hugh Studebaker (Charles Meredith), Betty Lou Gerson (Julia Meredith)

Discontinued in 1940.

When a Girl Marries

Benton and Bowles supervised for Prudential Insurance on CBS beginning on May 29, 1939.

Writer: Elaine Carrington

Actors: Noel Mills, Mary Jane Higby (Joan Field Davis); John Raby, Robert Haag, Lyle Sudrow, Whitfield Connor (Harry); Georgia Burke (Lily, the maid); Dolores Gillen (Little Sammy); Marion Barney (Mother Davis); Frances Woodbury (Mrs. Field)

Theme: "Serenade" (Drigo)

Mary Jane Higby assumed the role of Joan Davis after six months and carried it through the drama's remaining eighteen years. Raby's tenure as husband Harry was interrupted by World War II.

Caroline's Golden Store

Blackett-Sample-Hummert supervised for General Mills on NBC Red beginning on June 5, 1939. Moved to CBS on October 9.
Writer: Caroline Ellis
Actress: Caroline Ellis
Theme: "Song of Songs"

The Man I Married

Blackett-Sample-Hummert supervised for Procter and Gamble (Oxydol) on NBC Red beginning on July 3, 1939.

Writers: Carl Bixby, Don Becker
Actor: Van Heflin (Adam Waring)
Theme: Original composition by Don Becker

The story of a disinherited son of a millionaire trying to make a new start in a small town. Discontinued in 1942.

Woman of Courage

Benton and Bowles supervised for Colgate (Octagon) on CBS beginning on July 17, 1939.

Writer: Carl Buss
Actress: Selena Royale (Martha Jackson)
Theme: "Look for the Silver Lining"

Discontinued in 1942.

Meet the Dixons

Ruthrauff and Ryan supervised for Campbell Soup (Franco-American Spaghetti) on CBS beginning on July 31, 1939.

Writer: Robert Andrews
Actors: Richard Widmark (Wesley Dixon), Barbara Weeks (Joan Dixon)

The Trouble with Marriage

Blackett-Sample-Hummert supervised for Procter and Gamble (Oxydol) on NBC Blue from July 31 to December 29, 1939.

Actors: Mary Patton (Pat), Stanley Harris (Barry)
Theme: "Jealousy"

Brenda Curtis

Ward Wheelock supervised for Campbell Soup on CBS beginning on September 11, 1939.

Actors: Vicki Vola (Brenda), Hugh Marlowe (Jim Curtis)

Discontinued in January, 1940.

Orphans of Divorce

After a brief evening run, Blackett-Sample-Hummert supervised for Dr. Lyons on NBC Blue beginning in September, 1939.

Actors: Margaret Anglin, Effie Palmer (Nora Worthington); Richard Gordon, Richard Keith (Cyril Worthington); Joan Tompkins (Barbara Worthington)
Theme: "I'll Take You Home Again, Kathleen"

Discontinued in 1942.

The Serials

Thunder over Paradise

Kenyon and Eckhardt supervised for C. F. Mueller Macaroni on NBC Blue beginning on October 2, 1939.
Writer: Fayette Krum

Actors: Fern Parsons, Laurette Fillbrandt, Pat Murphy, Billy Idelson, Michael Romano

Discontinued in 1941.

Ellen Randolph

Benton and Bowles supervised for Colgate (Super Suds) on NBC Red beginning on October 9, 1939.
Writers: Vera Oldham, Margaret Sangster
Actors: Elsie Hitz (Ellen), John McGovern, Parker Fennelly, Jack Jordan
Theme: "Andante Cantabile" (Tchaikovsky)

Discontinued in 1941.

My Son and I

Young and Rubicam supervised for General Foods (Swansdown) on CBS beginning on October 9, 1939.
Actress: Betty Garde (Connie Vance)
Theme: "My Son and I" (Charles Paul)

Discontinued in 1940.

Society Girl

Hellwig-Miller supervised for Corn Products (Kre-mel, Linit) on CBS beginning on October 9, 1939.
Writers: David Davidson, Jerome Ross
Actors: Charlotte Manson (Bryn Clark Barrington), Alexander Kirkland (Russ)

Discontinued in 1940.

By Kathleen Norris

Knox-Reeves supervised for General Mills (Wheaties) on CBS beginning on October 9, 1939. The Phillips H. Lord staff prepared changing Norris stories, narrated by an actress impersonating Miss Norris. The first story (in a KYW tryout) was "Woman in Love."

462

Discontinued in 1941.

Beyond These Valleys

Blackett-Sample-Hummert supervised for General Mills on CBS from October 9, 1939, to September 27, 1940.

Writer: Don Becker
Actors: Gertrude Warner (Rebecca Lane), Santos Ortega (John)
Theme: Original composition by Don Becker

The Right to Happiness

Compton supervised for Procter and Gamble on NBC Blue beginning on October 16, 1939.

Writers: Irna Phillips, John M. Young
Actors: Eloise Kummer, Claudia Morgan (Carolyn Allen Kramer Nelson); Constance Crowder, Selena Royal, Irene Hubbard (Doris Cameron); Gary Merrill, John Larkin (Miles Nelson); Dick Wells (Dwight Kramer); Ruth Bailey (Rose Kransky); Mignon Schreiber (Mrs. Kransky); Seymour Young (Mr. Kransky)
Theme: "Song of the Soul" (Breil)

The program was developed from characters in *The Guiding Light*. Discontinued in 1960.

Against the Storm

Compton supervised for Procter and Gamble beginning on October 16, 1939.
Writer: Sandra Michael
Actors: Gertrude Warner, Claudia Morgan (Christy Allen Cameron); Arnold Moss, Alexander Scourby (Philip Cameron); Roger De-Koven (Professor Allen); Michael Ingram (Manuel); Philip Clarke (Dr. Reimer); Charlotte Holland (Kathy Reimer)
Theme: "Ich Liebe Dich"
Epigraph: "Against the storm keep thy head bowed
          For the greatest storm the world has ever known
          Came to an end one sunny morning."

Discontinued in 1942. Revived by ABC in 1951–52.

Young Dr. Malone

Benton and Bowles supervised for General Foods (Post Bran Flakes)

463

on NBC Blue beginning in November, 1939. (Moved to CBS on April 29, 1940.)

Actors: Alan Bunce, Sandy Becker (Dr. Jerry Malone); Elizabeth Reller, Barbara Weeks (Ann Richards Malone); Richard Coogan (Robbie Hughes); Nancy Coleman (Alice Hughes); Joan Lazer, Rosemary Rice (Jill Malone); Bill Lipton (Dr. David Malone); Amanda Randolph (Ruby)
Theme: Original composition by Johnny Winters.

Discontinued in 1960.

1940

Martha Webster (Life Begins)

Ward Wheelock supervised for Campbell Soup on CBS beginning on January 22, 1940.

Writer: Bess Flynn
Actors: Bess Flynn (Martha), Donald Cook (Dick Young), Ralph Dumke (Wilbur)
Theme: "Melody in F" (Rubinstein)

Amanda of Honeymoon Hill

Blackett-Sample-Hummert supervised for Phillips on NBC Blue beginning on February 5, 1940.
Actors: Joy Hathaway (Amanda, the humble southern girl), Boyd Crawford (her husband, Edward Leighton)
Discontinued in 1946.

The Light of the World

Blackett-Sample-Hummert supervised for General Mills on NBC Red beginning on March 18, 1940. Various writers dramatized these stories from the Bible. Dr. James B. Moffatt served as consultant. David Gothard, Arnold Moss, and Bret Morrison were the speaker-narrators. Performers included Bernard Lenrow (Nebuchadnezzar), Richard Coogan (Jonathan), William Hollenback (Daniel), Inge Adams (Slave girl, Elona), and many others.

Discontinued in 1950.

Lone Journey

Blackett-Sample-Hummert supervised for Procter and Gamble (Dreft) on NBC Red beginning on May 27, 1940.

Writers: Sandra and Peter Michael
Actors: Les Damon, Staats Cotsworth (Wolfe Bennett); Betty Winkler, Eloise Kummer, Claudia Morgan (Nita Bennett)
Theme: Original melody by Delos Owens
Discontinued in 1943. Revived by ABC in 1951–52.

This Small Town
Compton supervised for Procter and Gamble on NBC Red from September 30, 1940 to April 25, 1941. Allegedly based on stories from actual life.

Portia Faces Life
Benton and Bowles supervised for General Foods on CBS beginning on October 7, 1940.
Writer: Mona Kent
Actors: Lucille Wall (Portia Blake); Myron McCormick, Bartlett Robinson (Walter Manning); Henrietta Tedrow, Doris Rich (Miss Daisy)
Discontinued in 1951.

We, the Abbotts
Benton and Bowles supervised for Best Foods (Nucoa and Hellmans) on CBS beginning on October 7, 1940.
Writer: Bess Flynn
Actors: John McIntire (John Abbott), Ethel Everett (Emily Abbott), Cliff Carpenter (Jack), Audrey Egan (Barbara), Betty Jane Tyler (Linda)
Discontinued in 1942.

Kate Hopkins, Angel of Mercy
Benton and Bowles supervised for General Foods (Maxwell House) on CBS beginning on October 7, 1940.
Writers: Chester McCracken, Gertrude Berg
Actors: Margaret MacDonald (Kate), Clayton Coller (Tom Hopkins)
Discontinued in 1942.

Mother O'Mine
Young and Rubicam supervised for Clapp on NBC Blue beginning in October, 1940.

Actors: Agnes Young (Mother Morrison), Donald Cook (John), Ruth Yorke (Helen)

Discontinued in 1941.

1941

The Johnson Family *

After several years as a WLW and regional feature, this unique serial was carried in the afternoon by Mutual and Don Lee networks, Young and Rubicam supervising. Jimmy Scribner played all the roles in this ethnic comedy-drama.

Home of the Brave

Young and Rubicam supervised for General Foods on CBS beginning on January 6, 1941.

Actors: Sammie Hill (Casino), Tom Tully, Ed Latimer, Alan Bunce, Richard Widmark

Charlie and Jessie

Ward Wheelock supervised for Campbell Soup on CBS beginning in January, 1941.

Writer: Wyllis Cooper
Actors: Donald Cook, Diana Bourbon

The Mystery Man

Knox-Reeves supervised for General Mills (Wheaties) on NBC Red beginning on March 24, 1941. Jay Jostyn introduced changing mysteries by famous authors.
Theme: "Swan Lake" passage.

Discontinued in 1942.

The Story of Bess Johnson

Ward Wheelock supervised for Colgate on CBS beginning on March 31, 1941.

Derived from the Bess Johnson character of *Hilltop House*, this drama, in which the orphanage superintendent became a boarding-school director, was written by William Sweets and starred Miss Johnson.

Discontinued in 1942.

*The Bartons (Story of Bud Barton)**

After several months as a sustaining feature, it was supervised by Compton for Procter and Gamble on NBC Red under contract running from October, 1941, to June, 1942.

Writer: Harlan Ware (who pleased critics with his scripts)
Actors: Dick Holland (Bud Barton), Kathryn Card (Grandma Barton), Bill Bouchey (Pa).

Front Page Farrell

Blackett-Sample-Hummert supervised for Anacin on Mutual beginning on June 23, 1941. (Moved to NBC in 1942.)

Actors: Carleton Young, Richard Widmark, Staats Cotsworth (David Farrell); Virginia Dwyer, Florence Williams (Sally Farrell)
Theme: "You and I know."

This late-afternoon newspaper melodrama was discontinued in 1954.

Bright Horizon

BBD&O supervised for Lever on CBS, Young and Rubicam for CBS (Pacific Coast) beginning on August 25, 1941. Joe Julian and Richard Kollmar played vagabond restaurant singer Michael West (introduced on *Big Sister* several months earlier). Big Sister Ruth Wayne appeared in the first few episodes. Carol West was played by Sammie Hill and Joan Alexander.

Discontinued in 1945.

*The Second Mrs. Burton (Second Wife)**

Starting as *Second Wife* on CBS Pacific stations in 1940, it was supervised by Young and Rubicam for General Foods on CBS beginning on September 21, 1941.

Writers: Priscilla Kent, Martha Alexander; John M. Young, Hector Chevigny
Actors: Claire Niesen, Patsy Campbell, Teri Keane (Terry Burton); Evelyn Varden, Ethel Owen (Mother Burton); Dwight Weist (Stan Burton)

Under the authorship of Chevigny, and with the Keane-Owen-Weist cast, the drama became light comedy.

Discontinued in 1960.

467

The Serials

Helpmate

Blackett-Sample-Hummert supervised for Cudahy (Old Dutch) on NBC Red beginning in September, 1941.

Actors: Arlene Francis (Linda Harper), Myron McCormick (Steve Harper), Judith Evelyn (Grace Marshall)

Discontinued in 1944.

Stories America Loves (Kitty Foyle)

Knox-Reeves supervised for General Mills on CBS beginning October 6, 1941. American novels such as *So Big* and *The Virginian* were dramatized. *Kitty Foyle* was begun in June, 1942, became the show's title in October, and continued until the series ended in 1944. Julie Stevens and Clayton Collyer played Kitty Foyle and Wynn Strafford.

Helping Hand

Ruthrauff and Ryan supervised for Sterling (Ironized Yeast) on CBS beginning on October 13, 1941. John J. Anthony, the family advice man, conducted the dramatized series.

Discontinued in 1942.

1942

We Love and Learn (As the Twig Is Bent)*

Young and Rubicam supervised for General Foods on CBS beginning on April 13, 1942. (Started as transcription series—*As the Twig Is Bent*—in 1941.)

Writer: Don Becker

Actors: Frank Lovejoy (Bill Peters); Joan Banks, Betty Worth (Andrea Reynolds); Barbara Weeks (Madame Sophie)

Discontinued by CBS in 1944. Revived by NBC, 1949–51. Reworked as Negro serial, *Ruby Valentine*, in mid-1950s transcriptions.

Second Husband*

Blackett-Sample-Hummert supervised for Dr. Lyons on CBS beginning in April, 1942. (Started as evening serial, June 2, 1937.)

Actors: Helen Menken (Brenda Cummings), Joseph Curtin (Grant)

Themes: "If Love Were All," "Diane"

Discontinued in 1946.

Lonely Women (Today's Children)
Blackett-Sample-Hummert supervised for General Mills on NBC beginning in June, 1942.
Writer: Irna Phillips
Actors: Betty Lou Gerson (Marilyn Larimore), Eileen Palmer (Judith Evans), Patricia Dunlap (Bertha Schultz), Virginia Payne (Mrs. Schultz), Murray Forbes (Mr. Schultz), Nanette Sargent (Nora), Barbara Luddy (Judith Clark)
Theme: Original melody by Duane

Snow Village *
Compton supervised for Procter and Gamble on NBC beginning on December 28, 1942. (Heard as nighttime series as early as 1936.) These sketches of rural New England life by William Ford Manly were similar to his *Soconyland Sketches* (1928–34). Arthur Allen and Parker Fennelly starred in this and several other folksy dramas. Replaced on November 11, 1943.

1943
Woman of America
Benton and Bowles supervised for Procter and Gamble on NBC beginning January 25, 1943. A war inspired story of a nineteenth-century covered-wagon trek.

Actors: Anne Seymour (Prudence Dane), James Monks (wagonmaster Wade Douglas), Larry Robinson (John Dane)

When the trek ended, the story moved to the present and centered upon Pru's descendant of the same name, a newspaper editor (Florence Freeman).

Discontinued in 1946.

Lora Lawton
Duane Jones supervised for Babbitt on NBC beginning in May, 1943.

Actors: Joan Tompkins, Jan Miner (Lora), James Meighan, Ned Wever (Peter Carver, the shipbuilder-husband)

This premium-laden serial was discontinued in 1949.

The Open Door

Ted Bates supervised for Standard Brands on NBC from June 21, 1943, to June 30, 1944.

Writer: Sandra Michael

Actors: Reverend Alfred Dorf (Eric Hansen), Florence Freeman, Alexander Scourby, Joan Alexander, and Everett Sloan

Theme: "Sim Sala"

In this literate story of the dean of Vernon University the emphasis was upon brotherhood.

Dreft Star Playhouse (Hollywood Theatre of the Air)

Blackett-Sample-Hummert supervised for Procter and Gamble on NBC beginning on June 28, 1943. Adaptations of popular motion pictures (week-long originally, then lasting several weeks) included: *Bachelor Mother* (Jane Wyman), *5th Avenue Girl* (Ellen Drew), *The Bride Came C.O.D.* (Phil Harris), *One Way Passage* (Richard Carlson), *The Magnificent Ambersons* (Agnes Moorehead), *Hold Back the Dawn* (Maureen O'Sullivan), *All This and Heaven Too* (Martha Scott), *Suspicion* (Margo), *Intermezzo* (George Coulouris), and *Of Human Bondage* (Rosemary De Camp, Les Tremayne). The last drama, *An American Tragedy*, ran many months and closed the series on March 30, 1945.

American Women

Arthur Meyerhoff supervised for Wrigley on CBS beginning on August 2, 1943. Eloise Kummer and Charlotte Manson narrated these stories, by Frank and Doris Hursley, designed to spur women to the war effort.

Discontinued in 1944.

Brave Tomorrow

Compton supervised for Procter and Gamble on NBC beginning on October 11, 1943.

Writer: Ruth Knight

Actors: Frank Lovejoy (Brad Forbes), Raymond Edward Johnson, Jeannette Dowling, Nancy Douglass, Jone Allison

Discontinued in 1944.

Perry Mason

Pedlar and Ryan supervised for Procter and Gamble on CBS beginning on October 18, 1943.

Writers: Ruth Borden, Irving Vendig (Erle Stanley Gardner stories)
Actors: Bartlett Robinson, Santos Ortega, Donald Briggs, John Larkin (Perry Mason); Gertrude Warner, Jan Miner, Joan Alexander (Della Street); Matt Crowley (Paul Drake); Mandel Kramer (Lieutenant Tragg)

The first story was "The Case of the Unwanted Wife." Discontinued in 1955.

1944

Sweet River

Hill Blackett supervised for Staley on ABC beginning on January 3, 1944. (The series had been originated two years earlier.) Charles Jackson wrote this wartime story of minister-widower raising two sons in an industrial town and trying to foster tolerance toward outsiders.

Discontinued in 1944.

This Changing World

Ted Bates supervised for Standard Brands on CBS beginning on July 3, 1944.

Writers: Ted and Matilda Ferro
Actress: Fran Carlon
This forced replacement of *The Open Door* was discontinued before 1945.

Tena and Tim*

Grand Advertising supervised for Cudahy (Old Dutch Cleanser) on CBS beginning on August 7, 1944. (A transcription series from the mid-1930s.)

Writer: Peggy Beckmark
Actors: Peggy Beckmark (Tena); George Cisar, James Gardner, Frank Dane (Tim); Gladys Heen; Marge Calvert; Wilms Herbert

Discontinued in 1946.

471

Rosemary

Compton, Pedlar and Ryan and Benton and Bowles supervised for Procter and Gamble on NBC beginning on October 2, 1944.

Writer: Elaine Carrington

Actors: Betty Winkler, Virginia Kaye (Rosemary Dawson Roberts); George Keane, Bob Readick (Bill Roberts)

Rosemary was an ex-secretary who became both the spiritual and the financial prop of husband Bill, who endured such things as amnesia and trial for murder.

Discontinued in 1955.

Two on a Clue

Young and Rubicam supervised for General Foods on CBS beginning on October 2, 1944.

Writer: Harry Ingram

Actors: Ned Wever (Jeff), Louise Fitch (Debby Spencer)

This husband-and-wife detective comedy was discontinued in 1946.

The Strange Romance of Evelyn Winters

Duane Jones supervised for Sweetheart Soap on CBS beginning on November 20, 1944.

Actors: Toni Darnay (Evelyn); Karl Weber, Martin Blaine (Gary Bennett)

Discontinued in 1948.

1945

Barry Cameron (The Soldier Who Came Home)

Duane Jones supervised for Sweetheart Soap on NBC beginning on April 16, 1945.

Actors: Spencer Bentley (Barry), Florence Williams (Anna Cameron).

Criticized for its superficialities, this drama was discontinued in 1946.

A Woman's Life

Young and Rubicam supervised for Lever (Swan Soap) on CBS beginning on July 9, 1945. The story of a young couple trying to understand each other (*Bright Horizon* in a new dress).

Discontinued in 1946.

1946

Masquerade
Knox-Reeves supervised for General Mills on NBC from January 14, 1946, to August 29, 1947.

Writer: Art Gladd
Actor: Carlton Kadell (Tom Field)

A short-lived serial below the standard of creator Irna Phillips.

Rose of My Dreams
Duane Jones supervised for Sweetheart Soap on NBC beginning in November 25, 1946. Lasted only a few months, scarcely long enough for Jones to begin unloading the Sweetheart premiums.

1947

Katie's Daughter
Duane Jones supervised for Sweetheart Soap on NBC beginning in March, 1947. More premiums.

Discontinued in 1948.

Wendy Warren
Benton and Bowles supervised for General Foods (Jello) on CBS beginning June 23, 1947.

Writers: Frank Provo and John Pickard
Actors: Florence Freeman (Wendy), Les Tremayne (Gil Kendal), Lamont Johnson (Mark Douglas), Rod Hendrickson (Sam Warren), Tess Sheehan (Aunt Dorrie), Douglas Edwards (newscaster)
Theme: "My Home Town" (original composition by Clarke Morgan)

Discontinued in 1958.

The Story of Holly Sloan
Knox-Reeves supervised for General Mills on NBC beginning on September 1, 1947.

Actors: Gale Page (Holly), Marlene Ames (Lauralee McWilliams), Charles Seel (Henry Sloan), Georgia Backus (Keturah)

Discontinued in 1948.

Song of a Stranger

Ruthrauff and Ryan supervised for Pharmaco on Mutual beginning on September 29, 1947.

Writer: Doris Halman
Actor: Bret (The Shadow) Morrison (Pierre Varnay, the stranger)

Discontinued in 1948.

This Is Nora Drake

Foote, Cone, and Belding supervised for Toni on NBC beginning on October 27, 1947.

Writer: Milton Lewis
Actors: Charlotte Holland, Joan Tompkins, Mary Jane Higby (Nora); Everett Sloane, Ralph Bell (Arthur Drake); Douglas Parkhirst (David Brown); Lucille Wall (Lorraine Hartley); Lesley Woods, Joan Alexander, Mercedes McCambridge (Peg)

Discontinued in 1959.

1948

The Brighter Day

Dancer, Fitzgerald, and Sample supervised for Procter and Gamble on NBC beginning on October 11, 1948.

Writers: Irna Phillips, Orin Tovrov
Actors: Margaret Draper, Grace Matthews (Liz Dennis); Bill Smith (Reverend Richard "Poppa" Dennis); Jay Meredith (Althea); Lorna Lynn (Bobby)

This story of the people of Three Rivers began on TV in 1954, left radio in 1956.

1949

Marriage for Two

Sustained on NBC from July 11 to October 3, 1949, when J. Walter Thompson took charge for Kraft.

Writers: Elaine Carrington, Winifred Wolfe
Actor: Staats Cotsworth

Last broadcast on March 31, 1950.

1950

Nona from Nowhere

Duane Jones supervised for Babbitt on CBS beginning on January 9, 1950.

Actress: Toni Darnay (Nona)

Another premium vehicle, lasting only months.

1951

Dr. Paul

An NBC serial sponsored by Wesson Oil.

King's Row

William Esty supervised for Colgate on NBC beginning on February 26, 1951. Derived from the popular novel and film, it departed in October of the same year.

Woman in My House*

A Carlton E. Morse creation presented on NBC for Sweetheart Soap.

Writers: Gil Faust, Edward Borgers, others

Actors: Forrest Lewis (James Carter), Jane Scott (Jessie Carter), Les Tremayne (Jeff), Alice Reinheart (Virginia), William Idelson (Clay)

Discontinued in 1959.

1952

The Doctor's Wife

An NBC serial, sponsored by Ex-Lax, beginning on March 3, 1952.

Writer: Manya Starr

Actors: Donald Curtis, John Baragrey (Dan Palmer); Pat Wheel (Julie); Kenny Delmar; George Roy Hill

Discontinued in 1956.

1954

Hotel for Pets

An NBC serial sponsored by Quaker Oats.

Actors: Frank McHugh (Mr. Jolly), Charlotte Manson, Lloyd Richards, Abby Lewis

Discontinued in 1956.

1955

One Man's Family

A daytime edition of this venerable evening drama was added by NBC on July 4, 1955. (Heard first on KGO, San Francisco, on March 29, 1932. A Pacific regional show, April 13, 1932. First heard on East Coast on May 17, 1933.)

Writer: Carlton E. Morse

Actors: J. Anthony Smythe (Henry Barbour); Minetta Ellen (1932–55), Mary Adams (1955–59) (Fanny Barbour); Michael Raffetto (until 1955), Russell Thorson (until 1959) (Paul); Bernice Berwin (Hazel); Barton Yarborough (Clifford); Kathleen Wilson, Barbara Fuller (Claudia); Page Gilman (Jack); Walter Paterson (Nicky); Jean Rouverol (Betty Carter); Barbara Jo Allen (Beth Holly); Helen Musselman (Ann Waite); Naomi Stevens (Irene Franklyn); Bert Horton (Bill Herbert); Wally Maher (Dan Murray); Frank Provo (Johnny Roberts); Winifred Wolfe (Teddy); Ann Shelley (Joan); Anne Whitfield (Penny)

Themes: "Destiny Waltz" (Barnes), "Patricia" (Paul Carson)

Discontinued in 1959 (with Chapter 30, Book 134).

1957

The Affairs of Dr. Gentry

On NBC with various sponsors beginning in January, 1957.

Actors: Madeleine Carroll (Dr. Anne Gentry), Paul McGrath (Dr. Philip Hamilton)

Discontinued in 1959.

Five Star Matinee

An NBC serial with changing stories and various sponsors.

Discontinued in 1958.

1958

Real Life Stories

An NBC serial similar to *Five Star Matinee*.

Discontinued in 1959.

1959

Whispering Streets

Introduced as a daytime single-unit drama by ABC in 1953, this series adopted a five-part serial format on CBS in 1959. The stories were narrated by a fictional Hope Winslow, played in 1958 by Bette Davis. In 1959 Anne Seymour assumed the narration duties. The myriad stories were written by Margaret E. Sangster.

Discontinued in 1960.

1960

Best Seller

Five-part dramatizations of popular novels on CBS beginning on June 27, 1960. The first was Frank Yerby's *The Serpent and the Staff*, adapted by Greer Johnson. Radio's last serial drama.

APPENDIX B

THE DAYTIME NETWORK SERIALS OF TELEVISION
As of Summer, 1970

Title	Network	Date of Premiere
Search for Tomorrow	CBS	1951 (September 3)
Love of Life	CBS	1951 (September 24)
The Guiding Light	CBS	1952 (June 30)
The Secret Storm	CBS	1954 (February 1)
As the World Turns	CBS	1956 (April 2)
The Edge of Night	CBS	1956 (April 2)
General Hospital	ABC	1963 (April 1)
The Doctors	NBC	1963 (April 1)
Another World	NBC	1964 (May 4)
Days of Our Lives	NBC	1965 (November 8)
Dark Shadows	ABC	1966 (June 25)
Love Is a Many-Splendored Thing	CBS	1967 (September 18)
One Life to Live	ABC	1968 (July 15)

Where the Heart Is	CBS	1969 (September 15)
Bright Promise	NBC	1969 (September 29)
All My Children	ABC	1970 (January 5)
The Best of Everything	ABC	1970 (March 30)
A World Apart	ABC	1970 (March 30)
Another World—Somerset	NBC	1970 (March 30)

OTHER DAYTIME TELEVISION SERIALS

Title	Network	Date of Premiere
The First Hundred Years	NBC	1950
The Egg and I	CBS	1951
Miss Susan	NBC	
Hawkins Falls	NBC	
The House in the Garden	NBC	1952
Valiant Lady	CBS	1953
The Bennetts	NBC	
Follow Your Heart	NBC	
Three Steps to Heaven	NBC	
The World of Mr. Sweeney	NBC	
The Brighter Day	CBS	1954
Portia Faces Life	CBS	
Woman With a Past	CBS	
The Seeking Heart	CBS	
Road of Life	CBS	
One Man's Family	NBC	
A Time to Live	NBC	
Golden Windows	NBC	
First Love	NBC	
Concerning Miss Marlowe	NBC	
The Greatest Gift	NBC	
Modern Romances	NBC	
The Way of the World	NBC	1955
Date with Life	NBC	
Hotel Cosmopolitan	CBS	1957
The Verdict Is Yours	CBS	
Kitty Foyle	NBC	1958
Today Is Ours	NBC	
From These Roots	NBC	

The Serials

Young Dr. Malone	NBC	
House on High Street	NBC	1959
For Better or Worse	CBS	
Road to Reality	ABC	1960
Full Circle	CBS	
The Clear Horizon	CBS	
Dr. Hudson's Secret Journal	ABC	1962
Our Five Daughters	NBC	
Ben Jerrod: Attorney at Law	ABC	1963
The Young Marrieds	ABC	1964
The Nurses	ABC	1965
A Time for Us (*Flame in the Wind*)	ABC	
Never Too Young	ABC	
Morning Star	NBC	
Paradise Bay	NBC	
Moment of Truth	NBC	
Confidential for Women	ABC	1966
Hidden Faces	NBC	1968

BIBLIOGRAPHY

The source material for such a book as this is found not only in print and in conversation but on film, on tape, and in fleeting electronic impulses of sound and light. The dramas of radio were rarely recorded, and few scripts were saved; much of their story is lost beyond recovery. Not even the filmed serials survive in the quantity that might be expected.

Still much material is available to one interested in the history of serial drama. What seemed to me most relevant is included in the bibliography that follows. I have not listed the hundreds—no, thousands—of program logs, network file cards, and memoranda I consulted in developing the chronological framework of this account. Nor have I itemized the myriad episodes I monitored, though some are identified in the text. The references below were chosen primarily for the information they can give the scholar, serious or nostalgic, as the case may be.

481

1. BOOKS

All About Amos 'n' Andy. New York, Rand McNally and Company, 1929.

Arnold, Frank A. *Broadcast Advertising.* New York, John Wiley and Sons, Inc., 1931.

Balshofer, Fred J., and Arthur C. Miller. *One Reel a Week.* Berkeley and Los Angeles, University of California Press, 1967.

Barbour, Alan G. *The Serials of Columbia.* Kew Gardens, N.Y., Screen Facts Press, 1967.

———. *The Serials of Republic.* Kew Gardens, N.Y., Screen Facts Press, 1965.

Beaumont, Charles. *Remember? Remember?* New York, Macmillan Company, 1963.

Becker, Stephan. *Comic Art in America.* New York, Simon and Schuster, 1959.

Beville, H. M. *Social Stratification of the Radio Audience.* Princeton, Princeton Radio Research Project, November, 1939.

Blum, Daniel. *A Pictorial History of Television.* Philadelphia, Chilton Company, 1959.

———. *A Pictorial History of the Silent Screen.* New York, Grosset and Dunlap, 1953.

Bryson, Lyman. *Time for Reason About Radio.* New York, George W. Stewart, 1948.

Buxton, Frank, and Bill Owen. *Radio's Golden Age.* New York, Easton Valley Press, 1966.

Cantril, Hadley, and Gordon W. Allport. *The Psychology of Radio.* New York, Harper and Brothers, 1935.

Chase, Francis. *Sound and Fury.* New York, Harper and Brothers, 1942.

Correll, Charles, and Freeman Gosden. *Sam 'n' Henry.* Chicago, Shrewesbury Publishing Company, 1926.

Crosby, John. *Out of the Blue.* New York, Simon and Schuster, 1952.

Crowther, Bosley. *Hollywood Rajah.* New York, Holt, Rinehart and Winston, 1960.

Cuthbert, Margaret, ed. *Adventure in Radio.* N.p., Howell, Soskin, Publishers, Inc., 1945.

Dixon, Peter. *Radio Sketches.* New York, Frederick A. Stokes Company, 1936.

Dunlap, Orrin E., Jr. *Radio in Advertising.* New York, Harper and Brothers Publishers, 1931.

Bibliography

Essoe, Gabe. *Tarzan of the Movies.* New York, Citadel Press, 1968.

Federal Communications Commission. *Public Service Responsibility of Broadcast Licensees.* Washington, D.C., U.S. Government Printing Office, March 7, 1946.

Feiffer, Jules. *The Great Comic Book Heroes.* New York, Dial Press, 1965.

Fenin, George N., and William K. Everson. *The Western.* New York, Orion Press, 1962.

Fenton, Robert W. *The Big Swingers* [Edgar Rice Burroughs and Tarzan]. Englewood Cliffs, N.J., Prentice-Hall, Inc., 1967.

Fidler, William Perry. *Augusta Evans Wilson, 1835–1909.* Birmingham, University of Alabama Press, 1951.

Franklin, Joe. *Classics of the Silent Screen.* New York, Citadel Press, 1959.

Gaver, Jack, and Dave Stanley. *There's Laughter in the Air.* New York, Greenberg, 1945.

Green, Abel, and Joe Laurie, Jr. *Show Biz.* New York, Henry Holt and Company, 1951.

Griffith, Richard, and Arthur Mayer. *The Movies.* New York, Simon and Schuster, 1957.

Gross, Ben. *I Looked and Listened.* New York, Random House, 1954.

Harmon, Jim. *The Great Radio Heroes.* Garden City, N.Y., Doubleday and Company, 1967.

Higby, Mary Jane. *Tune In Tomorrow.* New York, Cowles, 1968.

Lahue, Kalton. *Continued Next Week: A History of the Moving Picture Serial.* Norman, University of Oklahoma Press, 1964.

Lawrence, Jerome, ed. *Off Mike.* New York, Essential Books, 1944.

Lawton, Sherman. *Radio Continuity Types.* Boston, Expression Company, 1938.

Lazarsfeld, Paul, and Frank Stanton. *Radio Research, 1942–43.* New York, Duell, Sloan and Pearce, 1944.

———, and Harry Field. *The People Look at Radio.* Chapel Hill, University of North Carolina Press, 1946.

Lupoff, Richard A. *Edgar Rice Burroughs: Master of Adventure.* New York, Ace Books, 1968.

Macgowan, Kenneth. *Behind the Screen.* New York, Delacorte Press, 1965.

Mott, Frank Luther. *American Journalism.* New York, Macmillan Company, 1947.

483

Niggli, Josephine. *Pointers on Radio Writing.* Boston, Writer, Inc., 1946.

Noel, Mary. *Villains Galore.* New York, Macmillan Company, 1954.

Overstreet, H. A. *The Mature Mind.* New York, W. W. Norton and Company, Inc., 1949.

Papashvily, Helen Waite. *All the Happy Endings.* New York, Harper and Brothers, Publishers, 1956.

Parker, Everett C., David W. Barry, and Dallas W. Smythe. *The Television-Radio Audience and Religion.* New York, Harper and Brothers, Publishers, 1955.

Perry, George, and Alan Aldridge. *The Penguin Book of Comics.* Harmondsworth, Middlesex, England, Penguin Books, 1967.

Radio and Television Bibliography. New York, Columbia Broadcasting System, 1942.

Ramsaye, Terry. *A Million and One Nights.* New York, Simon and Schuster, 1926.

Reeve, Arthur B. *The Exploits of Elaine.* New York, Harper and Brothers, 1915.

———. *The Romance of Elaine.* New York, Harper and Brothers, 1916.

Reynolds, Quentin. *The Fiction Factory* [Street and Smith]. New York, Random House, 1955.

Riley, Donald. *Handbook of Radio Drama Techniques.* Rev. ed. Ann Arbor, Edwards Brothers, Inc., 1941.

Scott, R. T. M. *The Spider Strikes* and *The Wheel of Death* [reprints of 1933 Spider pulp adventures]. New York, Berkeley Publishing Corporation, 1969.

Seldes, Gilbert. *The Great Audience.* New York, Viking Press, 1950.

Shepherd, Jean. *In God We Trust: All Others Pay Cash.* New York, Doubleday and Company, 1966.

Shulman, Arthur, and Roger Youman. *How Sweet It Was.* New York, Crown Publishers, Inc., 1966.

Shurick, E. P. J. *The First Quarter-Century of American Broadcasting.* Kansas City, Mo., Midland Publishing Company, 1946.

Siepmann, Charles. *Radio's Second Chance.* Boston, Little, Brown and Company, 1946.

Summers, Harrison B. *A Thirty-Year History of Programs Carried on National Radio Networks in the United States, 1926–1956.* Columbus, Department of Speech, Ohio State University, January, 1958.

Bibliography

Summers, Leda P. *Daytime Serials and Iowa Women*. Des Moines, Radio Station WHO, 1943.

Thurber, James. *The Beast in Me and Other Animals*. New York, Harcourt, Brace and Company, 1948.

Today's Children: A Story of Modern American Life. Minneapolis, Pillsbury Flour Mills, 1937.

Wagenknecht, Edward. *The Movies in the Age of Innocence*. Norman, University of Oklahoma Press, 1962.

Weaver, Luther. *The Technique of Radio Writing*. New York, Prentice-Hall, Inc., 1948.

Whipple, James. *How to Write for Radio*. New York, Whittlesey House, 1938.

White, David Manning, and Robert H. Abel, eds. *The Funnies: An American Idiom*. New York, Macmillan Company, 1963.

Wylie, Max, ed. *Best Broadcasts of 1939–40*. New York, Whittlesey House, 1940.

———. *Best Broadcasts of 1940–41*. New York, Whittlesey House, 1942.

———. *Radio and Television Writing*. Rev. ed. New York, Rinehart and Company, Inc., 1950.

2. PAMPHLETS

Cooperative Analysis of Broadcasting. Report of January 26, 1935.

Cooperative Analysis of Broadcasting. Report of January 28, 1936.

A Discussion of Radio. New York, Radio-TV Research Department, Batten, Barton, Durstine, and Osborn, Inc., Fall, 1956. (8 pp.)

The Forsyte Saga. National Educational Television folio, 1969.

Karol, John. *Confidence*. New York, CBS Radio, 1959. (15 pp.)

A Survey of Daytime Radio Listening Habits. New York, Foote, Cone and Belding, May, 1943. (65 pp.)

Wilder, Frances. *Radio's Daytime Serial*. New York, Columbia Broadcasting System, September, 1945. (27 pp.)

3. PERIODICALS

"The Affairs of Dr. Gentry," *Broadcasting*, January 21, 1957, 19.

"Ageless Heroine," *Time*, August 6, 1956, 48.

Alpert, Hollis. "French Nostalgia and Fun" [*Judex*], *Saturday Review*, May 7, 1966, 100.

"Bab-O Ad-$$$," *Sponsor*, November, 1946, 14–18.

485

"Bab-O Bounces Back," *Sponsor*, October 22, 1951, 29.

"Batman and Robin," *Screen Thrills Illustrated*, April, 1963, 10–15; July, 1963, 12–16.

Behlmer, Rudy. "The Saga of Flash Gordon," *Screen Facts* 2, No. 4 (1965), 53–62.

Best, Katherine. "Literature of the Air: Radio's Perpetual Emotion," *Saturday Review of Literature*, April 20, 1940, 11.

Billboard program reviews:

"*Bachelor's Children*," October 10, 1942, 8.

"*General Mills Hour*," August 3, 1946, 12.

"*The Open Door*," July 17, 1943, 12.

"*Those Websters*," August 10, 1946, 6.

Birnie, William. "Molly Goes Marching On," *American Magazine*, November, 1941, 24.

Boutell, C. B. "Hi-Yo Silver Lining," *The Nation*, January 11, 1941, 44–45.

"Boxtops and Broadcasting," *Broadcasting*, October 15, 1956, 112.

Bryan, J. "Hi-Yo-Silver," *Saturday Evening Post*, October 14, 1939, 20.

Bunzel, Peter. "A Final Fiancé for Helen Trent," *Life*, July 11, 1960, 49–52.

"CBS Radio Near 'SRO' Status," *Broadcasting*, August 6, 1956, 54.

Chappell, Matthew. "Soap Operas Need New Formula," *Printers' Ink*, November 20, 1942, 28–33.

Cheydleur, Raymond, and Robert Golter. "Graduate Theses and Dissertations on Broadcasting: A Topical Index," *Journal of Broadcasting*, Winter, 1957–58, 59–90.

"Clara, Em, and New Lu," *Newsweek*, June 15, 1942, 66–67.

Connor, Edward. "The First Eight Serials of Republic," *Screen Facts* 2, No. 1 (1964), 52–63.

———. "The Geneology of Zorro," *Films in Review*, August–September, 1957, 330.

———. "The Serial Lovers," *Films in Review*, August–September, 1955, 328–32.

———. "The Twelve Tarzans," *Films in Review*, October, 1960, 452–63.

"Continued Next Week," *Screen Thrills Illustrated*, June, 1962, 16–29.

Davies, Wallace E. "Truth About Pearl White," *Films in Review*, November, 1959, 537–48.

"Daytime Classics," *Time*, November 12, 1942, 45.

"Daytime Paradox," *Broadcasting*, March 1, 1940, 46.

"Dear Daughter," *Movie Radio Guide*, February 16, 1940, 10.

Bibliography

Demming, Ellen. "Comes a Pause in the Day's Occupation . . . ," *Who's Who in Television and Radio*, 1957, 53.

Denison, Merrill. "Soap Opera," *Harper's*, April, 1940, 498–505.

Dickinson, Hugh. "Soap Opera Down the Drain," *America*, October 29, 1955, 127–30.

"The Dick Tracy Story," *Screen Thrills Illustrated*, June, 1962, 52–59.

D. J. "Search for Tomorrow," *TV Guide*, May 14, 1954, 20.

"Don't Lose Out on Daytime TV," *Sponsor*, October 8, 1951, 72.

"Edgeville, U.S.A.," *Time*, March 17, 1961, 56.

Efron, Edith. "The Soaps—Anything But 99 44/100 Percent Pure," *TV Guide*, March 13, 1965, 6–11.

"Estimated Production Costs," *Variety*, October 22, 1941, 28.

"First Families of Radio," *Movie-Radio Guide*:
"*Backstage Wife*," August 10, 1944, 32.
"*Carters of Elm Street*," April 27, 1940, 47.
"*Lorenzo Jones*," November 9, 1940, 33.
"*Myrt and Marge*," October 5, 1940, 33.
"*We, the Abbotts*," December 28, 1940, 33.

"Frankenstein," *Broadcasting*, December 15, 1939, 56.

"From Tarzan to Lion Man," *Screen Thrills Illustrated*, April, 1963, 7–9.

Geltzer, George. "40 Years of Cliffhanging," *Films in Review*, February, 1957, 60–67.

———. "Ruth Roland," *Films in Review*, November, 1960, 539–48.

"Give Us Love—and Come Back Home" [*Myrt and Marge*], *Radioland*, December, 1934, 15.

"The Goldbergs," *TV Guide*, July 24, 1953, 17.

"Gothic Revival," *Time*, September 4, 1964, 59–60.

Grafton, Samuel. "The Tearful World of Soap Operas," *TV Guide*, August 12, 1961, 9–11; August 19, 1961, 20–23; August 26, 1961, 20–23.

Grant, Maxwell [Walter P. Gibson]. "Teeth of the Dragon," *The Shadow*, November 15, 1937, 12.

Green, Alice. "The Woman Behind Mary Marlin," *Radio Guide*, December 15, 1939, 26.

Hanley, Jack. "For Women Only," *Radio Stars*, July, 1937, 42.

Heuman, Bill. "The Word Merchants," *Writer's Digest*, March, 1964, 32–38.

Higgins, Robert. "Mickey Mouse, Where Are You?" *TV Guide*, March 23, 1968, 6–10.

487

"High Explosive Hero" [Joe Bonomo], *Screen Thrills Illustrated*, June, 1962, 10–15.

"Holy Flypaper!" *Time*, January 28, 1966, 61.

Howard, Lisa. "The Secret Lovers in Your Home," *People Today*, December, 1957, 46–48.

Hughes, Richard. "The Birth of Radio Drama," *Atlantic*, December, 1957, 145–48.

"Hummert Out of B-S-H," *Billboard*, August 21, 1943, 6.

"The Hummerts Super Soaps," *Newsweek*, January 10, 1944, 81.

"Irna Phillips' Ghost Writers," *Variety*, August 5, 1942, 40.

Jaffe, Alfred J. "Daytime Television's Quiet Little Revolution," *Sponsor*, April 19, 1958, 39.

Jenkins, Mrs. John Paul. "Are There Too Many Serials?" *Movie-Radio Guide*, July 27, 1940, 38.

Kensman, Karl. "Stella's Some Lady," *American Mercury*, April, 1955, 80–83.

"Kitty Foyle," *Broadcasting*, March 24, 1958, 20.

Lehman, Rick. "Give My Regards to Woodridge; Or, Kicking the Soap Opera Habit," *Los Angeles Magazine*, June, 1965, 63–64.

"Let's Chat With the Chain Gangs,," *Radio Digest*, January, 1931, 67.

"Life Can Be Beautiful," *Radio Mirror*, May, 1941, 36–39.

"Life with Ma," *Time*, August 26, 1957, 41–42.

"Linda Stirling: Siren of the Serials," *Screen Thrills Illustrated*, April, 1963, 44–47.

"The Lone Ranger Story," *Screen Thrills Illustrated*, February, 1965, 6–13.

McDonough, Robert. "Radio's Heart-Throbs," *Commonweal*, January 26, 1940, 229–300.

McKay, Peggy. "Daytime Serials," *Who's Who in Television and Radio*, 1955, 53.

"Major Networks Provide Numerous Premium Offers," *Broadcasting*, April 1, 1940, 34.

"The Man Who Cast the Shadow," *Newsweek*, January 16, 1967, 10.

"Mary Stuart's Problems," *TV Guide*, November 19, 1960, 17–19.

"Meet Vic and Sade," *Radio Stars*, March, 1935, 43.

Mitchell, George, and William K. Everson. "Tom Mix," *Films in Review*, October, 1957, 387–97.

Mitchener, James. "A Hit in Any Language," *TV Guide*, May 30, 1970, 4–9.

Bibliography

Mothner, Ira. "Peyton Place: Tales of a Town Where Good Prevails, but It Isn't Easy," *Look*, October 19, 1965, 78–86.
"Murder Necessitated," *Time*, August 24, 1962, 56.
"Mutual Serials," *Variety*, February 12, 1941, 25.
"My Son and I," *Movie-Radio Guide*, September 28, 1940, 33.
"NBC to Drop Weekday Programs," *Broadcasting*, June 25, 1956, 90.
"Nemesis of the Underworld" [the Spider], *Screen Thrills Illustrated*, May, 1964, 7–11.
"Net Programs and Net Shifts Mark Opening of 1936 Season," *Broadcasting*, January 1, 1936, 10.
"Network Daytime Programs," *Variety*, January 8, 1941, 96.
"New Sins in Soapland," *Newsweek*, December 9, 1968, 100–104.
"One Man's Two Families," *TV Guide*, May 14, 1954, 20.
"Pepper Young's Family," *Radio Mirror*, October, 1941, 22–25.
Price, Bob. Articles in *Screen Thrills Illustrated*:
   "King of Jungleland," September, 1962, 20–25.
   "The Man Behind the Mask," August, 1964, 7–15.
   "Serial Queens," January, 1963, 12–18.
   "Shazam," September, 1962, 12–19.
   "Tom Tyler," October, 1963, 34–39.
"Princess Marie," *Radioland*, June, 1934, 45.
"Problems of TV Soap Opera," *Sponsor*, January, 1951, 63.
"Promotion: The Batboom," *Time*, March 11, 1966, 88, 90.
"Queen of the Soap Opera," *Newsweek*, July 13, 1942, 59.
"Queen of the Soap Opera," *TV Guide*, December 11, 1953, 17–19.
"Queen of the Soaps," *Newsweek*, May 11, 1964, 66–67.
"The Radio Networks," *Broadcasting*, November 26, 1956, 31–36.
"Radio Revolution," *Variety*, May 28, 1941, 23.
"Reorganization Plan Outlined for Blackett-Sample-Hummert," *Broadcasting*, August 16, 1943, 12.
Rollin, Betty. "The Return of the (Whoosh! There Goes One!) Superhero!" *Look*, March 22, 1966, 113–14.
"Say Virtues of Daytime Serials Outweigh Shortcomings," *Printers' Ink*, February 12, 1943, 20.
"Scented Soaps," *Newsweek*, July 5, 1943, 110.
"Script Queen," *Time*, June 10, 1940, 66.
"Seven Deadly Daytime Sins," *Time*, April 8, 1966, 61.
Shayon, Robert Louis. "Here's Aunt Jenny in Your Eye," *Saturday Review*, July 14, 1956.

———. "The King of the Soaps Is Dead," *Saturday Review*, November 12, 1955, 26–27.

Sherman, Sam. "Republic Studios: Hollywood Thrill Factory," *Screen Thrills Illustrated*, January, 1963, 24–31; April, 1963, 12–16.

Sherwood, Mary Parker. "Welcome Little Strangers," *TV Radio Mirror*, October, 1956, 49.

Smith, Frank Leon. Letter to editor, *Films in Review*, February, 1958, 108–109.

———. "The Man Who Made Serials," *Films in Review*, October, 1956, 375.

"Soap Opera Librettos," *TV Guide*, August 16, 1958, 17–19.

"Soap Operas—and How They Grew," *TV Guide*, August 10, 1956, 11.

Spears, Jack. "Comic Strips on the Screen," *Films in Review*, August–September, 1956, 317–25, 333.

Stevens, Julie. "Tune In Again Tomorrow," *Who's Who in TV and Radio*, 1954, 83.

"Story of Mary Marlin," *Life*, September 11, 1944, 67.

"The Stuntmen," *Wildest Westerns*, May, 1961, 18–24.

"Superman," *Screen Thrills Illustrated*, June, 1962, 30–37; September, 1962, 42–48; January, 1963, 52–57.

"Ten Million Words," *Fortune*, June, 1938, 14.

"Theatre of the Air," *Movie-Radio Guide*, October 25, 1941, 36.

"They Turned Their Backs on Broadway" [Clara, Lu 'n' Em], *Radioland*, October, 1934, 56.

"The 13 Faces of Tarzan," *Screen Thrills Illustrated*, June, 1962, 4–9.

"The Three Mesquiteers," *Wildest Westerns*, May, 1961, 34–41.

"Trade Your Mirror for a Window," *Broadcasting*, April 29, 1957, 80–82.

"Triple Jeopardy," *Time*, August 20, 1965, 65.

"Two New Agencies Organized from Dissolution of Blackett-Sample-Hummert," *Broadcasting*, September 20, 1943, 8.

"Uptown-Milltown; Wagetown-Magazines," *Time*, March 25, 1957, 78.

Variety, program reviews:
"*Against the Storm*," November 5, 1941, 34.
"*The Andersons*," April 22, 1942, 30.
"*The Bartons*," April 30, 1941, 51.
"*Bracken's World*," September 24, 1969.
"*Bright Horizon*," August 27, 1941, 33.

Bibliography

"Bright Promise," October 8, 1969, 44.

"Chaplain Jim, U.S.A.," April 8, 1942, 34.

"Checking Up on the Washboard Weepers," July 2, 1941, 26, 28.

"Clara, Lu 'n' Em," June 17, 1942, 34.

"Edith Adams' Future," March 5, 1941, 34.

"Front Page Farrell," July 2, 1941, 26.

"Helen Holden," March 5, 1941, 37.

"I'll Find My Way," March 12, 1941, 34.

"Kitty Foyle" [radio], June 17, 1942, 34.

"Kitty Foyle" [TV], January 22, 1958, 47.

"Lonely Women," July 22, 1942, 7.

"Mary Marlin," September 29, 1943, 32.

"Myrt and Marge," March 26, 1941, 32.

"Our Gal Sunday," December 31, 1941, 34.

"The Rains Came," October 8, 1941, 29.

"Second Husband," April 29, 1942, 36.

"Story of Bess Johnson," March 26, 1941, 26; April 2, 1941, 30.

"Stories America Loves," October 15, 1941, 26.

"The Survivors," October 1, 1969.

"We Are Always Young," February 26, 1941, 30.

"Verdict Is In," *Time,* May 19, 1958, 50.

"Vic and Sade," *Time,* December 27, 1943, 42.

Warner, Lloyd, and William Henry. "The Radio Daytime Serial: A Symbolic Analysis," *Genetic Psychology Monographs,* February, 1948, 3–71.

"Washboard Dramas," *Broadcasting,* April 1, 1939, 52.

"What Happened to Mary," *The Ladies' World,* August, 1912, and subsequent months.

"Why Soap Opera Sponsors Stay Put 52 Weeks," *Sponsor,* April 9, 1951, 60.

Willey, George A. "The Soap Operas and the War," *Journal of Broadcasting,* Fall, 1963, 339–52.

The WLW Program, November 8, 1931.

"Woman of America," *Tune In,* November, 1945, 4.

Woodstone, Art. "Crime on Soap Street," *Golden Jubilee Variety,* January 4, 1956, 155.

Wright, Mack V. "Serials, Stunts, and Six Guns," *Screen Thrills Illustrated,* February, 1964, 26–31.

Wylie, Max. "Dusting Off Dr. Berg," *Printers' Ink,* February 12, 1943, 19.

491

The Serials

4. NEWSPAPERS

Adams, Val. Broadcasting articles in *New York Times*:
"Ann Sheridan Lends 'Oomph' to Soaps," November 21, 1965.
"CBS Soap Opera Is Going Off," August 3, 1965.
"Networks Cancel 2 TV Soap Operas," September 5, 1962.
"The Nighttime Adventures of Lisa," April 25, 1965.
"Sponsors Stay Put on *Peyton Place*," December 29, 1964.
"Suds for All Seasons," February 21, 1965.
"NBC Developing Evening TV Serial," January 23, 1965.
"NBC Plans to Make Dr. Kildare into a Serial," March 6, 1965.
"Returning, a 5 O'Clock Shadow," August 11, 1963.
"7 Soap Operas Face Extinction," August 11, 1960.

Baker, Russell. "Television's Bat Burlesque," *New York Times*, February 8, 1956.

"Barry Film Suit Settled," *New York Times*, October 18, 1916.

Bart, Peter. "Universal Plans TV Soap Operas," *New York Times*, October 22, 1964.

———. "Will TV Serials Find Success?" *New York Times*, June 26, 1964.

Barthel, Joan. "Out in Detergent Land: A Hard Day's Fright," *New York Times*, July 20, 1967.

———. "The World Has Turned More Than 3,200 Times . . . and 8 Million People Keep Watching," *New York Times Magazine*, September 8, 1968.

Bender, Marilyn. "Dr. Whistlebait Makes Them Say Ahhh," *New York Times*, July 14, 1968.

Blum, Sam. "De-escalating the Violence on TV," *New York Times*, December 8, 1968.

"Buck Jones Is Dead of Injuries in Fire," *New York Times*, December 1, 1942.

Burgess, Anthony. "Seen Any Good Galsworthy Lately?" *New York Times*, November 16, 1969.

Carey, Bernadette. "TV Couture: Good Girls Finish Dowdy," *New York Times*, April 27, 1966.

Colonna, Pat. "Mr. Hidden Faces Hides Away in Bucks," *Sunday Times Advertiser* (Trenton), April 20, 1969.

Crosby, John. "Nothing's New in Radioland," *Los Angeles Evening Mirror News*, August 27, 1958.

Crowther, Bosley. "Vampires," *New York Times*, September 14, 1965.

492

Bibliography

DuBrow, Rick. "Fugitive Leaves, but Format Stays," *Bucks County* (Pennsylvania) *Courier Times*, September 21, 1967.

———. "In Defense of the Soap Opera," *Trenton Evening Times*, January 28, 1968.

Dunlap, Orrin. "Spinning Endless Yarns," *New York Times*, February 11, 1940.

Editorial, *New York Times*, December 4, 1939.

Ewen, Edward T. "Eh-wa-au-wau-aoooow!" *New York Times Magazine*, September 23, 1962.

Ferretti, Fred. "Soap Opera: Winner for Spanish TV Here," *New York Times*, September 5, 1969.

"Final Curtain for the Soap Operas" [editorial], *Los Angeles Times*, November 23, 1960.

"Flame Grows Hotter," *Long Island Press*, March 21, 1965.

Fremont-Smith, Eliot. "The Great Comic Book Heroes" [book review], *New York Times*, November 22, 1965.

———. "He's Coming . . . He's Almost Here," *New York Times*, March 27, 1966.

Gates, Dorothy E. "Remember One Man's Family?" *The Christian Science Monitor*, January 21, 1966.

Gavzer, Bernard. "The Sad, Sad Story of Sudsville, U.S.A.," *Philadelphia Sunday Bulletin*, July 31, 1960.

Gent, George. "Serial Role Goes to Joan Bennett," *New York Times*, June 15, 1966.

"Gloria's Romance," *New York Times*, May 23, 1916.

Gould, Jack. "Pow! It's Batman, Robin—Alive," *New York Times*, January 13, 1966.

———. "Too Good to Be Camp," *New York Times*, January 23, 1966.

Hull, Bob. "Down the Drain Go Soap Operas," *Los Angeles Herald-Examiner*, August 22, 1960.

Humphrey, Hal. "Greater Woes of Daytime Drama," *Los Angeles Times*, April 19, 1967.

———. "Kids Desert Part I of Batman Stories," *Philadelphia Evening Bulletin*, February 1, 1967.

———. "Man from Milwaukee Writes Love of Life," *Philadelphia Evening Bulletin*, August 2, 1968.

Hutchens, John K. "Are The Soap Operas Only Suds?" *New York Times Magazine*, March 28, 1943.

———. "This One Is Good," *New York Times*, October 9, 1941.

493

———. "And Going Strong," *New York Times*, June 20, 1943; April 30, 1944.

LeShan, Eda J. "At War With Batman," *New York Times Magazine*, May 15, 1966.

Litwak, Leo E. "Visit to a Town of the Mind," *New York Times Magazine*, April 4, 1965.

Lowry, Cynthia. "Dr. Malone Ends 30 Years of Practice," *Ellwood City* (Pennsylvania) *Ledger*, March 5, 1963.

———. "Hidden Faces to Debut on Monday," *Los Angeles Times*, December 26, 1968.

———. "TV Forsyte Saga Glorified Soaper," *Pittsburgh Post Gazette*, October 8, 1969.

McManus, Margaret. " 'Queen Mary' Starts 17th Soapy Year," *Philadelphia Sunday Bulletin*, September 17, 1967.

Meehan, Thomas. "Not Good Taste, Not Bad Taste—It's Camp," *New York Times Magazine*, March 21, 1965.

———. "The Soaps Fade but Do Not Die," *New York Times Magazine*, December 4, 1960.

Metz, Stuart. Letter to *New York Times*, August 6, 1939.

Millstein, Gilbert. "Helen Trent—Chapter 5,900," *New York Times Magazine*, July 16, 1956.

Mooney, George. "Soap Opera Queen," *New York Times*, July 27, 1941.

Morehouse, Ward. "Eileen Plays Lisa and People Hate Her," *Trenton Evening Times*, July 6, 1965.

Morse, Carlton E. "Another Beacon Has Flickered Out," *Los Angeles Times*, June 6, 1959.

Musel, Robert. UPI profile on Irna Phillips and her new serial, *Bucks County* (Pennsylvania) *Courier Times*, August 14, 1967.

"New Programs of the Month," *New York Times*, September 25, 1932.

"New Sherlock Holmes Sleuthes on the Radio" [William Gillette as Holmes], *New York Times*, October 26, 1930.

Nichols, Paul. *Judge Parker* strip of March 24, 1958.

Nixon, Agnes Eckhardt. "They're Happy to Be Hooked," *New York Times*, July 7, 1968.

Page, Don. "Can the Shadow Stamp Out Beatles?" *Los Angeles Times*, February 16, 1964.

"Patria . . . ," *New York Times*, December 14, 1918.

Paturean, Alan. "Peyton Place To Spread Woe," *Newsday*, January 14, 1965.

Bibliography

Polier, Rex. Broadcasting articles in *Philadelphia Evening Bulletin*: "Batman Is Far Out—So What Else Is New?" January 13, 1966. "The Fade Out of Peyton Place Approaches," April 23, 1969. "The Forsyte Saga: Elegant Soap Opera," October 6, 1969. "George Hamilton Survives TV Bomb," November 17, 1969. "Soap Opera Queen Returns," January 23, 1967. "Tempus Fugits—and So Does *Fugitive*," August 30, 1967.

Post, Ted. "TV Serial—Mirror to Mankind," *Los Angeles Times*, May 16, 1965.

"Radio Serial Has Formula," *New York Times*, July 31, 1938.

Rotter, Clara. "An Open Letter to the Dear and Departed of Radio," *New York Times*, May 24, 1964.

Sarris, Andrew. "Suffering in TV's Suburban Soapland," *New York Times*, May 24, 1964.

Saunders, Allen, and Ken Ernst. *Mary Worth* strip of March 24, 1958.

Shanley, John P. "Comeback for the Shadow," *New York Times*, August 18, 1965.

Siegel, Joel. "Radio, It Was Magic!" *Los Angeles Times*, September 28, 1969.

Sloane, Leonard. "Networks Produce More TV Soap Operas," *New York Times*, August 31, 1969.

Smart, James. "The World for Two Boxtops and a Dime," *Philadelphia Sunday Bulletin*, September 8, 1968.

"Soap Opera a Term to Live with," *Los Angeles Times*, May 31, 1965.

Stone, Judy. "Caped Crusader of Camp," *New York Times*, January 9, 1966.

Sullivan, Dan. "In Today's Soap Operas, Men Are No Longer All Rotten," *New York Times*, June 23, 1968.

"Tarzan of the Apes," *New York Times*, January 28, 1918.

"TV Soap Operas—Trouble Without End," *New York Times*, September 1, 1957.

Weales, Gerald. "Doc Savage Returns," *New York Times Book Review*, January 24, 1965.

West, Jane. Letter to *New York Times*, November 5, 1939.

Windeler, Robert. "Harold Robbins' TV 'Novel' Has 52 Chapters for 2-Year Run," *Philadelphia Evening Bulletin*, March 28, 1969.

———. "Joan Crawford Takes Daughter's Soap Opera Role," *New York Times*, October 23, 1968.

———. "NBC Is Dropping Violent Cartoons," *New York Times*, November 25, 1968.

495

5. UNPUBLISHED MATERIALS

Blackadore, Dorothy. "The Advertising Effectiveness and Social Desirability of the Radio Daytime Serial." Master's thesis, Columbia University, 1949. (69 pp.)

Hext, Charlene Betty. "Thriller Drama on American Radio Networks: The Development in Regard to Types, Extent of Use, and Program Policies." Master's thesis, Ohio State University, 1949. (156 pp.)

Rodeman, Norbert R. "The Development of Academic Research in Radio and Television for the First Half of the Twentieth Century." Ph.D. dissertation, Northwestern University, 1951. (674 pp.)

Rowe, S. R. "The Radio Serial." Master's thesis, Boston University, 1949. (119 pp.)

Smith, Marie L. Shorthand notes of Nightbeat (television program), May 12, 1958. Author's files.

Stedman, Raymond William. "A History of the Broadcasting of Daytime Serial Dramas in the United States." Ph.D. dissertation, University of Southern California, 1959. (333 pp.)

Stewart, Raymond Frederic. "A Study of the Daytime Serial Radio Listener." Master's thesis, Iowa State University, 1949. (119 pp.)

Summers, Harrison B. Unpublished report H-13. Department of Speech, Ohio State University, n.d.

Willey, George A. "End of an Era: The Daytime Radio Serial." Institute for Communication Research, Stanford University, 1961. (37 pp.) (Published in different form in Journal of Broadcasting, Spring, 1961.)

FINIS

GENERAL INDEX

497

General Index

General Index

General Index

TITLE INDEX

MOTION PICTURES

Title Index

The Serials

Title Index

509

The Serials

RADIO AND TELEVISION

Title Index

The Serials

Title Index

The Serials

DATE DUE

E

A